D0231428

0 599 833 6

A Bibliography of

WILLIAM DEAN HOWELLS

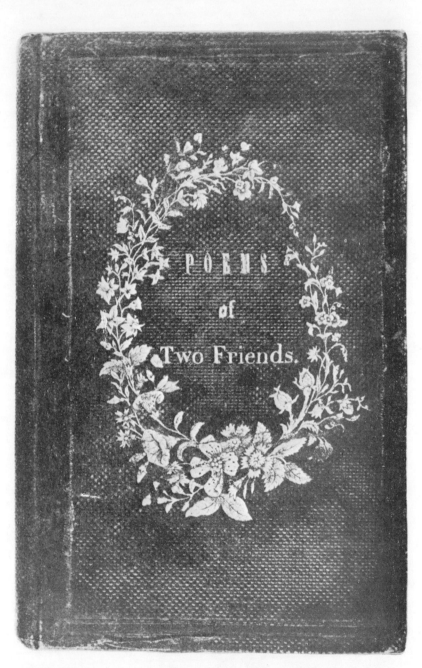

Original binding in the Berg Collection, NYPL, of "Poems of Two Friends," 60-A

A Bibliography of

WILLIAM DEAN HOWELLS

By WILLIAM M. GIBSON

Williams College

and

GEORGE ARMS

The University of New Mexico

THE NEW YORK PUBLIC LIBRARY

ASTOR, LENOX AND TILDEN FOUNDATIONS

&

ARNO PRESS INC.

A PUBLISHING AND LIBRARY SERVICE OF THE NEW YORK TIMES

New York

Originally published 1948 by
The New York Public Library

Reprint edition 1971
With an additional note by the compilers

LC 71-137708
NYPL ISBN 0-87104-512-5
ARNO ISBN 0-405-01743-X

REPRINTED WITH REVISIONS AND ADDITIONS FROM THE
BULLETIN OF THE NEW YORK PUBLIC LIBRARY
1946, 1947

Manufactured in the United States of America

Table of Contents

ILLUSTRATIONS

A Bibliography of William Dean Howells

By William M. Gibson and George Arms

PREFACE

THE chief goals in bibliography are to be accurate, consistent, complete, and usable. Of the first two qualities little can be said in the way of explanation or defense. We have worked hard to avoid inaccuracies. We still realize that some must exist and hope that the pleasure others will have in discovering them may outweigh our own alarm when they are found. As for consistency, although we have generally maintained it in our forms, we have sacrificed it when retention would seem to defeat its purpose.

At the outset of our work we hoped to include everything by Howells that had been published. This in the main we have done, with one major exception — the English and continental editions of his books. With such other and minor exceptions as will be pointed out, all Howells' books and periodical publications have been listed.

These begin with the first acknowledged poem, published at the age of fifteen, and end with a comment on post World War conditions in the last year of Howells' life. Within these sixty-eight years of continuous authorship, about 200 books wholly or in part by Howells and 1200 periodical pieces were published. The span of years and number of items have thus given us a vast opportunity for searching. Though in this preface emphasis will be on what we did not find, we feel justified in urging that what we did find affords essential completion.

The scope of our research is indicated by the list of libraries from which courtesies are later acknowledged. Many individuals have also been sought out or have come forward to give pertinent help. Letters, indexes, memoirs, and earlier check lists have brought to light much material not generally known. Of these latter, several predecessors deserve specific mention. P. K. Foley's *American Authors 1795–1895* and Merle Johnson's *American First Editions* have been used in determining or suggesting certain points of issue. But we have not always regarded these books as of final authority.[1]

Some work of a peripheral nature remains to be done. At a future date we hope to supplement this work with a check list of English and continental

[1] The collations of Albert Lee in the *Book Buyer* are to be regarded as untrustworthy.

editions, of manuscript material, and of the stage productions of the farces and plays, with a calendar of letters both printed [2] and in manuscript.

The omission (except when they are of special significance) of English editions and foreign translations has been caused by our inability under war conditions to make proper examination of these materials. Briefly, the procedure of English publication was that in the late 1880's and early 1890's Howells published book installments in England (as twenty-five copy pamphlet editions) simultaneously with magazine publication in the United States. He also had the plates for many of his books made in Edinburgh, since first publication in England was necessary to secure copyright. [3]

The principle upon which we have included American volumes for collation has been to list all books in whole or part by our author when they were first printings, or printings with additional material, or printings from new plates. It has thus been our intention to describe — in a few cases merely to mention — every volume in which Howells might have revised his original printed text. [4]

Certain publications, which may be found in previous check lists, have thus been excluded. In this category are books of reprinted material issued without Howells' editorial direction. These are: *The Sunnyside Book*, which reprints a portion of *No Love Lost;* the two paper-bound volumes in the "Riverside Literature Series," *A Doorstep Acquaintance and Other Sketches* and *The Parlor Car and the Sleeping Car;* and the ten Samuel French editions of the farces published in 1921. Certain anthologies have also appeared in previous lists which are here omitted: *Character and Comment Selected from the Novels of W. D. Howells,* by Minnie Macoun; *Boy Life,* edited by Percival Chubb; *The Howells Story Book,* compiled by Mildred Howells; and *Off Duty,* which reprints "A Case of Metaphantasmia." Three volumes customarily listed as first editions are "ghosts": "Love's Young Dream" is only a portion of *A Chance Acquaintance* reprinted in *Mark Twain's Library of Humor;* "Buying a Horse," which appeared first in volume form in *A Day's Pleasure and Other Sketches,* was not reprinted separately in 1881 as sometimes claimed, but in 1916; and the first separate publication of "The Country Printer" is in 1916, not 1896.

---

[2] Letters to the press, along with interviews, are however included in the present work. Among personal letters we would like to call attention to the generally unnoted series to T. W. Higginson, edited by George S. Hellman for the Bibliophile Society of Boston in 1929.

[3] Fuller information on this problem may be found in the Boston *Advertiser,* September 20, 1888, p. 5; the Boston *Transcript,* November 6, 1888, p. 2; and the *Literary World,* January 7, 1888, xix, 15.

[4] Paper-bound copies in "Harper's Franklin Square Library" are collated only when they precede the cloth-bound volumes from the same plates.

These unimportant volumes were easy enough to locate. Unfortunately a few highly desirable ones were not found, and our description of them is incomplete. They are the pamphlet poem written and published in Italy for the Zeni-Foratti nuptials; the Italian guidebook which Howells translated from German; the two pieces of sheet-music, *Don't Wake the Children* and the MacDowell lyrics; the *History of the Western Reserve;* and the 1916 edition of Garland's *They of the High Trails.* Thorough personal search and several public notices have failed to secure more information on these books than that little presented in our bibliography.

A few early periodical items, the existence of which we are fairly certain of, have not been located. They should appear in the *Broadway Journal,* the *Home Journal,* the New York *Ledger* (at least one poem — see 73-B), *Vanity Fair* (at least one poem), a "Columbus agricultural journal," and possibly the Louisville *Courier-Journal.* A letter on Lincoln's death is said to have been printed in the "consular books" (*Independent,* March 7, 1912, LXXII, 533–534). These items may well be signed by name, initials, or pseudonyms; but in any event, they have eluded us so far.

A great many unsigned periodical pieces have undoubtedly been omitted. Of these a number have been examined, but have been discarded because they were not indubitably by Howells. We have passed over such items during the 1850's and 1860's in the *Ohio State Journal,* the Ashtabula *Sentinel,* the *Ohio Farmer,* the *Nation,* and the New York *Times.* On the question of German translations, see the discussion under 57–10. Further investigation of Howells' early life and writing may be rewarded with additional entries from these volumes. In his later career there are principally two groups of unsigned writing. The early numbers of "The Contributor's Club" in the *Atlantic Monthly* contain such material, and the *Atlantic* index does not list all the Howells reviews. *Harper's Weekly* for 1902 and 1903 contains items that we have discarded reluctantly.

In spite of these omissions, a great deal of material — signed and unsigned — has been included which was not listed before. None of the early writing has previously been listed. Much of it is now identified through the discovery of Howells' pseudonyms — Chispa, Godfrey or Geoffrey or Wilhelm Constant, and Will Narlie. Unsigned material has been identified from both internal and external evidence. If some of the attributions may seem overbrief or not sufficiently substantiated, examination of the items in question with careful consideration of Howells' interest and ideas at the time will, we feel, justify our assigning them to him. All such anonymous items are of course so indicated. Our practice was to include only those unsigned items on which we were solidly agreed; consequently, we have discarded a body of material that seemed Howellsian.

The check list of selected critical articles has been derived, according to the criteria of selection stated at its head, from a list three or four times as long. Perhaps it is a heinous enough offense to resurrect all the writings of an author without compounding it by a complete enumeration of all that has been written about him.

It is hoped that the usableness of this bibliography will prove itself to readers. Since it is constructed fundamentally in the manner of most bibliographies, a little patience and a glance at the table of contents ought to be adequate preparation for those acquainted with works of this sort. A few features — collations (especially dating and cross-referencing), the annual register, and the index — may properly receive some comment.

Collations of the Howells books are brief in form since there are over 200 volumes to describe, but a careful attempt has been made to retain the most valuable features of a full collation. Where portions or chapters of the books first appeared in periodicals, full reference to the periodical is given in the collation. Likewise, reprinted periodical items are cross-referenced to the book in which they later appear. For books partially written by Howells, the collations are very short, consisting of the first portion of the title page, the name of the publisher, the place and date of publication, and the pages written by Howells.

Publication dates for the books have been determined by copyright dates when available. In the collations dates so determined are given without notation, while determination of dates by other means is signified in parentheses (as copyright *title* dates). The explanation in parentheses, "earliest notice observed," indicates that for publication date we have depended upon reviews or publication notices. Undated volumes are listed at the end of the year.

Publication dates in the House of Harper register are used when copyright deposit date is unknown and are entered concurrently when the difference is greater than seven days. The Harper register usually agrees closely with the copyright deposit date, and while more significant is far from complete. The code letters which appear on the title page verso of Harper books after 1913 refer to printing, rather than publication, date. The combinations entered in the collations are, we believe, those of earliest printing; but an "earlier" second letter (the year) or an "earlier" first letter (the month) when the second letter is the same would mark an earlier issue.

A Bibliography of William Dean Howells 9

The annual register includes the books by their title and date, but has as its principal purpose the listing of periodical publications. Attention is called to the series of "departments" in magazines and newspapers — the later ones known though seldom given proper recognition, the earlier ones almost entirely unknown. For these series, and for all other items the titles of which do not sufficiently explain their content, we have written brief descriptions, and have thus made the entries for the travel series, the *Atlantic* reviews, and the literary columns usable. We have not described chapters or articles or portions of articles which have been reprinted in volume form, and merely give at such times a cross-reference to the volume by its item-number.

This system of numbering is our greatest departure from customary bibliographical practice. The first number signifies the last two digits of the year in which the item was published; the second number indicates the order of publication for a periodical item within any given year, and the capital letters indicate such order for books. Thus 60–14 is the fourteenth periodical item published in 1860, and 00–A is the first book published in 1900.

The numbering system here described seems to us relatively economical and informative. Another reason for adopting it was that it enabled us to construct less onerously a name-index which would cover all the discussion of literary figures (beyond bare allusion) in all the critical articles and books that Howells wrote from 1852 to 1920. The names of Howells' illustrators both in periodicals and in books will also be found in the name-index. The scholar who wishes to read Howells' published comments on any person or to ascertain his illustrators may theoretically discover them by reference to this index, though in practice he will probably discover omissions. Through the system of numbering he will also be instantly cognizant of the year. Reference to the index of *Life in Letters of William Dean Howells* will reveal all other comments in published writings except for those in the letters which have been published occasionally in scattered books and periodicals.

We wish finally to make acknowledgment to those institutions and individuals whose work this is as well as our own. We appreciate particularly the services of the libraries in which we have done the major part of our work: The New York Public Library, Williams College Library, Mary Washington College Library, University of Chicago Library, Newberry Library. Dartmouth College Library, University of New Mexico Library, and the Library of Congress. For the courtesy of the staff in libraries where we have more briefly visited or with which we have corresponded we are also grateful: Harvard College Library, Boston Public Library, American Antiquarian

Society Library, New York University Library (Index), Columbia University Library, Chicago Public Library, Northwestern University Library, Public Library of Columbus, Ohio State Archaeological and Historical Society Library, Western Reserve Historical Society Library, Huntington Library, and University of Michigan Library.

To certain other groups we owe an especial debt: the President and Trustees of Williams College for a grant of fifty dollars from the 1900 Fund for microfilm, the Committee on Research of the faculty of The University of New Mexico for a grant of eighty dollars, the publishers of the *Nation* for the use of their marked files, and the editors of Harper & Brothers for the use of their register.

We wish to thank again the following individuals for their generous help: Mr. E. H. O'Neill, Mr. and Mrs. Rudolf Kirk, Mr. Hallett D. Smith, Mr. Frederick C. Marston, jr., Mr. Kenneth B. Murdock, Mr. David Borowitz, Mr. William H. Briggs, Messrs. Howard S. Mott and Robert K. Black, Mr. John C. Pearson, Miss M. M. Fréchette, Miss Florence Murdoch, Miss Hannah G. Belcher, Mrs. Leonard W. Jones, Mr. Edward Ellis, Mr. Howard M. Munford, Mr. Charles T. Miller, Mr. Edwin H. Cady, Mr. Robert Price, Mr. R. H. Ballinger, Mr. Louis J. Budrewicz, Mrs. Margaret D. Gidney, Mr. W. D. Howells II, Mr. Arnold B. Fox, and Mr. William R. Keast. Mr. Miller has materially aided us in locating several items and in the cross-referencing of *Criticism and Fiction.* From Mr. Marston's correspondence and dissertation we received particular help. By using our manuscript in the writing of his dissertation he has been in a position to point out errors and to supply us with a number of items. For generous permission to print several manuscript items of William Dean Howells, we wish to thank Miss Mildred Howells and Mr. John Mead Howells; Miss Howells' *Life in Letters of William Dean Howells* has been a constant help in our work. At a later date we hope to make specific acknowledgment to the many individuals and libraries who have copied letters or notified us of them, the value of which for this work has been indirect but nevertheless real. For proofreading and editing in the final preparation of the bibliography, we are indebted to Mr. Daniel C. Haskell, Bibliographer of The New York Public Library, to Mrs. R. S. Crane, and to our wives.

As corrections and additions are from time to time discovered, we should appreciate news of them.

WILLIAM M. GIBSON, *Williams College*

GEORGE ARMS, *The University of New Mexico*

CHECK LIST OF WORKS AND PARTIAL WORKS

1860

A Poems of two friends.
B "Old Brown," Echoes of Harper's Ferry.
C Lives and speeches of Abraham Lincoln and
 Hannibal Hamlin, first issue.
D Lives and speeches of Abraham Lincoln and
 Hannibal Hamlin, second issue.
E [Poems and notices,] The poets and poetry
 of the West.

1861

A Three years in Chili, edited and rewritten.

1863

A [Report,] Commercial relations of the United
 States with foreign countries.
B [Zeni-Foratti pamphlet.]
C [Translation of a guidebook.]

1864

A The battle in the clouds, song and chorus
 inscribed to the Army of the Cumberland.

1865

A [Report,] Commercial relations of the United
 States with foreign countries.
B [Report,] Commercial relations of the
 United States with foreign nations.

1866

A Venetian life, first English edition.
B Venetian life.
C [Report,] Commercial relations of the United
 States with foreign nations.

1867

A Venetian life, second edition.
B Italian journeys.

1869

A No love lost, a romance of travel.
B "BoPeep, a pastoral," The Atlantic almanac,
 1870.

1871

A Suburban sketches.

1872

A Their wedding journey.
B Italian journeys, enlarged edition.
C Venetian life, enlarged edition.
D Jubilee days, written and edited with T. B.
 Aldrich.
E Suburban sketches, enlarged edition.

1873

A A chance acquaintance.
B Poems.

1874

A A chance acquaintance, illustrated edition.

1875

A A foregone conclusion.

1876

A "Dorothy Dudley," Theatrum Majorum, the
 Cambridge of 1776.
B A day's pleasure.
C Sketch of the life and character of Ruther-
 ford B. Hayes.
D The parlor car, farce.
E The first cricket.

1877

A Out of the question, a comedy.
B A counterfeit presentment, comedy.
C [Essay,] Memoirs of Frederica Sophia Wil-
 helmina, two volumes.
D [Essay,] Lives of Lord Herbert of Cherbury
 and Thomas Ellwood.
E [Essay,] Life of Vittorio Alfieri.
F [Essay,] Memoirs of Carlo Goldoni.
G [Essay,] Memoirs of Edward Gibbon, Esq.

1878

A [Essay,] Memoirs of Jean François Marmontel, two volumes.

1879

A The lady of the Aroostook, Feb. 27.
B [Letters,] Editorial right, June.

1880

A The undiscovered country.

1881

A A fearful responsibility and other stories.
B "My first friend in Cambridge," The city
 and the sea with other Cambridge con-
 tributions.
C Dr. Breen's practice, a novel.
D A day's pleasure and other sketches.

Check list of works and partial works, cont'd

1882

A "Introduction," Living truths from the writings of Charles Kingsley.
B A modern instance, a novel.
C "The sleeping-car, a farce," Harper's Christmas.

1883

A The sleeping car, a farce.
B A woman's reason, a novel.

1884

A A little girl among the old masters.
B The register, farce.
C Three villages.
D Niagara revisited.

1885

A The elevator, farce.
B The rise of Silas Lapham.
C Venetian life, two volumes, Aldine edition.

1886

A Tuscan cities.
B The garroters, farce.
C Poems, enlarged edition.
D Indian summer.
E "Sketch of George Fuller's life," George Fuller, his life and works.

1887

A The minister's charge, or, the apprenticeship of Lemuel Barker.
B "Leo Tolstoï," Sebastapol.
C Modern Italian poets, essays and versions.
D Their wedding journey, enlarged edition.

1888

A April hopes.
B Mark Twain's library of humor, edited, with introduction.
C Library of universal adventure by sea and land, edited with T. S. Perry.
D A sea change, or love's stowaway, a lyricated farce.

1889

A Annie Kilburn, a novel.
B The mouse trap and other farces.
C The sleeping-car and other farces.
D Samson, a tragedy in five acts, translated.

1890

A A hazard of new fortunes, a novel, first edition, paper.
B A hazard of new fortunes, a novel, two volumes.
C "The prose poem," Pastels in prose.
D The shadow of a dream, a story, first edition, paper.
E The shadow of a dream, a story, cloth.
F "Introduction," The house by the medlar-tree.
G A boy's town.
H "W. D. Howells," The art of authorship.

1891

A [Winifred Howells]
B Criticism and fiction.
C Venetian life, English and American editions, two volumes, illustrated.

1892

A The Albany depot, farce, first printed issue.
B The Albany depot.
C An imperative duty, a novel.
D The quality of mercy, a novel.
E A letter of introduction, farce.
F A little Swiss sojourn.
G "Introductory letter," South-sea idyls.

1893

A Christmas every day and other stories told for children.
B The world of chance, a novel.
C The unexpected guests, a farce.
D "Niagara, first and last," The Niagara book, a complete souvenir of Niagara Falls.
E "Introduction," The poems of George Pellew.
F My year in a log cabin.
G Evening dress, farce.
H "Judgment day," The first book of the Authors Club, Liber scriptorum.
I The coast of Bohemia, a novel.
J "Introduction," Main-travelled roads.
K "Folksong," "The sea," "Through the meadow," [Eight songs.]
L "Except as little children," Fame's tribute to children.

1894

A A likely story, farce, first separate edition.
B A traveler from Altruria, romance.
C The mouse trap, farce, first separate edition.
D Five o'clock tea, farce, first separate edition.
E Tuscan cities, new preface.

1895

A Their wedding journey, illustrated edition.
B "Introduction" and "Chapter xviii," Recollections of life in Ohio from 1813 to 1840.
C "Introduction," Master and man.
D [Don't wake the children, song.]
E My literary passions.
F Stops of various quills.

1896

A "Introduction," Doña Perfecta.
B The day of their wedding, a novel.
C A parting and a meeting, story.
D "An Appreciation," Maggie, a child of the streets.
E Impressions and experiences.
F "Introduction," Lyrics of lowly life.

1897

A "George du Maurier," English society.
B A previous engagement, comedy.
C The landlord at Lion's Head, a novel.
D An open-eyed conspiracy, an idyl of Saratoga.
E Stories of Ohio.
F "Lyof Tolstoy," A library of the world's best literature, volume 27.

1898

A The story of a play, a novel.
B "Prefatory sketch," The blindman's world and other stories.

1899

A Ragged lady, a novel.
B The coast of Bohemia, biographical edition.
C Their silver wedding journey, two volumes.

1900

A "Success and unsuccess," "The mulberries in Pay's garden," The Hesperian tree.
B Bride roses, a scene.
C Room forty-five, a farce.
D An Indian giver, a comedy.
E The smoking car, a farce.
F Literary friends and acquaintance, a personal retrospect of American authorship.

1901

A "How William Dean Howells worked to secure a foothold," How they succeeded.
B A pair of patient lovers.
C Heroines of fiction, two volumes.
D Italian journeys, revised and illustrated edition.
E Italian journeys, illustrated English edition.
F Florence in art and literature, edited with Russell Sturgis.

1902

A The Kentons, a novel.
B The flight of Pony Baker, a boy's town story.
C Literature and life, studies.

1903

A "Success — a parable," "Hot," "Awaiting his exequatur," The Hesperian tree.
B Questionable shapes.
C Letters home.

1904

A "Meetings with Clarence King," Clarence King memoirs.
B The son of Royal Langbrith, a novel.

1905

A Miss Bellard's inspiration, a novel.

1906

A London films.
B "Introduction," Their husbands' wives.
C "Introduction," Under the sunset.
D "Introduction," Different girls.
E "Introduction," Quaint courtships.
F Certain delightful English towns with glimpses of the pleasant country between.
G "Introduction" and "The amigo," The heart of childhood.

1907

A "Introduction," Southern lights and shadows.
B Through the eye of the needle, a romance with an introduction.
C "Introduction," Shapes that haunt the dusk.
D Between the dark and the daylight, romances.
E Venetian life, enlarged and illustrated edition.
F Life at high tide, edited with H. M. Alden.
G Minor dramas, two volumes, English edition.
H The mulberries in Pay's garden.

1908

A Fennel and rue, a novel.
B Christmas every day, a story told a child, illustrated edition.
C "The father," The whole family, a novel by twelve authors.
D Roman holidays and others.

1909

A The mother and the father, dramatic passages.
B Seven English cities.

1910

A "A counsel of consolation," In after days, thoughts on the future life.
B "Introduction," Mark Twain's speeches.
C My Mark Twain, reminiscences and criticisms.
D Imaginary interviews.
E [Letter,] History of the Western Reserve.

1911

A Parting friends, a farce.
B "Bibliographical," My literary passions [and] Criticism and fiction, Library edition.
C "Bibliographical," The landlord at Lion's Head, a novel, Library edition.
D "Bibliographical," Literature and life, studies, Library edition.
E "Bibliographical," London films and Certain delightful English towns, Library edition.
F "Bibliographical," Literary friends and acquaintance [and My Mark Twain], Library edition.
G "Bibliographical," A hazard of new fortunes, Library edition.
H "The poetry of Madison Cawein," Poems.
I "Introduction," Tom Brown's school-days.
J [Prefaces for incomplete Library edition.]

1912

A [Letter,] The house of Harper.
B "One of the public to the author," The Henry James year book.
C [Introduction,] Artemus Ward's best stories.

1913

A New Leaf Mills, a chronicle.
B Familiar Spanish travels.
C "Introduction," Gulliver's travels.

1914

A The seen and unseen at Stratford-on-Avon, a fantasy.
B [Untitled anecdotes,] 300 latest stories.

1915

A [Letter,] Sixty American opinions on the war.

1916

A "The little children," The book of the homeless.
B "Preface," They of the high trails.
C The daughter of the storage and other things in prose and verse.
D Buying a horse, first separate edition.
E The leatherwood god.
F Years of my youth, first issue.
G [Letter,] Tributes to Canada.
H The country printer, an essay.

1917

A [Paragraph,] The books of Kathleen Norris.
B "Introduction," The second odd number.
C "Letter" and "An appreciation," The story of a country town.
D Years of my youth, illustrated edition.
E [Letter,] The Harper centennial.

1918

A [Letter,] Defenders of democracy.
B "Introduction," Pride and prejudice.
C "Introduction," Daisy Miller [and] An international episode.
D The daughter of the storage, first separate edition.

1919

A "Introduction," The shadow of the cathedral.
B "Introduction," The actor-manager.
C "The incredible cruelty of the Teutons," The World War.

1920

A Hither and thither in Germany.
B Immortality and Sir Oliver Lodge.
C "A reminiscent introduction," The great modern American stories.
D The vacation of the Kelwyns, an idyl of the middle eighteen-seventies.

1921

A Eighty years and after.
B Mrs. Farrell, a novel.

1922

A [Address,] Public meeting...in memory of Samuel Langhorne Clemens.

1923

A Don Quixote, edited.

1924

A "Emile Zola," Germinal.
B [Letter,] Vivisection according to representative people.

1928

A Life in letters of William Dean Howells, two volumes.

CHECK LIST OF PERIODICALS, NEWSPAPERS, & "DEPARTMENTS"
(with dates of Howells material)

PERIODICALS

Ainslee's, 1900
American Academy. Proceedings, 1910–11, 1914–16
American Fabian, 1898
American Hebrew, 1885
Athenaeum, 1882
Atlantic monthly, 1860–62, 1866–83, 1885, 1896, 1898, 1900, 1907, 1917
Author, 1889, 1891
Authors League of America. Bulletin, 1916
Book news monthly, 1908
Bookbuyer, 1897, 1900
Booklover's, 1902
Bookman, 1912
Broadway journal (see "Preface")
Cambridge Historical Society. Publications,1907
Casket, 1853
Century, 1881–86, 1895–96, 1898, 1901, 1916
Commonwealth, 1863–64
Cornhill magazine, 1911
Cosmopolitan, 1892–95
Critic, 1886–88, 1892, 1897–99
Current literature, 1898.
Dial, 1860
Every Saturday, 1871
Forum, 1895
Frank Leslie's, 1892, 1898–99
Galaxy, 1866
Harper's bazar, 1893–96, 1898, 1900–03, 1906–07, 1909–10
Harper's monthly, 1863, 1865–66, 1882–97, 1899–1920
Harper's weekly, 1887–89, 1892–93, 1895–98, 1900–09, 1912
Harper's young people, 1890
Harvard graduates magazine, 1907
Harvard register, 1881
Home journal (see "Preface")
Independent, 1883
Knickerbocker, 1861
Ladies' home journal, 1892–95
Lamp, 1904
Lippincott's, 1887, 1899
Literary digest, 1898–1900.
Literary news, 1886, 1897
Literary world, 1886
Literature, 1898–99
Longman's, 1882
McClure's, 1893–94, 1897
Metropolitan, 1903
Munsey's, 1897
Nation, 1865–67, 1916
National era, 1855, 1858
New York ledger (see "Preface")
North American review, 1864–69, 1872, 1888, 1894, 1899–1916
Odd-Fellows' casket and review, 1859

Outlook, 1894, 1895
Overland monthly, 1902
Prang's chromo, 1868
Putnam's, 1868
Round table, 1865–66
Saint Nicholas, 1886
Saturday press, 1859–60, 1865
Scribner's, 1881, 1893, 1895, 1897, 1900
Success, 1898
Temple Bar, 1886
Vanity Fair (see "Preface")
World's work, 1909
Youth's companion, 1887, 1895, 1898–1901

NEWSPAPERS

Ashtabula *Sentinel*, 1853–55, 1857–60, 1862–66
Balloon post, 1871
Boston *Advertiser*, 1863–65, 1888
Boston *Transcript*, 1873, 1877, 1892–93
Cincinnati *Commercial*, 1852
Cincinnati *Gazette*, 1857–58, 1860, 1865–66
Cleveland *Herald*, 1858
Daily tatler, 1896
New York *Herald*, 1900–01.
New York *Post*, 1900, 1916
New York *Sun*, 1891–92, 1899, 1907–08, 1912
New York *Times*, 1865, 1892, 1894, 1900, 1908, 1912, 1914–15, 1917–18
New York *Tribune*, 1881, 1887, 1892, 1897
New York *World*, 1861, 1896
Newton *Journal*, 1883
Ohio farmer, 1854–55, 1857–58, 1860
Ohio state journal, 1852, 1855, 1858–62
Ohio state weekly journal, 1858–60.
Philadelphia *Press*, 1894

"DEPARTMENTS"

"American letter," *Literature*, 1898
"Diversions of the higher journalist," *Harper's weekly*, 1903
"Editor's easy chair," *Harper's monthly*,1900–20.
"Editor's study," *Harper's monthly*, 1886–92
"En passant," *Ohio state journal*, 1860
"From Ohio," New York *World*, 1861
"Glimpses of summer travel," Cincinnati *Gazette*, 1860
"Life and letters," *Harper's weekly*, 1895–98
"Letter from Columbus," Cincinnati *Gazette*, 1857–58
"Letter from Europe," *Ohio state journal*, 1862
"Letter from New York," Cincinnati *Gazette*, 1865–66
"Letters from Venice," Boston *Advertiser*, 1863–64
"Literary gossip," *Ohio state journal*, 1860–61
"Minor topics," *Nation*, 1865–66
"News and humors of the mail," *Ohio state journal*, 1858–60

COLLATIONS OF WORKS AND PARTIAL WORKS

60-A

Poems | of | two friends. | [*rule*] | Columbus: | Follett, Foster and Company. | 1860.

Collation: p. –ii + x + 134, 7¼ x 4½ inches: blank leaf; title page, [i]; 1–132, text; blank leaf. Yellow end papers. Howells' poems appear on p. 83–132; John J. Piatt's on p. 1–79.

Brown pebbled cloth over boards. Lettering and ornamental wreath on front cover gold-stamped; heavy rule-box blind-stamped. Wreath and rule-box blind-stamped on back cover. Top edge gilt. Published Dec. 23, 1859 (earliest notice observed).

"Prelude."
"The movers."
"The old bouquet."
"Through the meadow," reprinted 93-K.
"Gone," first printed *National era*, Oct. 21, 1858, xii, 168. "Wilhelm Constant."
"The throstle," first printed Ashtabula *Sentinel*, Aug. 5, 1858, xxvii, 41.
"The autumn-land," first printed *Ohio farmer*, Nov. 21, 1857, vi, 188. "Godfrey Constant."
"All four."
"Thistles."
"The mysteries," first printed *Ohio farmer*, Oct. 2, 1858, vii, 320. "Will Narlie."
"The shepherd."
"The sarcastic fair."
"Evening voices," first printed Ashtabula *Sentinel*, May 20, 1858, xxviii, 153. "W. D. H."
"The heaven-wreath," first printed as "The wreath in heaven — a fancy," *Ohio farmer*, May 26, 1855, iv, 84. "Will Narlie."
"Liebeswonne," first printed *Saturday press*, Oct. 22, 1859, ii, 1.
"The violets."
"Sonnet," first printed as "Leonora," *Saturday press*, April 12, 1855, ix, 60.
"The death of May," first printed *National era*, June 21, 1855, ix, 97.
"Compliment."
"Drifting away," first printed *Saturday press*, Sept. 10, 1859, ii, 1. Reprinted *Commonwealth*, Dec. 6, 1862, i, 1.
"Dead," first printed *Saturday press*, Nov. 12, 1859, ii, 1.
"Spring," first printed *National era*, May 3, 1855, ix, 70. "W. D. H."
"The caged robin."
"The doubt," first printed *National era*, Sept. 16, 1858, xii, 145. "Wilhelm Constant." Re-printed Ashtabula *Sentinel*, Sept. 23, 1858, xxvii, 297 under same pseudonym; reprinted *Ohio farmer*, Sept. 25, 1858, vii, 312. "Will Narlie." Reprinted *Saturday press*, June 21, 1860, iii, 4.
"The thorn," first printed *Saturday press*, Dec. 3, 1859, ii, 1.
"Drowned."
"Under the locusts," first printed *Saturday press*, June 18, 1859, ii, 1.
"Midnight rain," first printed *Ohio farmer*, reprinted as "Nightly rain," Ashtabula *Sentinel*, Oct. 5, 1854, xxiii, 1. "Will Narlie."
"The bird," first printed as "The bird song," *National era*, Dec. 2, 1858, xii, 189. "Wilhelm Constant."
"The fisher-maiden," first printed as "The fishermaid," Ashtabula *Sentinel*, April 1, 1858, xxvii, 103.
"Words of warning."
"The straw hat," first printed *Saturday press*, Nov. 19, 1859, ii, 2. Reprinted *Ohio state journal*, Nov. 24, 1859, xxiii, 2.
"Sir Philip Sidney."

60-B

Echoes | of | Harper's Ferry. | [*rule*] | "By the rude bridge that arched the flood, | their flag to April's breeze unfurled; | here once the embattled farmers stood, | and fired the shot heard round the world." | R. W. Emerson.

Thayer and Eldridge: Boston, 1860. Published May 12, 1860 (earliest notice observed).

"Old Brown," poem, p. 316, first printed Ashtabula *Sentinel*, Jan. 25, 1860, xxix, 1, and reprinted *Commonwealth*, June 24, 1865, iii, 1.

60-C

Lives and speeches | of | Abraham Lincoln | and | Hannibal Hamlin. | [*rule*] | Columbus, O: | Follett, Foster & Co. | 1860.

Collation: p. 170, 7⅝ x 4⅝ inches: title page, [3]; text of Howells' life of Lincoln, 17–94; "Memorabilia of the Chicago Convention," 99–111;

"Speech delivered at Cincinnati, Ohio, September, 1859," 115–153; life of Hannibal Hamlin [by John L. Hayes], 157–170.

Yellow paper covers. Portrait of Lincoln, lettering, publishers' imprint, and ornamental rule-box on front cover in black. Engraving of "The Republican Wigwam at Chicago" on back cover in black. Published June 25, 1860 (earliest notice observed).

Pages 17–153 are identical with the corresponding pages of the later 1860 edition, 60-D; p. 157–170 correspond exactly to p. 307–321 of the later edition, except that a concluding paragraph on p. 321 is dropped in the later edition.

60-D

Lives and speeches | of | Abraham Lincoln | and | Hannibal Hamlin. | [*rule*] | Columbus, O: | Follett, Foster & Co. | 1860.

Collation: p. ii + 410, 7⅜ x 4¾ inches: title page, [3]; text of Howells' life of Lincoln, 17–94; "Memorabilia of the Chicago Convention," 99–111; text of Lincoln's speeches, 115–304; John L. Hayes' life of Hamlin, 307–406; two blank leaves. Engraved portraits of Lincoln and Hamlin tipped in before each biography. End papers pink.

Dark purple-brown pebbled cloth over boards. Lettering and rules on spine gold-stamped. Rule-boxes and ornament on both covers blind-stamped. Published July 5, 1860 (earliest notice observed).

The Boston imprint differs only in that: "Boston: Brown & Taggard. | 1860." appears on the title page; lettering on the spine differs; and the rule-box blind-stamped on the cover is ornamental. The New York imprint differs only in that: "New York: | W. A. Townsend & Co., | Columbus: Follett, Foster & Co. | 1860." appears on the title page; lettering on the spine differs; there is no ornament on the covers; and both portraits are tipped in together at the beginning of the volume. The Cincinnati imprint differs only in that: "Cincinnati: Rickey, Mallory & Co." appears on the title page.

The second issue of this edition from the same plates alters the footnote on p. 33 from

"near Petersburgh" to "now Petersburgh" and adds an errata slip facing p. 74.

For information on the writing and publishing of this campaign biography, see *Life of Abraham Lincoln*, the facsimile edition published by the Abraham Lincoln Association, Springfield, 1938, p. v–xvii, and *Years of my youth*, 16-F, p. 202–204.

60-E

The | poets and poetry | of | the West; | with biographical and critical notices. | By William T. Coggeshall. | [*rule*] | "Here is a wreath | with many an unripe blossom garlanded, | and many a weed, yet mingled with some flowers | that will not wither." | Southey.

Follet, Foster and Company: Columbus, 1860. Published Sept. 1, 1860 (earliest notice observed).

"Helen Louisa Bostwick," p. 550, biographical notice first printed at greater length *Ohio state journal*, Oct. 1, 1860, xxiv, 2.

"John Herbert A. Bone," p. 589, biographical notice.

"Gordon A. Stewart," p. 612, biographical notice.

"Mary A. Whittlesey," p. 640, biographical notice.

"Drifting away," p. 678–679, reprinted from *Poems of two friends*.

"The movers," p. 679–680, reprinted from *Poems of two friends*.

"Dead," p. 680, reprinted from *Poems of two friends*.

"The poet's friends," p. 680, first printed *Atlantic monthly*, Feb., 1860, v, 185.

"The bobolinks are singing," p. 681, first printed *Saturday press*, Feb. 11, 1860, iii, 1. Reprinted *Ohio state journal*, Feb. 17, 1860, xxiii.

"Summer dead," p. 681, first printed as "Pleasure-pain, v," *Atlantic monthly*, April, 1860, v, 470.

61-A

Three years in Chili. | By | a lady of Ohio. | [*rule*] | Columbus: Follett, Foster and Company. | Boston: Brown & Taggard. | New York: Sheldon & Co. | 1861.

Collation: p. [–ii] + viii + 162, 7⅜ x 4¾ inches: title page, [i]; iii–viii, con-

Collations of Works... — 61-A, continued
tents; 1–158, text; two blank leaves.
End papers yellow.

Dark gray-green pebbled cloth over boards. Lettering on spine gold-stamped. Ornament and rule-boxes on covers and spine blind-stamped. Published after Sept. 15, 1861 (earliest notice observed).

Howells edited and rewrote this volume, which was submitted to Follett and Foster when he was their reader. Its author was Mrs. C. B. Merwin. Follett and Foster reissued the book in New York in 1863.

63-A

Letter | of | the Secretary of State, | transmitting a report on the | commercial relations of the United States | with | foreign countries, | for | the year ended September 30, 1862.
Government Printing Office: Washington, 1863.

The consular report, p. 376–380, here first printed.

63-B

[Poem translated into Italian by the Abbè Fratini, University of Padua Printing Office, Padua.]

See *Life in letters*, I, 76: "I enclose for father a poem of mine, translated and printed at Padua, on occasion of the Zeni-Foratti Nuptials. It is the custom in Italy, when people get married, to print little copies of verses and circulate among their friends. The abbè Fratini, a professor in the University of Padua, made this translation, which has been much admired in that ancient city. It was printed at the University office. The original English has never been printed."

Circa 63-C

[Translation of a guidebook.]

"In Venice my wife wrote from my dictation the translation of a guide-book which I made there..." *Life in letters*, II, 136.

64-A

The | battle in the clouds | song & chorus | inscribed to the Army of the Cumberland. | Written by | Wm. D.

Howells. | U. S. consul at Venice. | Composed by | M. Keller. | 4 [*within ornate rules*] | Jefferson, Ohio | published by J. A. Howells & Co. Sentinel building. | Chicago, New Haven Conn, Rochester, | Root & Cady. Skinner & Sperry. Jo^s. P. Shaw. | Entered according to act of congress AD 1864 by Wm. D. Howells in the clerks office of the dis^t. court of the s^o. dis^t of N. Y. [*All the foregoing in triple-rule box.*]

Collation: p. 8, 14 $^1/_{16}$ x 10 $^{13}/_{16}$ inches: [1], title page; 2, blank; 3–7, text; 8, blank. No end papers.

No cover. Sheet music, the two folded leaves not sewed or bound.

Text here first printed. Except for careless punctuation and spelling it is essentially the same as the 1873 text.

65-A

Letter | of | the Secretary of State, | transmitting a report on the | commercial relations of the United States | with | foreign countries, | for | the year ended September 30, 1863.
Government Printing Office: Washington, 1865.

The consular report, dated October 5, 1863, p. 360–362, here first printed.

65-B

Letter | of | the Secretary of State, | transmitting a report on the | commercial relations of the United States | with | foreign nations, | for | the year ended September 30, 1864.
.Government Printing Office: Washington, 1865.

The consular report, dated September 30, 1864, p. 462–467, is by far the most interesting of the four reports Howells wrote from Venice; he says: "I propose here to review very succinctly the whole history of Venetian commerce, and to develop as far as possible the causes of its rise and decline." Reprinted in second edition of *Venetian life*. See 67-A.

66-A

Venetian life. | [*short ornamental rule*] | By | Wm. D. Howells. | [*Publisher's device*] | London: | N. Trübner & Co., 60, Paternoster Row. | MDCCCLXVI. | [Right of translation and reproduction reserved.] [*Brackets as above.*]

Collation: p. xiv + 360, 7¾ x 4¾ inches: A⁷, 1–22⁸, 23⁴: title page, [v]; 1–359, text; 360, "John Childs and Son, Printers." End papers chocolate brown.

Green or purple-red pebbled cloth over boards. Figure of gondola on front cover gold-stamped. Lettering, ornament, and rules on spine gold-stamped. Front and back cover blind-stamped with triple rule-box running into ornamented corners. Published by June 2, 1866 (earliest notice observed).

In copies of this edition as above, A⁵⁻⁷ or p. ix–xiv consist of a single leaf and two conjugate leaves tipped in. A⁵ recto bears an "Advertisement" dated New York, February 15, 1866 and A⁶ verso with A⁷ recto and verso list errata. In other copies the collation reads A⁵, 1–22⁸, 23⁶, the difference being that the two conjugate leaves of errata are tipped in at the end of gathering 23.

"Venice in Venice," p. 1–7, first printed as "Letters from Venice, IX, i. Sentimental errors about Venice," Boston *Advertiser*, Nov. 26, 1863, CII, 2. Pages 7–18 here first printed.

"Arrival and first days in Venice," p. 19–23, first printed as "Letters from Venice, IX, ii. Arriving in Venice," Boston *Advertiser*, Nov. 26, 1863, CII, 2. Pages 26–29, 30–31, first printed as "Letters from Venice, XXIII, Fatti diversi," Boston *Advertiser*, June 25, 1864, CIII, 2. The rest here first printed.

"The winter in Venice," p. 32–37, 41, 42–45, first printed Boston *Advertiser*, Dec. 8, 1863, CII, 2. Pages 40–41 first printed in different form as "Letters from Venice, XV, ii. The cold," Boston *Advertiser*, March 12, 1864, CIII, 2. The rest here first printed.

"Comincia far Caldo," p. 46–53 here first printed. Pages 53–61 first printed Boston *Advertiser*, May 7, 1864, CIII, 2.

"Opera and theatres," p. 63, 63–64, first printed as "Letters from Venice, XV, i. Opera," Boston *Advertiser*, March 12, 1864, CIII, 2. Pages 66–75 first printed as "Letters from Venice, XIV, Alle marionette," Boston *Adver-*

tiser, March 5, 1864, CIII, 2. The rest here first printed.

"Venetian dinners and diners," first printed Boston *Advertiser*, Jan. 18, 1864, CIII, 2.

"Housekeeping in Venice," p. 87–98 first printed Boston *Advertiser*, July 9, 1864, CIV, 2. Pages 98–102, 103–106, first printed Boston *Advertiser*, July 16, 1864, CIV, 2. Pages 106–116 first printed Boston *Advertiser*, July 23, 1864, CIV, 2. The rest here first printed.

"The balcony on the Grand Canal," p. 117–120, 122–124, 126–129, first printed as "Letters from Venice, XXIV," Boston *Advertiser*, July 2, 1864, CIV, 2. Pages 120–121, 121–122 first printed as "Letters from Venice, VIII, ii," Boston *Advertiser*, Nov. 21, 1863, CII, 2. Page 125 first printed as "Letters from Venice, VI, i," Boston *Advertiser*, Sept. 11, 1863, CII, 2. The rest here first printed.

"A day-break ramble," p. 130–136, here first printed.

"The mouse," first printed Boston *Advertiser*, April 22, 1864, CIII, 2.

"Churches and pictures," p. 145–151, 153–163, here first printed. Pages 151–152 (and 152–153, note) first printed as "Letters from Venice, VI, iii," Boston *Advertiser*, Sept. 11, 1863, CII, 2.

"The islands of the lagoons," p. 164–182, here first printed.

"The Armenians," p. 183–185, 191–195, first printed in different form as "Letters from Venice, VII, Commencement at the Armenian College in Venice," Boston *Advertiser*, Sept. 29, 1863, CII, 2. Pages 185–186, 189–191, first printed as "Letters from Venice, VII, i," Boston *Advertiser*, Nov. 21, 1863, CII, 2. Pages 186–189 here first printed.

"The Ghetto and the Jews of Venice," first printed with different second paragraph, Boston *Advertiser*, Feb. 27, 1864, CIII, 2.

"Some memorable places," p. 208–219, first printed as "Letters from Venice, XVII, Fra Paolo Sarpi," Boston *Advertiser*, March 19, 1864, CIII, 2. Pages 219–224 here first printed.

"Venetian holidays," p. 225–240, here first printed. Pages 240–250 first printed as "Letters from Venice, IV," Boston *Advertiser*, June 29, 1863, CII, 2.

"Christmas holidays," first printed as "Letters from Venice, XII, Christmas and New Years in Venice," Boston *Advertiser*, Feb. 6, 1864, CIII, 2.

"Love-making and marrying, baptisms and burials," p. 263–272, 273–274, 275–280 here first printed. Pages 272–273, 275 first printed as "Letters from Venice, XXII, Traits of Venetian society," Boston *Advertiser*, June 16, 1864, CIII, 2. Pages 280–285 first printed as "Letters

Collations of Works... — 66-A, continued

from Venice, XIII, A Venetian funeral," Boston *Advertiser,* Feb. 4, 1864, CIII, 2.

"Venetian traits and characters," p. 286–297, first printed in different order as "Letters from Venice, XIX, Gondoliers and their stories," Boston *Advertiser,* April 7, 1864, CIII, 2. Pages 297–305 first printed Boston *Advertiser,* March 26, 1864, CIII, 2. Pages 305–317 here first printed.

"Venetian society," p. 318–330, 332–359 here first printed. Pages 330–332, first printed in different form, Boston *Advertiser,* June 16, 1864, CIV, 2.

66-B

Venetian life. | [*ornamental rule*] | by | Wm. D. Howells. | New York: | Hurd & Houghton. | MDCCCLXVI.

Collation: p. x + 362, $7\,^{7}/_{16}$ x 4¾ inches: A⁵, 1–22⁸, 23⁵; A¹ and 23⁵ are tipped in: two blank leaves; title page, [vii]; 1–359, text; 360–362, blank. End papers yellow.

In "The author to the reader," *Venetian life,* 1907, Howells says: "As for the American edition, I spent my whole percentage from it in replacing certain portions of the London sheets with corrected pages, where the errors seemed too gross. I had then gone to live in Cambridge, where errors, especially in foreign languages, were not tolerated; these were in Italian, and worse yet, they were my own blunders." This edition of five hundred copies, then, was made up from imported English first edition sheets (see 66-A), but because of errors, Howells cancelled 33 leaves in the English sheets and replaced them with 33 corrected leaves printed in the United States. These leaves are as follows: 4¹ and 4⁸ conjugate; 6⁵ tipped in on stub; 9¹ and 9⁸ conjugate; 9² and 9⁷ conjugate; 10⁶ tipped in on stub; 12² and 12⁷ conjugate; 12³ and 12⁶ conjugate; 13⁴ tipped in on stub; 14² and 14⁷ conjugate; 14³ and 14⁶ conjugate; 19¹ and 19⁸ conjugate; 19⁴ and 19⁵ conjugate; 20¹ and 20⁸ conjugate; 21¹ and 21⁸ conjugate; 21² and 21⁷ conjugate; 22³ and 22⁶ conjugate; 22⁴ and 22⁵ conjugate; 23¹ and 23⁴ are tipped in. These 33 cancellans were printed on a much flimsier wove paper than the English paper, and are also distinguishable from the English leaves because of differences in type faces and the length of the type pages.

Dark brown cloth with imitation leather grain over boards. Front and back covers blind-stamped with two rule-boxes and ornament in each corner. Lettering, rules, and ornament on spine gold-stamped. Published Aug. 24, 1866 (earliest notice observed).

Except for the corrections made in the cancellans noted above, the text of this edition is the same as that of the first London edition.

66-C

Letter | of | the Secretary of State, transmitting a report on the | commercial relations of the United States | with | foreign nations, | for | the year ended September 30, 1865.

Government Printing Office: Washington, 1866.

The consular report, p. 355–356, no more than a table of goods exported from Venice to the United States and vice versa, here first printed.

67-A

Venetian life. | By | W. D. Howells. | Second edition. | [*publisher's device*] | New York: | published by Hurd and Houghton, | 1867.

Collation: p. ii + 404, $6\,^{15}/_{16}$ x $4\,^{9}/_{16}$ inches: title page, [3]; 5, "Advertisement to the Second Edition"; 9–398, text; 399–401, index; 402–404, blank. End papers yellow. Published Jan., 1867 (cf. preface date).

Brown pebbled cloth over boards. Front and back covers blind-stamped with three rule-boxes. Rules, ornament, and lettering on spine gold-stamped.

This second edition was printed from new plates. The "Advertisement," dated Jan. 1, 1867, states: "I have given a new chapter sketching the history of Venetian Commerce and noticing the present trade and industry of Venice; I have amplified somewhat the chapter on the national holidays, and have affixed an index . . . ." There are other revisions in text throughout.

"Advertisement to the Second Edition," p. 5, here first printed.

"Commerce," p. 237–257 first printed in unexpanded form as Howells' "Consular report," in *Commercial relations of the United States,* p. 462–467; see 65-B.

67-B

Italian journeys. | By | W. D. Howells. | Author of "Venetian life." | [*publisher's device*] | New York: | published by Hurd and Houghton, | 459 Broome Street. | 1867.

Collation: p. ii + 332, 7⅛ x 4⅝ inches: title page, [5]; 9–320, text; one blank leaf. End papers yellow.

Green or brown pebbled cloth over boards. Front and back covers blind-stamped with double rule-box, rules ending in solid circles enclosed within each side of the box. Rules, lettering, and ornament on spine gold-stamped. Imitation laid paper throughout. Published Dec. 8, 1867 (earliest notice observed).

"Leaving Venice," p. 9, here first printed.

"From Padua to Ferrara," p. 10–13, here first printed.

"The picturesque, the improbable, and the pathetic in Farrara," p. 21–27, first printed Boston *Advertiser*, March 4, 1865, cv, 2; p. 27–36 first printed Boston *Advertiser*, April 13, 1865, cv, 1; p. 37–42 first printed as "Men and manners on the way from Ferrara to Genoa," *Nation*, Feb. 15, 1866, II, 205–206.

"Through Bologna to Genoa," p. 43–51, first printed as "Men and manners on the way from Ferrara to Genoa," *Nation*, Feb. 15, 1866, II, 206–207.

"Up and down Genoa," p. 52–64, first printed as "A glimpse of Genoa," *Atlantic monthly*, March, 1867, XIX, 359–363.

"By sea from Genoa to Naples," p. 65–74, first printed Boston *Advertiser*, May 3, 1865, cv, supplement, 2.

"Certain things in Naples," p. 75–88, first printed *Nation*, Jan. 25, 1866, II, 108–110.

"A day in Pompeii," p. 89–105, first printed *Nation*, Oct. 5, 1865, I, 430–432.

"A half-hour at Herculaneum," p. 106–115, first printed *Nation*, April 5, 1866, II, 429–430.

"Capri and Capriotes," p. 116–135, first printed *Nation*, July 5–12, 1866, III, 14–15, 33–34.

"The Protestant ragged schools at Naples," p. 136–146, here first printed.

"Between Rome and Naples," p. 147–150, here first printed.

"Roman pearls," p. 151–177, first printed *Nation*, Sept. 27, Nov. 29, Dec. 27, 1866, III, 253–254, 433–435, 523–525.

"Forza Maggiore," p. 178–195, first printed *Atlantic monthly*, Feb., 1867, XIX, 220–227.

"At Padua," p. 196–215, first printed *Atlantic monthly*, July, 1867, xx, 25–32.

"A pilgrimage to Petrarch's house at Arqua," p. 216–234, first printed *Nation*, Nov. 30, 1865, I, 685–688.

"A visit to the Cimbri," p. 235–250, first printed *Nation*, Oct. 19, 1865, I, 495–497.

"Pisa," p. 251–258, first printed as "Minor travels," *Atlantic monthly*, Sept., 1867, xx, 337–339.

"The Ferrara road," p. 259–263, here first printed.

"Trieste," p. 264–273, first printed as "Minor travels," *Atlantic monthly*, Sept., 1867, xx, 342–346.

"Bassano," p. 274–276, first printed as "Minor travels," *Atlantic monthly*, Sept., 1867, xx, 346–347; p. 276–279 here first printed.

"Possagno," p. 281–284, first printed as "Minor travels," *Atlantic monthly*, Sept., 1867, xx, 347–348.

"Como," p. 285–292, first printed as "Minor travels," *Atlantic monthly*, Sept., 1867, xx, 339–342.

"Stopping at Vicenza, Verona, and Parma," p. 293–320, here first printed.

69-A

No love lost | a romance of travel | by W. D. Howells | author of "Venetian life," etc. | New York | G. P. Putnam & Son 661 Broadway | 1869.

Collation: p. iv + 60, 6¹¹⁄₁₆ x 5¼ inches: engraved frontispiece, [iv]; engraved title page, [1]; title page, [3]; 5–58, text; blank leaf. One illustrated leaf tipped in and not paginated. Red-brown end papers.

Pebbled green or brown cloth over bevelled boards. Blind-stamped rule-boxes on covers; front cover gold-stamped with lettering and cupid figure. All edges gilt. Illustrations by Elinor Mead Howells. Published Nov. 12, 1868 (earliest notice observed).

First printed *Putnam's*, n. s., Dec., 1868, II, 641–651.

69-B

The | Atlantic almanac | 1870 | [*illustrations and contents*] | Boston: | Fields, Osgood, & Co., | office of the Atlantic Monthly. | [*All the foregoing in a rule-box*]

Fields, Osgood, & Co.: Boston, 1869. Published Dec., 1869 (earliest notice observed).

"BoPeep: a pastoral," p. 12–13, 15–16, here first printed.

71-A

Suburban sketches. | By | W. D. Howells, | author of "Venetian life" and "Italian journeys." | [*publisher's device*] | New York: | published by Hurd and Houghton. | Cambridge: Riverside Press. | 1871.

Collation: p. 240, 7 ⁵/₁₆ x 5 inches: title page, [7]; 11–234, text; three blank leaves. End papers cream-yellow.

Green or brown pebbled cloth over bevelled boards. Publisher's device stamped in gold on front cover; lettering on backstrip gold-stamped. Top edge gilt; fore and bottom edges rough-trimmed. Imitation laid paper throughout except for end papers. Published Dec. 19, 1870.

In some copies of this edition, the collation reads p. ii + 238, the only difference being that a blank page precedes the arabic pagination and that there are two instead of three blank leaves at the end.

"Mrs. Johnson," first printed *Atlantic monthly*, Jan., 1868, xxi, 97–106.

"Doorstep acquaintance," first printed *Atlantic monthly*, April, 1869, xxiii, 484–493.

"A pedestrian tour," first printed *Atlantic monthly*, Nov., 1869, xxiv, 591–603.

"By horse-car to Boston," first printed *Atlantic monthly*, Jan., 1870, xxv, 114–122.

"A day's pleasure," first printed *Atlantic monthly*, July – Sept., 1870, xxvi, 107–114, 223–230, 341–346.

"A romance of real life," first printed *Atlantic monthly*, March, 1870, xxv, 305–312.

"Scene," here first printed. Reprinted in *Every Saturday*, Jan. 7, 1871, x, 11.

"Jubilee days," first printed *Atlantic monthly*, Aug., 1869, xxiv, 245–254.

"Flitting," first printed *Atlantic monthly*, Dec., 1870, xxvi, 734–739.

72-A

Their wedding journey. | By | W. D. Howells, | author of "Venetian life," "Italian journeys," etc. | With illustrations by | Augustus Hoppin. |

[*publisher's device*] | Boston: | James R. Osgood and Company. | late Ticknor & Fields, and Fields, Osgood, & Co. | 1872.

Collation: p. vi + 290, 7⅜ x 4⅞ inches: title page, [iii]; 1–287, text; 288–290, blank. End papers cream-yellow.

Brown cloth with fine crosshatching over boards. Lettering and ornament on front cover stamped in gold and black. Lettering and publisher's device on spine raised or gold-stamped; ornament stamped in gold and black. Rule-boxes and ornament on back cover blind-stamped. Published Dec. 27, 1871.

According to Merle Johnson, *American first editions* (New York, 1942), the first state has a period after "Co" in "Osgood, & Co.", later copies dropping the period.

First printed *Atlantic monthly*, July, 1871, xxviii, 29–40, chapter i; Aug., 162–176, ii–iii; Sept., 345–357, iv–v; Oct., 442–459, vi; Nov., 605–623, vii–viii; Dec., 721–740, ix–x.

72-B

Italian journeys. | By | W. D. Howells, | author of "Suburban sketches," "Venetian life," etc. | New and enlarged edition. | [*publisher's device*] | Boston: | James R. Osgood and Company. | late Ticknor & Fields, and Fields, Osgood, & Co. | 1872.

Collation: p. 400, 7⅜ x 4⅞ inches: title page, [3]; 9–398, text; blank leaf. End papers chocolate brown.

Brown or green cloth blind-stamped with fine crosshatching over boards. Lettering and ornament on front cover stamped in gold and black. Lettering and publisher's device on spine gold-stamped; ornament stamped in gold and black. In some copies a blank leaf precedes the regularly paginated leaves, the collation thus reading "p. ii + 400." The text, p. 9–320, is here reprinted from the first edition plates. Published May 18, 1872.

"Ducal Mantua," p. 321–398, first printed *North American review*, Jan., 1866, cii, 48–100.

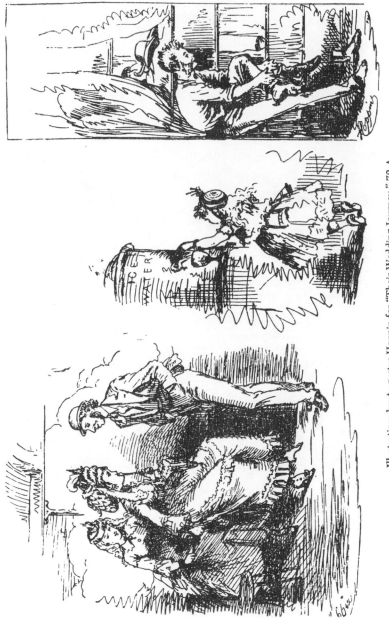

Illustrations by Augustus Hoppin for "Their Wedding Journey," 72-A

72-C

Venetian life. | By | W. D. Howells, | author of "Suburban sketches," "Italian journeys," etc. | New and enlarged edition. | [*publisher's device*] | Boston: | James R. Osgood and Company. | late Ticknor & Fields, and Fields, Osgood, & Co. | 1872.

Collation: p. ii + 440, 7 ⁵/₁₆ x 4 ¹⁵/₁₆ inches: advertisements, [2]; title page, [3]; preface, [5]; 9–434, text; 435–437, index; 438–440, blank. End papers chocolate brown.

Brown cloth blind-stamped with fine cross-hatching over boards. Lettering and ornaments on front cover stamped in gold and black. Rules and ornaments on back cover blind-stamped. Lettering and publisher's device on spine gold-stamped; ornament stamped in gold and black. Pages 5, 9–398 are reprinted from the 1867 plates. Published May 18, 1872.

"Our last year in Venice," p. 399–434, first printed as "A year in a Venetian palace," *Atlantic monthly,* Jan., 1871, xxvii, 1–14.

72-D

Jubilee days. [*in scroll*] | An illustrated daily record | of the | humorous features of the world's peace jubilee. | With illustrations by Augustus Hoppin, | engraved by the Chemical Engraving Company. | [*Hoppin engraving*] | Boston: | James R. Osgood and Company, | (late Ticknor & Fields, and Fields, Osgood, & Co.) | 1872.

Collation: p. iv + 72, 11 ⁵/₁₆ x 8⅛ inches: title page, [i]; publisher's note, [iii]; list of plates, [iv]; 1–68, text of the sixteen numbers of the four-page journal; 69–72, advertisements and engravings. End papers.

Paper over boards. Title page repeated on front cover; advertisements for books by Howells on back cover. Leather backstrip. It is known that Aldrich and Howells edited this work jointly; a Howells manuscript indicates that he and Aldrich also wrote everything in

it. The publisher's notice on p. [iii] reads: "The daily issues of *Jubilee Days* have been received with such favor, that the publishers feel warranted in presenting them in a more permanent form." Published July 4, 1872 (date of last number).

72-E

Suburban sketches. | By W. D. Howells, | author of "Venetian life," "Italian journeys," etc. | New and enlarged edition. | With illustrations by | Augustus Hoppin. | [*publisher's device*] | Boston: | James R. Osgood and Company. | late Ticknor & Fields, and Fields, Osgood, & Co. | 1872.

Collation: p. ii + 258, 7⅜ x 4⅛ inches; title page, [3]; 11–255, text; 256–258, blank. Frontispiece and nine illustrated leaves tipped in and not paginated. End papers cream-yellow.

Brown cloth with fine diagonal grain, or brown or green cloth with fine vertical-horizontal grain, over boards; or salmon-red pebbled cloth over boards, end papers chocolate. In all bindings, ornament and lettering on front cover stamped in black and gold; lettering, ornament, and publisher's device on spine stamped in black and gold; double-rule-box on back cover blind-stamped. Pages 11–219, 241–255 printed from Hurd and Houghton first edition plates. See 71-A.

"Some lessons from the school of morals," first printed as "The new taste in theatricals," *Atlantic monthly,* May, 1869, xxiii, 635–644.

73-A

A chance acquaintance. | By | W. D. Howells. | [*publisher's device*] | Boston: | James R. Osgood and Company, | late Ticknor & Fields, and Fields, Osgood, & Co. | 1873. [*All the foregoing in two rule-boxes.*]

Collation: p. viii + 288, 5 ¹³/₁₆ x 4 inches: title page, [v]; 1–279, text; 280–288, colophon, advertisements, blank leaf. Blue-black end papers.

Tan or green or blue cloth over boards. Covers and spine blind-stamped; gold-stamped

Collations of Works . . . — 73-A, continued

ornaments and lettering. All edges stained red-tan. Published May 27, 1873.

First printed *Atlantic monthly*, Jan., 1873, xxxi, 17–28; Feb., 181–196; March, 339–356; April, 431–448; May, 563–578; June, 693–704.

For textual change from magazine serialization to volume publication see *Life in letters*, i, 174.

73-B

Poems | by | W. D. Howells. | [*publisher's device*] | Boston: | James R. Osgood and Company, | late Ticknor & Fields, and Fields, Osgood, & Co. | 1873. [*All the foregoing in two rule-boxes.*]

Collation: p. iv + 176, $5^{13}/_{16}$ x 4 inches: title page, [iii]; 3–172, text; two blank leaves. Blue-black end papers.

Tan or green or dark blue cloth over boards. Covers and spine blind-stamped; lettering and ornaments on spine and front cover gold-stamped. All edges stained red. Published Sept. 30, 1873.

"The pilot's story," first printed *Atlantic monthly*, Sept., 1860, vi, 323–325.

"Forlorn," first printed *Nation*, Aug. 16, 1866, iii, 134–135. Reprinted Ashtabula *Sentinel*, Sept. 5, 1866, xxxv, 1.

"Pleasure — pain," first printed as "Andenken" and "Pleasure — pain" at greater length *Atlantic monthly*, Jan., 1860, v, 100–102, and April, 1860, v, 468–470.

"In August," reprinted from "Summer dead," *The poets and poetry of the West*. See 60-E.

"The empty house," first printed as "The old homestead," *Atlantic monthly*, Feb., 1861, vii, 213.

"Bubbles," first printed *Atlantic monthly*, April, 1861, vii, 415.

"Lost beliefs," first printed *Atlantic monthly*, April, 1860, v, 486.

"Louis Lebeau's conversion," first printed *Atlantic monthly*, Nov., 1862, x, 534–538.

"Caprice," first printed *Saturday press*, April 14, 1860, iii, 1. Reprinted *Ohio state journal*, April 18, 1860, xxiv, 4.

"Sweet clover," first printed *Harper's monthly*, Feb., 1866, xxxii, 322.

"The royal portraits," first printed *Harper's monthly*, Dec., 1865, xxxii, 43.

"The faithful of the Gonzaga," first printed

New York *Ledger* (1865?); see F. C. Marston, jr., *The early life*, p. 280.

"The first cricket," first printed *Atlantic monthly*, Sept., 1869, xxiv, 351.

"The mulberries," first printed *Atlantic monthly*, March, 1871, xxvii, 377–379.

"Before the gate," first printed *Atlantic monthly*, Aug., 1869, xxiv, 176.

"Clement," first printed *Galaxy*, June 1, 1866, i, 210–212.

"By the sea," first printed *Commonwealth*, May 1, 1863, i, 1. Dated "Venice, March 24th." Reprinted Boston *Advertiser*, May 6, 1863, ci, 1.

"Saint Christopher," first printed *Harper's monthly*, Dec., 1863, xxviii, 1–2.

"Elegy on John Butler Howells," first printed Ashtabula *Sentinel*, June 29, 1864, xxxiii, 1.

"Thanksgiving," first printed in "Minor topics," *Nation*, Dec. 7, 1865, i, 8.

"A springtime," first printed *Commonwealth*, April 1, 1864, ii, 1. Dated "Columbus, O., June, 1861."

"In earliest spring," first printed *Atlantic monthly*, May, 1872, xxix, 619.

"The bobolinks are singing," reprinted from *The poets and poetry of the West*. See 60-E.

"Prelude," reprinted from *Poems of two friends*. See 60-A.

"The movers," reprinted from *Poems of two friends*.

"Through the meadow," reprinted from *Poems of two friends*.

"Gone," reprinted from *Poems of two friends*.

"The sarcastic fair," reprinted from *Poems of two friends*.

"Rapture," reprinted from "Liebeswonne," *Poems of two friends*.

"Dead," reprinted from *Poems of two friends*.

"The doubt," reprinted from *Poems of two friends*.

"The thorn," reprinted from *Poems of two friends*.

"The mysteries," reprinted from *Poems of two friends*.

"The battle in the clouds," first printed in *The battle in the clouds*; see 64-A.

"For one of the killed," here first printed.

"The two wives," first printed with dedication, "To Colonel J.[ohn] G. M.[itchell]," in Memory of the Event before Atlanta," Boston *Advertiser*, Nov. 12, 1864, civ, 2.

"Bereaved," first printed *Ohio state journal*, March 2, 1860, xxiii, 4. Reprinted *Ohio farmer*, March 3, 1860, ix, 72.

"The snow-birds," first printed *Ohio farmer*, Jan. 28, 1860, ix, 32 and *Ohio state journal*, Jan. 28, 1860, xxiii, 2.

"Vagary," first printed *Saturday press,* March 24, 1860, III, 4. Reprinted Ashtabula *Sentinel,* April 18, 1860, XXIX, 1.

"Feuerbilder," first printed *Saturday press,* Jan. 14, 1860, III, 1. Reprinted *Ohio state journal,* Jan. 18, 1860, XXIII, 4, and *Ohio farmer,* Feb. 25, 1860, IX, 64.

"Avery," first printed *Their wedding journey,* p. 139–141. See 72-A.

"BoPeep: a pastoral," first printed *The Atlantic almanac.* See 69-B.

"While she sang," first printed as portion of "Mortuaviva," *Saturday press,* Dec. 10, 1859, II, 1.

"Naming the bird."

"A poet," first printed *Dial,* June, 1860, I, 371. Reprinted *Saturday press,* June 2, 1860, III, and *Commonwealth,* Feb. 14, 1863, I, 1.

"Convention," first printed *Dial,* June, 1860, I, 371. Reprinted *Ohio farmer,* June 16, 1860, IX, 192.

"The poet's friends," reprinted from *The poets and poetry of the West.* See 60-E.

74-A

A chance acquaintance. | By | William D. Howells. | Illustrated by William L. Sheppard. | [*publisher's device*] | Boston: | James R. Osgood and Company, | late Ticknor & Fields, and Fields, Osgood, & Company. | 1874.

Collation: p. iv + 272, 7 $^7/_{16}$ x 4⅞ inches: title page, [5]; 13–271, text; 272, blank. Frontispiece leaf paginated; six illustrated leaves tipped in and not paginated. End papers cream-yellow.

Brown or green cloth over boards. Lettering and ornament on front cover stamped in gold and black; rules, lettering, ornament, publisher's device on spine stamped in gold and black. Double rule-box on back cover blind-stamped. Published Nov. 17, 1873.

Printed with illustrations and from new plates. See 73-A.

75-A

A foregone conclusion. | By | W. D. Howells, | author of | "Venetian life," "Their wedding journey," | "A chance acquaintance," etc. | Boston: | James R. Osgood and Company. | Late Tick-

nor & Fields, and Fields, Osgood, & Co. | 131 Franklin Street. | 1875.

Collation: p. iv + 268, 7⅜ x 4¾ inches; advertisements, [ii]; title page, [iii]; 1–265, text; 266–268, blank. End papers chocolate brown.

First issue brown cloth with fine cross-hatching over boards with advertisements on p. [ii]; second issue green cloth. Lettering on front cover gold-stamped; ornament stamped in black and gold. On spine, lettering raised and gold-stamped, ornament and publisher's device in black or gold. Double-rule-box blind-stamped on back cover. Published Dec. 3, 1874.

First printed *Atlantic monthly,* July, 1874, XXXIV, 1–15, chapters i–ii; Aug., 145–160, iii–vi; Sept., 345–360, vii–ix; Oct., 475–487, x–xii; Nov., 534–550, xiii–xv; Dec., 641–658, xvi–xviii.

76-A

Theatrum majorum. | The Cambridge of 1776: | . . . | with which is incorporated | the diary of Dorothy Dudley, | now first publish'd.

The Ladies' Centennial Committee, Cambridge; Lockwood, Brooks, & Co., Boston; Hurd & Houghton, New York, 1876. Published Nov., 1875 (title page date).

"Dorothy Dudley," sonnet, p. 1, here first printed.

76-B

A day's pleasure. | By | William D. Howells. | Illustrated. | [*floral design*] | Boston: | James R. Osgood and Company, | late Ticknor & Fields, and Fields, Osgood, & Co. | 1876.

Collation: p. 92, 4 $^{11}/_{16}$ x 3¼ inches: title page, [3]; 11–91, text; 92, blank. Frontispiece and two illustrated leaves paginated. End papers of light stock with advertisements in red.

Green or brown cloth over boards. Lettering on front cover gold-stamped; rule-box, floral design, and publisher's device stamped in black. Lettering and ornament on spine stamped in

Collations of Works... — 76-B, continued
black; rule-box and ornament on back cover stamped in black. "Vest-pocket series." Published Feb. 18, 1876.

Reprinted from *Suburban sketches*, p. 115–170. New plates were used in this edition.

76-C

Sketch | of the | life and character | of | Rutherford B. Hayes. | By Wm. D. Howells. | Also a biographical sketch of | William A. Wheeler. | With portraits of both candidates | New York: | published by Hurd and Houghton. | Boston: H. O. Houghton and Company. | Cambridge: the Riverside Press. | 1876.

Collation: p. –iv + vi + 196 [+ 38 separately paginated], 6¾ x 4¼ inches: two blank leaves; title page, [i]; iii–iv, preface; 1–195, text; 196, blank; [3–31, text in second pagination; 32–38, blank and advertisements]. Two tipped-in portrait leaves not paginated. End papers yellow.

Brick-red or dark blue cloth with diagonal grain over boards. Ornamental band (stamped in black on front cover and spine, blind-stamped on back cover) runs across lower portion of covers and spine. Lettering and ornament on front cover stamped in black; on spine in gold. The first issue of the first edition is distinguished by the words "seven hundred days" in the eighth line from the bottom of p. 96, and by an erratum slip tipped in between p. 96–97 correcting the phrase to read "about one hundred days." Published Sept. 15, 1876.

76-D

The parlor car. | Farce. | By | William D. Howells. | [*ornament*] | Boston: | James R. Osgood and Company, | late Ticknor & Fields, and Fields, Osgood, & Co. | 1876.

Collation: p. 76, 4¹¹/₁₆ x 3¼ inches: title page, [1]; 3–74, text; blank leaf. End papers printed with advertisements in purple-red.

Green or brown cloth over thin boards. Lettering on front cover gold-stamped; on

spine stamped in black. Publisher's device on front cover raised from ornament stamped in black; rule-boxes and ornament on front cover and spine stamped in black. Ornament and rule-box on back cover blind-stamped. "Vest-pocket series." Published Dec. 4, 1876.

First printed *Atlantic monthly*, Sept., 1876, xxxviii, 290–300.

76-E

The first cricket | words by | W. D. Howells, | music by | F. Booth. | 3 [*within star*] | Boston | Oliver Ditson & C° 451 Washington Sᵗ. | N. York. C. H. Ditson & Co. Philᵃ. J. E. Ditson & Co. | 711 Broadway. Sucʳˢ. to Lee & Walker. | Cinn, J. Church & Co. Boston, J. C. Haynes & Co. Chicago, Lyon & Healy. | Copyright 1876 by D. Ditson & Co. [*All the foregoing in rule-box.*]

Collation: p. 6, 13¹⁵/₁₆ x 10¹¹/₁₆ inches: title page, [1]; 2, blank; 3–5, text; 6, blank. No end papers.

No cover. Sheet music. One folded leaf and one single leaf not sewed or bound.

Reprinted from *Poems*. See 73-B.

77-A

Out of the question. | A comedy. | By | W. D. Howells. | [*publisher's device*] | Boston: | James R. Osgood and Company. | Late Ticknor & Fields, and Fields, Osgood, & Co. | 1877. [*All the foregoing in two rule-boxes.*]

Collation: p. vi + 186, 5¾ x 4³/₁₆ inches: title page, [v]; 5–183, text; 184–186 blank. First and last leaves, of lighter stock than text, tipped in. End papers blue-black.

Green or brown cloth over boards. Lettering and ornament on front cover and spine gold-stamped. Rule-boxes and ornament on covers and spine blind-stamped. All edges stained red. Published April 25, 1877.

First printed *Atlantic monthly*, Feb.–April, 1877, xxxix, 195–208, 317–329, 447–461.

77-B

A counterfeit presentment. | Comedy. | By | W. D. Howells. | [*publisher's device*] | Boston: | James R. Osgood and Company. | Late Ticknor & Fields, and Fields, Osgood, & Co. | 1877. [*All the foregoing in two rule-boxes.*]

Collation: p. iv + 160, 5¾ x 4⅛ inches; title page, [1]; 7–155, text; 156–160, blank. Dull black end papers.

Green or brown or gray cloth over boards. Covers and spine blind-stamped; gold-stamped ornaments and lettering. All edges stained red. Published Oct. 5, 1877.

First printed *Atlantic monthly*, Aug.–Oct., 1877, XL, 148–161, 296–305, 448–460.

77-C

Autobiography. | [*rule*] | Memoirs | of | Frederica Sophia Wilhelmina, | Princess Royal of Prussia, | ... | With an essay | by William D. Howells.

James R. Osgood and Company: Boston, 1877. Two volumes. Published Oct. 12, 1877.

The essay, I, 1–28, here first printed.

77-D

Autobiography. | [*rule*] | Lives | of | Lord Herbert of Cherbury | and | Thomas Ellwood. | With essays | by William D. Howells.

James R. Osgood and Company: Boston, 1877. Published Oct. 15, 1877.

The essays, p. 1–14, 169–179, here first printed.

77-E

Autobiography. | [*rule*] | Life | of | Vittorio Alfieri. | [*rule*] | With an essay | by William D. Howells.

James R. Osgood and Company: Boston, 1877. Published Nov. 6, 1877.

The essay, p. 5–51, first printed *Atlantic monthly*, May, 1875, XXXV, 533–549.

77-F

Autobiography. | [*rule*] | Memoirs | of | Carlo Goldoni. | Translated from the original French, | by John Black. | With an essay | by William D. Howells.

James R. Osgood and Company: Boston, 1877. Published Nov. 13, 1877.

"Carlo Goldoni," p. 4–29, first printed *Atlantic monthly*, Nov., 1877, XL, 601–613.

77-G

Autobiography. | [*rule*] | Memoirs | of | Edward Gibbon, Esq. | [*rule*] | With an essay | by William D. Howells.

James R. Osgood and Company: Boston, 1877. Published Dec. 20, 1877.

The essay, p. 5–41, first printed *Atlantic monthly*, Jan., 1878, XLI, 99–111.

78-A

Autobiography. | [*rule*] | Memoirs | of | Jean François Marmontel. | With an essay | by William D. Howells.

Houghton, Osgood and Company: Boston, 1878. Two volumes. Published May 17, 1878.

The essay, I, 5–27, first printed *Atlantic monthly*, March, 1878, XLI, 332–343.

79-A

The | lady of the Aroostook. | By | W. D. Howells, | author of "A foregone conclusion," "A chance acquaintance," | "Venetian life," etc. | Boston: | Houghton, Osgood and Company. | The Riverside Press, Cambridge. | 1879.

Collation: p. iv + 328, 7⅜ x 4¾ inches: title page, [iii]; 1–326, text; blank leaf. End papers dark gray with fine purple floral design.

Light or dark green cloth with fine diagonal grain over boards. Ornamental band running across front cover and spine stamped in black and gold; lettering on front cover in gold, on spine black and gold. Published Feb. 27, 1879. Variant copies exist with one extra flyleaf preceding the title page and one extra flyleaf following the text.

First printed *Atlantic monthly*, Nov., 1878, xlii, 597–618, chapters i–vi; Dec., 727–746, vii–x; Jan., 1879, xliii, 25–41, xi–xiv; Feb., 193–216, xv–xxi; March, 338–367, xxii–xxvii.

79-B

Editorial right | a question of honesty and plain speech | W. J. Linton *v.* the Atlantic Monthly.

Appledore Press: Hamden, Connecticut [1879]. Dated New Haven, Connecticut, June, 1879.

Letters, dated April 18 and May 14, 1879, Editorial Office of the Atlantic Monthly, p. 1–2 and 3 here first printed. This eight-page pamphlet contains correspondence between Linton and Howells, and Linton and Houghton, Osgood and Company regarding alterations made in the proof of Linton's article, "Art engraving on wood," which appeared in the June *Atlantic.*

80-A

The | undiscovered country. | By | W. D. Howells, | author of "The lady of the Aroostook," "A foregone conclusion," | "A chance acquaintance," "Venetian life," etc. | [*publisher's device*] | Boston: | Houghton, Mifflin and Company. | The Riverside Press, Cambridge. | 1880.

Collation: p. vi + 422, 7⅜ x 4¾ inches: title page, [v]; 1–419, text; 420–422, blank. End papers gray.

Dark blue, brown, green, or drab olive cloth with diagonal grain over boards. Over-all floral design stamped in black on front cover and spine (present in all issues). Rule-box blind-stamped on back cover. Lettering on front cover and spine gold-stamped. Published June 24, 1880. Variant copies bound in brown cloth exist with no comma after "1880" and a period after "Company" on p. [vi], the verso of the title page.

First printed *Atlantic monthly*, Jan., 1880, xlv, 66–84, chapters i–ii; Feb., 216–240, iii–

vii; March, 336–355, viii–xi; April, 499–523, xii–xiv; May, 641–660, xv–xvii; June, 780–805, xviii–xxii; July, xlvi, 83–111, xxiii–xxviii.

81-A

A fearful responsibility | and other stories | by | William D. Howells | author of "The lady of the Aroostook," "The undiscovered | country," etc. | [*publisher's device*] | Boston | James R. Osgood and Company | 1881

Collation: p. vi + 258, 7⅜ x 4⅞ inches: title page, [v]; 3–255, text; 256–258, blank. Gray-green end papers.

Light-brown or green cloth over boards. Ornaments and publisher's device stamped in black and gold on front cover and spine. Published July 13, 1881.

"A fearful responsibility," first printed *Scribner's*, June–July, 1881, xxii, 276–293, 390–414.

"At the sign of the Savage," first printed *Atlantic monthly*, July, 1877, xl, 36–48.

"Tonelli's marriage," first printed *Atlantic monthly*, July, 1868, xxii, 96–110.

81-B

"The city and the sea," | with other Cambridge contributions, | in aid of | the hospital fund.

John Wilson and Son: Cambridge, 1881. Published Nov. 9, 1881.

"My first friend in Cambridge," p. 73–78, here first printed.

81-C

Doctor Breen's practice | a novel | by | William D. Howells | author of "The lady of the Aroostook," "The undiscovered | country," "Venetian life," etc. | [*publisher's device*] | Boston | James R. Osgood and Company | 1881

Collation: p. iv + 276, 7⅜ x 4¾ inches: title page, [1]; 3–272, text; two blank leaves. End papers tan or green with floral design.

Dark blue or green cloth with diagonal grain over boards. Ornamental band running across front cover and spine stamped in black and gold. Lettering on front cover and spine raised or gold-stamped. Publisher's device on front cover stamped in black. Published Dec. 2, 1881.

First printed *Atlantic monthly*, Aug., 1881, xlviii, 145–164, chapters i–iii; Sept., 289–309, iv–vi; Oct., 433–452, vii–viii; Nov., 577–593, ix–x; Dec., 721–734, xi–xii.

81-D

Modern classics. | [*rule*] | A day's pleasure, and | other sketches. | By W. D. Howells. | Illustrated. | [*ornament*] | Boston: | Houghton, Mifflin and Company. | The Riverside Press, Cambridge. | 1881.

Collation: p. iv + 242, 5¼ x 3⅝ inches: title page, [1]; 11–240, text; blank leaf. Five illustrated leaves paginated, flimsy protective leaf over first illustrated leaf tipped in and not paginated. End papers with advertisements in red.

Dark green cloth over flexible boards. Lettering on front cover raised from band stamped in gold or black; ornament, publisher's device, and rule-box stamped in black. Lettering, rules, ornament, publisher's device on spine in black or gold. Back cover blind-stamped with double rule-box.

"A day's pleasure," p. 11–91, reprinted from first edition plates of *A day's pleasure*. See 76-B.

"Buying a horse," p. 95–138, first printed *Atlantic monthly*, June, 1879, xliii, 741–750.

"Flitting," p. 141–166, reprinted from *Suburban sketches*. See 71-A.

"The mouse," p. 169–180, reprinted from *Venetian life*. See 66-B.

"A year in a Venetian palace," p. 183–240, reprinted from enlarged edition of *Venetian life*. See 72-C.

There is no separate edition of "Buying a horse" until 1916. (See 16-D.) At the time that P. K. Foley was compiling his bibliography, *American authors 1795–1895*, he must have written to Howells for titles and dates, and Howells evidently called the above volume (which prints the sketch in volume form for the first time, it will be noted) *Buying a horse*. Foley later wrote to Howells asking him if he had not made a mistake; Howells returned Foley's letter with the pencilled notation that he had. This letter, and a note from Houghton, Mifflin and Company stating that

they had not published a separate edition and knew of none, may be found in Foley's own interleaved copy of *American authors* at the American Antiquarian Society Library in Worcester, Massachusetts.

82-A

Spare minute series. | [*rule*] | Living truths | from the writings of Charles Kingsley | selected by | E. E. Brown | introduction by | W. D. Howells.

D. Lathrop and Company: Boston [1882]. Published July 20, 1882.

"Introduction," p. 3–4, here first printed.

82-B

A modern instance | a novel | by | William D. Howells | author of "The lady of the Aroostook," "The undiscovered | country," "Dr. Breen's practice," etc. | [*publisher's device*] | Boston | James R. Osgood and Company | 1882

Collation: p. iv + 516, 7⅜ x 4¾ inches: title page, [1]; 3–514, text; blank leaf. End papers light gray, of heavier stock than text.

Brown or green cloth with diagonal grain over boards. Ornamental band running across top of front cover and spine stamped in black and gold. Lettering on front cover and spine raised or gold-stamped. Publisher's device on front cover stamped in black. Published Oct. 7, 1882. Merle Johnson, *American first editions* (New York, 1942) states that it is probable that the "first state" of this book is 1¼ inches across the top of the covers, later copies being printed on a lighter stock wove paper. Published Oct. 7, 1882.

The Howells letter which follows, laid in the copy of *A modern instance* in the David A. Borowitz collection, throws a very interesting light on Howells' attitude toward the ending of his novel as it exists in print. It was probably written to a *Century* editor.

"Boston, March 24, 1882 Dear Sir: I have shortened this a little, and I am very sorry that I can't have out the last chapter. I can assure you that I wish the story had not grown to such length on my hands: it has cost me nearly twice the labor of anything I've written before; I will compress it all I can. Yours truly, W. D. Howells."

First printed *Century*, Dec., 1881, xxiii, 241–258, chapters i–iv; Jan., 1882, 362–375, v–vii; Feb., 577–591, viii–x; March, 753–760, xi–xii; April, 921–931, xiii–xv; May, xxiv, 114–127, xvi–xviii; June, 257–272, xix–xxii; July, 409–425, xxiii–xxvi; Aug., 569–586, xxvii–xxx; Sept., 740–763, xxxi–xxxv; Oct., 897–919, xxxvi–xli.

82-C

Harper's Christmas | pictures & papers | [*illustration with wide floral border, at bottom* Christmas 1882] | Done by the | Tile Club | & its literary friends | Published by Harper & Brothers | Harpers Square, New York

Collation: p. iv + 32, 21½ x 16¼ inches: title page, [front cover recto]; index and prospectus, [front cover verso]; supplement illustration, [ii–iii]; 1–31, text; 32 and [back cover recto and verso], advertisements. No end papers.

Paper covers of heavier stock than text. Lettering and illustrations on front and back covers printed in green and light brown. Published Nov., 1882.

"The sleeping-car, a farce," p. 6–7, here first printed.

83-A

The | sleeping-car | a farce | by William D. Howells | [*publisher's device*] | Boston | James R. Osgood and Company | 1883

Collation: p. iv + 76, 5½ x 3½ inches: title page, [1]; 3–74, text; blank leaf. End papers with advertisements printed in red.

Dark green cloth over thin boards. Front cover design stamped in black, publisher's device in black, lettering raised from gold panel. Back cover blind-stamped with double rulebox. All edges stained red. Published March 21, 1883.

First printed *Harper's Christmas*: see 82-C.

83-B

A woman's reason | a novel | by | William D. Howells | author of "A modern instance," "Doctor Breen's practice," | "A foregone conclusion," etc. | [*publisher's device*] | Boston | James R. Osgood and Company | 1883

Collation: p. viii + 468, 7 ⁷/₁₆ x 4¾ inches: title page, [v]; 1–466, text; blank leaf. End papers gray.

Dark blue or tan cloth with diagonal grain over boards. Ornamental band running across front cover and spine stamped in black and gold. Lettering on front cover and spine raised or gold-stamped. Publisher's device on front cover stamped in black. Published Sept. 24, 1883.

First printed *Century*, Feb., 1883, xxv, 513–528, chapters i–ii; March, 753–768, iii–v; April, 887–898, vi–vii; May, xxvi, 115–127, viii–ix; June, 233–248, x–xi; July, 433–449, xii–xiv; Aug., 592–611, xv–xvi; Sept., 659–671, xvii–xix; Oct., 907–921, xx–xxi.

84-A

A little girl | among the old masters | with introduction and comment | by W. D. Howells | [*floral ornament*] | Boston | James R. Osgood and Company | 1884

Collation: p. [132], 5¾ x 8⅞ inches: the 66 leaves printed on the recto of each leaf only and numbered 3–65; title page, [3]; text, [5–129]; 130–132, blank; 54 leaves of illustrations are tipped in and not paginated. End papers with green floral design.

Olive green or brown cloth over boards. Ornamental figure on front cover stamped in black; lettering in red. Lettering on spine stamped in black. Text and illustrations on wove paper, somewhat heavier for illustrations. All edges stained orange. Drawings by Mildred Howells. Published Nov. 15, 1883.

A deluxe edition also appeared. The English edition was published by Trübner and Company, London, n. d.

84-B

The | register | farce | by W. D. Howells | [*publisher's device*] | Boston |

James R. Osgood and Company | 1884

Collation: p. ii + 94, 5¼ x 3½ inches: title page, [3]; 5–91, text; 92–94, blank. End papers with advertisements in red.

Dark green cloth over thin boards. Front cover design stamped in black, publisher's device in black, lettering raised from gold panel. Back cover blind-stamped with double rule-box. All edges stained red. Published March 17, 1884.

First printed *Harper's monthly*, Dec., 1883, LXVIII, 70–86.

84-C

[*Ornament*] | Three villages | by | W. D. Howells | author of | "A modern instance," "Dr. Breen's practice," etc. | [*publisher's device*] | Boston | James R. Osgood and Company | 1884

Collation: p. ii + 200, 5¾ x 4⅛ inches: title page, [5]; 11–198, text; blank leaf. End papers black.

First issue gray-green or brown cloth over boards. Spine and covers blind-stamped; lettering on spine and front cover gold-stamped. All edges stained orange. Second issue chocolate brown cloth over boards, lettering and ornament on front cover stamped in black. Published May 22, 1884.

"Lexington," first printed *Longman's*, Nov., 1882, I, 41–61.

"Shirley," first printed as "A Shaker village," *Atlantic monthly*, June, 1876, XXXVII, 699–710.

"Gnadenhütten," first printed *Atlantic monthly*, Jan., 1869, XXIII, 95–115.

84-D

Niagara | revisited [*the foregoing on a scroll*] | (· by · William · Dean · Howells ·) | Published · by · D · Dalziell · Chicago · [*All the foregoing on a colored sketch of Niagara Falls, within four rule-boxes.*] [1884].

Collation: p. ii + 16 + [16], 8¾ x 7 inches: blank leaf; title page, [i]; text, 1–12; 13–16, blank. Frontispiece leaf, with illustration on verso, and six leaves (twelve colored illustrations)

tipped in and not paginated; a gathering of sixteen unnumbered pages of advertisements is also bound between p. 12–[13]. End papers light tan with black floral design.

Cream-tan paper over boards. Lettering on front cover (including full title, "Niagara revisited, 12 years after their wedding journey by the Hoosac Tunnel route") pink, on colored background of train entering the Hoosac Tunnel. Colored illustration on back cover. This pirated edition was suppressed by Howells for financial reasons.

First printed *Atlantic monthly*, May, 1883, LI, 598–610.

85-A

The | elevator | farce | by W. D. Howells | [*publisher's device*] | Boston | James R. Osgood and Company | 1885

Collation: p. ii + 86, 5¼ x 3½ inches: [ii], advertisements; title page, [1]; 5–84, text; blank leaf. End papers with advertisements in red.

Dark green cloth over thin boards. Front cover design stamped in black, publisher's device in black, lettering raised from gold panel. Back cover blind-stamped with double rule-box. All edges stained red. Published Jan. 30, 1885.

First printed *Harper's monthly*, Dec., 1884, LXX, 111–125.

85-B

The | rise of Silas Lapham | by | William D. Howells | author of "A modern instance," "A woman's reason," etc. | [*publisher's device*] | Boston | Ticknor and Company | 1885

Collation: p. vi + 518, 7⅜ x 4¾ inches; title page, [v]; 1–515, text; 516–518, blank. End papers gray.

The first edition of this novel was issued in medium blue (as in the August 19 copy described below), dark blue, green, olive-green, tan, and brown cloth over boards. In all copies the ornamental band running across the top of the front cover is stamped in black and gold; lettering on the front cover and spine is

Collations of Works... — 85-B continued

raised or gold-stamped; and the publisher's device on the front cover is stamped in black.

The first issue of the first edition reads, within the rule-box-enclosed advertisements on p. [iv], "Mr. Howells's Latest Works" rather than "Mr. Howells's Latest Novels." (Note the *'s* form in both headings; the *s'* form in Merle Johnson appears to be a typographical error.) Perfect type in the words "thick" and "sojourner" at the bottom of p. 176 characterizes a number of copies, which were clearly printed before those with blurred or broken type in these words. The earliest dated copy known to us, however, which bears Howells' inscription, "First copy...Aug. 19, 1885," is characterized by "Works" and broken type; and other early-dated copies with the same characteristics exist. It is apparent then that the type on p. 176 wore down and broke early in the printing of the first edition sheets, and that the novel was first *issued* or *sold* to the public in both an earlier and a later *printed* state. The second issue of the first edition is distinguished, as noted above, by the alteration of "Works" to "Novels" in the advertisement page.

A variant copy of the second issue, probably printed for presentation, exists in the Howe collection of The New York Public Library; it is characterized by "Novels" and broken type. Two extra leaves are blanks; the volume measures 7¹¹/₁₆ x 5⅛ inches. End papers wove and slightly heavier than text; bound in yellow paper over boards; leaves untrimmed and uncut. A printed label on the spine reads "W. D. Howells, 1st Ed."

Library of Congress copyright deposit copies, dated October 5, read "Novels" and have broken type. Copyright deposit date was August 21 and the novel was being reviewed by September 1.

First printed *Century*, Nov., 1884, xxix, 13–26, chapters i–ii; Dec., 242–254, iii–v; Jan., 1885, 370–384, vi–viii; Feb., 581–592, ix–x; March, 663–676, xi–xii; April, 858–872, xiii–xiv; May, xxx, 15–27, xv–xviii; June, 241–255, xix–xxi; July, 353–373, xxii–xxv; Aug., 513–526, xxvi–xxvii.

85-C

The Riverside Aldine series | [*rule*] | Venetian life | by | W. D. Howells | author of "Italian journeys," "Suburban sketches," | "Their wedding journey," "A chance | acquaintance," etc. | In two volumes | Vol. ɪ | [*publisher's device*] | Boston | Houghton, Mifflin and Company | New York: 11

East Seventeenth Street | the Riverside Press, Cambridge | 1885 [*Title page of second volume as above except that "Vol. ɪɪ" appears in place of "Vol. ɪ."*]

Collation: Vol. ɪ, p. ii + 288, 6⁵/₁₆ x 4¼ inches: title page, [5]; 9–279, text; 281–284, advertisements; two blank leaves. Vol. ɪɪ, p. iv + 290: title page, [3]; 7–284, text; 285–287, index; 288–290, blank. End papers of slightly heavier stock than text in both volumes.

Both volumes bound in red cloth over boards with cream paper labels printed in black on spine "Riverside Aldine Series | First Edition." All edges uncut. Imitation laid paper throughout. A later issue of this edition was bound in dark blue cloth over boards, the lettering and volume numbers gold-stamped on the spine.

Reprinted from the text of the enlarged edition of *Venetian life,* but from new plates.

86-A

Tuscan cities | by | William D. Howells | with illustrations | from drawings and etchings by Joseph Pennell and others | [*publisher's device*] | Boston | Ticknor and Company | 1886

Collation: p. –iv + vi + 258, 8¾ x 6½ inches; two blank leaves; title page, [i]; 3–251, text; 252–258, blank and advertisements. End papers tan with floral design; first and last leaves of lighter stock than text.

Tan or blue cloth over beveled boards. Lettering and ornament on front cover and spine stamped in black and gold. All edges gilt. Illustrations by Joseph Pennell and Van J. Published Oct. 26, 1885.

"A Florentine mosaic," first printed *Century*, Feb., 1885, xxix, 483–501, chapters i–xiv; April, 803–819, xv–xxv; June, xxx, 199–219, xxvi–xl.

"Panforte di Siena," first printed *Century*, Aug., 1885, xxx, 534–549; Sept., 659–673.

"Pitiless Pisa," "Industrious Lucca," "Pistoja, Prato, and Fiesole," first printed as "Tuscan cities," *Century,* Oct., 1885, xxx, 890–910.

86-B

The | garroters | farce | by W. D. Howells | [rule] | New York | Harper & Brothers | 1886

Collation: p. ii + 98, 5¼ x 3½ inches: title page, [3]; 5–90, text; 91–98, advertisements. Frontispiece and two illustrated leaves tipped in and not paginated. End papers and advertisement leaves of heavier stock than text.

Dark green cloth over thin boards. Front cover design stamped in black, publisher's device in black, lettering raised from gold panel. Back cover blind-stamped with double rule-box. All edges stained red. Illustrations by C. S. Reinhart. Published Dec. 18, 1885.

First printed *Harper's monthly*, Dec., 1885, LXXII, 146–162.

86-C

[Ornament] | Poems | by | William D. Howells | [publisher's device] | Boston | Ticknor and Company | 211 Tremont Street | MDCCCLXXXVI

Collation: p. iv + 224, 7¼ x 4¾ inches: title page, [iii]; 3–223, text; 224, blank. End papers of heavier stock.

Vellum over flexible boards with lettering and publisher's device on front cover and spine in black and red. Or vellum over boards with rule on front cover and lettering on spine gold-stamped; this issue has one extra flyleaf following p. 224. Laid paper with watermark and watermark name "John Dickin[s]on & Co." throughout. Top edge gilt; fore and bottom edges untrimmed. Published by Jan. 30, 1886 (earliest notice observed).

The first forty-three poems in this edition were printed from the plates of *Poems*, 1873; see 73-B. But "Naming the bird" is omitted from this edition and consequently the pages for "A poet," "Convention," and "The poet's friends" are renumbered. Collected for the first time in volume form with other poems are:

"No love lost," reprinted from *No love lost*. See 69-A.

"The song the oriole sings," first printed as "While the oriole sings," *Atlantic monthly*, July, 1874, XXXIV, 83–84.

"Pordenone," first printed *Harper's monthly*, Nov., 1882, LXV, 829–835.

"The long days," first printed *Atlantic monthly*, June, 1874, XXXIII, 663.

86-D

Indian summer | by | William D. Howells | author of "The rise of Silas Lapham," "A modern instance," | "A woman's reason," etc. | [publisher's device] | Boston | Ticknor and Company | 1886

Collation: p. vi + 398, 7⅜ x 4¾ inches: title page, [v]; 1–395, text; 396–398, blank. End papers gray.

Blue-green or tan cloth over boards. Ornamental band in black and gold-stamping over front cover and spine. Publisher's device stamped in black on front cover. Merle Johnson, *American first editions*, 1942, notes that some copies were issued wholly untrimmed, white cloth, label on spine. Published Feb. 19, 1886.

First printed *Harper's monthly*, July, 1885, LXXI, 261–277, chapters i–iv; Aug., 433–451, v–vii; Sept., 616–634, viii–x; Oct., 780–797, xi–xiii; Nov., 854–872, xiv–xvi; Dec., LXXII, 25–34, xvii–xix; Jan., 1886, 283–293, xx; Feb., 448–460, xxi–xxiv.

86-E

George Fuller | his life and works | with illustrations | [engraving].

Houghton, Mifflin and Company: Boston and New York, 1886. Published April 19, 1886.

"Sketch of George Fuller's life," p. 1–52, here first printed.

87-A

The minister's charge | or | The apprenticeship of Lemuel Barker | by | William D. Howells | author of "The rise of Silas Lapham," "A modern instance," | "Indian summer," etc. | [publisher's device] | Boston | Ticknor and Company | 1887

Collation: p. vi + 464 + 26 separately paginated, 7⅜ x 4¾ inches: title page, [v]; 1–463, text; 464, blank; 1–

Collations of Works . . . — 87-A, continued

24, separately paginated advertisements; blank leaf. End papers light tan.

Red-brown, blue-green, olive-green, or dark blue cloth with diagonal grain over boards. Ornamental band running across front cover and spine stamped in black and gold. Lettering on front cover and spine raised from gold panel or gold-stamped. Publisher's device on front cover stamped in black. Published Dec. 11, 1886.

First printed *Century*, Feb., 1886, xxxi, 500–515, chapters i–iv; March, 718–729, v–vii; April, 860–872, viii–x; May, xxxii, 21–36, xi–xiii; June, 249–259, xiv–xvi; July, 350–360, xvii–xix; Aug., 511–521, xx–xxi; Sept., 734–744, xxii–xxiii; Oct., 881–892, xxiv–xxvii; Nov., xxxiii, 38–46, xxviii–xxxi; Dec., 183–192, xxxii–xxxvi.

87-B

Sebastopol | by | Count Leo Tolstoï | Translated from the French | by | Frank D. Millet | with an introduction by W. D. Howells.

Harper & Brothers: New York, 1887. Published July 2, 1887.

"Leo Tolstoï," p. 5–12, first printed as "Lyof Tolstoï," *Harper's weekly*, April 23, 1887, xxxi, 299–300.

87-C

Modern | Italian poets | essays and versions | by | W. D. Howells | with portraits | New York | Harper & Brothers, Franklin Square | 1887

Collation: p. viii + 372, 5⅝ x 4³/₁₆ inches: title page, [iii]; 1–369, text; 370, bibliography; errata slip tipped in between 370 and 371; 371–372, blank. Eleven illustrated leaves tipped in and not paginated. Four end paper leaves of heavier stock than text.

Green cloth over boards with vellum backstrip. Lettering on spine gold-stamped. Top edge gilt; fore and bottom edges rough-trimmed. Published Oct. 1, 1887.

"Introduction," p. 1–10, here first printed.
"Arcadian shepherds," p. 11–23, first printed in slightly briefer form as "Some Arcadian shepherds," *Atlantic monthly*, Jan., 1872, xxix, 84–89. Pages 23–24, here first printed.

"Giuseppe Parini," p. 25–50, first printed as "An obsolete fine gentleman," *Atlantic monthly*, July, 1875, xxxvi, 98–106.

"Vittorio Alfieri," p. 55–101, reprinted from "Essay," *Life of Vittorio Alfieri*, p. 5–51.

"Vincenzo Monti," p. 102–115, first printed in briefer form as review, *North American review*, Oct., 1866, ciii, 323–328.

"Ugo Foscolo," p. 116–125, first printed as review, *North American review*, Oct., 1866, ciii, 328–333.

"Alessandro Manzoni," p. 126–174, first printed in part as "Modern Italian poets," *North American review*, April, 1867, civ, 317–323.

"Silvio Pellico," p. 175–177, first printed in part as "Modern Italian poets," *North American review*, April, 1867, civ, 317–323.

"Tommaso Grossi," p. 178–183, first printed as "Modern Italian poets," *North American review*, April, 1867, civ, 323–327.

"Luigi Carrer," p. 184–185, first printed as "Modern Italian poets," *North American review*, April, 1867, civ, 327–330.

"Giovanni Berchet," p. 189–195, here first printed.

"Giambattista Niccolini," p. 196–243, first printed as "Niccolini's anti-Papal tragedy," *North American review*, Oct., 1872, cxv, 333–366.

"Giacomo Leopardi," p. 244–274, first printed as "The laureate of death," *Atlantic monthly*, Sept., 1885, lvi, 311–322.

"Giuseppe Giusti," p. 275–299, first printed as "The Florentine satirist, Giusti," *North American review*, July, 1872, cxv, 31–47.

"Francesco Dall' Ongaro," p. 300–322, first printed as review, *North American review*, Jan., 1868, cvi, 26–42.

"Giovanni Prati," p. 323–332, first printed in briefer form as "Modern Italian poets," *North American review*, April, 1867, civ, 330–336.

"Aleardo Aleardi," p. 333–359, first printed as "Modern Italian poets," *North American review*, April, 1867, civ, 336–352.

"Giulio Carcano," p. 360–361, first printed as "Modern Italian poets," *North American review*, April, 1867, civ, 352–353.

"Arnaldo Fusinato," p. 362–364, here first printed.

"Luigi Mercantini," p. 366–368, here first printed.

"Conclusion," p. 369, here first printed.

87-D

Their wedding journey | by | W. D. Howells, | author of "Venetian life," "Italian journeys" | etc., etc. | With illustrations by Augustus Hoppin | [*publisher's device*] | Boston: | Houghton, Mifflin and Company. | New York: | 11 East Seventeenth Street. | The Riverside Press, Cambridge. | 1887.

Collation: p. –iv + iv + 334, 7⅜ x 4¾ inches: title page, [i]; 1–319, text; 320, blank; [321–332], advertisements, 1–12 in separate pagination; blank leaf. End papers chocolate brown.

Green cloth with diagonal grain over boards. Ornamental border on front cover blind-stamped, ornament gold-stamped. Lettering on spine gold-stamped. Published by Dec. 25, 1887 (inscribed copy).

An edition printed from the same plates appeared in 1888. The title page is of glazed stock tipped in on stub. Besides the date, it differs slightly from the 1887 title page, and contains the phrase, "with an additional chapter on Niagara revisited."

"Niagara revisited, twelve years after their wedding journey," reprinted from *Niagara revisited*. See 84-D.

88-A

April hopes | by | W. D. Howells | author of | "Indian summer" "The rise of Silas Lapham" | "Modern Italian poets" etc. | New York | Harper & Brothers, Franklin Square | 1888

Collation: p. iv + 492, 7⅜ x 4¾ inches: title page, [iii]; 1–484, text; 485–492, advertisements. End papers imitation laid. In some copies an extra flyleaf precedes the title page and one follows the text, the collation thus reading: "p. vi + 494: title page, [v]; 1–484, text; 485–492, advertisements; blank leaf." End papers in these copies of same stock as text.

Red cloth over boards. Lettering on front cover and spine gold-stamped; signature on front cover gold-stamped. Published Dec. 10, 1887.

First printed *Harper's monthly*, Feb., 1887, LXXIV, 381–396, chapters i–vii; March, 589–606, viii–xiii; April, 788–801, xiv–xviii; May,

934–951, xix–xxiii; June, LXXV, 99–112, xxiv–xxvii; July, 246–258, xxviii–xxxii; Aug., 344–352, xxxiii–xxxvi; Sept., 605–620, xxxvii–xlii; Oct., 713–729, xliii–xlviii; Nov., 925–943, xlix–lii.

88-B

Mark Twain's | library of humor | [*rule*] | illustrated by E. W. Kemble.

Charles L. Webster & Company: New York, 1888. Published Dec. 15, 1887 (title-copyright).

Howells was editor of this volume, which includes six selections reprinted from *Their wedding journey* and *A chance acquaintance*. *Life in letters*, II, 407, lists "Love's young dream" as a volume contributed to by Howells: it is actually no more than a portion of *A chance acquaintance* reprinted in this work. Compare 73-A, chapter vii, p. 141–155. See also article by Harold Blodgett in *American literature*, March, 1938, x, 78–80, which ascribes the introduction to Howells.

88-C

Library of universal | adventure by sea and land | [*rule*] | including original narratives and authentic | stories of personal prowess and peril in all | the waters and regions of the globe … | … | Compiled and edited by | William Dean Howells | and Thomas Sergeant Perry.

Harper and Brothers: New York, 1888. Published May 17, 1888.

T. S. Perry, "His friends greet William Dean Howells at eighty," New York *Sun*, Feb. 25, 1917, v, 10, comments on this book, which the compilers would not let their own children see because of the quality of horror in its narratives.

88-D

A sea-change | or | Love's stowaway | a lyricated farce | in two acts and an epilogue | by | W. D. Howells | All rights reserved | Boston | Ticknor and Company | 211, Tremont Street | 1888

Collation: p. iv + 154, 5¾ x 4⅛ inches: two blank leaves; title page,

Collations of Works... — 88-D, continued

[1]; 5–151, text; 152–154, blank. End papers black.

Gray-green or chocolate-brown cloth over boards. Spine and covers blind-stamped; lettering on spine and front cover gold-stamped. All edges stained red. Copies in brown and some copies in green have an extra flyleaf following the text and the collation reads "p. iv + 156." Published Aug. 8, 1888.

First printed *Harper's weekly*, July 14, 1888, xxxii, 505, supplement, 521–524.

89-A

Annie Kilburn | a novel | by | W. D. Howells | author of | "Indian summer" "The rise of Silas Lapham" | "April hopes" etc. | New York | Harper & Brothers, Franklin Square | 1889

Collation: p. vi + 338, 7¼ x 4¾ inches: title page, [v]; 1–331, text; 332–338, blank and advertisements. End papers of lighter stock than text.

Red cloth over boards. Lettering on front cover and spine gold-stamped. Signature on front cover gold-stamped. Published Dec. 15, 1888.

First printed *Harper's monthly*, June, 1888, lxxvii, 128–144, chapters i–v; July, 270–285, vi–ix; Aug., 407–422, x–xii; Sept., 569–584, xiii–xviii; Oct., 700–718, xix–xxiv; Nov., 869–888, xxv–xxx.

89-B

The mouse-trap | and | other farces | by | W. D. Howells | author of "April hopes" "Annie Kilburn" etc. | Illustrated | New York | Harper & Brothers, Franklin Square | 1889

Collation: p. x + 188, 7¼ x 4¾ inches: title page, [v]; 3–184, text; advertisement leaf; blank leaf, frontispiece and eight illustrated leaves tipped in and paginated. End papers imitation laid.

Red cloth over boards. Lettering on front cover and spine gold-stamped. Signature on front cover gold-stamped. Imitation laid paper throughout, except for frontispiece and

illustrated leaves, which are wove. Illustrations by C. S. Reinhart. Published April 17, 1889; (Harper register) April 26.

The collection was printed from new plates and in a larger format by Harper & Brothers in 1909, the collation in part reading, "p. viii + 144, 8¹/₁₆ x 5⅜ inches: title page, [iii]; 3–141, text; 142–143, blank."

"The garroters," reprinted from *The garroters;* see 86-B.

"Five o'clock tea," first printed *Harper's monthly*, Dec., 1887, lxxvi, 86–96.

"The mouse-trap," first printed *Harper's monthly*, Dec., 1886, lxxiv, 64–75.

"A likely story," first printed *Harper's monthly*, Dec., 1888, lxxviii, 26–38.

89-C

The | sleeping-car | and | other farces | by | William D. Howells | [*publisher's device*] | Boston and New York | Houghton, Mifflin and Company | the Riverside Press, Cambridge | 1889

Collation: p. ii + 216, 7¼ x 4⅞ inches: advertisement, [2]; title page, [5]; 11–212, text; 213–216, blank. End papers of heavier stock.

Red cloth over boards. Lettering on front cover and spine gold-stamped; signature on front cover gold-stamped. Published May 13, 1889.

"The parlor-car," p. 11–48, reprinted from 76-D.

"The sleeping-car," p. 51–97, reprinted from 83-A.

"The register," p. 101–157, reprinted from 84-B.

"The elevator," p. 161–212, reprinted from 85-A.

89-D

Samson | [*rule*] | a tragedy in five acts, by | Ippolito d'Aste. | [*rule*] | Translated by W. D. Howells. | With the English and Italian words, | as performed by | Signor Salvini, | during his farewell American tour, under the direction of | Mr. A. M. Palmer. | [*rule*] | Charles D. Koppel, publisher,

A HAZARD OF NEW FORTUNES

A Novel

BY

WILLIAM DEAN HOWELLS

AUTHOR OF

"APRIL HOPES" "ANNIE KILBURN" "MODERN ITALIAN POETS" ETC.

ILLUSTRATED

NEW YORK

HARPER & BROTHERS, FRANKLIN SQUARE

1890

Title page of the first, paper bound, edition, 90-A

115 & 117 Nassau Street, | New York. | Copyright, 1889, by C. D. Koppel.

Collation: p. ii + 52, 9½ x 6¾ inches: title page, [1]; text, 3–51; 52, blank. Published Oct. 19, 1889.

Salmon-colored paper wrappers, printed in black; portrait of Salvini on front wrapper.

90-A

A hazard of new fortunes | a novel | by | William Dean Howells | author of | "April hopes" "Annie Kilburn" "Modern Italian poets" etc. | Illustrated | [*publisher's device*] | New York | Harper & Brothers, Franklin Square | 1890

Collation: p. iv + 172, 9⅜ x 6⅝ inches: title page, [i]; 1–171, text; 172, blank. Frontispiece and fifteen illustrated leaves tipped in and not paginated. No end papers.

Brown paper covers. Lettering, ornament, publisher's device, and solid-circle rule-box printed in darker shades of brown. Pasted to the front cover are two paper labels, one printed "November, | 1889 | Extra | Harper's Franklin Square | Library | New Series" and the other "661." Advertisements on back cover. Illustrations by W. A. Rogers and C. R. S. Published Nov. 27, 1889.

First printed *Harper's weekly*, March 23, 1889, xxxiii, 217, 222–223, i–ii, Part i; March 30, 241–242, iii–iv; April 6, 261–262, v–vi; April 13, 281–282, vii; April 20, 301–303, viii–x; April 27, 329–330, xi; May 4, 346–347, xii; May 18, 385–386, i, Part ii; May 25, 409–411, ii–iv; June 1, 429–430, v–vi; June 8, 454–455, vii–viii; June 15, 474–475, ix–x; June 22, 494, xi; June 29, 517–518, xii–xiii; July 6, 538–539, xiv–xv; July 13, 558–559, i–ii, Part iii; July 20, 574–575, iii–iv; July 27, 606–607, v–vi; Aug. 3, 622–623, vii–viii; Aug. 10, 646–647, ix; Aug. 17, 662–663, i, Part iv; Aug. 24, 682–683, ii–iii; Aug. 31, 701–703, iv–v; Sept. 7, 722–723, vi; Sept. 14, 742–744, vii–viii; Sept. 21, 757–758, viii [ix]; Sept. 28, 774–775, i, Part v; Oct. 5, 798–799, ii; Oct. 12, 810–811, iii–iv; Oct. 19, 829–831, vi–ix; Oct. 26, 858–859, x–xii; Nov. 2, 874–875, xiii–xiv; Nov. 9, 898–899, xv–xvi; Nov. 16, 914, xvii–xviii.

90-B

A hazard | of new fortunes | a novel | by | William D. Howells | author of "Annie Kilburn" "April hopes" | "Modern Italian poets" etc. | In two volumes | Vol. i. | New York | Harper & Brothers, Franklin Square | 1890 [*Title page of the second volume as above except that "Vol. ii" appears in place of "Vol. i."*]

Collation: Vol. i, p. vi +334, 7¼ x 4¾ inches: title page, [v]; 1–332, text; blank leaf. Vol. ii, p. vi + 334; title page, [v]; 1–332, text; blank leaf. End papers.

Both volumes bound in red cloth over boards. Title and signature on front cover gold-stamped; volume number and lettering on spine gold-stamped. Published Jan. 27, 1890.

Reprinted from the text of the first edition: see 90-A. Printed from new plates.

90-C

From the French | [*rule*] | Pastels in prose | [*rule*] | translated by Stuart Merrill, | with illustrations by Henry W. McVicar, and an introduction | by William Dean Howells.

Harper & Brothers: New York, 1890. Published April 5, 1890.

"The prose poem," dated "New York, April 1890," p. v–viii, here first printed.

90-D

The shadow of a dream | a story | by | W. D. Howells | author of "April hopes" "Annie Kilburn" | "A hazard of new fortunes" etc. | New York | Harper & Brothers, Franklin Square | 1890

Collation: p. iv + 220, 7⅛ x 4¾ inches: title page, [iii]; 1–218, text; 219–220, advertisements. No end papers.

Paper covers. Ornament and lettering on front cover and spine dark blue. Harper's

38   The New York Public Library

Collations of Works... — 90-D, continued

Franklin Square Library, 672. Advertisements on back cover. On spine, "May, 1890, extra." Top edges trimmed; fore and bottom edges uncut and untrimmed. Published May 31, 1890.

First printed *Harper's monthly*, March, 1890, LXXX, 510–529, part first; April, 766–782, part second; May, 865–881, part third.

90-E

The shadow of a dream | a story | by | W. D. Howells | author of "April hopes" "Annie Kilburn" | "A hazard of new fortunes" etc. | New York | Harper & Brothers, Franklin Square | 1890

Collation: p. iv + 220, 7⅛ x 4¾ inches: title page, [iii]; 1–218, text; 219–220, advertisements. End papers.

Red cloth over boards. Lettering on front cover and spine stamped in black; signature on front cover stamped in black. Published June 7, 1890.

Reprinted from first edition plates: see 90-D.

90-F

Giovanni Verga | [*rule*] | The | house by the medlar-tree | the translation | by Mary A. Craig | an introduction | by W. D. Howells.

Harper & Brothers: New York, 1890. "Odd number series." Published Aug. 13, 1890.

The introduction, p. iii–vii, here first printed.

90-G

A boy's town | described for "Harper's young people" | by | W. D. Howells | author of "The shadow of a dream" "April hopes" | "A hazard of new fortunes" etc. | Illustrated | New York | Harper & Brothers, Franklin Square | 1890

Collation: p. –iv + vi + 250, 7¼ x 4¾ inches: [–i] to [–iv], blank; title page, [i]; 1–247, text; 248–250, blank. Frontispiece and twenty-two illus-

trated leaves are tipped in and not paginated. End papers of lighter stock than text.

Dark green cloth with diagonal grain over boards. Title and signature on front cover gold-stamped as is lettering on spine. Ornamental box, rules, and floral design on front cover and spine stamped in silver. Illustrations by H. F. Farny. According to Merle Johnson, *American first editions* (New York, 1942), the first state of this book has the illustrated leaf at p. iv which occurs in later copies at p. 44. Published Oct. 11, 1890.

First printed *Harper's young people*, April 8, 1890, XI, 386–387, i; April 15, 402–403, ii; April 22, 421–423, iii; April 29, 447–449, iv; May 6, 458–460, v; May 13, 470–472, vi; May 20, 499–501, vii; May 27, 510–512, viii; June 3, 531–533, ix; June 10, 537–540, x; June 17, 563–566, xi; June 24, 573–576, xii; July 1, 598–600, xiii; July 8, 610–612, xiv; July 15, 629–632, xv; July 22, 641, 646–648, xvi; July 29, 658–659, xvii; Aug. 5, 678–680, xviii; Aug. 12, 703–705, xix; Aug. 19, 718–721, xx; Aug. 26, 734–736, xxi.

90-H

The | art of authorship | literary reminiscences, | methods of work, and advice to young beginners, | personally contributed by | leading authors of the day. | Compiled and edited by | George Bainton.

James Clarke & Co.: London, 1890. An American edition was also issued by D. Appleton and Company, New York, 1890.

Howells' contribution under the title "W. D. Howells," p. 334–335, here first printed.

91-A

[Winifred Howells, 1891] Privately printed.

Collation: p. 28, 8⅝ x 5¾ inches: text, 3–26. Three photograph leaves of glazed paper tipped in and not paginated. No end papers.

Cream colored paper covers. Lettering on front cover dark brown. Poems by Winifred Howells are included in the text. One hundred copies were printed. Published by Feb. 1, 1891 (date of manuscript letter to S. Weir Mitchell).

91-B

Criticism | and fiction | by | W. D. Howells | [*publisher's device*] | New York | Harper and Brothers | MDCCCXCI

Collation: p. iv + 192, 5⅞ x 3⅜ inches: title page, [iii]; 1–188, text; two leaves of advertisements. Frontispiece portrait leaf and flimsy protective leaf over portrait are tipped in and not paginated. End papers of heavier stock than text.

First issue is bound in white cloth over boards. The torch design, ornament, and lettering on front cover and spine are gold-stamped. Pages i–iv are printed on laid paper with the watermark "Old Berkshire Mills 1889," the title page printed in red and black and the publisher's device both stamped blind and in light tan and black. Imitation laid paper otherwise throughout, including end papers. Top edges gilt, fore and bottom edges untrimmed. Published May 9, 1891.

The second issue differs from the first only in that the cloth is dark green, the top and fore edges trimmed.

Except for several brief transitional passages here first printed, all the volume is reprinted from the "Editor's study" in *Harper's monthly*.

Page 1, first printed Dec., 1887, LXXVI, 153.

Pages 1–2, first printed Nov., 1887, LXXV, 964–965.

Pages 3–14, first printed Dec., 1887, LXXVI, 153–155.

Pages 14–18, first printed May, 1886, LXXII, 973.

Pages 18–20, first printed June, 1886, LXXIII, 156–157.

Pages 21–22, first printed with inversions in order, May, 1889, LXXVIII, 983.

Pages 22–24, first printed June, 1886, LXXIII, 154.

Pages 25–28, first printed Feb., 1886, LXXII, 486.

Pages 29–38, first printed in slightly longer form, June, 1887, LXXV, 155–157.

Page 38, first printed July, 1886, LXXIII, 317–318.

Pages 38–41, first printed in slightly longer form, June, 1887, LXXV, 157–158.

Pages 42–44, first printed in slightly longer form, Aug., 1886, LXXIII, 475–476.

Pages 45–53, first printed in slightly longer form, Aug., 1890, LXXXI, 476–479.

Pages 53–55, first printed in slightly longer form, July, 1887, LXXV, 318–319.

Page 55, first printed Aug., 1890, LXXXI, 479–480.

Pages 56–57, first printed Aug., 1890, LXXXI, 480.

Pages 57–77, first printed Nov., 1889, LXXIX, 962–967.

Pages 78–82, first printed in slightly longer form, Oct., 1887, LXXV, 802–803.

Pages 82–85, first printed Nov., 1886, LXXIII, 962–963.

Pages 85–86, first printed April, 1886, LXXII, 809.

Pages 86–87, first printed June, 1886, LXXIII, 154.

Pages 88–91, first printed March, 1886, LXXII, 649.

Pages 92–104, first printed in slightly longer form, April, 1887, LXXIV, 824–826.

Page 104, first printed May, 1887, LXXIV, 987.

Page 105, transition.

Pages 105–107, first printed in slightly longer form, July, 1887, LXXV, 318.

Page 107, first printed July, 1890, LXXXI, 317.

Page 107, first printed Oct., 1890, LXXXI, 801.

Pages 108–112, first printed Sept., 1887, LXXV, 638–639.

Pages 113–114, first printed Feb., 1888, LXXVI, 480.

Pages 115–116, first printed May, 1886, LXXII, 972–973.

Pages 116–117, first printed Aug., 1886, LXXIII, 478.

Page 117, first printed Oct., 1890, LXXXI, 800.

Pages 117–118, first printed Sept., 1890, LXXXI, 642.

Page 118, first printed June, 1888, LXXVII, 155.

Page 118, transition.

Pages 118–120, first printed Sept., 1890, LXXXI, 639–640.

Pages 121–123, first printed Feb., 1890, LXXX, 481–482.

Pages 123–124, first printed Jan., 1886, LXXII, 322.

Pages 124–127, first printed in slightly longer form, Oct., 1890, LXXXI, 803–804.

Pages 127–129, first printed Sept., 1886, LXXIII, 641–642.

Pages 129–130, first printed May, 1889, LXXVIII, 985.

Pages 130–131, first printed Nov., 1888, LXXVII, 964.

Pages 131–133, first printed Feb., 1887, LXXIV, 484.

Page 134, first printed Feb., 1887, LXXIV, 485.

Pages 134–138, first printed in slightly longer form, Jan., 1886, LXXII, 324–325.

Collations of Works... — 91-B, continued

Pages 138–140, first printed July, 1888, LXXVII, 317–318.

Pages 141–143, first printed Sept., 1887, LXXV, 639–640.

Pages 144–146, first printed with inversion in order, Sept., 1887, LXXV, 641.

Pages 147–162, first printed June, 1889, LXXIX, 151–154.

Pages 163–170, first printed Dec., 1889, LXXX, 157–159.

Pages 171–182, first printed Jan., 1887, LXXIV, 321–323.

Pages 183–184, first printed Aug., 1889, LXXIX, 479–480.

Pages 184–186, first printed Dec., 1888, LXXVIII, 159–160.

Pages 186–187, first printed Jan., 1888, LXXVI, 320.

Pages 187–188, first printed Sept., 1887, LXXV, 639.

91-C

Venetian life | by William Dean Howells | with illustrations from | original water colors | [*publisher's device*] | Volume | I | London | Longman's, Green, and Co. | 1891 | [*The second volume differs only in that "II" replaces "I" above.*]

Collation: Vol. I, p. ii + 280, 7 x 4⅝ inches: title page, [3]; preface, v–vi [i. e., 5–6]; 9–279, text; 280, blank. Frontispiece and eight illustrated leaves tipped in and not paginated. Vol. II, p. ii + 288; title page, [3]; 7–284, text; 285–287, index; 288, blank. Frontispiece and eight illustrated leaves tipped in and not paginated. End papers blue with blue and gold floral design.

Both volumes bound in white cloth over boards. Ornamental wreath, lettering, rules, and rule-boxes on front cover and spine gold-stamped. Rule-boxes on back cover blind-stamped. Illustrations by Childe Hassam, Ross Turner, R. H. Nichols, and F. Hopkinson Smith. The two-volume American edition was printed from the same plates and was bound in the same fashion, the only differences being that after "Volume | I" the title page reads "Boston and New York | Houghton, Mifflin and Company | the Riverside Press, Cambridge | MDCCCXCII," that the end papers bear a gold

floral design, that both volumes contain an extra flyleaf at the end, and that the edition though published Oct. 7, 1891 (title copyright) probably simultaneously with the English edition, bears the date 1892 on title page.

"Preface," I, v–vi, dated Sept., 1891, here first printed.

92-A

The Albany depot. | Farce. | By W. D. Howells. [*All the foregoing at the top of the first page of text.*] [No place, no date.]

Collation: p. 52, 8¼ x 5¼ inches, printed on recto only, and with rectos numbered 1–26.

Gray blank paper covers, the binding sewed. Printed ca. Oct., 1891 (cf. 92-B).

This is the first issue of the play, privately printed for stage use only. First printed *Harper's weekly*, Dec. 14, 1889, XXXIII, 989, supplement 1005–1008.

92-B

The Albany depot | by | W. D. Howells | [*publisher's device*] | New York | Harper and Brothers | 1892

Collation: p. 72, 5 ³/₁₆ x 3⅝ inches; title page, [3]; 7–68, text; 69–72, advertisements. Frontispiece leaf tipped in and not paginated. End papers imitation laid.

White cloth over thin boards. Lettering and ornament on spine and covers in black. Illustrations by W. T. Smedley. "Harper's black & white series." Published Oct. 10, 1891.

Printed from new plates; see 92-A.

92-C

An imperative duty. | A novel | by | W. D. Howells | author of | "A hazard of new fortunes" "Annie Kilburn" etc. | New York | Harper & Brothers, Franklin Square | 1892

Collation: p. ii + 158, 7 ³/₁₆ x 4¾ inches: title page, [i]; 1–150, text; 151–156, advertisements; blank leaf. End papers imitation laid.

Red cloth over boards. Lettering on front cover and spine gold-stamped; signature on front cover gold-stamped. Published Nov. 14, 1891.

First printed *Harper's monthly*, July, 1891, LXXXIII, 191–204, chapters i–v; Aug., 416–428, vi–vii; Sept., 517–527, viii–x; Oct., 765–776, xi–xiii.

92-D

The quality of mercy | a novel | by | W. D. Howells | author of "An imperative duty" "Annie Kilburn" | "A hazard of new fortunes" etc. | New York | Harper & Brothers, Franklin Square | 1892

Collation: p. ii + 478, 7 ³/₁₆ x 4¾ inches; title page, [i]; 1–474, text; 475–478, advertisements. End papers imitation laid.

Red cloth over boards. Lettering on front cover and spine gold-stamped. Signature on front cover gold-stamped. Published March 26, 1892.

First printed as "The quality of mercy, a story of contemporary American life," New York *Sun*, Oct. 4, 1891, p. 21, Part I, chapters i–v; Oct. 11, 1891, p. 21, vi–x; Oct. 18, p. 23, xi–xii; Oct. 25, p. 23, xiii–xvi; Nov. 1, p. 23, xvii–xx; Nov. 8, p. 23, xxi–xxiv, Part II, Chapter i; Nov. 15, p. 23, ii–vi; Nov. 22, p. 23, vii–x; Nov. 29, p. 21, xi–xvi; Dec. 6, p. 22, xvii–xx; Dec. 13, p. 21, xxi, Part III, chapters i–ii; Dec. 20, p. 21, iii–iv; Dec. 27, p. 17, v–vii; Jan. 3, 1892, p. 17, 18, viii–xi.

Published simultaneously in the Chicago *Inter ocean*, Philadelphia *Inquirer*, Cincinnati *Commercial gazette*, Boston *Herald*, and Toronto *Globe*.

92-E

A letter of introduction | farce | by | W. D. Howells | illustrated | [*publisher's device*] | New York | Harper and Brothers | 1892

Collation: p. 72, 5 ³/₁₆ x 3⅝ inches: title page, [3]; 7–61, text; 62, blank; 63–70, advertisements; blank leaf. Frontispiece and three illustrated leaves tipped in and paginated. End papers imitation laid.

White cloth over thin boards. Lettering on front cover and spine stamped in black; ruleboxes, ornament on cover and spine stamped in black. Frontispiece and illustrations by W.

T. Smedley. "Harper's black & white series." Published July 25, 1892.

First printed *Harper's monthly*, Jan., 1892, LXXXIV, 243–256.

92-F

A little Swiss sojourn | by | W. D. Howells | illustrated | [*publisher's device*] | New York | Harper & Brothers, Franklin Square | 1892

Collation: p. viii + 120, 5 ³/₁₆ x 3⅝ inches: title page, [v]; 1–119, text; 120, blank. End papers imitation laid.

White cloth over thin boards. Lettering and ornament on spine and covers stamped in black. Illustrations by C. S. Reinhart. "Harper's black & white series." Published Sept. 28, 1892; (Harper register) Oct. 27.

First printed *Harper's monthly*, Feb. – March, 1888, LXXVI, 452–467, 572–587, chapters i–xiii, i–viii.

92-G

South-sea idyls | by | Charles Warren Stoddard.

Charles Scribner's Sons: New York, 1892.

"Introductory letter," p. v–vi, dated "Yorke [*sic*] Harbor, August 11, 1892."

93-A

Christmas every day | and other stories | told for children | by W. D. Howells | [*ornament*] | [*publisher's device*] | New York | Harper & Brothers publishers | 1893

Collation: p. x + 152, 7 ³/₁₆ x 4¾ inches: title page, [v]; 3–150, text; 151–152, advertisements. End papers imitation laid.

Brown cloth over boards. Lettering on front cover and spine stamped in dark brown. Ornament on front cover and spine stamped in dark brown and gold. Illustrations by Frank Verbeer. Published Dec. 7, 1892.

"Christmas every day," first printed *Saint Nicholas,* Jan., 1886, XIII, 163–167.

"Turkeys turning the tables."

"The pony engine and the Pacific express."

"The pumpkin-glory."

"Butterflyflutterby and flutterbybutterfly."

93-B

The world of chance | a novel | by | W. D. Howells | author of "A hazard of new fortunes" | "The quality of mercy" etc. | [*publisher's device*] | New York | Harper & Brothers publishers | 1893

Collation: p. ii + 382, 7¼ x 4¾ inches: title page, [i]; 1–375, text; 376–382, blank and advertisements. End papers imitation laid.

Red cloth over boards. Lettering on front cover and spine gold-stamped; signature on front cover gold-stamped. Published March 29, 1893.

First printed *Harper's monthly*, March, 1892, LXXXIV, 604–618, chapters i–vii; April, 669–681, viii–xii; May, 856–868, xiii–xvi; June, LXXXV, 36–46, xvii–xx; July, 229–239, xxi–xxiv; Aug., 400–410, xxv–xxviii; Sept., 544–560, xxix–xxxiv; Oct., 740–756, xxxv–xxxix; Nov., 927–942, xl–xlvi.

93-C

The unexpected guests | a farce | by | W. D. Howells | illustrated | [*publisher's device*] | New York | Harper & Brothers publishers | 1893

Collation: p. iv + 60, 5³/₁₆ x 3⅝ inches: title page, [i]; 1–54, text; 55–58, advertisements; blank leaf. Frontispiece and five illustrated leaves tipped in and not paginated. End papers imitation laid.

White cloth over thin boards. Lettering and ornament on covers and spine stamped in black. Illustrations by W. T. Smedley. "Harper's black & white series." Published May 17, 1893.

First printed *Harper's monthly*, Jan., 1893, LXXXVI, 211–225.

93-D

The Niagara book | a complete souvenir of Niagara Falls | ... | written exclusively for this book. | By | W. D. Howells, Mark Twain, | Prof. Nathaniel S. Shaler, and others. | Fully illustrated by Harry Fenn.

Underhill and Nichols: Buffalo, 1893. Published June 27, 1893. Issued in both paper wrappers and in boards.

Howells' reminiscences, "Niagara first and last," p. 1–27, here first printed.

93-E

The poems of | George Pellew | edited, with an introduction, | by W. D. Howells.

W. B. Clarke & Co.: Boston, [1893]. Published July 1, 1893.

"Introduction," p. v–xi, first printed *Cosmopolitan*, Sept., 1892, XIII, 527–530.

93-F

My year in a log cabin | by | W. D. Howells | illustrated | [*publisher's device*] | New York | Harper & Brothers publishers | 1893

Collation: p. ii + 62, 5³/₁₆ x 3¹¹/₁₆ inches: title page, [i]; 1–62, text, frontispiece and one illustrated leaf tipped in and not paginated. End papers imitation laid.

White cloth over thin boards. Lettering and ornament on covers and spine stamped in black. "Harper's black & white series." Published Oct. 10, 1893.

First printed as "Year in a log-cabin, a bit of autobiography," *Youth's companion*, May 12, 1887, LX, 213–215.

93-G

Evening dress | farce | by | W. D. Howells | illustrated | [*publisher's device*] | New York | Harper & Brothers publishers | 1893

Collation: p. iv + 62, 5³/₁₆ x 3⅝ inches: title page, [i]; 1–59, text; 60, blank; advertisement leaf. Frontispiece and two illustrated leaves tipped in and not paginated. End papers imitation laid.

White cloth over thin boards. Lettering and ornament on spine and covers stamped in black. Illustrations by Edward Penfield. "Harper's black & white series." Published Oct. 25, 1893.

First printed *Cosmopolitan*, May, 1892, XIII, 116–127.

93-H

The first book | of the Authors Club | [*ornament*] | Liber scriptorum.

The Authors Club: New York, 1893. Published Oct. 31, 1893 (title copyright).

"Judgment day," poem, p. 288, here first printed. A broadside entitled *Judgment day* was issued in 1893, n. p., from the plate used in the book; it measures 9 ⁵/₁₆ x 6 ⁵/₁₆ inches and was printed on stiff paper with the original ornamental border at the top, the elaborate initial letter, and the open book for a tailpiece.

93-I

The coast of Bohemia | a novel | by | W. D. Howells | author of "A hazard of new fortunes" | "The world of chance" etc. | Illustrated | [*publisher's device*] | New York | Harper & Brothers publishers | 1893

Collation: p. iv + 344, 7 ³/₁₆ x 4⅞ inches: title page, [i]; 1–340, text; 341–344 advertisements. Frontispiece and seven illustrated leaves are tipped in and not paginated. End papers imitation laid.

Red cloth over boards. Lettering on front cover and spine gold-stamped. Signature on front cover gold-stamped. Frontispiece and illustrations by Frank O. Small. Published Nov. 3, 1893.

First printed *Ladies' home journal*, Dec., 1892, x, 3–4, chapters i–v; Jan., 1893, 3–4, vi–ix; Feb., 5–6, x–xiii; March, 5–6, xiv–xvi; April, 5–6, xvii–xix; May, 7–8, xx–xxii; June, 3–4, xxiii–xxiv; July, 7–8, 25, xxv–xxvii; Aug., 7–8, xxviii–xxxi; Sept., 7–8, xxxii–xxxvi; Oct., 3–4, 32, xxxvii–xl.

93-J

Main-travelled roads | being six stories of the | Mississippi Valley by | Hamlin Garland, with an | introduction by W. D. | Howells and decora- | tions by H. T. Carpenter.

Stone and Kimball: Cambridge and Chicago, 1893. This is the large-paper edition published on Dec. 4, 1893. A trade edition with a Chicago imprint only was issued in 1894.

"Introduction," p. 1–6, first printed "Editor's study," *Harper's monthly*, Sept., 1891, LXXXIII, 638–640.

93-K

[Eight songs with pianoforte accompaniment composed by E. A. MacDowell. Op. 47.]

Breitkopf & Härtel: New York, 1893. Published Dec. 30 (title copyright). "Actually deposited on 'Jan. 12, 1894.'" This collation is made from O. G. Sonneck's MacDowell catalogue (1917), no first edition having been found. A new revised edition issued in 1906 has German translations by Joh. Bernhof.

III. "Folksong," first printed as "Gone." See 60-A.

VII. "The sea," first printed as II of "Pleasure — pain." See 73-B.

VIII. "Through the meadow," reprinted from 60-A.

93-L

Fame's | tribute to children | being a collection of autograph sentiments con- | tributed by famous men and women.

Hayes and Company: Chicago, 1893. Edited by Martha S. Hill.

"Except as little children," a four-line poem reproduced in holograph on p. 24 of part two (which is newly paginated), here first printed. Signed W. D. Howells.

94-A

A likely story | farce | by | W. D. Howells | illustrated | [*publisher's device*] | New York | Harper and Brothers | 1894

Collation: p. 64, 5 ³/₁₆ x 3⅝ inches; title page, [3]; 7–54, text; 55–62, advertisements; blank leaf. Frontispiece and one illustrated leaf tipped

Collations of Works . . . — 94-A, continued

in and not paginated. End papers imitation laid.

White cloth over thin boards. Lettering and ornament on covers and spine in black. "Harper's black & white series." Published May 28, 1894 (Harper register).

Reprinted from *The mouse-trap and other farces;* see 89–B. New plates were used in this edition.

94-B

A traveler from Altruria | romance | by | W. D. Howells | author of | "The coast of Bohemia" "The quality of mercy" | "A hazard of new fortunes" etc. | [*publisher's device*] | New York | Harper & Brothers publishers | 1894

Collation: p. ii + 318, 7¼ x 4¾ inches: title page, [i]; 1–318, text. End papers imitation laid.

Red cloth over boards. Lettering on front cover and spine gold-stamped; signature on front cover gold-stamped. Published May 28, 1894 (Harper register).

The novel was printed from new plates and in a larger format by Harper & Brothers in 1908, the collation in part reading "p. iv + 216, 8 ¹/₁₆ x 5 ⁸/₁₆ inches: title page, [iii]; 3–216, text." Published Oct. 8, 1908 (Harper register).

First printed *Cosmopolitan,* Nov., 1892, xiv, 52–58, chapter i; Dec., 251–256, ii; Jan., 1893, 341–347, iii; Feb., 495–500, iv; March, 633–640, v; April, 697–705, vi; May, xv, 39–46, vii; June, 249–256, viii; July, 305–310, ix; Aug., 449–456, x; Sept., 635–640, xi; Oct., 738–749, xii.

94-C

The mouse-trap | farce | by | W. D. Howells | illustrated | [*publisher's device*] | New York | Harper and Brothers | 1894

Collation: p. 60, 5 ³/₁₆ x 3¾ inches: title page, [3]; 7–52, text; 53–60, advertisements. Frontispiece and one illustrated leaf tipped in and not paginated. End papers imitation laid.

White cloth over thin boards. Lettering, rule-boxes, and ornament on covers and spine in black. Illustrations by C. S. Reinhart. "Harp-

er's black & white series." Published June 8, 1894.

Reprinted from *The mouse-trap and other farces;* see 89–B. New plates were used in this edition.

94-D

Five o'clock tea | farce | by W. D. Howells | illustrated | [*publisher's device*] | New York | Harper and Brothers | 1894

Collation: p. 48, 5¼ x 3¾ inches; title page, [3]; 7–46, text; 47–48, advertisements. Frontispiece and one illustrated leaf tipped in and not paginated. End papers imitation laid.

White cloth over thin boards. Lettering and ornament on covers and spine in black. Illustrations by C. S. Reinhart. "Harper's black & white series." Published June 19, 1894.

Reprinted from *The mouse-trap and other farces;* see 89–B. New plates were used in this edition.

94-E

Tuscan cities | by | William Dean Howells | author of "Venetian life," "Italian journeys," etc. | [*publisher's device*] | Boston and New York | Houghton, Mifflin and Company | the Riverside Press, Cambridge | 1894

Collation: p. viii + 274, 7⅛ x 4¾ inches: title page, [v]; preface, [vii]; 1–272, text; blank leaf. End papers imitation laid.

Red cloth over boards. Lettering on front cover and spine gold-stamped; signature on front cover gold-stamped.

Preface, p. [vii], here first printed. Printed from new plates; see 86–A.

95-A

Their wedding journey | by William Dean Howells | with illustrations by | Clifford Carleton | [*publisher's device*] | Cambridge | printed at the Riverside Press | MDCCCXCV

Collation: p. –iv + viii + 402, 8 ⁹/₁₆ x 5⅝ inches; title page, [i]; 1–399, text; 400–402, blank. Eighty-five illustrations on very light glazed stock glued to paginated leaves, often with text. End papers of heavier stock than text.

Vellum over boards. Ornamental rules and lettering on spine and front cover gold-stamped. Top edge gilt; fore and bottom edges rough-trimmed. This is the large-paper edition; a trade edition was issued by Houghton, Mifflin and Company in white or light green cloth over boards, the ornamental rules, ornament, and lettering on front cover and spine gold-stamped. Houghton Mifflin also issued another edition in 1895, bound in red cloth, from the plates of the 1887 edition; see 87-D. Published Oct. 26, 1894.

95-B

Recollections of life | in Ohio, | from 1813 to 1840, | by | William Cooper Howells. | With an introduction by his son, | William Dean Howells.

The Robert Clarke Company: Cincinnati, 1895. Published Feb. 13, 1895.

The introduction, p. iii–viii, here first printed, and the conclusion and editing as well are Howells'.

95-C

Master and man | by | Count Leo Tolstoy | translated by | A. Hulme Beaman | with an introduction | by W. D. Howells.

D. Appleton and Company: New York, 1895. Published May 17, 1895.

"Introduction," dated "New York, May 1, 1895," p. v–xv, here first printed.

95-D

[Don't wake the children. Song. Words by William Dean Howells music by Clarence W. Bowers J. A. Howells & Co. Jefferson, Ohio 1895.]

Record of title copyright only, Aug. 19, 1895. An edition was printed, though perhaps no copies were sold (*Critic*, Nov., 1899, xxxv, 26–28).

95-E

My literary passions | by | W. D. Howells | author of | "A traveler from Altruria" "The coast of Bohemia" | "A hazard of new fortunes" etc. | [*publisher's device*] | New York | Harper & Brothers publishers | 1895

Collation: p. iv + 268, 7 $^3/_{16}$ x 4¾ inches: title page, [i]; 1–258, text; 259–261, index; 262–268, blank and advertisements. End papers imitation laid.

Red cloth over boards. Lettering on front cover and spine gold-stamped; signature on front cover gold-stamped. Published June 18, 1895 (Harper register).

Pages 1–12, first printed *Ladies' home journal*, Dec., 1893, xi, 10; p. 12–32, Jan., 1894, 13; p. 32–49, Feb., 17; p. 49–65, March, 13; p. 66–81, April, 15; p. 82–97, May, 13; p. 97–113, June, 15; p. 114–131, July, 13; p. 132–148, Aug., 14; p. 148–164, Sept., 12; p. 165–181, Oct., 15; p. 181–197, Nov., 15; p. 198–214, Dec., xii, 17; p. 214–231, Jan., 1895, 13; p. 231–247, Feb., 14; p. 247–258, March, 15.

95-F

[*Ornament*] Stops | of various | quills [*ornament*] | by W. D. Howells | illustrated by | Howard | Pyle | [*publisher's device*] | New York | Harper and Brothers | MDCCCXCV

Collation: p. 116, 8¼ x 5¾ inches: title page, [3]; 9–115, text; 116, blank; all pages un-numbered, with text on recto only of each leaf. End papers imitation laid.

Tan cloth over boards. Ornament and lettering on front cover and spine gold-stamped. Top edge gilt; fore and bottom edges rough-trimmed. Glazed paper throughout. Published Oct. 25, 1895.

An edition limited to fifty copies was published later, the title page as above except that MDCCCXCVI appears in place of MDCCCXCV. This edition was printed in two colors throughout on heavy rag paper, the pages measuring 10¼ x 7½ inches; it has three more leaves than the regular edition above, one bearing the notice of limitation and two holograph signatures, the other two blank. The volume is bound in gray cloth over boards, the cream backstrip with rule-boxes and lettering in dark

Collations of Works . . . — 95-F, continued

brown. The two editions, it should be noted, were printed from the same plates.

"November," first printed *Harper's monthly,* Nov., 1891, LXXXIII, 906.

"Midway," first printed *Harper's monthly,* Dec., 1894, XC, 39.

"Time," first printed *Harper's monthly,* Dec., 1894, XC, 36.

"From generation to generation," first printed *Harper's monthly,* March, 1893, LXXXVI, 549.

"The bewildered guest," first printed *Harper's monthly,* March, 1893, LXXXVI, 549.

"Company," first printed *Harper's monthly,* March, 1893, LXXXVI, 548.

"Heredity," first printed *Harper's monthly,* Dec., 1894, XC, 37.

"Twelve P. M.," first printed *Harper's monthly,* Dec., 1894, XC, 35.

"Change," first printed *Harper's monthly,* Dec., 1894, XC, 38.

"In the dark," first printed *Harper's monthly,* Dec., 1894, XC, 37.

"Tomorrow," first printed *Harper's monthly,* March, 1893, LXXXVI, 548.

"Living," first printed *Harper's monthly,* March, 1893, LXXXVI, 548.

"If," first printed as "Hope," *Harper's monthly,* March, 1893, LXXXVI, 550.

"Solitude," first printed *Harper's monthly,* Dec., 1894, XC, 38.

"Respite," first printed *Harper's monthly,* March, 1893, LXXXVI, 550.

"Question," first printed *Harper's monthly,* March, 1893, LXXXVI, 547.

"Hope," first printed *Harper's monthly,* Sept., 1895, XCI, 517.

"The burden," first printed *Harper's monthly,* Sept., 1895, XCI, 517.

"Calvary," first printed *Harper's monthly,* Dec., 1894, XC, 39.

"Conscience," first printed *Harper's monthly,* Dec., 1894, XC, 39.

"Reward and punishment," first printed *Harper's monthly,* Sept., 1895, XCI, 518.

"Sympathy," first printed *Harper's monthly,* Sept., 1895, XCI, 518.

"Statistics," first printed *Harper's monthly,* Sept., 1895, XCI, 519.

"Parable," first printed *Harper's monthly,* Sept., 1895, XCI, 519.

"Vision," first printed *Harper's monthly,* Sept., 1895, XCI, 518.

"Society," first printed *Harper's monthly,* March, 1895, XC, 630.

"Good society," first printed as "Society," *Harper's monthly,* Dec., 1894, XC, 36.

"Friends and foes," first printed *Harper's monthly,* March, 1893, LXXXVI, 548.

"Sphinx," first printed *Harper's monthly,* Dec., 1894, XC, 35.

"Materials of a story," first printed *Harper's monthly,* May, 1892, LXXXIV, 942.

"The king dines."

"Labor and capital."

"Equality."

"Judgment day," first printed *The first book of the Authors Club;* see 93–H.

"Mortality," first printed *Harper's monthly,* May, 1891, LXXXII, 848–849.

"Another day," first printed *Harper's monthly,* March, 1891, LXXXII, 608.

"Some one else," first printed *Harper's monthly,* March, 1891, LXXXII, 609.

"Life," first printed *Harper's monthly,* March, 1891, LXXXII, 608.

"Weather-breeder," first printed *Harper's monthly,* March, 1891, LXXXII, 609.

"Peonage," first printed *Harper's monthly,* March, 1891, LXXXII, 609.

"Race," first printed *Harper's monthly,* April, 1894, LXXXVIII, 677.

"Temperament," first printed *Harper's monthly,* March, 1891, LXXXII, 608.

"What shall it profit?" first printed *Harper's monthly,* Feb., 1891, LXXXII, 384.

96-A

B. Perez Galdos | [*rule*] | Doña Perfecta | translation by Mary J. Serrano | introduction by | William Dean Howells.

Harper & Brothers: New York, 1896. "Odd number series." Published Nov. 8, 1895 (Harper register).

"Introduction," p. v–xiii, first printed as "A great novel," *Harper's bazar,* Nov. 2, 1895, XXVIII, 886.

96-B

The day of their wedding | a novel | by | W. D. Howells | author of "A hazard of new fortunes" | "A traveler from Altruria" etc. | Illustrated | [*publisher's device*] | New York | Harper & Brothers publishers | 1896

Collation: p. iv + 160, 7 $^8/_{16}$ x 4¾ inches: title page, [i]; 1–158, text; 159–160, advertisements. Frontispiece and six illustrated leaves tipped in and not paginated. End papers imitation laid.

Red cloth over boards. Lettering on front cover and spine gold-stamped; signature on front cover gold-stamped. Illustrations by T. de Thulstrup. Published Feb. 14, 1896 (Harper register).

The inscription in the copy of this book in the Howells collection of Mr. David Borowitz reads: "A fact given me by Hamilton Mabie. W. D. Howells. 1894–1915."

First printed *Harper's bazar*, Oct. 5, 1895, xxviii, 801–802, chapters i–ii; Oct. 12, 825–826, iii–iv; Oct. 19, 845–846, v–vi; Oct. 26, 869–871, vii–viii; Nov. 2, 889–890, ix–x; Nov. 9, 909–910, xi–xii; Nov. 16, 933–934, xiii–xiv.

96-C

A parting and a meeting | story | by | W. D. Howells | illustrated | [*publisher's device*] | New York | Harper & Brothers publishers | 1896

Collation: p. iv + 104, 5¾ x 4¼ inches: title page, [i]; 1–99, text; 100–104, blank and advertisements. Frontispiece and illustrated leaves tipped in and not paginated. End papers of heavier stock than text.

Light tan cloth over boards. Ornamental hinges in silver and dark brown stamped over spine and covers. Lettering on front cover and spine gold-stamped. Illustrations by C. Y. Turner. "Harper's little novels" series. Published April 7, 1896.

First printed *Cosmopolitan*, Dec., 1894, xviii, 183–188, chapters i–ii; Jan., 1895, 307–316, iii–iv; Feb., 469–474, v.

96-D

Maggie | a child of the streets | by | Stephen Crane | author of | "The red badge of courage."

William Heinemann: London, 1896. Published about June, 1896 (earliest notice observed).

"An appreciation," p. v–vii, here first printed.

96-E

Impressions and experiences | by | W. D. Howells | author of "A hazard

of new fortunes" | "The quality of mercy" etc. | [*publisher's device*] | New York | Harper & Brothers publishers | 1896

Collation: p. iv + 284, 7⅜ x 5 inches; title page, [i]; 1–281, text; 282–284, blank and advertisements. End papers of heavier stock.

Red cloth over boards. Lettering, ornament, and rule-boxes on front cover and spine stamped in black and gold; publisher's device stamped in gold on back cover. Top edge gilt; fore and bottom edges untrimmed. Published Sept. 25, 1896; (Harper register) Nov. 23.

The collection was printed from new plates and in a larger format by Harper & Brothers in 1909, the collation in part reading, "p. vi + 210, 8 ¹/₁₆ x 5⅜ inches: title page, [iii]; 3–207, text; 208–210, blank."

"The country printer," first printed *Scribner's*, May, 1893, xiii, 539–558.

"Police report," first printed *Atlantic monthly*, Jan., 1882, xlix, 1–16.

"I talk of dreams," first printed *Harper's monthly*, May, 1895, xc, 836–845.

"An East-Side ramble."

"Tribulations of a cheerful giver," first printed *Century*, June – July, 1895, l, 181–185, 417–421.

"The closing of the hotel," first printed "Life and letters," *Harper's weekly*, Sept. 28, Oct. 5, Oct. 19, 1895, xxxix, 916–917, 941, 988–989.

"Glimpses of Central Park," first printed more fully as "Letters of an Altrurian traveller, a bit of Altruria in New York," *Cosmopolitan*, Jan., 1894, xvi, 259–277.

"New York streets," first printed more fully as "Letters of an Altrurian traveller, aspects and impressions of a plutocratic city," and "Plutocratic contrasts and contradictions," *Cosmopolitan*, Feb. – March, 1894, xvi, 415–425, 558–569.

96-F

Lyrics of lowly life | by | Paul Laurence Dunbar | with | an introduction by W. D. Howells.

Dodd, Mead and Company: New York, 1896. Published Dec. 2, 1896.

"Introduction," p. xiii–xx, here first printed. Reprinted *Bookman*, April, 1906, xxiii, 185–186.

97-A

English society | sketched by | George du Maurier.

Harper & Brothers: New York, 1897. Published Dec. 17, 1896 (copyright stamp).

"George du Maurier," p. 1–9, here first printed.

97-B

A previous engagement | comedy | by | W. D. Howells | illustrated | [*publisher's device*] | New York | Harper & Brothers publishers | 1897

Collation: p. vi + 70, 6 x 4⅝ inches: title page, [i]; illustrated half-title, [v]; 1–65, text; 66, illustrations; 67–68, advertisements; blank leaf. Frontispiece and two illustrated leaves tipped in and not paginated. No end papers.

Red paper covers. Lettering and rule-boxes on front cover in black; ornamental masks on covers in black. Illustrations by Albert E. Sterner. Published Jan. 29, 1897; (Harper register) Feb. 11.

First printed *Harper's monthly*, Dec., 1895, xcii, 29–44.

97-C

The | landlord at Lion's Head | a novel | by | W. D. Howells | author of "A hazard of new fortunes" | "The day of their wedding" etc. | Illustrated | by W. T. Smedley | [*publisher's device*] | New York | Harper & Brothers publishers | 1897

Collation: p. –ii + vi + 464, 7¼ x 4¾ inches: blank leaf; title page, [i]; 1–461, text; 462–464, blank and advertisements. Frontispiece and twenty-two illustrated leaves tipped in and not paginated. End papers imitation laid.

Red cloth over boards. Lettering on front cover and spine gold-stamped; signature on front cover gold-stamped. Published April 9, 1897.

The novel was reprinted from the same plates by the International Book and Publishing Company: New York, 1900. It was printed from new plates and in a larger format by Harper & Brothers in 1908, the collation in part reading: "p. vi + 410, 8⅛ x 5 ⁵/₁₆ inches: title page, [iii]; 3–408, text; 409–410 blank." Published Oct. 22, 1908 (Harper register).

First printed *Harper's weekly*, July 4, 1896, xl, 657–659, chapters i–v; July 11, 687–688, vi–viii; July 18, 707–708, ix–x; July 25, 735–736, xi–xii; Aug. 1, 753–755, xiii–xiv; Aug. 8, 777–779, xv–xvii; Aug. 15, 808–810, xviii–xx; Aug. 22, 830–832, xxi–xxiii; Aug. 29, 854–856, xxiv–xxvi; Sept. 5, 878–880, xxvii–xxix; Sept. 12, 902–904, xxx–xxxii; Sept. 19, 926–928, xxxiii–xxxv; Sept. 26, 951–952, xxxvi–xxxvii; Oct. 3, 969–971, xxxviii–xxxix; Oct. 10, 1007–1008, xl–xli; Oct. 17, 1025–1026, xlii; Oct. 24, 1055–1056, xliii–xliv; Oct. 31, 1073–1074, xlv–xlvi; Nov. 7, 1097–1098, xlvii–xlviii; Nov. 14, 1126–1127, xlix; Nov. 21, 1145–1147, l–li; Nov. 28, 1169–1170, lii–liii; Dec. 5, 1193–1194, liv–lv.

97-D

An open-eyed conspiracy | an idyl of Saratoga | by | W. D. Howells | author of "The landlord at Lion's Head" | "The coast of Bohemia" "April hopes" | "A hazard of new fortunes" etc. | [*publisher's device*] | New York and London | Harper & Brothers publishers | 1897

Collation: p. iv + 188, 7 ³/₁₆ x 4¾ inches: title page, [iii]; 1–181, text; 182–188, blank and advertisements. End papers imitation laid.

Red cloth over boards. Lettering on front cover and spine gold-stamped; signature on front cover gold-stamped. Published Sept. 3, 1897.

First printed *Century*, July, 1896, lii, 345–357, chapters i–iv; Aug., 607–620, v–ix; Sept., 659–671, x–xiv; Oct., 836–848, xv–xviii.

97-E

Stories of Ohio | by | William Dean Howells | [*publisher's device*] | New

York .:. Cincinnati .:. Chicago |
American Book Company | 1897

Collation: p. 290, 7¼ x 5 inches:
title page, [3]; preface, 5; 9–287, text;
288–290, blank. End papers of heavier stock than text.

Gray cloth over boards. Lettering, ornament, and rule-boxes on covers and spine stamped in dark blue. Illustrations by De Cost Smith, W. M. Cary, Dan Beard, A. I. Keller, E. P. Upjohn, Max F. Klapper (?). Published Dec. 15, 1897.

97-F

University edition | [*rule*] | A library
of the | world's best literature | ancient and modern | Charles Dudley
Warner | editor | Hamilton Wright
Mabie | Lucia Gilbert Runkle |
George Henry Warner | associate editors | Forty-five volumes | Vol.
xxxvii.

The International Society: New
York, 1897. Published Feb. 17, 1898.

"Lyof Tolstoy," p. 14985–14994, here first printed.

98-A

The story of a play | a novel | by |
W. D. Howells | author of "The landlord at Lion's Head" | "An open-eyed
conspiracy" etc. | [*publisher's device*]
| New York and London | Harper &
Brothers publishers | 1898

Collation: p. iv + 312, 7³/₁₆ x 4¾
inches: title page, [iii]; 1–312, text.
End papers imitation laid.

Red cloth over boards. Lettering on front cover and spine gold-stamped; signature on front cover gold-stamped. Published June 15, 1898.

First printed *Scribner's,* March, 1897, xxi, 290–305, chapters i–iii; April, 477–492, iv–vii; May, 641–651, viii–x; June, 764–775, xi–xiii; July, xxii, 99–120, xiv–xx; Aug., 245–254, xxi–xxv.

98-B

The | blindman's world | and other
stories | by | Edward Bellamy | with
a prefatory sketch by | W. D. Howells.

Houghton, Mifflin and Company:
Boston and New York, 1898. Published Oct. 5, 1898.

"Prefatory sketch," p. v–xiii, first printed *Atlantic monthly,* Aug., 1898, lxxxii, 253–256.

99-A

Ragged lady | a novel | by | W. D.
Howells | author of "A hazard of
new fortunes" | "The landlord at
Lion's Head" etc. | Illustrated | by
A. I. Keller | [*publisher's device*] |
New York and London | Harper &
Brothers publishers | 1899

Collation: p. iv + 364, 7³/₁₆ x 4⅞
inches: title page, [i]; 1–357, text;
358, blank; 359–364, advertisements.
Frontispiece and nine illustrated
leaves tipped in and not paginated.
End papers imitation laid.

Red cloth over boards. Lettering on front cover and spine gold-stamped; signature on front cover gold-stamped. Published Feb. 16, 1899.

The novel was printed from new plates and in a larger format by Harper & Brothers in 1908, the collation in part reading, "p. vi + 314, 8⅛ x 5⅜ inches: title page, [iii]; 3–311, text; 312–314, blank."

First printed *Harper's bazar,* July 2, 1898, xxxi, 561–563, chapters i–ii; July 9, 582–583, iii–iv; July 16, 601–602, v–vi; July 23, 626–627, vii–viii; July 30, 645–646, ix–x; Aug. 6, 666–667, xi–xii; Aug. 13, 687–689, xiii–xiv; Aug. 20, 706–707, xv–xvi; Aug. 27, 737–739, xvii–xix; Sept. 3, 750–751, xx–xxi; Sept. 10, 769–771, xxii–xxiii; Sept. 17, 790–791, xxiv–xxv; Sept. 24, 821–822, xxvi–xxvii; Oct. 1, 834–835, xxviii–xxix; Oct. 8, 866–868, xxix (continued)–xxxi; Oct. 15, 890–891, xxxii–xxxiii; Oct. 22, 909–911, xxxiv–xxxv; Oct. 29, 930–931, xxxvi–xxxvii; Nov. 5, 950–952, xxxviii–xl.

99-B

The | coast of Bohemia | [*rule*] | by W. D. Howells | [*publisher's device*] | Biographical edition | [*rule*] | New York and London | Harper & Brothers, publishers | 1899 [*All the foregoing in a rule-box.*]

Collation: p. viii + 344, 7⅜ x 5 inches: title page, [i]; "Introductory sketch," iii–vii; 1–340, text; 341–344, advertisements. Frontispiece portrait tipped in and not paginated. End papers imitation laid.

Green cloth with vertical grain over boards. Lettering, ornament, and rule-boxes on front cover stamped in black. Lettering and publisher's device on spine gold-stamped. Top edge gilt; fore and bottom edges uncut. Imitation laid paper throughout. Published Nov. 2, 1899.

"Introductory sketch," p. iii–vii, here first printed. Reprinted from first edition plates; see 93-I.

99-C

Their | silver wedding | journey | [*rule*] | by | W. D. Howells | author of "A hazard of new fortunes" | "The landlord at Lion's Head" etc. | Illustrated | in two volumes | Vol. i. | [*publisher's device*] | New York and London | Harper & Brothers publishers | MDCCCXCIX [*Title page of second volume as above except that "Vol.* ii.*" appears in place of "Vol.* i.*"]

Collation: Vol. i, p. –iv + vi + 404, 8 x 5⅛ inches: [–iv], frontispiece; title page, [i]; 1–401, text; 402–404, blank. Vol. ii, p. –iv + vi + 464; [–iv], frontispiece; title page, [i]; 1–464, text. End papers imitation laid.

Light gray cloth over boards. Lettering and ornament on front cover and spine stamped in silver; volume numbers stamped in silver on spine. Top edges trimmed and cut, fore edges uncut, bottom edges untrimmed. Glazed paper throughout. Illustrations by W. T. Smedley. Published Dec. 8, 1899.

The novel was printed from new plates in a one-volume edition by Harper & Brothers

in 1900, the collation in part reading, "p. iv + 604, 7 ⁵/₁₆ x 4 ¹¹/₁₆ inches: title page, [i]; 1–601, text; 602, blank; 603–604, advertisements." It was printed in 1909, again from new plates and this time in a larger format, the collation in part reading, "p. ii + 494, 8 ¹/₁₆ x 5 ⁵/₁₆ inches; title page, [i]; 3–493, text; 494, blank."

First printed *Harper's monthly*, Jan., 1899, XCVIII, 193–210, chapters i–viii; Feb., 392–408, ix–xiv; March, 546–560, xv–xxi; April, 787–802, xxii–xxvii; May, 923–938, xxviii–xxxii; June, XCIX, 109–124, xxxiii–xxxviii; July, 269–286, xxxix–xlv; Aug., 374–392, xlvi–l; Sept., 570–588, li–lvi; Oct., 763–781, lvii–lxii; Nov., 926–949, lxiii–lxx; Dec., C, 85–106, lxxi–lxxv.

Volume I includes chapters i–xxxviii; volume II, chapters xxxix–lxxv.

00-A

The [*three ornaments*] | Hesperian tree | a souvenir of the Ohio Valley | [*double rule*] | edited by John James Piatt.

John Scott & Co.: Three Rivers Elm, North Bend, Ohio, [1900]. Published May 17, 1900.

"Success and unsuccess," poem dated 1860, p. 38, reprinted from the first two stanzas of "Old Brown," *Echoes of Harper's Ferry*. See 60-B.

"The mulberries in Pay's garden," a reminiscent sketch, p. 431–436, here first printed.

00-B

Bride roses | a scene | by W. D. Howells | [*publisher's device*] | Boston and New York | Houghton, Mifflin and | Company MDCCCC [*All the foregoing in two double-rule boxes.*]

Collation: p. ii + 56, 5⅞ x 3⅝ inches: title page, [1]; 3–48, text; 49–56, blank, colophon, advertisements, blank. End papers imitation laid, of slightly heavier stock than text.

Dark blue cloth over thin boards. Ornamental stamping and lettering on spine and front cover in silver; lettering on front cover gold-stamped. Top edge stained yellow. Imitation laid throughout. Published May 21, 1900.

First printed *Harper's monthly*, Aug., 1893, LXXXVII, 424–430.

00-C

Room forty- | five a farce | by W. D. Howells | [*publisher's device*] | Boston and New York | Houghton, Mifflin and | Company MDCCCC [*All the foregoing in two double-rule boxes.*]

Collation: p. ii + 66, 5⅞ x 3⅝ inches: title page, [1]; 3–61, text; 62–66, colophon, advertisements, and blank. End papers imitation laid.

Dark blue cloth over thin boards. Lettering and ornament on spine, and rule-boxes and ornament on front cover, in silver. Lettering on front cover gold-stamped. Top edge stained yellow. Imitation laid paper throughout. Published May 21, 1900.

First printed *Frank Leslie's*, Dec., 1899, XLIX, 132–148.

00-D

An Indian giver | a comedy | by W. D. Howells | [*publisher's device*] | Boston and New York | Houghton, Mifflin and | Company MDCCCC [*All the foregoing in two double-rule boxes.*]

Collation: p. ii + 104, 5⅞ x 3⅝ inches: title page, [1]; 3–99, text; 100–104, colophon, advertisements, blank. End papers imitation laid.

Dark blue cloth over thin boards. Lettering and ornament on spine, and rule-boxes and ornament on front cover, in silver. Lettering on front cover gold-stamped. Top edge stained yellow. Imitation laid paper throughout. Published Aug. 15, 1900.

First printed *Harper's monthly*, Jan., 1897, XCIV, 235–252.

00-E

The smoking car | a farce | by W. D. Howells | [*publisher's device*] | Boston and New York | Houghton, Mifflin and | Company MDCCCC [*All the foregoing in two double-rule boxes.*]

Collation: p. ii + 74, 5⅞ x 3⅝ inches: blank leaf; title page, [i]; 3–70, text; 71–74, colophon, advertise-ments, and blank. End papers imitation laid.

Dark blue cloth over thin boards. Lettering and ornament on spine, and rule-boxes and ornament on front cover, in silver. Lettering on front cover gold-stamped. Top edge stained yellow. Imitation laid paper throughout. Published Aug. 15, 1900.

First printed *Frank Leslie's*, Dec., 1898, XLVII, 183–199.

00-F

Literary friends | and | acquaintance | a personal retrospect of | American authorship | by W. D. Howells | illustrated | [*publisher's device*] | Harper & Brothers publishers | New York and London | 1900

Collation: p. x + 292, 8⅛ x 5⅜ inches: title page, [i]; "Note," [iii]; 1–288, text; 289–292, blank and advertisements. Frontispiece and seventy-one illustrated leaves are not paginated. End papers imitation laid.

Green cloth with fine vertical lines over boards. Lettering on front cover and spine gold-stamped. Initial L on front cover stamped in red. Top edge gilt; fore and bottom edges rough-trimmed. Or red cloth with fine vertical lines over boards, lettering and rules on front cover and spine gold-stamped. Illustrations by H. Sandham, C. Broughton, V. Perard, C. D. Graves, W. T. Smedley, Lucius Hitchcock, W. H. Drake. Published Nov. 17, 1900.

A limited edition printed from the same plates as the trade edition above was also issued, the collation reading: "p. –iv + x + 288, 8¼ x 5⅜ inches: blank leaf; [–iv], notice of limitation to 150 copies and holograph signature; title page, [i]; text, 1–288." Tan buckram over boards, with lettering on leather inset on front cover and rule-box enclosing the inset gold-stamped, top edge gilt, fore and bottom edges uncut and untrimmed.

"Note," here first printed.

"My first visit to New England," first printed *Harper's monthly*, May, 1894, LXXXVIII, 816–824, chapters i–v; June, 1894, LXXXIX, 40–52, vi–viii; July, 1894, 228–235, ix–xii; Aug., 1894, 441–451, xiii–xvii.

"First impressions of literary New York," first printed *Harper's monthly*, June, 1895, XCI, 62–74.

Collations of Works . . . — 00-F, continued

"Roundabout to Boston," first printed *Harper's monthly*, Aug., 1895, xci, 427–438.

"Literary Boston as I knew it," first printed as "Literary Boston thirty years ago," *Harper's monthly*, Nov., 1895, xci, 865–879.

"Oliver Wendell Holmes," first printed *Harper's monthly*, Dec., 1896, xciv, 120–134.

"The white Mr. Longfellow," first printed *Harper's monthly*, Aug., 1896, xciii, 327–343.

"Studies of Lowell," first printed as "A personal retrospect of James Russell Lowell," *Scribner's*, Sept., 1900, xxviii, 363–378.

"Cambridge neighbors," first printed as "Some literary memories of Cambridge," *Harper's monthly*, Nov., 1900, ci, 823–839.

01-A

How | they succeeded | [*four ornaments*] | life stories of successful | men told by themselves | [*rule*] | by Orison Swett Marden.

Lothrop Publishing Company: Boston, [1901]. Published April 25, 1901.

"How William Dean Howells worked to secure a foothold," p. 171–184, in different form first printed as "How he climbed fame's ladder," by Theodore Dreiser, *Success*, April, 1898, p. 5–6. See articles by John F. Huth, Jr., *Colophon*, Winter, 1938, p. 120–133, Summer, 1938, p. 406–410.

01-B

A pair of | patient lovers | by | W. D. Howells | author of | "The landlord at Lion's Head" | "Ragged lady" etc. | [*publisher's device*] | New York and London | Harper & Brothers publishers | 1901 [*All the foregoing in an ornamental rule-box.*]

Collation: p. iv + 368, 7⅝ x 5⅛ inches: title page, [i]; 1–368, text. Frontispiece leaf (colored photograph) tipped in and not paginated. Ornamental end papers with design in light green and brown.

Brown cloth backstrip and corners and marbled paper over boards. Lettering, orna-

ment, and medallion portrait gold-stamped. Top edge gilt; fore and bottom edges uncut and untrimmed. "Harper's portrait collection of short stories" series. Published May 23, 1901.

"A pair of patient lovers," first printed *Harper's monthly*, Nov., 1897, xcv, 832–851.

"The pursuit of the piano," first printed *Harper's monthly*, April, 1900, c, 725–746.

"A difficult case," first printed *Atlantic monthly*, July – Aug., 1900, lxxxvi, 24–36, 205–217.

"The magic of a voice," first printed *Lippincott's*, Dec., 1899, lxiv, 901–928.

"A circle in the water," first printed *Scribner's*, March – April, 1895, xvii, 293–303, 428–440.

01-C

Heroines of fiction | by W. D. Howells | author of | "Literary friends and acquaintance" etc. | With illustrations by H. C. Christy | A. K. Keller, and others | Volume i. | [*publisher's device*] | Harper & Brothers publishers | New York and London | 1901 [*Title page of second volume as above except that "Volume ii." appears in place of "Volume i."*]

Collation: Volume i, p. viii + 240, 8⅛ x 5⅜ inches: title page, [i]; 1–239, text; 240, blank. Frontispiece and forty illustrated leaves tipped in and not paginated. Volume ii, p. viii + 276; title page, [i]; 1–274, text; 275, blank; 276, advertisements. Frontispiece and twenty-seven illustrated leaves tipped in and not paginated. End papers imitation laid.

Green cloth with fine vertical lines over boards. Lettering on front cover and spine gold-stamped with initial H in red. Top edges gilt, fore edges untrimmed, bottom edges rough-trimmed. Illustrations by Howard Chandler Christy, A. I. Keller, Henry Hutt, Rosing E. Sherwood, Otto H. Bacher, W. T. Smedley, George T. Tobin, Albert Sterner, Fletcher C. Ransom, and William L. Jacobson. Published Oct. 26, 1901.

Volume i, chapters i–xix, first printed *Harper's bazar*, May 5, 1900, xxxiii, 3–8; May 12, 67–72; May 26, 195–201; June 9, 323–328;

June 23, 453–460; June 30, 517–523; July 14, 647–652; July 28, 775–780; Aug. 11, 903–908; Aug. 25, 1031–1036; Sept. 8, 1192–1197; Sept. 22, 1287–1292; Oct. 6, 1415–1421; Oct. 20, 1543–1548; Nov. 3, 1671–1677; Nov. 17, 1799–1804; Dec. 1, 1945–1950; Dec. 15, 2094–2100; Dec. 29, 2224–2230. Volume II, chapters i–xii, first printed *Harper's bazar*, · Jan. 12, 1901, xxxiv, 79–83; Jan. 26, 195–201; Feb. 16, 409–415; March 2, 537–545; March 16, 675–681; March 30, 808–813; April 13, 947–953; April 27, 1075–1080; June, xxxv, 103–109; Aug., 303–309; Oct., 538–544; Jan., 1902, xxxvi, 9–14 (serialized after volume publication).

Chapters xiii–xix here first printed.

01-D

Italian journeys | by W. D. Howells | with illustrations by | Joseph Pennell | [*device*] | Cambridge | printed at the Riverside Press | MDCCCCI

Collation: p. –ii + xii + 384, 8¾ x 5¾ inches: title page, [iii]; copyright and notice of limitation to 300 copies, [iv]; "A confidence," v–vi; 3–369, text; index, 371–380; two blank leaves. Frontispiece and forty-seven illustrated leaves of glazed paper tipped in and not paginated; twenty-three other illustrations are reproduced on text leaves as chapter headpieces. End papers.

Brown cloth over boards. Cream cloth backstrip with paper label printed in black, ornament and rules in red. Imitation laid paper throughout except as noted. Published Nov. 12, 1901.

A trade edition was issued at the same time by Houghton, Mifflin and Company from the same plates: "The Park Street library" series. In 1907, Houghton, Mifflin used the plates again to issue *Italian journeys* as Volume v of "The Atlantic library of travel" series.

Revised from the 1892 edition of *Italian journeys.* See 72-C. "A confidence," p. v–vi, here first printed.

01-E

Italian journeys | by | W. D. Howells | [*engraved ornament*] | with one hundred and three illustrations by |

Joseph Pennell | London | William Heinemann | 1901

Collation: p. xii + 292, 8 x 5¾ inches: title page, [iii]; "A confidence," v–vi; 1–292, text; frontispiece leaf and ten illustrated leaves tipped in and not paginated. End papers of lighter stock than text.

Olive green cloth over boards. Lettering and ornament on front and back covers and flat spine stamped in black and gold. Top edge gilt; bottom edge untrimmed. Published ca. Nov., 1901 (cf. 01-D).

Text and illustrations are the same as in the American edition; see 01-D.

01-F

Florence in art | and literature | [*rules*] | [*rule*] | course x: Booklovers Reading Club | [*rule*] | books selected | for this reading course | by William Dean Howells | and | Russell Sturgis.

The Booklovers Library: Philadelphia, [1901]. Published Dec. 13, 1901.

"Supplementary books recommended for this course by William Dean Howells," p. 113–114, here first printed.

02-A

The Kentons | a novel· | by | W. D. Howells | author of "Their silver wedding journey" | "Literary friends and acquaintance" | "Heroines of fiction" etc. | [*publisher's device*] | New York and London | Harper & Brothers publishers | 1902

Collation: p. iv + 320, 7⅛ x 4¾ inches: title page, [iii]; 1–317, text; 318–320, blank. End papers imitation laid.

Red cloth over boards. Lettering on front cover and spine gold-stamped; signature on front cover gold-stamped. Published April 18, 1902.

02-B

The flight | of Pony Baker | a boy's town story | by | W. D. Howells | author of | "A boy's town" | "Christmas every day" etc. | Illustrated | [*publisher's device*] | New York and London | Harper & Brothers | publishers 1902 [*All the foregoing in a rule-box.*]

Collation: p. –ii + vi + 224, 7 $^3/_{16}$ x 4¾ inches: blank leaf; title page, [i]; 3–223, text; 224, blank. Frontispiece and seven illustrated leaves tipped in and not paginated. End papers imitation laid.

Red cloth over boards. Lettering on front cover and spine stamped in silver; rule-boxes and ornament on front cover stamped in black. Illustrations by Florence Scovel Shinn. Published Sept. 26, 1902; (Harper register) Sept. 19.

"Pony's mother and why he had a right to run off."

"The right that Pony had to run off, from the way his father acted."

"Jim Leonard's hair-breadth escape," first printed *Youth's companion,* May 10, 1900, LXXIV, 237–238.

"The scrape that Jim Leonard got the boys into," first printed as "The abandoned watermelon patch," *Youth's companion,* Dec. 1, 1898, LXXII, 602–603.

"About running away to the Indian reservation on a canal-boat, and how the plan failed."

"How the Indians came to the boy's town and Jim Leonard acted the coward."

"How Frank Baker spent the Fourth at Pawpaw Bottom, and saw the Fourth of July boy," first printed as "The Fourth-of-July boy," *Harper's weekly,* July 5, 1902, XLVI, 867–870.

"How Pony Baker came pretty near running off with a circus."

"How Pony did not quite get off with the circus."

"The adventures that Pony's cousin, Frank Baker, had with a pocketful of money," first printed as "A pocketful of money," *Youth's companion,* Nov. 16–23, 1899, LXXIII, 602–603, 617–618.

"How Jim Leonard planned for Pony Baker to run off on a raft."

"How Jim Leonard backed out, and Pony had to give it up."

The Newberry Library copy of the first edition of *The flight of Pony Baker* has laid in the following holograph MS. verse:

"All the long August afternoon
 The little, drowsy stream,
Whispers a melancholy tune,
 As if it dreamed of June,
 And whispered in its dream.
                        W. D. HOWELLS"

02-C

Literature and life | studies | by W. D. Howells | author of | "Literary friends and acquaintance" | "Heroines of fiction" | "My literary passions" etc. | Illustrated | [*publisher's device*] | Harper & Brothers publishers | New York and London | 1902

Collation: p. –ii + x + 324, 8⅛ x 5⅜ inches: blank leaf; title page, [i]; "A word of explanation," iii–iv; 1–323, text; 324, blank. Frontispiece and thirty-one illustrated leaves are tipped in and not paginated. End papers imitation laid.

Dark green cloth with fine vertical lines over boards. Lettering on front cover and spine heavily stamped in gold; initial L on front cover in red. Top edge gilt; fore and bottom edges untrimmed. Illustrated by A. Sterner, T. de Thulstrup, J. Conacher. Published Oct. 14, 1902.

"A word of explanation," here first printed.

"The man of letters as a man of business," first printed *Scribner's,* Oct., 1893, XIV, 429–445.

"Worries of a winter walk," first printed "Life and letters," *Harper's weekly,* April 3, 1897, XLI, 338–339.

"Confessions of a summer colonist," first printed *Atlantic monthly,* Dec., 1898, LXXXII, 742–750.

"The editor's relations with the young contributor," here first printed.

"Summer isles of Eden," first printed "Editor's easy chair," June, 1901, CIII, 146–151.

"Wild flowers of the asphalt," first printed "Life and letters," *Harper's weekly,* July 17, 1897, XLI, 706.

"Last days in a Dutch hotel," first printed "Life and letters," *Harper's weekly,* Nov. 13–20, 1897, XLI, 1134, 1147.

"Some anomalies of the short story," first printed *North American review,* Sept., 1901, CLXXIII, 422–432.

All the long August afternoon
The little, drowsy stream,
Whispers a melancholy tune,
As if it dreamed of June,
And whispered in its dream.

W. D. Howells.

Previously unpublished holograph poem laid in The Newberry Library
copy of "The Flight of Pony Baker," 02-B

"A circus in the suburbs," first printed "Life and letters," *Harper's weekly*, Aug. 8, 1896, XL, 774.

"A she Hamlet," first printed "Editor's easy chair," *Harper's monthly*, March, 1901, CII, 640–643.

"Spanish prisoners of war," first printed "Life and letters," *Harper's weekly*, Aug. 20, 1898, XLII, 826–827.

"The midnight platoon," first printed "Life and letters," *Harper's weekly*, May 4, 1895, XXXIX, 416–417.

"The beach at Rockaway," first printed "Life and letters," *Harper's weekly*, Sept. 5–12, 1896, XL, 870, 894.

"American literary centres," first printed *Literature*, June 4, 18, 1898, II, 649–651, 704–706.

"Sawdust in the arena," first printed "Life and letters," *Harper's weekly*, Oct. 3, 1896, XL, 966.

"At a dime museum," first printed "Life and letters," *Harper's weekly*, April 25, 1896, XL, 415.

"American literature in exile," first printed *Literature*, March 3, 1899, n. s. I, 169–170.

"The horse show," first printed "Life and letters," *Harper's weekly*, Nov. 28, 1896, XL, 1171.

"The problem of the summer," first printed "Life and letters," *Harper's weekly*, July 11, 1896, XL, 678.

"Aesthetic New York fifty-odd years ago," first printed *Literature*, Aug. 11, 1899, n. s. II, 105–106.

"From New York into New England," first printed *Literature*, July 30, 1898, III, 87–90.

"The standard household effect company," first printed "Life and letters," *Harper's weekly*, July 6–13, 1895, XXXIX, 628, 653.

"Staccato notes of a vanished summer," first printed *Literature*, Oct. 13 – Nov. 10, 1899, n. s. II, 321–322, 345, 369, 393–394, 417–418.

"The art of the adsmith," first printed "Life and letters," *Harper's weekly*, May 9, 1896, XL, 462.

"The psychology of plagiarism," first printed *Literature*, Aug. 18, 1899, n. s. II, 129–130.

"Puritanism in American fiction," first printed *Literature*, May 14, 1898, n. s. II, 563–564.

"The what and the how in art," first printed "Life and letters," *Harper's weekly*, March 21, 1896, XL, 270.

"Politics of American authors," first printed *Literature*, July 16, 1898, III, 41–42.

"Storage," first printed "Editor's easy chair," *Harper's monthly*, Dec., 1901, CIV, 162–166.

"Floating down the river on the O-hi-o," first printed "Editor's easy chair," *Harper's monthly*, June, 1902, CV, 146–151.

03-A

The [*three ornaments*] | Hesperian tree | an annual of the Ohio Valley — 1903 | [*double rule*] | edited by John James Piatt.

S. F. Harriman: Columbus, 1903. Published Dec. 10, 1902.

"Success – a parable," poem dated 1860, p. 50, first printed *Ohio farmer*, May 5, 1860, IX, 144.

"Hot," a sketch, p. 86–88, first printed *Ohio state journal*, June 29, 1859, XXIII, 2.

"Awaiting his exequatur (returned from the dead-letter office)," a letter to J. J. Piatt dated "Venice, January 27, 1862," p. 425–429, here first printed.

03-B

Questionable | shapes | by | W. D. Howells | author of | "Literary friends and acquaintance" | "Literature and life" "The Kentons" | "Their silver wedding journey" | etc. etc. | Illustrated | [*publisher's device*] | New York and London | Harper & Brothers publishers | 1903

Collation: p. vi + 226, 7¼ x 4¾ inches: title page, [iii]; 5–219, text; 220–226, blank and advertisements. Frontispiece and three illustrated leaves tipped in and not paginated. End papers imitation laid.

Red cloth over boards. Lettering on front cover and spine gold-stamped; signature on front cover gold-stamped. Illustrations by W. T. Smedley. Published May 19, 1903.

"His apparition," first printed *Harper's monthly*, March, 1902, CIV, 621–648.

"The angel of the Lord," first printed as "At third hand, a psychological inquiry," *Century*, Feb., 1901, LXI, 496–506.

"Though one rose from the dead," first printed *Harper's monthly*, April, 1903, CVI, 724–738.

03-C

Letters home | by | W. D. Howells | author of | "Literary friends and acquaintance" | "Literature and life" "The Kentons" | "Their silver wedding journey" | etc. etc. | [*publisher's device*] | New York and London | Harper & Brothers publishers | 1903

Collation: p. iv + 300, 7¼ x 4¾ inches: title page, [i]; 1–299, text; 300, blank. End papers imitation laid.

Red cloth over boards. Lettering on front cover and spine gold-stamped; signature on front cover gold-stamped. Illustrations by William Glackens. Published Sept. 18, 1903.

First printed *Metropolitan*, April, 1903, xviii, 94–109, i–vii; May, 210–224, viii–xiii; June, 337–352, xiv–xxi; July, 467–480, xxii–xxx; Aug., 591–611, xxxi–xliv; Sept., 759–770, xlv–xlix.

04-A

Clarence King | Memoirs | the | helmet of Mambrino | [*device*] | published for the King Memorial Committee of | the Century Association.

G. P. Putnam's Sons: New York and London, 1904. Published May 9, 1904.

"Meetings with Clarence King," p. 135–156, here first printed.

04-B

The son of | Royal Langbrith | [*double rule*] | a novel | by | W. D. Howells | author of | "Questionable shapes" "Letters home" | "Literary friends and acquaintance" | "Their silver wedding journey" | etc. etc. | [*publisher's device*] | [*double rule*] | New York and London | Harper & Brothers publishers | 1904 [*All the foregoing enclosed in a double-rule box within a rule-box.*]

Collation: p. vi + 372, 8⅛ x 5¼ inches: title page, [v]; 1–369, text; 370, blank; 371–372, tipped in leaf of imitation laid. End papers whiter and of heavier stock than text.

Purple cloth with diagonal grain over boards. Ornamental panelling and corners on front

cover and spine stamped in ivory; lettering on spine gold-stamped. Top edge gilt; fore and bottom edges rough-trimmed. Published Oct. 6, 1904.

First printed *North American review*, Jan., 1904, clxxviii, 133–160, chapters i–viii; Feb., 296–320, ix–xiii; March, 454–480, xiv–xvii; April, 617–640, xviii–xxii; May, 783–800, xxiii–xxv; June, 933–952, xxvi–xxix; July, clxxix, 136–160, xxx–xxxiv; Aug., 301–320, xxxv–xxxvii.

05-A

Miss Bellard's inspiration | a novel | by W. D. Howells | author of | "Letters home" "Questionable shapes" | "Literary friends and acquaintance" | "Literature and life" etc. | [*publisher's device*] | New York and London | Harper & Brothers publishers | 1905

Collation: p. vi + 226, 7⁵⁄₁₆ x 4⅞ inches: title page, [iii]; 1–224, text; 225–226, blank. End papers of same stock as text.

Light green or gray cloth over boards. Floral decoration on front cover and spine in light shade of green, yellow and white. Lettering on front cover and spine gold-stamped. Published June 8, 1905.

06-A

London films | by W. D. Howells | illustrated | [*publisher's device*] | Harper & Brothers publishers | New York and London | 1906.

Collation: p. x + 246, 8⅛ x 5¼ inches: title page, [iii]; 1–241, text; 242–246, blank. Frontispiece and twenty-three illustrated leaves tipped in and not paginated. End papers of heavier stock than text.

Green cloth with fine vertical lines over boards. Lettering on front cover and spine gold-stamped. Initial L and F stamped in red. Top edge gilt; fore edge rough-trimmed and partially uncut; bottom edge rough-trimmed.

Illustrations by Sydney Adamson. Published Oct. 12, 1905.

Pages 1–26, first printed as "London films," *Harper's monthly*, Dec., 1904, cx, 67–78.

Pages 26–34.

Pages 35–55, first printed as "In the season, London films," *Harper's monthly*, March, 1905, cx, 559–569.

Pages 55–67, first printed as "English feeling toward Americans," *North American review*, Dec., 1904, clxxix, 815–823.

Pages 68–76, first printed as "In the season, London films," *Harper's monthly*, March, 1905, cx, 559–569.

Pages 77–105, first printed at greater length and with different paragraph sequence as "In summer, London films," *Harper's monthly*, June, 1905, cxi, 104–116.

Pages 106–164.

Pages 165–177, first printed with slight differences as "A day at Henley," *Harper's weekly*, June 10, 1905, xlix, 826–828, 843.

Pages 178–181, first printed as "In summer, London films," *Harper's monthly*, June, 1905, cxi, 114–116.

Pages 181–202, first printed as "American origins, London films," *Harper's monthly*, July, 1905, cxi, 185–197.

Pages 203–223, first printed in different form as "American origins, London films," *Harper's monthly*, Aug., 1905, cxi, 368–380.

Pages 223–241.

06-B

Their husbands' wives | Harper's novelettes | [*rule*] | edited by | William Dean Howells | and | Henry Mills Alden.

Harper & Brothers: New York and London, 1906. Published March 8, 1906; (Harper register) March 15.

"Introduction," p. v–vi, here first printed.

06-C

Under the sunset | Harper's novelettes | edited by | William Dean Howells | and | Henry Mills Alden.

Harper & Brothers: New York and London, [1906]. Published May 11, 1906.

"Introduction," p. v–vii, here first printed.

06-D

Different girls | Harper's novelettes | edited by | William Dean Howells | and | Henry Mills Alden.

Harper & Brothers: New York and London, [1906]. Published Aug. 17, 1906.

"Introduction," p. v–vii, here first printed.

06-E

Quaint courtships | Harper's novelettes | edited by | William Dean Howells | and | Henry Mills Alden.

Harper & Brothers: New York and London, [1906]. Published Aug. 17, 1906.

"Introduction," p. v–vi, here first printed.

06-F

Certain delightful | English towns | with glimpses of the pleasant | country between | W. D. Howells | illustrated | [*publisher's device*] | Harper & Brothers publishers | New York and London | 1906

Collation: p. –ii + viii + 294, 8⅛ x 5⅜ inches: blank leaf; title page, [i]; 1–290, text; two blank leaves. Frontispiece and forty-seven illustrated leaves tipped in and not paginated. End papers of heavier stock than text.

Green cloth with fine vertical lines over boards. Lettering on front cover and spine gold-stamped. Initial C on front cover stamped in red. Top edge gilt. Illustrated by Joseph Pennell, V. Perard, T. A. Brever, and Ernest Haskell. Published Oct. 26, 1906.

"The landing of a pilgrim at Plymouth," first printed *Harper's monthly*, April, 1905, cx, 707–718.

"Twenty-four hours at Exeter," first printed *Harper's monthly*, Sept., 1905, cxi, 497–506.

"A fortnight at Bath," first printed *Harper's monthly*, Nov., 1905, cxi, 811–824.

"A country town and a country home," first printed *Harper's monthly*, July, 1906, cxiii, 165–175.

"Afternoons in Wells and Bristol," here first printed.

Collations of Works... — 06-F, continued

"By way of Southampton to London," first printed *Harper's monthly*, Nov., 1906, cxiii, 892–903.

"In Folkestone out of season," first printed in slightly briefer form *Harper's monthly*, Nov., 1904, cix, 821–830.

"Kentish neighborhoods, including Canterbury," first printed *Harper's monthly*, Sept., 1906, cxiii, 550–563.

"Oxford," first printed *North American review*, Oct. 5, 1906, clxxxiii, 620–638.

"The charm of Chester," first printed as "Our nearest point in antiquity," *Harper's monthly*, June, 1906, cxiii, 99–109.

"Malvern among her hills," here first printed.

"Shrewsbury by way of Worcester and Hereford," here first printed.

"Northampton and the Washington country," first printed *Harper's monthly*, April, 1906, cxii, 651–661.

06-G

The heart of childhood | Harper's novelettes | [*rule*] | edited by | William Dean Howells | and | Henry Mills Alden.

Harper & Brothers: New York and London, 1906. Published Dec. 1, 1906.

"Introduction," p. iii–iv, here first printed.
"The Amigo," first printed *Harper's monthly*, Dec., 1905, cxii, 51–53.

07-A

Southern | lights and shadows | Harper's novelettes | edited by | William Dean Howells | and | Henry Mills Alden.

Harper & Brothers: New York and London, [1907]. Published Feb. 28, 1907.

"Introduction," p. v–vi, here first printed.

07-B

Through the | eye of the needle | a romance | with an introduction | by | W. D. Howells | [*publisher's device*]

| Harper & Brothers publishers | New York and London | 1907

Collation: p. xiv + 234, $8\,^1/_{16}$ x $5\frac{3}{8}$ inches: title page, [i]; "Introduction," v–xiii; 3–233, text; 234, blank. End papers of same stock as text.

Dark green cloth over boards, the front cover blind-stamped with vertical rules and torch design. Lettering on front cover and spine gold-stamped. Top edge gilt. Published April 18, 1907.

"Introduction," p. v–xiii, here first printed.

Part I, i–vi, first printed as "Letters of an Altrurian traveller, how people live in a plutocratic city," *Cosmopolitan*, April, 1894, xvi, 696–704.

Part I, vii–xi, first printed as "Letters of an Altrurian traveller, plutocratic housekeeping," *Cosmopolitan*, May, 1894, xvii, 46–58.

Part I, xii–xvi, first printed as "Letters of an Altrurian traveller, dinner, very informal," *Cosmopolitan*, June, 1894, xvii, 221–228.

Part I, xvii–xviii, first printed as "Letters of an Altrurian traveller, the selling and the giving of dinners," *Cosmopolitan*, July, 1894, xvii, 356–359.

Part I, xix–xxi, first printed as "Letters of an Altrurian traveller, an altruistic plutocrat," *Cosmopolitan*, Aug., 1894, xvii, 495–499.

Part I, xxii–xxvii, first printed as "Letters of an Altrurian traveller, a plutocratic triumph," *Cosmopolitan*, Sept., 1894, xvii, 610–618.

Part II here first printed. See *Life in letters*, II, 235: "Just now I am writing a sequel to the Altrurian business which you stereotyped for me twelve years ago under the title *The Eye of the Needle*."

07-C

Shapes that | haunt the dusk | Harper's novelettes | edited by | William Dean Howells | and | Henry Mills Alden.

Harper & Brothers: New York and London, 1907. Published June 14, 1907.

"Introduction," p. v–vii, here first printed.

07-D

Between the dark | and the daylight | romances | by | W. D. Howells | [*publisher's device*] | Harper & Brothers publishers | New York and London | 1907

Collation: p. x + 186, 8 ³/₁₆ x 5¼ inches: title page, [v]; 3–185, text; 186, blank. Frontispiece and five illustrated leaves tipped in and not paginated.

Dark green cloth over boards. Front cover blind-stamped with vertical rules and torch design. Lettering and ornament on front cover and spine gold-stamped. Top edge gilt. Illustrations by W. D. Stevens. A second issue was bound in red cloth with black stamping. Published Oct. 24, 1907.

"A sleep and a forgetting," first printed *Harper's weekly*, Dec. 15, 1906, L, 1781–1784, 1805, chapters i–ii; Dec. 22, 1862–1865, iii–v; Dec. 29, 1899–1901, vi–vii; Jan. 5, 1907, LI, 24–27, vii concluded.

"The eidolons of Brooks Alford," first printed *Harper's monthly*, Aug., 1906, CXIII, 377–397.

"A memory that worked overtime," first printed *Harper's monthly*, Aug., 1907, CXV, 415–418.

"A case of metaphantasmia," first printed *Harper's weekly*, Dec. 16, 1905, XLIX, 20–22, Christmas supplement, 40–41.

"The chick of the Easter egg," first printed *Harper's weekly*, April 14, 1906, L, 509–512.

"Braybridge's offer," first printed *Harper's monthly*, Jan., 1906, CXII, 229–236.

"Editha," first printed *Harper's monthly*, Jan., 1905, CX, 214–224.

07-E

Venetian life | by William Dean Howells | with illustrations by | Edmund H. Garrett | in two volumes | Volume I | [*seal of Venice*] | Cambridge: printed at the | Riverside Press: MDCCCCVII [*Title page of the second volume as above except that "Volume II" appears in place of "Volume I."*]

Collation: Vol. I, p. –ii + xx + 240, 9 ¹¹/₁₆ x 6⅛ inches: title page tipped in; preface, ix–xviii; 1–238, text; 239, blank; 240, colophon. Vol. II, p. xii + 188: title page tipped in; 1–185, text; 186, colophon; blank leaf. Both frontispieces, title pages and eighteen

illustrations on light manila stock glued to brown leaves tipped in and not paginated. End papers.

Both volumes bound in white paper over boards. Over-all flower pattern on front and back covers printed in yellow. Backstrips white linen bearing brown paper-labels with lettering in black. All edges rough trimmed. This edition was limited to 550 copies, signed by the author, artist, and publishers. Published Nov. 1, 1907.

A trade edition with a new title page and re-numbered pages (1–423 text) but with the same illustrations and plates was issued in one volume by Houghton, Mifflin & Company in the same year. Another edition from these plates was issued in the red cloth of the "Library edition" in 1908 with a three-page index and without the illustrations.

"Author to the reader," vol. I, p. ix–xviii, and "Venice revisited," vol. II, p. 168–185, here first printed.

07-F

Life at high tide | Harper's novelettes | edited by | William Dean Howells | and | Henry Mills Alden.

Harper & Brothers: New York and London, [1907]. Published Sept. 24, 1908; copyright deposit late, possibly through neglect.

Howells was co-editor of this volume.

07-G

Minor dramas | by | William D. Howells | Volume I | [*publisher's device*] | Edinburgh | David Douglas, Castle Street | 1907 | All rights reserved [*Title page of the second volume as above, except "Volume II" appears in place of "Volume I."*]

Both volumes bound in green cloth over boards. Lettering on front cover and spine gold-stamped. Full details of the collation are lacking; pages run somewhat over 400 in both volumes and measure 5¼ x 3¾ inches.

Of the nineteen farces, seventeen appear in earlier editions.

[Introduction,] p. v–xii, here first printed.

"A masterpiece of diplomacy," first printed *Harper's monthly*, Feb., 1894, LXXXVIII, 371–385.

"Her opinion of his story," first printed *Harper's bazar*, May, 1907, XLI, 429–437.

07-H

The | mulberries | in | Pay's | garden | Wm. Dean Howells | [*all the foregoing in ornamental rule-box*] | John Scott & Co., Three Rivers Elm, North Bend, O. | [*double rule*] | The Western Literary Press. | Cincinnati. | [*1907*]

Collation: p. ii + 30, 7 x 4½ inches: title page, [3]; 7–21, text; 22, blank; 23–27, appendix, poem, "The mulberries"; 28–30, advertisements. Frontispiece leaf tipped in and not paginated. End papers.

White cloth over boards. Lettering and ornament on front cover gold-stamped and printed in gray. "The swallow-flight series."

"The mulberries in Pay's garden," p. 7–21, reprinted from *The Hesperian tree*. See 00-B.

"The mulberries," poem dated Venice, 1862–1865, reprinted from *Poems*. See 73-B.

Printed from new plates.

08-A

Fennel and rue | a novel | by | W. D. Howells | illustrated by | Charlotte Harding | [*publisher's device*] | Harper & Brothers publishers | New York and London | 1908

Collation: p. vi + 130, 8⅛ x 5⅜ inches: title page, [i]; 1–130, text. Frontispiece and three illustrated leaves tipped in and not paginated. End papers of same stock as text.

Dark green cloth over boards. Front cover blind-stamped with vertical rules and torch design. Lettering and ornament on front cover and spine gold-stamped. Top edge gilt. Published March 13, 1908.

08-B

Christmas every day | a story told a child | [*ornament*] | by | W. D. Howells | with illustrations and decorations by | Harriet Roosevelt Richards | [*publisher's device*] | New York and London | Harper & Brothers publishers | 1908 [*All the foregoing with-*

in an ornamental rule-box and a rule-box.]

Collation: 16 double leaves, folded at top, printed on recto and verso only, the two recto and verso pages within the fold thus left blank, 11½ x 8⅝ inches: [1], blank; title page, [2 recto]; [3 recto], list of illustrations; [5–15], text, p. 1–22; [16 recto], conclusion of text; [16 verso], blank. Frontispiece and five illustrations printed on six single leaves, tipped in and not paginated.

Red cloth over boards. Ornamental holly border stamped in green on front cover; lettering gold-stamped. Lettering on spine gold-stamped. Published Oct. 15, 1908.

Reprinted from *Christmas every day and other stories told for children;* see 93-A.

08-C

The whole | family | a novel by | twelve authors | William Dean Howells | Mary E. Wilkins Freeman | Mary Heaton Vorse | Mary Stewart Cutting | Elizabeth Jordan | John Kendrick Bangs | Henry James | Elizabeth Stuart Phelps | Edith Wyatt | Mary R. Shipman Andrews | Alice Brown [space] Henry van Dyke.

Harper & Brothers: New York and London, 1908. Published Oct. 15, 1908.

"The father," p. 3–29, first printed *Harper's bazar*, Dec., 1907, XLI, 1161–1170.

08-D

Roman holidays | and others | W. D. Howells | illustrated | [*publisher's device*] | Harper & Brothers publishers | New York and London | 1908

Collation: p. viii + 304, 8⅛ x 5⅜ inches: title page, [i]; 1–303, text; 304, blank. Frontispiece and fifty-one illustrated leaves tipped in and not paginated. End papers of heavier stock than text.

Green cloth with fine vertical lines over boards. Lettering on front cover and spine gold-stamped. Initial R on front cover stamped in red. Top edge gilt. Illustrations by A. Castaigne and "DOS." Published Oct. 22, 1908.

Except for sections noted here as first printed, all the volume is reprinted from New York *Sun.*

"Up and down Madeira," first printed March 8, 1908, 6–7.

"Two up-town blocks into Spain," first printed as "Two short blocks into Spain," March 15, 1908, 6–7.

"Ashore at Genoa," first printed March 22, 1908, 8–9.

"Naples and her joyful noise," first printed as "Naples and her joyous noise," March 29, 1908, 8–9.

"Pompeii revisited," first printed April 12, 1908, 8–9.

"Roman holidays:"

"Hotels, pensions, and apartments," first printed April 26, 1908, 8–9.

"A praise of new Rome," first printed May 3, 1908, 8–9.

"The Colosseum and the Forum," first printed May 10, 1908, 8–9.

"The Anglo-American neighborhood of the Spanish Steps," first printed May 17, 1908, 8–9.

"An effort to be honest with antiquity," first printed May 24, 1908, 8–9.

"Personal relations with the past," first printed May 31, 1908, 6–7.

"Chances in churches," first printed June 7, 1908, 6–7.

"A few villas," first printed June 14, 1908, 8–9.

"Dramatic incidents," first printed June 21, 1908, 6–7.

"Seeing Rome as Romans see us," first printed July 5, 1908, 6–7.

"In and about the Vatican," first printed July 12, 1908, 6–7.

"Superficial observations and conjectures," first printed as "Some superficial observations and conjectures," July 19, 1908, 6–7.

"Casual impressions," first printed as "Amiable impressions," July 26, 1908, 6–7.

"Tivoli and Frascati," here first printed.

"A few remaining moments," first printed Aug. 2, 1908, 6–7.

"A week at Leghorn," first printed Sept. 20, 27, 1903, p. 6–7, 6–7.

"Over at Pisa," first printed Oct. 4, 1908, 6–7.

"Back at Genoa," here first printed.

"Eden after the fall," first printed as "Eden after the fall," and "Looking on at Monte Carlo," Oct. 11, 18, 1908, p. 6–7, 6–7.

08- *and 09-note*

In 1908 and 1909 several earlier volumes by Howells were published in uniform bindings from new plates. For partial collations see 89-B, 94-B, 96-E, 97-C, 99-A, 99-C.

09-A

The mother | and the father | dramatic passages | by | W. D. Howells | illustrated | [*publisher's device*] | Harper & Brothers publishers | New York and London | 1909

Collation: p. viii + 56, $8\frac{1}{8}$ x $5\frac{1}{8}$ inches: title page, [v]; 3–55, text; 56, blank. Frontispiece and three illustrated leaves tipped in and not paginated. End papers.

Green cloth over boards; front cover blind-stamped with vertical lines and torch design. Lettering and ornament on front cover and spine gold-stamped. Top edge gilt. Or second issue, red cloth blind-stamped as above over boards, the lettering and ornament on front cover and spine stamped in black. Illustrations on glazed paper by Wolcott Hitchcock. Published May 20, 1909.

"The mother," first printed *Harper's monthly,* Dec., 1902, cvi, 21–26.

"The father and the mother," first printed as "After the wedding," *Harper's monthly,* Dec., 1906, cxiv, 64–69.

"The father," first printed as "Father and mother, a mystery," *Harper's monthly,* May, 1900, c, 869–874.

09-B

Seven | English cities | by | W. D. Howells | illustrated | [*publisher's device*] | Harper & Brothers publishers | New York and London | 1909

Collation: p. x + 202, 8 x $5\frac{3}{16}$ inches: title page, [v]; 3–201, text; 202, blank. Frontispiece and thirty-one illustrated leaves tipped in and not paginated. End papers of heavier stock than text.

Green cloth with fine vertical lines over boards. Lettering on front cover and spine gold-stamped. Initial S on front cover stamped in red. Or light green cloth over boards, the lettering on front cover and spine stamped in black. Illustrations by Ernest Haskell, Frank Craig, and Albert S. Sterner. Published Oct. 22, 1909.

"A modest liking for Liverpool," "Some merits of Manchester," "In smokiest Sheffield," first printed as "Three English capitals of industry," *Harper's monthly*, May, 1909, CXVIII, 891–902.

"Nine days' wonder in York," first printed *Harper's monthly*, Feb., 1908, CXVI, 349–361.

"Two Yorkish episodes," first printed as "Two little English episodes," *Harper's monthly*, July, 1909, CXIX, 241–244.

"A day at Doncaster and an hour out of Durham," first printed *Harper's monthly*, June, 1907, CXV, 58–66.

"The mother of the American Athens," first printed *Harper's monthly*, Sept., 1908, CXVII, 514–525.

"Aberystwyth, a Welsh watering-place."

"Llandudno, another Welsh watering-place."

"Glimpses of English character," first printed as "English idiosyncrasies," *North American review*, Nov. – Dec., 1905, CLXXXI, 649–664, 897–911.

10-A

In after days | thoughts on the future life | by | W. D. Howells, Henry James, John | Bigelow, Thomas Wentworth | Higginson, Henry M. Alden | William Hanna Thomson | Guglielmo Ferrero | Julia Ward Howe | Elizabeth Stuart | Phelps.

Harper & Brothers: New York and London, 1910. Published Feb. 11, 1910.

"A counsel of consolation," p. 3–16, first printed as "In the house of mourning," *Harper's bazar*, April, 1909, XLIII, 360–363.

10-B

Mark Twain's | speeches | with an introduction by | William Dean Howells.

Harper & Brothers: New York and London, 1910. Published May 24, 1910; (Harper register) June 22. A revised edition appeared in 1923.

"Introduction," p. vii–viii, here first printed.

10-C

My Mark Twain | reminiscences and criticisms | by | W. D. Howells | illustrated | [*publisher's device*] | Harper & Brothers publishers | New York and London | 1910

Collation: p. viii + 188, 8⅛ x 5¼ inches: title page, [iii]; 3–187, text; 188, blank. Frontispiece (two leaves) and six illustrated leaves not paginated. End papers of heavier stock than text.

Green cloth with fine vertical lines over boards. Lettering on front cover and spine gold-stamped. Initial M on front cover stamped in red. Top edge gilt. There are two states of this edition: in one the photograph of Mark Twain shows him with shoulders nearly parallel with the camera lens, and in the other with shoulders almost at a right angle to the camera lens. Published Sept. 10, 1910.

Part First — Memories:

"My Mark Twain," first printed as "My memories of Mark Twain," *Harper's monthly*, July – Sept., 1910, CXXI, 165–178, 340–348, 512–529.

Part Second — Criticisms:

"Introduction," here first printed.

"The innocents abroad," first printed *Atlantic monthly*, Dec., 1869, XXIV, 764–766.

"Roughing it," first printed *Atlantic monthly*, June, 1872, XXIX, 754–755.

"The play from 'The gilded age,'" first printed *Atlantic monthly*, June, 1875, XXXV, 749–751.

"Mark Twain's 'Sketches, old and new,'" first printed *Atlantic monthly*, Dec., 1875, XXXVI, 749–751.

"The adventures of Tom Sawyer," first printed *Atlantic monthly*, May, 1876, XXXVII, 621–622.

"A tramp abroad," first printed *Atlantic monthly*, May, 1880, XLV, 686–688.

"Mark Twain," first printed *Century*, Sept., 1882, XXIV, 780–783.

Part Second — Criticisms, continued

"A Connecticut Yankee in King Arthur's court," first printed "Editor's study," *Harper's monthly*, Jan., 1890, LXXX, 318–323.

"Joan of Arc," first printed "Life and letters," *Harper's weekly*, May 30, 1896, XL, 535–536.

"Review of an Italian's views of Mark Twain," first printed *North American review*, Nov., 1901, CLXXIII, 709–720.

"Mark Twain: an inquiry," first printed *North American review*, Feb., 1901, CLXXII, 306–321.

"The American joke," a "double-barreled" sonnet to Mark Twain, first printed *Harper's weekly*, Dec. 23, 1905, XLIX, 1885.

10-D

Imaginary | interviews | by | W. D. Howells | illustrated | [*publisher's device*] | Harper & Brothers publishers | New York and London | 1910

Collation: p. viii+360, 8 $^1/_{16}$ x 5 $^5/_{16}$ inches: title page, [i]; 1–359, text; 360, blank. Frontispiece and seven illustrated leaves tipped in and not paginated. End papers of heavier stock than text.

Green cloth with vertical lines over boards. Lettering on front cover and spine gold-stamped; initial I stamped in red. Top edge gilt. Or light green cloth over boards, the lettering on front cover and spine stamped in black. Frontispiece by Howard Chandler Christy. Published Oct. 15, 1910.

Except for "Readings for a grandfather," this volume is reprinted from the "Editor's easy chair" in *Harper's monthly*.

"The restoration of the Easy chair by way of introduction," first printed Dec., 1900, CII, 153–158.

"A year of spring and a life of youth," first printed July, 1907, CXV, 309–312.

"Sclerosis of the tastes," first printed July, 1908, CXVII, 309–312.

"The practices and precepts of vaudeville," first printed April, 1903, CVI, 810–815.

"Intimations of Italian opera," first printed May, 1904, CVIII, 964–968.

"The superiority of our inferiors," first printed Jan., 1908, CXVI, 309–312.

"Unimportance of women in republics," first printed June, 1909, CXIX, 147–150.

"Having just got home," first printed Dec., 1908, CXVIII, 155–158.

"New York to the home-comer's eye," first printed Feb., 1909, CXVIII, 479–482.

"Cheapness of the costliest city on earth," first printed March, 1909, CXVIII, 641–644.

"Ways and means of living in New York," first printed April, 1909, CXVIII, 803–806.

"The quality of Boston and the quantity of New York," first printed Jan., 1909, CXVIII, 317–320.

"The whirl of life in our first circles," first printed May, 1910, CXX, 957–960.

"The magazine muse," first printed March, 1907, CXIV, 641–644.

"Comparative luxuries of travel," first printed Feb., 1910, CXX, 471–474.

"Qualities without defects," first printed Jan., 1910, CXX, 309–312.

"A wasted opportunity," first printed March, 1910, CXX, 633–636.

"A niece's literary advice to her uncle," first printed Aug., 1906, CXIII, 473–475.

"A search for celebrity," first printed May, 1907, CXIV, 965–968.

"Practical immortality on earth," first printed Oct., 1904, CIX, 803–806.

"Around a rainy-day fire," first printed Oct., 1903, CVII, 802–806.

"The advantages of quotational criticism," first printed Jan., 1904, CVIII, 317–320.

"Readings for a grandfather," first printed *Harper's bazar*, Dec., 1903, XXXVII, 1153–1157.

"Some moments with the muse," first printed Jan., 1903, CVI, 324–328.

"A normal hero and heroine out of work," first printed Aug., 1905, CXI, 471–473.

"Autumn in the country and city," first printed Feb., 1908, CXVI, 471–474.

"Personal and epistolary addresses," first printed Dec., 1907, CXVI, 148–151.

"Dressing for hotel dinner," first printed July, 1906, CXIII, 310–313.

"The counsel of literary age to literary youth," first printed Nov., 1904, CIX, 965–969.

"The unsatisfactoriness of unfriendly criticism," first printed May, 1905, CX, 965–968.

"The fickleness of age," first printed Nov., 1905, CXI, 956–959.

"The renewal of inspiration," first printed July, 1905, CXI, 309–312.

"The summer sojourn of Florindo and Lindora," first printed Sept., 1903, CVII, 641–645.

"To have the honor of meeting," first printed Feb., 1903, CVI, 486–490.

"A day at Bronx Park," first printed Sept., 1909, CXIX, 633–636.

10-E

[History of the Western Reserve by Harriet Taylor Upton.]

The Lewis Publishing Company: Chicago and New York, 1910. Three volumes.

Howells' letter concerning his mother, vol. I, p. 576, here first printed. The title given above, it will be noted, is not transcribed from the title page.

11-A

Parting friends | a farce | by | W. D. Howells | illustrated | [*publisher's device*] | Harper & Brothers publishers | New York and London | MCMXI

Collation: p. 58, 5 $^3/_{16}$ x 4¼ inches: title page, [3]; 9–57, text; 58, blank. Frontispiece and four illustrated leaves tipped in; only frontispiece leaf included in pagination.

Dark blue cloth over thin boards. Lettering, rule-boxes, and ornament on front cover and spine stamped in white. Illustrations by W. T. Jacobs. Published June 17, 1911.

First printed as "Parting friends, tragedy," *Harper's monthly*, Oct., 1910, CXXI, 670–677.

11-B

My literary passions | Criticism & fiction | W. D. Howells | illustrated | [*publisher's device*] | Harper & Brothers publishers | New York and London | [1911]

Collation: p. xii + 292, 8⅝ x 5¾ inches: one leaf with half-title on recto, verso blank: engraved title page in red and black, "The writings of | William Dean Howells | Library edition"; title page, [iii]; "Bibliographical" preface, ix–xiii; 3–283, text; 284, blank; 285–290, index; blank leaf. Frontispiece leaf, engraved title page, and six illustrated leaves tipped in and not paginated. End papers of heavier stock than text.

Dark olive-green cloth with fine vertical lines over boards. Lettering and double-rule box

on spine gold-stamped. Top edge gilt; fore and bottom edges rough-trimmed. Illustrations by Samuel Laurence and Giotto. Published July 26, 1911.

The "Bibliographical" preface, p. ix–xiii, is here first printed. In it Howells asserts of *Criticism and fiction:* "When the author came to revise the material, he found sins against taste which his zeal for righteousness could not sufficiently atone for. He did not hesitate to omit the proofs of these... He hopes that in other and slighter things he has bettered his own instruction, and that in form and in fact the book is altogether less crude and rude than the papers from which it has here been a second time evolved."

11-C

The landlord | at Lion's Head | a novel | W. D. Howells | illustrated | [*publisher's device*] | Harper & Brothers publishers | New York and London | [1911]

Collation: p. x + 410, 8⅝ x 5¾ inches: blank leaf; engraved title page in black and red, "The writings of | William Dean Howells | Library edition"; title page, [iii]; "Bibliographical" preface, vii–x; 3–408, text; blank leaf. Frontispiece leaf, engraved title page, and six illustrated leaves tipped in and not paginated. End papers of heavy stock.

Dark olive-green cloth with fine vertical lines over boards. Lettering and double-rule box on spine gold-stamped. Top edge gilt; fore and bottom edges rough-trimmed. Illustrations by W. T. Smedley. Published July 26, 1911.

The edition was reprinted from the plates of the 1908 edition; see 97-C.

The "Bibliographical" preface, p. vii–x, is here first printed.

11-D

Literature | and life | studies | W. D. Howells | illustrated | [*publisher's device*] | Harper & Brothers publishers | New York and London | [1911]

Collation: p. xii + 324, 8⅝ x 5¾ inches: one leaf with half-title on recto, verso blank; engraved title page in black and red, "The writings of | William Dean Howells | Library edition"; title page, [iii]; "Bibliographical" preface, ix–xii; 1–323, text; 324, blank. Frontispiece leaf, engraved title page, and six illustrated leaves tipped in and not paginated. End papers of heavy stock.

Dark olive-green cloth with fine vertical lines over boards. Lettering and double-rule box on spine gold-stamped. Top edge gilt; fore and bottom edges rough-trimmed. Published July 26, 1911.

Text, p. 1–323, reprinted from first edition plates. See 02-C. The "Bibliographical" preface, p. ix–xii, here first printed.

11-E

London films | and | Certain delightful English towns | W. D. Howells | illustrated | [*publisher's device*] | Harper & Brothers publishers | New York and London | [1911]

Collation: p. xiv + 530, 8⅝ x 5¾ inches: one leaf with half-title on recto, verso blank; engraved title page in red and black, "The writings of | William Dean Howells | Library edition"; title page, [iii]; "Bibliographical" preface, ix–xi; 1–522, text; 523–529, index; 530, blank. Frontispiece leaf, engraved title page, and seven illustrated leaves tipped in and not paginated. End papers of heavier stock than text.

Dark olive-green cloth with fine vertical lines over boards. Lettering and double-rule box on spine gold-stamped. Top edge gilt; fore and bottom edges rough-trimmed and partially uncut. Illustrations by Vernon H. Bailey. Published July 26, 1911.

The "Bibliographical" preface, p. ix–xi, is here first printed.

11-F

Literary friends | and | acquaintance | a personal retrospect | of American authorship | W. D. Howells | illustrated | [*publisher's device*] | Harper

& Brothers publishers | New York and London | [1911]

Collation: p. xiv + 410, 8⅝ x 5¾ inches: leaf with half-title on recto, verso blank; engraved title page in red and black, "The writings of | William Dean Howells | Library edition," tipped in; title page, [iii]; "Bibliographical" preface, ix–xi; 1–405, text; 407–410, index. Frontispiece leaf, engraved title page, and six illustrated leaves tipped in and not paginated. End papers of heavier stock than text.

Dark olive-green cloth with fine vertical lines over boards. Lettering and double-rule box on spine gold-stamped. Top edge gilt, fore and bottom edges rough-trimmed. Published July 26, 1911.

The "Bibliographical" preface, p. ix–xi, is here first printed.

Pages 1–288 reprinted from *Literary friends and acquaintance*, first edition plates. See 00-F.

Pages 289–305, "A belated guest [Bret Harte]," first printed in slightly different form "Editor's easy chair," *Harper's monthly*, Dec., 1903, cviii, 153–159.

Pages 307–405 reprinted from *My Mark Twain* [Part First], but from new plates. See 10-C.

11-G

A hazard of new fortunes | W. D. Howells | illustrated | [*publisher's device*] | Harper & Brothers publishers | New York and London | [1911]

Collation: p. –ii + x + 576, 8⅝ x 5¾ inches: one leaf with half-title on recto, verso blank; engraved title page in red and black, "The writings of | William Dean Howells | Library edition"; title page, [i]; "Bibliographical" preface, v–ix; 3–575, text; 576, blank. Frontispiece leaf, engraved title page, and seven illustrated leaves tipped in and not paginated. End papers of heavy stock.

Dark olive-green cloth with fine vertical lines over boards. Lettering and double-rule box on spine gold-stamped. Top edge gilt; fore and bottom edges rough-trimmed. Illustrations by G. C. Cox and W. A. Rogers. Published July 26, 1911.

The "Bibliographical" preface, p. v–ix, is here first printed.

11-H

Poems | by | Madison Cawein | (selected by the author) | with | a foreword by William Dean Howells.

The Macmillan Company: New York, 1911. Published Sept. 14, 1911.

"The poetry of Madison Cawein," p. xiii–xix, first printed at slightly greater length *North American review*, Jan., 1908, CLXXXVII, 124–131.

11-I

Tom Brown's | school-days | by an old boy | (Thomas Hughes).

Harper & Brothers: New York and London, [c. 1911]. Published Oct. 16, 1911.

"Introduction by W. D. Howells," p. ix–xii, here first printed.

ca. 11-J

[Prefaces for incomplete Library edition.] "Heroines of fiction | bibliographical," p. v, vol. VII, group II; "Son of Royal Langbrith | bibliographical," p. ii, group II, vol. VIII; "The shadow of a dream | bibliographical," p. iii, group II, vol. x [*for the March group of stories*]; "Coast of Bohemia and Story of a plap [*sic*] | bibliographical," p. iii, group II, vol. XI; "A traveler from Altruria Through the eye, etc. | bibliographical," p. iii, group II, vol. XII.

Proofs, 5⅛ x 3¾ inches, cut and affixed to sheets of paper folded to form leaves, 7½ x 4 ¹⁵/₁₆ inches, are in the Harvard Library Howells Collection. All are signed W. D. H. They are undated, but through their title and approach are classified as belonging with the partly completed Library edition, which as published contains six volumes. It should be noted that no preface exists here for a ninth

volume, and that the portion of the preface which deals with *The coast of Bohemia* is not the same as that of the Biographical edition (99-B).

All prefaces reprinted *New England quarterly*, Dec., 1944, XVII, 580–591.

12-A

The house | of Harper | a century of publishing | in Franklin Square | by | J. Henry Harper.

Harper & Brothers: New York and London, 1912. Published Feb. 17, 1912.

Howells' "paper," p. 319–327, here first printed. Letter to J. H. Harper, from 40 West 59th Street, January 6, 1895, p. 637, here first printed.

12-B

The | Henry James | year book | [*rule*] | selected and arranged by | Evelyn Garnaut Smalley | with an introduction by | Henry James and William Dean Howells.

Richard G. Badger: Boston, [1912]. Published Sept. 27, 1912. An English edition was also issued by Dent, London, 1912.

"One of the public to the author," p. [12–13], here first printed.

12-C

Artemus Ward's | best stories | edited by Clifton Johnson | with an introduction by | W. D. Howells | illustrated by | Frank A. Nankivell.

Harper & Brothers: New York and London, 1912. Published Oct. 5, 1912.

"Introduction," p. vii–xvi, here first printed.

13-A

New Leaf Mills | a chronicle | W. D. Howells | [*publisher's device*] | Harper & Brothers publishers | New York and London | MCMXIII

Collation: p. vi + 154, 8⅛ x 5¼ inches: title page, [iii]; 1–154, text. End papers.

Dark green cloth over boards; front cover blind-stamped with vertical lines and torch design. Lettering and ornament on front cover and spine gold-stamped. Top edge gilt. Or light green cloth over boards, the lettering on front cover and spine stamped in black. Published Feb. 21, 1913. Title page verso, M–M [Dec., 1912]; although accompanied by the date "January, 1912" (note the "2" is not aligned), the copies lettered F–O are later.

13-B

Familiar | Spanish travels | W. D. Howells | illustrated | [*publisher's device*] | Harper & Brothers publishers | New York and London | MCMXIII

Collation: p. xiv + 330, 8⅛ x 5⅜ inches: title page, [v]; 1–327, text; 328–330, blank. Frontispiece and thirty-one illustrated leaves tipped in and not paginated. End papers.

Pebbled green cloth over boards. Ornament, rule-boxes, and lettering on front cover gold-stamped. Lettering on spine gold-stamped. Top edge gilt; fore and bottom edges rough-trimmed. Illustrations by Norman I. Black and Walter Hale. Published Oct. 18, 1913. Title page verso, K–N [Oct., 1913].

"Autobiographical approaches."
"San Sebastian and beautiful Biscay."
"Burgos and the bitter cold of Burgos," first printed as "The austere attraction of Burgos," *Harper's monthly,* May, 1912, cxxiv, 813–827.
"The variety of Valladolid," first printed *Harper's monthly,* July, 1912, cxxv, 165–178.
"Phases of Madrid," first printed *North American review,* Nov., 1912, cxcvi, 608–634.
"A night and day in Toledo," first printed *Harper's monthly,* Aug., 1912, cxxv, 429–442.
"The great gridiron of St. Lawrence."
"Cordova and the way there," first printed *Harper's monthly,* Dec., 1912, cxxvi, 112–125.
"First days in Seville," first printed *Harper's monthly,* March, 1913, cxxvi, 568–581.
"Sevillian aspects and incidents," first printed as "Some Sevillan incidents," *Harper's monthly,* June, 1913, cxxvii, 71–86.
"To and in Granada," first printed *North American review,* April, 1913, cxcvii, 501–521.
"The surprises of Ronda."
"Algeciras and Tarifa."

13-C

Gulliver's | travels | .... world | by | Jonathan Swift.

Harper & Brothers: New York and London, MCMXIII. Published Oct. 18, 1913. Title page verso, K–N [Oct., 1913].

"Introduction by W. D. Howells," p. xv–xvi, here first printed.

14-A

The seen and unseen | at | Stratford-on-Avon | a fantasy | by | W. D. Howells | [*publisher's device*] | Harper & Brothers publishers | New York and London | MCMXIV

Collation: p. vi + 114, 8⅛ x 5¼ inches: title page, [iii]; 1–112, text; blank leaf. End papers of same stock as text.

Dark green cloth with vertical lines and torch design over boards. Lettering and ornament on front cover and spine gold-stamped. Top edge gilt. Published May 11, 1914. Title page verso, D–O [April, 1914].

Not first printed but anticipated in "Experiences of a true Baconian in Shakespeare's town," *North American review,* Jan., 1912, cxcv, 120–127.

14-B

300 | latest stories | by | 300 famous story tellers | as told by | Marshall P. Wilder [space] O. Henry | George M. Cohan [space] Jack London | Simeon Ford [space] George Ade | David Belasco [space] Joseph Choate | Bourke Cockran [space] Chauncey M. Depew.

Star Library Company: New York, [1914]. First printing? Copyright notices on the verso of title page read: "Copyright, 1912, 1913, by | International Magazine Co. | Copyright, 1914, by | Hearst's International Library Co., Inc."

Untitled anecdotes attributed to Howells, p. 22 and 249, here first printed (?).

15-A

Sixty American | [*short rule*] opinions [*short rule*] | on the war.

T. Fisher Unwin, Ltd.: London, [1915].

Letter, p. 90–91, first printed New York *Sun*, Feb. 1, 1915.

16-A

The | book of the homeless | (Le livre des sans-foyer) | edited by Edith Wharton | ˙.˙ | original articles in verse and prose | illustrations reproduced from original paintings & drawings | [*ornament*] | the book is sold | for the benefit of the American hostels for refugees | (with the Foyer franco-belge) | and of the Children of Flanders Rescue Committee.

Charles Scribner's Sons: New York, 1916. Published Jan. 25, 1916. In addition to the regular edition described above, there were issued 175 copies de luxe, 1–50 with four facsimiles of MSS and a second set of illustrations, and 51–175 on Van Gelder paper.

"The little children," poem, p. 17, here first printed.

16-B

[They of the high trails | by | Hamlin Garland.]

Harper & Brothers: New York and London, [c. 1916]. Published April 20, 1916 (Harper register). The data are compiled from secondary sources and later editions; a first edition has not been found.

"Preface," p. xi-xvi, here first printed.

16-C

The daughter | of the storage | and other things | in prose and verse | W. D. Howells | [*publisher's device*]

| Harper & Brothers publishers | New York and London | [1916]

Collation: p. viii + 352, 7¼ x 4¾ inches: title page, [v]; 3–352, text. End papers of heavier stock than text.

Light blue cloth over boards. Formalized tree-ornament on front cover and spine stamped in dark green and gold. Lettering on front cover and spine gold-stamped. Published April 27, 1916; (Harper register) April 20. Title page verso, D–Q [April, 1916].

"The daughter of the storage," first printed *Harper's monthly*, Sept., 1911, CXXIII, 572–583.

"A presentiment," first printed as "Talking of presentiments," *Harper's monthly*, Dec., 1907, CXVI, 76–78.

"Captain Dunlevy's last trip."

"The return to favor," first printed *Harper's monthly*, July, 1915, CXXXI, 278–280.

"Somebody's mother," first printed *Harper's monthly*, Sept., 1915, CXXXI, 523–526.

"The face at the window," first printed *Harper's weekly*, Dec. 14, 1907, LI, 1825.

"An experience," first printed *Harper's monthly*, Nov., 1915, CXXXI, 940–942.

"The boarders," first printed *Harper's monthly*, March, 1916, CXXXII, 540–543.

"Breakfast is my best meal," first printed *Frank Leslie's*, Aug., 1899, XLVIII, 388–391. Reprinted *Windsor magazine*, Jan., 1901, XIII, 223–226.

"The mother-bird," first printed *Harper's monthly*, Dec., 1909, CXX, 126–128.

"The amigo," first printed *Harper's monthly*, Dec., 1905, CXII, 51–53, and 06-G.

"Black Cross Farm."

"The critical bookstore," first printed *Harper's monthly*, Aug., 1913, CXXVII, 431–432.

"A feast of reason," first printed as "Editor's easy chair," *Harper's monthly*, Oct., 1915, CXXXI, 796–799.

"City and country in the fall," first printed *Harper's weekly*, Nov. 29, 1902, XLVI, 1792.

"Table talk," first printed as "Editor's easy chair," *Harper's monthly*, June, 1910, CXXI, 149–152.

"The escapade of a grandfather," first printed as "Editor's easy chair," *Harper's monthly*, Feb., 1916, CXXXII, 473–476.

"Self-sacrifice, a farce-tragedy," first printed *Harper's monthly*, April, 1911, CXXII, 748–757.

"The night before Christmas," first printed *Harper's monthly*, Jan., 1910, CXX, 207–216.

16-D

Buying a | horse | by | William Dean Howells | [*double rule*] | [*ornamental device*] | [*double rule*] | Boston and New York | Houghton Mifflin Company | the Riverside Press Cambridge | 1916 [*All the foregoing in two rule-boxes.*]

Collation: p. iv + 48, 6½ x 4⅜ inches: title page, [iii]; 3–44, text; 45, ornament; 46, colophon; blank leaf. End papers.

Tan paper over boards. Lettering and ornamental rule-boxes printed in black on paper label on front cover. Published Sept. 21, 1916.

First separate edition. Reprinted from *A day's pleasure and other sketches;* see 81-D.

16-E

The | leatherwood god | [*rule*] | by | William Dean Howells | with illustrations by | Henry Raleigh | [*publisher's device*] | [*rule*] | New York | the Century Co. | 1916 [*All the foregoing in a double-rule box.*]

Collation: p. x + 238, 7⅜ x 5 inches: title page, [v]; 3–236, text; blank leaf. Frontispiece and seven illustrated leaves on glazed paper. End papers.

Red cloth over boards. Lettering and ornament on front cover raised from gold-stamped box. Lettering and ornament on spine gold-stamped. Published Nov. 2, 1916.

First printed *Century*, April, 1916, xci, 801–816, chapters i–iv; May, xcii, 60–74, v–viii; June, 212–222, ix–x; July, 431–441, xi–xii; Aug., 574–583, xiii–xiv; Sept., 768–777, xv; Oct., 912–920, xvi–xviii; Nov., xciii, 140–153, xix–xxii.

16-F

Years of my youth | W. D. Howells | [*publisher's device*] | Harper & Brothers publishers | New York and London | [1916]

Collation: p. vi + 242, 8¹/₁₆ x 5¼ inches: title page, [v]; 3–239, text; 240–242, blank. End papers.

Green cloth with fine vertical lines over boards. Lettering on front cover and spine gold-stamped; initial Y on front cover stamped in red. Top edge gilt. Published Nov. 7, 1916. Title page verso, F–Q [June, 1916].

Pages 3–44 here first printed with references to *A boy's town*, 90-G, and *My literary passions*, 95-E.

Pages 44–65 reprinted from *My year in a log cabin*, 93-F.

Pages 66–81 here largely first printed, with some passages from "In an old-time state capital," *Harper's monthly*, Sept., 1914, cxxix, 593–596.

Pages 82–87 reprinted from *Impressions and experiences*, 96-D, p. 6–14.

Pages 87–90 reprinted from *Impressions and experiences*, 96-D, p. 19–27.

Pages 91–123 here first printed.

Pages 124–137 first printed in compressed form in "In an old-time state capital," *Harper's monthly*, Sept., 1914, cxxix, 596–597.

Pages 137–138 here first printed.

Pages 138–146 first printed in different form in "In an old-time state capital," *Harper's monthly*, Sept., 1914, cxxix, 597–599.

Pages 146–147 here first printed.

Pages 148–157 first printed as "In an old-time state capital," *Harper's monthly*, Sept., 1914, cxxix, 599–603.

Pages 157–203 first printed as "In an old-time state capital," *Harper's monthly*, Oct., 1914, cxxix, 740–751.

Pages 204–239 first printed as "In an old-time state capital," *Harper's monthly*, Nov., 1914, cxxix, 921–930.

16-G

Tributes to Canada.

Pamphlet. [Boston?, 1916.] Published Dec. 9, 1916 (letter date).

Letter, p. 2, dated St. Augustine, Florida, Dec. 9, 1916.

16-H

The country printer | an essay by | William Dean Howells | [*publisher's device*] | Privately printed [1916]

Collation: p. vi + 50, 8 x 5¹/₁₆ inches: title page, [v]; 3–48, text; 49, colophon; 50, advertisements. Mounted frontispiece. End papers.

Imitation laid olive paper over boards. Backstrip dark green cloth; lettering on backstrip gold-stamped. Note on p. [ii] reads: "Reprinted for private distribution only | by the Plimpton Press for its friends | through the courteous permission of | Harper & Brothers and the Author | Limited to Four Hundred Copies." Printed in 1916: see Plimpton Press letter to P. K. Foley in American Antiquarian Society Library, Worcester, Mass.

Reprinted from *Impressions and experiences.* See 96–E.

17-A

The books of Kathleen Norris | and the reasons for their sale and influence.

[Doubleday, Page & Company: Garden City, 1917.] Prior to April, 1917.

A paragraph by Howells, on p. [1] of this leaflet advertising Kathleen Norris's books and a uniform library edition, first printed in "A number of interesting novels," *North American review,* Dec., 1914, cc, 913.

17-B

The second | odd number | thirteen tales | by | Guy de Maupassant | the translation by | Charles Henry White | an introduction by | William Dean Howells.

Harper & Brothers: New York and London, [1917]. Published May 5, 1917. Title page verso, C–R [March, 1917].

"Introduction," p. vii–xii, here first printed.

17-C

The story of a | country town | by | E. W. Howe.

Harper & Brothers: New York and London, [c. 1917]. Published Sept. 25, 1917 (Harper register). Title page verso, I–R [Sept., 1917].

"Letter from W. D. Howells [to Howe]," p. [iv], here first printed.

"An appreciation," p. [vii–viii], first printed as "Two notable novels," *Century*, Aug., 1884, xxviii, 632–633.

17-D

Years of my youth | by | W. D. Howells | with introduction and illustrations | from photographs taken expressly | for this book by Clifton Johnson | [*publisher's device*] | Harper & Brothers publishers | New York and London [1917]

Collation: p. x + 246, 8¼ x 5½ inches: title page, [i]; illustrator's preface, [v–x]; 3–239, text; 240–246, blank. Frontispiece and fifteen illustrated leaves tipped in and not paginated. End papers of different stock from text.

Green cloth with fine vertical lines over boards. Lettering on front cover and spine gold-stamped; initial Y on front cover stamped in red. Top edge gilt; fore and bottom edges rough-trimmed. Published Nov. 5, 1917; (Harper register) Oct. 26. Title page verso, K–R [Oct., 1917].

Printed from the first edition plates; see 16-F.

17-E

The | Harper Centennial | 1817–1917 | a few of the greetings | and congratulations.

Harper & Brothers: New York, [1917]. Published Dec., 1917 (verso of title page).

[Letter], dated 1917, p. 9, here first printed.

18-A

President's edition | Defenders of democracy | contributions from representative men| and women of letters and other arts | from our allies and our own country | edited by | the Gift Book Committee | of | the Militia of Mercy | [*quotation of John Lewis Griffiths*].

John Lane Company: New York, 1918. Copyrighted and published late in 1917.

Letter, dated Kittery Point, Maine, October 14, 1917, p. xiv, here first printed. A reproduction of W. Orlando Rouland's portrait of Howells, opposite p. 274.

18-B

Pride and prejudice | by | Jane Austen | with an introduction | by | William Dean Howells.

Charles Scribner's Sons: New York, [1918]. "The modern student's library." Published April 4, 1918.

"Introduction," dated January, 1918, p. v–xxiii, here first printed.

18-C

Daisy Miller | An international | episode | [*rule*] | by Henry James.

Boni and Liveright, Inc.: New York, [1918]. "The modern library."

"Introduction," p. i–ix, here first printed.

18-D

The daughter | of the storage | W. D. Howells | [publisher's device] | Harper & Brothers publishers | New York and London | [1918]

Collation: p. vi + 42, 7⅜ x 4⅞ inches: title page [v]; 3–42, text. End papers of heavier stock than text.

Light blue cloth over boards. Formalized tree-ornament on front cover stamped in dark green and gold. Lettering on front cover gold-stamped. "Compliments of | David Fireproof Storage Warehouses | Chicago | Christmas | 1918." Title page verso M-S [Dec., 1918].

Another edition was reprinted from the same plates in 1928 as "Special edition for the | Security Storage Company | of Washington, D. C."

First separate edition. Reprinted from the plates of *The daughter of the storage and other things in prose and verse;* see 16-C.

19-A

The shadow of the | cathedral | a novel | by | Vicente Blasco Ibañez | translated from the Spanish | by | Mrs. A. W. Gillespie | with a critical introduction | by | W. D. Howells.

E. P. Dutton & Company: New York, 1919. Published Jan. 14, 1919.

"Introduction," p. v–xiv, here first printed.

19-B

The | actor-manager | [*ornament*] | by Leonard Merrick | [*ornament*] | with an introduction by | William Dean Howells.

E. P. Dutton and Company: New York, [1919]. Published Aug. 4, 1919. Limited to 1550 copies. A Canadian edition was also issued by Hodder & Stoughton, London and Toronto, 1919.

"Introduction," p. v–xiv, here first printed.

19-C

The World War | utterances concerning its issue and conduct | by members of | the American Academy of Arts | and Letters | printed for its archives and for | free circulation.

American Academy of Arts and Letters: New York, 1919. Published Aug. 18, 1919 (date of presentation copy).

"The incredible cruelty of the Teutons," p. 20–21, first printed as "Editor's easy chair," *Harper's monthly*, Aug., 1918, cxxxvii, 444, 445–446.

20-A

Hither and thither | in Germany | W. D. Howells | illustrated | [*publisher's device*] | Harper & Brothers publishers | New York and London [1920]

Collation: p. x + 132, 7⅜ x 4⅝ inches: title page, [v]; [1], "Hither

Collations of Works... — 20-A, continued

and thither in Germany"; 3–132, text. Frontispiece and seven illustrated leaves tipped in and not paginated. End papers.

Dark brown cloth over thin boards. Lettering and ornament on front cover and spine gold-stamped. "Harper's travel companions" series. Published Jan. 16, 1920. Title page verso, M–T [Dec., 1919].

Text is a condensation of *Their silver wedding journey.* See 99-C. "Hither and thither in Germany," p. 1, here first printed.

20-B

Immortality | and | Sir Oliver Lodge | by | William Dean Howells | Editor's easy chair, Harper's Magazine.

Collation: p. [4], 6½ x 4 ¹⁵/₁₆ inches.

Pamphlet. No date and no place of publication, but the last page lists fourteen "New-Church book rooms." Published March 1, 1920 (earliest notice observed).

First printed as "Editor's easy chair," *Harper's monthly,* Nov., 1917, cxxxv, 884–885.

20-C

The | great modern | American stories | an anthology | compiled and edited | with an introduction | by | William Dean Howells.

Boni and Liveright: New York, 1920. "The great modern stories series." Published July 3, 1920.

"A reminiscent introduction," p. vii–xiv, here first printed.

20-D

The vacation | of the Kelwyns | an idyl of the middle | eighteen-seventies | by | William Dean Howells | [*publisher's device*] | Harper & Brothers publishers | New York and London | [1920]

Collation: p. vi + 258, 7⅞ x 5¼ inches: title page, [iii]; 1–257, text; 258, blank. Portrait frontispiece leaf

tipped in and not paginated. End papers of different stock from text.

Dark gr en cloth over boards; front cover blind-stamped with vertical lines and torch design. Lettering and ornament on front cover and spine gold-stamped. Published Sept. 25, 1920. Title page verso, H–U [Aug., 1920].

21-A

Harpers magazine | [*ornament*] | Eighty years and after | by William Dean Howells | [*rule*] | reprinted from Harper's | magazine, December, 1919 | [*rule*] | presented with the | compliments of the | publishers at the meet- | ing in commemoration | of the eighty-fourth | anniversary of the | birth of Mr. Howells | [*ornament*] | MCMXXI [*Except for the first line, all the foregoing in an ornamental double-rule box.*]

Collation: p. 8, 9⅜ x 6⅜ inches: title page, [front cover]; frontispiece, [verso of front cover]; [1–8,] text; [recto of back cover,] advertisements. No end papers.

Glazed manila paper covers. Lettering on front cover and publisher's device on back cover in brown. Published March 1, 1921 (date of meeting).

First printed *Harper's monthly,* Dec., 1919, cxl, 21–28.

21-B

Mrs. Farrell | a novel by | William Dean Howells | with an introduction by | Mildred Howells | [*publisher's device*] | Harper & Brothers publishers | New York and London | [1921]

Collation: p. xii + 268, 8 x 5¼ inches: title page, [iii]; v–ix, introduction; 1–266, text; 267–268, advertisements. End papers of same stock as text.

Dark green cloth over boards. Front cover blind-stamped with vertical rules and torch design. Lettering and ornament on front cover and spine gold-stamped. Published Sept. 3, 1921. Title page verso, G–V [July, 1921].

For information on the suppression of this novel, see "Ricus," "A suppressed novel of Mr. Howells," *Bookman*, Oct., 1910, xxxii, 201–203. The *Vollständiges Bücher Lexicon* indicates a translation by Heichen-Abenheim was published in Germany — *Bühnenspiel ohne Coulissen*, Berlin, 1878. "Ricus" rumors an Edinburgh edition in the 1870's.

First printed as "Private theatricals," *Atlantic monthly*, Nov., 1875, xxvi, 513–522, chapters i–ii; Dec., 674–687, iii–iv; Jan., 1876, 1–20, v–vii; Feb., 182–195, viii; March, 329–344, ix–x; April, 437–449, xi–xii; May, 559–574, xiii–xv.

22-A

Public meeting | under | the auspices of | the American Academy | and the National Institute of | Arts and Letters | held at Carnegie Hall | New York, November 30, 1910 | in memory of | Samuel Langhorne Clemens.

American Academy of Arts and Letters: New York, 1922. Published June 30, 1922.

Howells' address and remarks introducing J. H. Choate, p. 1–7; introducing J. H. Twichell, p. 28–29; introducing J. G. Cannon, p. 44–45; introducing Champ Clark, p. 55–56; introducing G. W. Cable, p. 68; introducing Henry Watterson, p. 82; introducing Henry Van Dyke, p. 102; concluding the meeting, p. 103. First printed as "In memory of Mark Twain," *American Academy Proceedings*, Nov. 1, 1911, i, 5–6, 11–12, 15, 18, 21, 24, 29.

23-A

Don Quixote | by Miguel de Cervantes Saavedra | edited by William Dean Howells | with an introduction by Mildred Howells.

Harper & Brothers: New York and London, 1923. Published Sept. 14, 1923. Title page verso, E–X [May, 1923].

Howells' abridgement of Charles Jervas' translation (1742), the abridgement here first printed.

24-A

Émile Zola | [*rule*] | Germinal | translated from the French | by | Havelock Ellis | with an essay by | William D. Howells.

Boni and Liveright: New York, 1924.

"Emile Zola," p. v–xviii, first printed *North American review*, Nov., 1902, clxxv, 587–596.

24-B

Vivisection | according to | representative people.

Vivisection Investigation League: New York, 1924.

Howells' three-line letter to Mrs. C. P. Farrell, p. 26, dated April 15, 1909, is probably reprinted, like the entire pamphlet, from an earlier pamphlet entitled *Vivisection: from the viewpoint of some great minds*, published c. 1909 by the Anti-Vivisection Society of New York. We have not been able to locate a copy of this earlier pamphlet.

28-A

Life in letters of | William | Dean Howells | edited by Mildred Howells | [*rule*] | Volume one | [*rule*] | illustrated | [*publisher's device*] | Garden City, New York | Doubleday, Doran & Company, Inc. | 1928 [*Title page of second volume as above except that* "Volume two" *replaces* "Volume one."]

Collation: Volume i, p. –ii + xiv + 434, 9⅜ x 6¼ inches: title page, [iii]; preface, v–vi; 1–429, text; 430–434, blank; frontispiece and five illustrated leaves of glazed stock tipped in and not paginated; volume ii, p. xii + 430: title page, [iii]; 1–399, text; 403–409, chronological list of books; 413–426, index; two blank leaves; frontispiece and six illustrated leaves tipped in and not paginated. End papers of heavier stock than text.

Gray cloth over boards, red-tan backstrip bearing cream paper-label with lettering, rule-boxes, and volume number in red and black. "First edition" so indicated on verso of title page. Top edge gilt; fore and bottom edges rough-trimmed. Published Nov. 19, 1928.

I, 1–125, in small part first printed as "The ante-room to fame, letters of William Dean Howells, 1856–1867," *Bookman*, May, 1928, LXVII, 258–266.

I, 155–280, in small part first printed as "Howells and 'The Atlantic', letters of William

Dean Howells, 1870–1880," *Bookman*, June, 1928, LXVII, 392–400.

I, 281–429, in small part first printed as "A decade of change, letters of William Dean Howells, 1880–1889," *Bookman*, Aug., 1928, LXVII, 667–676.

II, 1–399, in small part first printed as "'The dean', letters of William Dean Howells, 1890–1920," *Bookman*, Oct., 1928, LXVIII, 188–203.

All numbers have introductory notice by "H. S. G."

ANNUAL REGISTER: CHRONOLOGICAL LIST OF PERIODICAL
PUBLICATIONS, INCLUDING VOLUME TITLES

1852

52–1. "[Old winter, loose thy hold on us.] For the Ohio State Journal," *Ohio state journal*, March 23, 1852, xv, 2.

Dated March 20. Signed V. M. H. *Years of my youth*, p. 74, states: "[It is his father] who presently steals into the print of the newspaper employing them both a poem on the premature warm weather which has invited the bluebirds and blackbirds into the northern March." Reprinted 52–2.

Old Winter, loose thy hold on us
　And let the Spring come forth;
And take thy frost and ice and snow
　Back to the frozen North.

The gentle, warm, and blooming Spring,
　We thought had come at last;
And thou, with all thy cold and woe,
　Wast for a season past; —
The blackbird on his glossy wing,
　Was soaring in the sky;
And pretty red breast robin, too,
　Was caroling on high . . .

52–2. "Old winter let go thy hold," Cincinnati *Commercial*, April 24, 1852, xv, 4.

Signed V. M. H. *Years of my youth*, p. 74, refers to Howells' "joy in finding his verse copied into a New York paper and also in the Cincinnati *Commercial*. I mean the piece on Winter." First printed 52–1.

52–3. "For the Ohio State Journal, The emigrant's last meal in the old

house," *Ohio state journal*, June 3, 1852, xv, 1.

Signed W. D. H. *My literary passions*, p. 43, refers to this second poem.

1853

53–1. "Translated for the Casket, Don Pedro II, emperor of Brazil, from the Spanish," *Casket*, Aug., 1853, II, 121–124.

Signed W. As E. H. Cady, who has supplied us with this and all Kingsville, Ohio, *Casket* items, points out, an editorial notice (p. 141) identifies "W." as a self-taught student of Spanish "only about sixteen years old." For each number of the *Casket* (printed at Jefferson on the *Sentinel* press) "W." was invited to "favor us with at least one article."

53–2. "Written for the Casket, Beauties of mythology," *Casket*, Sept., 1853, II, 154–155.

Signed W. For attribution see 53–1.

53–3. "A tale of love and politics, adventures of a printer boy," Ashtabula *Sentinel*, Sept. 1, 1853, XXII, 1.

Unsigned: attribution made through background and narrator of story and its publication in the Howells newspaper.

53–4. "The journeyman's secret, stray leaves from the diary of a journeyman printer," Ashtabula *Sentinel*, Nov. 3, 1853, XXII, 1.

Unsigned: attribution as in 53–3.

53–5. "A Christmas story, written expressly for the Casket," *Casket*, Dec., 1853, II, 235–237.

Narrative poem. Signed W. For attribution see 53–1.

1854

54–1. "How I lost a wife, an episode in the life of a bachelor," Ashtabula *Sentinel*, May 18, 1854, XXIII, 1.

Unsigned: it is highly probable that the fear of dogs in this story reflects Howells' own phobia described in *Years of my youth*, p. 91–94.

54–2. "The old farmer's elegy," Ashtabula *Sentinel*, May 25, 1854, XXIII, 1.

Unsigned: attribution made on basis of bluebird and robin motif and elegiac tone. Compare 52–1 and 52–3.

54–3. "Our emended edition of Shakspeare," Ashtabula *Sentinel*, Aug. 24, 1854, XXIII, 2.

Thirty-five lines of dialogue between Pistol, Nym, and Bardolph, describing the heat in diction imitating Shakespeare's. Attributed through *My literary passions*, p. 57–58.

54–4. "Ye childe and ye angell," Ashtabula *Sentinel*, Aug. 31, 1854, XXIII, 1.

Signed Will Narlie; possibly the first use of this pseudonym. See 54–7.

54–5. "The emigrant of 1802, a chapter from an unpublished history, for the Ashtabula Sentinel," Ashtabula *Sentinel*, Feb. 9, March 9, March 30, April 20, 1854, XXIII, p. 1.

Signed Lereo. Attribution made on the basis of similarity of material with *My year in a log cabin*.

54–6. "Original stories, An old-time love-affair," Ashtabula *Sentinel*, Sept. 14, 1854, XXIII, 1.

Unsigned: attribution through *Years of my youth*, p. 96–97.

54–7. "Nightly rain, from the Ohio Farmer," Ashtabula *Sentinel*, Oct. 5, 1854, XXIII, 1.

Signed Will Narlie. First printed *Ohio farmer*, date unknown. Reprinted 60–A.

54–8. "Original story – The independent candidate, a story of today," Ashtabula *Sentinel*, Nov. 23, Nov. 30, Dec. 7, Dec. 21, Dec. 28, 1854, Jan. 4, Jan. 11, Jan. 18, 1855, XXIII–XXIV, p. 1.

Unsigned: attribution made through printing office background, the use of a quotation from "Don Quijote," and the description of the story in *My literary passions*, p. 85–87. Thorough examination of Howells' authorship also appears in E. H. Cady, "William Dean Howells and the Ashtabula Sentinel," *Ohio state archaeological and historical quarterly*, Jan. – March, 1944, LIII, 43–46.

1855

55–1. "A little about jokes," Ashtabula *Sentinel*, March 1, 1855, XXIV, 1.

Signed "The looker-on." Attributed through strong similarity to the punning, whimsical, highly social kind of humor appearing in Howells' "News and humors of the mail," "Literary gossip," "Glimpses of summer travel," and "Minor topics."

55–2. "For the National Era, Leonora," *National era*, April 12, 1855, IX, 60.

Reprinted 60–A.

55–3. "For the National Era, Spring," *National era*, May 3, 1855, IX, 70.

Reprinted 60–A.

55–4. "The wreath in heaven – a fancy, written for the Ohio Farmer," *Ohio farmer*, May 26, 1855, IV, 84.

Reprinted 60–A.

55–5. "Original miscellany, Love through a key-hole, Felicity compared, A gastronome," Ashtabula *Sentinel*, June 7, 1855, XXIV, 1.

Unsigned: attribution made on basis of an editorial note indicating the sketches were

Periodical Publications... — 1855, continued

translated from a Spanish paper for the Ashtabula *Sentinel*. See *Years of my youth*, p. 146–147, on translation from Spanish and French sources, particularly newspaper exchanges and the *Courrier des États-Unis*. The same basis for attribution exists for all Spanish translations in the Ashtabula *Sentinel* and the *Ohio state journal*.

55–6. "For the National Era, The death of May," *National era*, June 21, 1855, IX, 97.

Reprinted 60–A.

55–7. "Notices of magazines," Ashtabula *Sentinel*, June 28, July 12, Aug. 2, 1855, XXIV, p. 4.

This was the season of Howells' great interest in the British quarterlies, and the style of these reviews of both British and American magazines is his.

55–8. "The Dutch mother, translated for the Sentinel from the Spanish of Jacinto de Solas y Quiroga," Ashtabula *Sentinel*, Aug. 16, 23, 1855, XXIV, p. 1.

Unsigned: for attribution see 55–5.

55–9. "The magazines for November," Ashtabula *Sentinel*, Oct. 25, 1855, XXIV, 4.

Reviews of "Ladies magazines." For attribution see 55–7.

55–10. "Chapter from *Lazarillo de Tormes*, Diego Hurtado de Mendoza," Ashtabula *Sentinel*, Nov. 15, 1855, XXIV, 1.

Unsigned: for attribution see 55–5.

55–11. "The poisoned bouquet — a story of the Italian opera, from the Courrier des Etats Unis," *Ohio state journal*, Nov. 29, 1855, XIX, 1.

Unsigned: for attribution see 55–5 and the reprinting of the story in the Ashtabula *Sentinel*, Jan. 17, 1856.

1856

56–1. [Editorial comment] including "The Pittsburgh convention," "Culpa

nostra," "The reviews," "Ohio disgraced," Ashtabula *Sentinel*, Jan. 24, Feb. 14, Feb. 21, Feb. 28, March 6, 1856, XXV, p. 4.

F. C. Marston, jr., has noted, in calling our attention to these items, that William Cooper Howells left "the business and home editorials" to J. and W. D. Howells, quoting the Ashtabula *Sentinel*, Jan. 10, 1856, XXV, 4. Between January and April, 1856, however, the father returned occasionally for visits from Columbus, and both his name and Giddings' remained on the masthead of the *Sentinel*.

56–2. "Gossip," Ashtabula *Sentinel*, March 13, 1856, XXV, 2.

Literary miscellany including comment on Heine. For attribution see 57–10.

56–3. "Editorial table talk," Ashtabula *Sentinel*, March 20, 27, April 3, 1856, XXV, p. 2 and 5.

Comment on the *Edinburgh review, London quarterly, Blackwood's,* and other British magazines. For attribution see 55–7.

1857

57–1. "From Columbus, correspondence of the Cincinnati Gazette," Cincinnati *Gazette*, Jan. 6, 1857, LXV, 2.

Unsigned: for attribution see 57–2.

57–2. "Letter from Columbus," Cincinnati *Gazette*, Jan. 7, 1857, LXV, 1 (signed "Jefferson"); Jan. 8, 1857, 2; Jan. 9, 1857, 1; Jan. 10, 1857, 2; Jan. 12, 1857, 1; Jan. 13, 1857, 2 (insane asylum outrage); Jan. 14, 1857, 1; Jan. 15, 1857, 2; Jan. 16, 1857, 2 (as "Columbus correspondence"); Jan. 17, 1857, 2; Jan. 19, 1857, 1; Jan. 20, 1857, 2; Jan. 21, 1857, 2; Jan. 22, 1857, 2; Jan. 23, 1857, 2; Jan. 24, 1857, 1 (report of Monroe's speech on slavery and word "white" in Constitution); Jan. 26, 1857, 1; Jan. 27, 1857, 2; Jan. 28, 1857, 2 (unsigned); Jan. 29, 1857, 2; Jan. 30, 1857, 2; Feb. 2, 1857, 1 (Corry-Slough fight aftermath); Feb. 3, 1857, 2; Feb. 4, 1857,

2; Feb. 5, 1857, 2; Feb. 6, 1857, 2; Feb. 7, 1857, 2; Feb. 9, 1857, 2; Feb. 10, 1857, 2 (unsigned); Feb. 11, 1857, 2; Feb. 12, 1857, 2; Feb. 13, 1857, 2; Feb. 14, 1857, 1; Feb. 16, 1857, 1; Feb. 18, 1857, 2; Feb. 19, 1857, 2 (mentions Don Quixote); Feb. 20, 1857, 2; Feb. 21, 1857, 2; Feb. 23, 1857, 1 (game and bird bill); Feb. 25, 1857, 2; Feb. 26, 1857, 2; Feb. 27, 1857, 2; Feb. 28, 1857, 2; March 2, 1857, 1; March 4, 1857, 2; March 6, 1857, 1, 2; March 7, 1857, 2; March 9, 1857, 2 (on M. D. Conway); March 11, 1857, 2; March 12, 1857, 2; March 13, 1857, 2 (on Corry's speech on unicameralism); March 14, 1857, 1; March 16, 1857, 2; March 17, 1857, 2; March 18, 1857, 2; March 19, 1857, 2 (Corry on marriage and legislative salaries); March 20, 1857, 2; March 21, 1857, 2; March 23, 1857, 1; March 24, 1857, 2 (mural sketch of Perry's Lake Erie victory); March 25, 1857, 2; March 26, 1857, 2; March 27, 1857, 2; March 28, 1857, 2; March 31, 1857, 2; April 1, 1857, 2; April 2, 1857, 2; April 3, 1857, 1; April 4, 1857, 2; April 6, 1857, 1; April 8, 1857, 2; April 9, 1857, 2; April 11, 1857, 2; April 13, 1857, 1; April 15, 1857, 2; April 16, 1857, 2; April 17, 1857, 2; April 18, 1857, 2; April 20, 1857, 2 ("The closing scene").

Except as noted, all signed "Jeffersonian": attribution through *Years of my youth*, p. 137–139. F. C. Marston, jr., in his unpublished dissertation, p. 133, asserts: "Just when he ceased writing this correspondence is a problem. The letters went on to April 20 — that is, the last is dated April 18 and printed the 20th — but it would appear that Will was no longer the author after March 31; on April 10th, he was in Cincinnati and evidently had been there for some days already on a new job. Probably after March 31st, when five lines assert that there is 'really nothing to report,' Will's father took over." The evidence for How-

ells' being in Cincinnati on April 10, Marston has found, is a letter of that date to his brother. See *American literature*, May, 1946, xviii, 163–164.

57–3. "The State House warming at Columbus," Cincinnati *Gazette,* Jan. 8, 1857, lxv, 1.

Unsigned: *Years of my youth,* p. 138–139, refers to this letter: "The first winter of my legislative correspondence began with a letter to my Cincinnati newspaper in which I described the public opening of the new State House." The first "Letter from Columbus" had however been printed the day before; see 57–2 above.

57–4. "News and humors of the mail," Cincinnati *Gazette,* May 4, 1857, lxv, 1.

Unsigned: attribution made on basis of similarity of material and manner with the later department of the same name in the *Ohio state journal.*

57–5. "The paper-readers. From the German, [Cincinnati *Republikaner*]," Ashtabula *Sentinel,* Aug. 27, 1857, xxvi, 6.

For attribution see 57–10.

57–6. "Blackwood for October," Ashtabula *Sentinel,* July 16, 1857, xxvi, 4.

High praise of the current issue of *Blackwood's magazine.* For attribution see 55–7.

57–7. "Blackwood's magazine," Ashtabula *Sentinel,* Nov. 12, 1857, xxvi, 3.

For attribution see 55–7.

57–8. "The Republican Party," "What will they do now?" Ashtabula *Sentinel,* Nov. 19, 1857, xxvi, 4.

These editorials were translated from the Cincinnati *Volksblatt* and the *Waechter am Erie* respectively. For attribution see 57–10.

57–9. "The autumn land, written for the Ohio Farmer," *Ohio farmer,* Nov. 21, 1857, vi, 188.

Signed Godfrey Constant. Reprinted 60–A.

57–10. "A fragment, Heine," Ashtabula *Sentinel,* Nov. 26, 1857, xxvi, 7.

A translation from the German of Heine. Unsigned: attribution made on basis of sim-

Periodical Publications... — 1857, continued

ilarity with 58–6 (a Heine poem translated by Howells for the *Sentinel* and reprinted in 60–A), and of Howells' new interest in German, which he says, "replaced Spanish in my affections through the witchery of Heine" (*Years of my youth*, p. 100.) The problem of determining Howells' unsigned translations from the German, both verse and prose, is difficult. In the case of translations from French or Spanish sources, *Years of my youth*, p. 146–147, specifically mentions *Courrier des États-Unis* and *La Crónica* as exchange sources from which he translated, but no such source is mentioned for German translation. Additionally, the probability of contributions to the *Sentinel* by readers of French and Spanish in Ashtabula other than W. D. Howells seems slight, whereas the number of German reading and speaking people there who might have done German translations was relatively large. Hence we have listed separately unsigned translations from the German only when the introductory phrase, or the choice of material to translate, or the style of the translation indicates very strongly Howells' authorship. Of the body of suspected Howells translations the following may be noted: "From the German of Schiller. Fame," Ashtabula *Sentinel*, July 20, 1854, XXIII, 1; "The minstrel, from the German," *National era*, Aug. 13, 1857, XI, 132; "The solitary," *Ohio state journal*, Nov. 19, 1858, XXII, 1; "Massacre of the Jews at Lisbon, from the German of John Frederic Jacobs," Ashtabula *Sentinel*, Nov. 26, Dec. 3, 10, 24, 1857 and Jan. 7, 1858, XXVI–XXVII, p. 1; "Three poems from the German," *Ohio state journal*, Dec. 17, 1858, XXII, 4. Serial stories by Jacobs and Zschokke in the *Sentinel* in 1855 and 1857 may have been translated by Howells. See in this connection E. H. Cady, "William Dean Howells and the Ashtabula Sentinel," *Ohio state archaeological and historical quarterly*, Jan. – March, 1944, LIII, 42–43. Additional suggestions have been made by Robert Price and F. C. Marston, jr.

1858

58–1. "Letter from Columbus, chiefly conjective and anticipatory," Cincinnati *Gazette*, Jan. 4, 1858, LXVII, 1.

Signed Chispa. See *My literary passions*, p. 39: "The hero's rogue servant, Chispa, seemed...so fine...that I chose his name for my first [*sic*] pseudonym when I began to write for the newspapers."

58–2. "Letter from Columbus" [in twenty-five cases] "From Columbus,"

Cincinnati *Gazette*, LXVII–LXVIII, Jan. 5, 1858, 3; Jan. 6, 1858, 2; Jan. 7, 1858, 2 (under variant title); Jan. 8, 1858, 2; Jan. 11, 1858, 3 (Klippert and agricultural societies); Jan. 13, 1858, 2; Jan. 15, 1858, 2; Jan. 16, 1858, 2; Jan. 20, 1858, 2; Jan. 21, 1858, 2; Jan. 22, 1858, 2; Jan. 23, 1858, 2; Jan. 25, 1858, 1; Jan. 27, 1858, 1, 2; Jan. 30, 1858, 3; Feb. 1, 1858, 1; Feb. 2, 1858, 2; Feb. 3, 1858, 2; Feb. 4, 1858, 2; Feb. 5, 1858, 2; Feb. 6, 1858, 2; Feb. 8, 1858, 1; Feb. 9, 1858, 3; Feb. 10, 1858, 2 (*Commercial* correspondent's expulsion); Feb. 12, 1858, 3; Feb. 13, 1858, 2; Feb. 15, 1858, 1; Feb. 16, 1858, 2; Feb. 17, 1858, 2; Feb. 19, 1858, 1; Feb. 22, 1858, 1; Feb. 24, 1858, 2; Feb. 25, 1858, 2; Feb. 26, 1858, 2; March 1, 1858, 1; March 3, 1858, 3; March 4, 1858, 2; March 5, 1858, 3; March 6, 1858, 2; March 8, 1858, 3; March 9, 1858, 2; March 10, 1858, 2; March 12, 1858, 3; March 15, 1858, 1; March 17, 1858, 2; March 19, 1858, 2; March 20, 1858, 2; March 22, 1858, 2 (condemns Sargent for assaulting *Commercial* correspondent); March 24, 1858, 2; March 25, 1858, 3 ("Ohio legislature"); March 26, 1858, 2; March 27, 1858, 2; March 29, 1858, 1; March 30, 1858, 3; March 31, 1858, 2; April 2, 1858, 3; April 3, 1858, 3; April 5, 1858, 3; April 6, 1858, 3; April 7, 1858, 3; April 8, 1858, 3; April 10, 1858, 1; April 12, 1858, 1; April 13, 1858, 3.

Signed Chispa. Attribution made through *Years of my youth*, p. 143–144. Items in this series signed "C." (possibly John Esten Cooke) and unsigned items are not entered. Note, however, that Howells asserts that his father took over the correspondence "almost before my labors began." F. C. Marston, jr., in his unpublished dissertation, p. 144, states: "Some time around January 20th, his health seems to have broken down 'under the strain of earlier over-study and later over-work,' or as the after-effects of the rheumatic fever he had had during the summer. From then on he 'dragged drearily through the winter,' helping his father as much as he could to carry on the letters. He seems to have been incapacitated by his vertigo from about January 20 to February 12 and again between March 29 and April 12. If so, we can safely accept Will as the author only of correspondence from the middle of February to the end of March [and for the earlier period in January]." Marston has derived the above dates from the father's letters to the *Sentinel;* he asserts that "Letters printed in the Ashtabula *Sentinel* from February 18 through March 25 are evidently by Will, signed with his customary 'W.' " It is probable then that the father continued the son's pseudonym (Chispa) in this series during his illness as in the previous year the son had used the father's pseudonym (Jeffersonian).

Years of my youth, p. 137, indicates unmistakably that Howells also wrote a series of "Letters from Columbus" for the Cleveland *Herald* during the spring of 1858. These letters appeared Jan. 11–16, 20–23, 23–30, Feb. 1, 3–6, 8–13, 15–20, 22–27, March 1–6, 8, 10, 12, 13, 15, 16, 18–20, 22–27, 29–31, and April 1, and were signed "Genug." Thereafter through the end of the legislative session the signature changed from "Genug" to "Enough." Marston's dissertation, p. 143, states: "The *Herald* correspondence (signed 'Genug') is almost the same as that to the *Gazette;* sometimes the two accounts are identical, but in general they bear only a generic similarity." The illness mentioned above, however, makes at least a portion of these letters suspect, and "Enough" rather than "Genug" may be Howells' signature.

"Columbus correspondence" signed "W." (rather than "W. C. H.," the customary initial signature of Howells' father) also appeared in the Ashtabula *Sentinel,* Jan. 7, 14, 21, and Feb. 18, 1858. Unsigned items in the series appeared Feb. 25 and March 4, 1858. Marston cites the Ashtabula *Sentinel,* Dec. 24, 1857, as authority for assigning this sequence of letters to Howells.

58–3. "The artesian well at Columbus," Cincinnati *Gazette,* Jan. 14, 1858, LXVII, 1.

Signed Chispa. This item with 58–4 and 58–5 is subject to none of the doubts indicated for portions of the series in 58–2. It was written early in the year and is markedly Howellsian in manner; the father's using the Chispa pseudonym outside the son's column is improbable.

58–4. "The military convention at Columbus," Cincinnati *Gazette,* Jan. 20, 21, 1858, LXVIII, p. 1.

Speech of Governor Chase and an accident with a runaway horse. Signed Chispa.

58–5. "Anti Lecompton meeting at Columbus," Cincinnati *Gazette,* Feb. 22, 1858, LXVIII, 1.

Signed Chispa.

58–6. "Translated for the Sentinel from the German of Heine," Ashtabula *Sentinel,* April 1, 1858, XXVII, 103.

Reprinted 60–A.

58–7. "Evening voices," Ashtabula *Sentinel,* May 20, 1858, XXVII, 153.

Poem. Signed W. D. H.

58–8. "For the Sentinel from the German of Heine," Ashtabula *Sentinel,* Aug. 5, 1858, XXVII, 241.

Reprinted 60–A.

58–9. "From the Courrier des Etats-Unis," Ashtabula *Sentinel,* Aug. 5, 1858, XXVII, 241.

Story. Unsigned: for attribution see 55–5 and 57–10.

58–10. "The doubt," *National era,* Sept. 16, 1858, XII, 145.

Reprinted 60–A.

58–11. "The dream," *Ohio farmer,* Sept. 18, 1858, VII, 304.

Poem. Signed Will Narlie.

58–12. "The mysteries, written for the Ohio Farmer," *Ohio farmer,* Oct. 2, 1858, VII, 320.

Reprinted 60–A.

58–13. "For the National Era, Gone," *National era,* Oct. 21, 1858, XII, 168.

Signed Wilhelm Constant. Reprinted 60–A and 93–K.

58–14. "Have we household poetry in the West? Literary matters," *Ohio state journal*, Nov. 20, 1858, XXII, 2.

Unsigned: although F. C. Marston, jr., finds this item a day or two early for Howells' appointment to the *Journal* staff, tentatively suggesting W. T. Coggeshall as the author, Howells' conduct of literary columns in the *Journal* and his part as critic and poet in *The poets and poetry of the West* (see 60–E) lead us to believe it is his.

Many of the *Ohio state journal* articles were reprinted from one to fourteen days later in the *Ohio state weekly journal*. In addition to this article those reprinted are: 58–19, 59–5, 59–6, 59–7, 59–10, 59–13, 59–14, 59–17, 59–24, 59–26, 59–27, 59–34, 59–36, 59–37, 60–4, 60–5, 60–6, 60–10, 60–12, 60–14, 60–16, 60–42, and 60–43. The column, "Literary gossip" was also reprinted in the weekly *Journal*, Jan. 24, 31, Feb. 14, 21, 28, April 17, 24, May 1, 8, 15, Sept. 11, 1860, XLIX–L, p. 1, 2, and 4. (Some of these "Literary gossip" columns may be printed in longer form, or for the first time, in the weekly *Journal*.)

58–15. "News and humors of the mail," *Ohio state journal*, Nov. 22, 23, 24, 25, 27, 29, 30, Dec. 1, 2, 3, 4, 6, 7, 8, 9, 10, 11, 13, 14, 15, 16, 17, 18, 20, 21, 22, 23, 24, 25, 27, 28, 29, 30, 31, 1858, XXII, p. 1.

Unsigned: attribution through *Years of my youth*, p. 146: "I called my column or two 'News and Humors of the Mail,' and I tried to give it an effect of originality by recasting many of the facts, or, when I could not find a pretext for this, by offering the selected passages with applausive or derisive comment." Many of the "News and humors of the mail" columns were reprinted in the *Ohio state weekly journal*, sometimes with additional material. A few may be printed in the weekly *Journal* for the first time. The column appeared in the *Ohio state weekly journal* Nov. 30, Dec. 7, 13, 21, 28, 1858, XLVIII, pages varying from 1 through 4; Jan. 4, 11, 18, Feb. 8, 15, March 8, April 5, 19, July 5, Oct. 4, 11, 18, 25, Nov. 1, 8, 15, 23, 29, Dec. 6, 1859, XLVIII–XLIX, pages varying from 1 through 4; and Jan. 10, Feb. 14, 1860, XLIX, p. 1, 3.

58–16. "The bird song," *National era*, Dec. 2, 1858, XII, 189.

Signed Wilhelm Constant. Reprinted 60–A.

58–17. "Local affairs, Dick Dowdy, study of a first-rate fellow," [followed by other local items], "Our state exchange," *Ohio state journal*, Dec. 6, 1858, XXII, 2.

In a letter to J. M. Comly of Aug. 5, 1869, cited by Robert Price (MS. at Ohio State Archaeological and Historical Society), Howells named "Dick Dowdy" as a sketch he had published in the *Ohio state journal*. A number of other unsigned columns at this time ("Literary matters," "State items," "News items," "Local affairs," "Our state exchange,") may also be by Howells, as Robert Price has suggested on the basis of internal evidence. F. C. Marston, jr., in his unpublished doctoral dissertation, "The early life of William Dean Howells, a chronicle, 1837–1871," p. 152, cites "Local affairs," *Ohio state journal*, July 20, 1861, as by Howells, quoting the following passage: "The news department of the *Journal* in 1858 and 59 was full of spice and information — a ragout of original talent and attractive clippings... The present writer feels the more freedom in speaking of this department, because he himself had charge of it, and is modestly conscious of then wielding scissors of metropolitan brilliancy."

58–18. "Literary notices," "Our state exchange," "Local affairs," *Ohio state journal*, Dec. 7, 1858, XXII, 2.

Review of D. P. Kidder's *Brazil and the Brazilians* (quoting a letter from Prescott and distributed by Follett, Foster and Company); notices of magazines; a note on prostitution. Unsigned: for attribution see 58–14 and 58–17.

58–19. "Bobby, study of a boy," *Ohio state journal*, Dec. 14, 1858, XXII, 1.
Signed W. D. H.

1859

59–1. "News and humors of the mails," *Ohio state journal*, Jan. 1, 3, 4, 6, 7, 8, 10, 11 (p. 3), 12, 13 (p. 3), 14, 15, 17, 18, 19, 20, 21, 22, 24, 25, 26, 27, 28, 29, 31, Feb. 1, 2, 3, 4, 18, 22, 23, 26, 28, March 1, 3, 4, 5, 8, April 8, 9, 11, 12, 13, 14, 15, 16, 18 (p. 3), 20, 21, 27, 28, May 5, 24, 25, 27, 30, 31, June 30 (p. 2), July 1 (p. 2), 2, 11, Aug. 17, 18, 19, 20, 22,

Sept. 1, 2, 3, 5, 6, 9, 12, 16, 19, 20, 22, 23, 24, 26, 27, 28, 30, Oct. 3, 4, 5, 7, 8, 10, 11, 14, 15, 17, 18, 19, 20, 21, 22, 25, 26, 27, 28, 29, 31, Nov. 1, 2, 3, 5, 8, 10, 11, 12, 14, 15, 16, 17, 18, 19, 21, 22, 23, 24, 26, 27, 28, 30, Dec. 1, 2, 5, 6, 7, 8, 9, 13, 14, 16, 17, 22, 24, 1859, xxii–xxiii, p. 1 (through Oct. 11), p. 2 (from Oct. 14) except as noted.

Unsigned: attribution through *Years of my youth*, p. 146. See 58–15.

59–2. "The modern Danaides," *Ohio state journal*, Jan. 14, 1859, xxii, 2.

Translated from *Courrier des États-Unis*. Unsigned: for attribution see 55–5, as in all following instances of translations from French or Spanish for the *Journal*.

59–3. "Three French stories, Romantic marriage, An unfortunate state of things, Royer's verses," *Ohio state journal*, Jan. 18, 1859, xxii, 2.

"We translate from the *Courrier des Etats-Unis*..." Unsigned.

59–4. "How a duel was prevented," *Ohio state journal*, Jan. 20, 1859, xxii, 2.

Translated from the *Courrier*. Unsigned.

59–5. "Marvellous story," *Ohio state journal*, Jan. 22, 1859, xxii, 2.

Translated from the *Courrier*. Unsigned.

59–6. "Princely incident," *Ohio state journal*, Jan. 31, 1859, xxii, 2.

Translated from the *Courrier*. Unsigned.

59–7. [Spanish proverbs translated,] *Ohio state journal*, Jan. 31, 1859, xxii, 2.

Unsigned.

59–8. "Not a love story," *Odd-Fellows casket*, Feb., 1859, i, 222–224.

Assigned in volume index.

59–9. "Castorology," *Ohio state journal*, Feb. 8, 1859, xxii, 1.

Translated from the *Courrier*. Unsigned.

59–10. "The conciergerie," *Ohio state journal*, Feb. 22, 1859, xxii, 1.

Translated from the *Courrier*. Unsigned.

59–11. "The Atlantic for March," *Ohio state journal*, Feb. 23, 1859, xxii, 2.

Unsigned: attribution as in 58–14.

59–11a. "Making love between heaven and earth," and "The new Machiavelli," *Ohio state weekly journal*, March 1, 1859, xlviii, 4.

Unsigned: this "sprightly little story" and the maxims "from the German" follow "The conciergerie," reprinted from 59–10.

59–12. "Morceaux," *Ohio state journal*, March 4, 1859, xxii, 1.

Translated from a Spanish exchange. Unsigned.

59–13. "The lost child – a street scene," *Ohio state journal*, March 4, 1859, xxii, 1.

Unsigned: attribution on basis of similarity to the sketch "Hot," 59–24. See also 54–3.

59–13a. "The perilous charity," *Ohio state weekly journal*, March 15, 1859, xlviii, 1.

Unsigned: story translated from the *Courrier*.

59–13b. "A French view of Byron," *Ohio state weekly journal*, March 15, 1859, xlviii, 1.

Editorial: Unsigned.

59–13c. "A terrible suspicion," *Ohio state weekly journal*, March 29, 1859, xlix, 4.

Unsigned. Satirical criticism of Saxe's poem "Love."

59–13d. "Cooper's novels," *Ohio state weekly journal*, April 5, 1859, xlix, 3.

Unsigned: review of *The pioneers* and *The red rover*, volumes in the W. A. Townsend collected edition of Cooper with Darley illustrations. For attribution see 58–14.

59–14. "A marvellous boy," *Ohio state journal,* April 11, 1859, xxii, 2.

Comment on an article in *La Crónica.* Unsigned.

59–15. "A summer Sunday in a country village," *Odd-Fellows casket,* April, 1859, i, 354–357.

Assigned in volume index.

59–16. "A perfect goose," *Odd-Fellows casket,* April, 1859, i, 379–380.

Signed Chispa.

59–17. "The spring fever (in suitable hexameters)," *Ohio state journal,* April 14, 1859, xxii, 2.

Unsigned: attribution on basis of subject, and lines, "exchanges to us are a loathing / And the scissors a burden."

59–18. "New books, Letters of a traveller, W. C. Bryant," *Ohio state journal,* April 16, 1859, xxii, 2.

Unsigned: attribution based on writer's notation of misspelled Spanish words and as in 58–14.

59–18a. "Spring birds and spring thoughts," *Ohio state weekly journal,* April 26, 1859, xlix, 4.

Unsigned: compare 59–21 and 59–22.

59–19. "The Germans in Italy," *Ohio state journal,* April 27, 1859, xxii, 2.

Translated from the *Courrier.* Unsigned.

59–20. "Romance of the crossing," *Odd-Fellows casket,* May, 1859, i, 443–444.

Signed Chispa.

59–20a. "Unworthy Mr. Thackeray!" *Ohio state weekly journal,* May 17, 1859, xlix, 1.

Unsigned: criticism of Thackeray's portrait of the American coquette of *The Virginians.*

59–21. "In the country, Es is [sic] lieber nichts zu schreiben, als nichts zu schreiben," *Ohio state journal,* June 9, 10, 1859, xxiii, p. 1.

Signed Chispa.

59–22. "In the country, birds and things," *Ohio state journal,* June 11, 1859, xxiii, 1.

Signed Chispa.

59–23. "Under the locusts," *Saturday press,* June 18, 1859, ii, 1.

Reprinted 60–A.

59–24. "Hot," *Ohio state journal,* June 29, 1859, xxiii, 2.

Reprinted 03–A.

59–25. "The day we celebrate," *Ohio state journal,* July 4, 1859, xxiii, 2.

Unsigned: quotation and names confirm attribution of this editorial written in the absence of the local and senior editors.

59–26. "A day at White Sulphur," *Ohio state journal,* July 6, 1859, xxiii, 2.

Signed Chispa.

59–26a. "Local affairs," *Ohio state weekly journal,* July 12, 1859, xlix, 3.

Unsigned: compare 58–17, and *Their wedding journey,* p. 98.

59–26b. "Local affairs," *Ohio state weekly journal,* Aug. 30, Sept. 6, 1859, xlix, p. 3.

A gala week at Camp Harrison. Unsigned: compare 59–27.

59–27. "I visit Camp Harrison," *Ohio state journal,* Aug. 31, 1859, xxiii, 2.

Signed Chispa.

59–28. "Drifting away," *Saturday press,* Sept. 10, 1859, ii, 1.

Reprinted 60–A.

59–29. "Death of Leigh Hunt," *Ohio state journal,* Sept. 15, 1859, xxiii, 1.

Unsigned: for attribution see 58–14 and *My literary passions,* p. 120.

59–30. [Review of Aldrich's *Ballad of Babie Bell,*] *Saturday press,* Sept. 17, 1859, ii, 1 (?).

Reprinted in Ferris Greenslet, *The life of Thomas Bailey Aldrich* (Boston, 1908), p. 47–48.

59–31. "The royal road to music," *Ohio state journal*, Sept. 23, 1859, XXIII, 2.

Translated from the *Courrier*. Unsigned.

59–32. "Liebeswonne," *Saturday press*, Oct. 22, 1859, II, 1.

Reprinted 60–A.

59–33. "Dead," *Saturday press*, Nov. 12, 1859, II, 1.

Reprinted 60–A.

59–34. "Gerrit Smith," *Ohio state journal*, Nov. 15, 1859, XXIII, 2.

Anti-slavery poem. Reprinted Ashtabula *Sentinel*, Dec. 1, 1859, XXVIII, 381.

59–35. "Bitters," *Ohio state journal*, Nov. 18, 1859, XXIII, 2.

Heine's detestation of American slavery. Unsigned: for attribution see 57–10.

59–36. "The straw hat, a picture at the doctor's," *Saturday press*, Nov. 19, 1859, II, 2.

Reprinted 60–A.

59–37. "Heinesque, for the Ohio State Journal," *Ohio state journal*, Nov. 23, 1859, XXIII, 2.

Poem. Unsigned: for attribution see 57–10.

59–38. "The thorn," *Saturday press*, Dec. 3, 1859, II, 1.

Reprinted 60–A.

59–39. "Mortuaviva," *Saturday press*, Dec. 10, 1859, II, 1.

Reprinted in part 73–B.

59–40. Review of *Poems of two friends*, *Ohio state journal*, Dec. 26, 1859, XXIII, 2.

Unsigned: attribution on basis of the sentence (after review of Piatt's portion), "Of the subordinate part of this volume it is not for us to speak."

59–41. "At the circus," *Saturday press*, Dec. 31, 1859, II, 3.

Poem.

1860

60–A. *Poems of two friends*, Dec. 23, 1859.

60–1. "Andenken," *Atlantic*, Jan., 1860, v, 100–102.

Unsigned as all early *Atlantic* items; attribution through *Atlantic* index. In part reprinted 73–B, and reprinted *The Riverside song book* (Boston [c. 1893]), p. 142–144, with music by Halfden Kjerulf.

60–2. "News and humors of the mail," *Ohio state journal*, Jan. 5, 6, 7, 9, 20, 21, 26, 31, Feb. 9 (Whitman), 10, 11, 13, 14, 15, 16, 17, 21, 27, 28, 1860, XXIII, p. 2 (through Jan. 26), p. 1 (after Jan. 31).

Unsigned: attribution through *Years of my youth*, p. 146.

60–3. "Literary gossip," *Ohio state journal*, Jan. 5, 17, 25, 31, Feb. 7, 14, 27, March 16, 22, 29, April 12, 20, 26, May 4, 10, 21, 1860, XXIII, p. 1.

Unsigned: for attribution see 58–14 and 58–17.

60–4. "Feuerbilder.—Germanesque," *Saturday press*, Jan. 14, 1860, III, 1.

Reprinted 73–B.

60–5. "The editorial convention at Tiffin," *Ohio state journal*, Jan. 21, 1860, XXIII, 2.

Signed Chispa.

60–6. "The coming," *Ohio state journal*, Jan. 23, 1860, XXIII, 4.

Poem read at the Tiffin convention. Reprinted 12–14 and in part reprinted 16–F.

60–7. "Old Brown," Ashtabula *Sentinel*, Jan. 25, 1860, XXIX, 1.

Dated Nov. 26, 1859. Reprinted 60–B. Along with several other investigators we have not located this poem in the *Ohio state journal* for Nov. 26, 1859; see *Life in letters*, I, 25. It is likely that the dates of composition and publication were confused.

60–8. "The snow birds, written for the Ohio Farmer," *Ohio farmer*, Jan. 28, 1860, IX, 32.

Reprinted 73–B.

60–9. "The poet's friends," *Atlantic,* Feb., 1860, v, 185.
Reprinted 60–E.

60–10. "The bobolinks are singing," *Saturday press,* Feb. 11, 1860, III, 1.
Poem. Reprinted *Ohio state journal,* Feb. 17, 1860, XXIII, and 60–E.

60–11. "The Dial," *Ohio state journal,* Feb. 15, 1860, XXIII, 2.
Critical notice. Unsigned: attribution through M. D. Conway's *Autobiography* (Boston, 1904), I, 307, which quotes from notice.

60–12. "Bereaved," *Ohio state journal,* March 2, 1860, XXIII, 4.
Credited from the *Ohio farmer* in which it appeared as "Bereaved, written for the Ohio Farmer," *Ohio farmer,* March 3, 1860, IX, 72. Reprinted 73–B.

60–13. "Phantoms," *Saturday press,* March 17, 1860, III, 4.
Poem.

60–14. "Hawthorne's Marble Faun," *Ohio state journal,* March 24, 1860, XXIII, 2.
Unsigned: for attribution see 58–14.

60–15. "Vagary," *Saturday press,* March 24, 1860, III, 4.
Reprinted 73–B.

60–16. "Bardic symbols," *Ohio state journal,* March 28, 1860, XXIII, 2.
Review of Whitman's poem in April *Atlantic.* Unsigned: attribution on basis of similarity with a later Whitman notice, 60–25.

60–17. "Pleasure-pain," *Atlantic,* April, 1860, v, 468–470.
In part reprinted 60–E, 73–B and 93–K.

60–18. "Lost beliefs," *Atlantic,* April, 1860, v, 486.
Reprinted 73–B.

60–19. "Romance of the mummy," *Ohio state journal,* April 2, 1860, XXIII, 2.
Unsigned: attributed on the basis of Howells' editorial position with Follett & Foster,

who were to publish Gautier's book. See *Years of my youth,* p. 202.

60–20. "Caprice," *Saturday press,* April 14, 1860, III, 1.
Reprinted 73–B.

60–21. "Success — a parable, written for the Ohio Farmer," *Ohio farmer,* May 5, 1860, IX, 144.
Reprinted 03–A.

60–22. "Poets and poetry of the West," *Ohio state journal,* May 5, 1860, XXIV, 2.
Notice of book from advance sheets. Unsigned: see 58–14 and note Howells' own interest in the work.

60–B. "Old Brown," *Echoes of Harper's Ferry,* May 12.

60–23. "[We wept when we saw in the meadow] for the New York *Saturday Press,"* *Saturday press,* May 26, 1860, III, 1.

60–24. "Convention" and "A poet," *Dial,* June, 1860, I, 371.
Reprinted 73–B.

60–24a. "Letters from the country I. June 30, 1860," *Ohio state weekly journal,* July 10, 1860, L, 1.
Unsigned: quotes Whitman and describes train trip from Columbus to Ashtabula, in the company of Barclay Coppac, one of John Brown's men.

60–C. Lives and speeches of Abraham Lincoln and Hannibal Hamlin, first issue, June 25.

60–D. Lives and speeches of Abraham Lincoln and Hannibal Hamlin, second issue, July 5.

60–25. "New publication, Leaves of grass," *Ashtabula Sentinel,* July 18, 1860, XXIX, 4.
Unsigned: attribution based on mention of Heine and later appearance in *Saturday press* following Howells' New York visit. Reprinted

A Bibliography of William Dean Howells   85

as "A Hoosier's opinion of Walt Whitman," *Saturday press,* Aug. 11, 1860, III, 1.

60–26. "Glimpses of summer travel," Cincinnati *Gazette,* July 21, 1860, LXXI, 2.

Letter dated Buffalo, July 16. Signed Chispa. Reprinted Ashtabula *Sentinel,* Aug. 1, 1860, XXIX, 1, with notice, "The following letters are copied from the Cincinnati *Gazette* for which they are written by W. D. Howells, who is now on a trip to the New England states..."

60–27. "Letters en passant," *Ohio state journal,* July 23, 1860, XXIV, 1.

Letter dated Buffalo, July 17. Unsigned: for attribution see Cincinnati *Gazette,* 60–26 and 60–37.

60–28. "Glimpses of summer travel," Cincinnati *Gazette,* July 24, 1860, LXXI, 1.

Letter dated Niagara Falls, July 17. Signed Chispa. Reprinted Ashtabula *Sentinel,* Aug. 1, 1860, XXIX, 1.

60–29. "En passant," *Ohio state journal,* July 24, 1860, XXIV, 1.

Letter dated Niagara Falls, July 19. Unsigned: for attribution see Cincinnati *Gazette,* 60–26 and 60–37.

60–30. "Glimpses of summer travel," Cincinnati *Gazette,* July 27, 1860, LXXI, 1.

Letter dated Toronto, July 20. Signed Chispa. Reprinted Ashtabula *Sentinel,* Aug. 8, 1860, XXIX, 1–2.

60–31. "En passant," *Ohio state journal,* July 28, 1860, XXIV, 1.

Letter dated Montreal, July 28. Unsigned: for attribution see Cincinnati *Gazette,* 60–26 and 60–37.

60–32. "Glimpses of summer travel," Cincinnati *Gazette,* July 31, 1860, LXXI, 1.

Letter dated Montreal, July 23. Signed Chispa. Reprinted Ashtabula *Sentinel,* Aug. 8, 1860, XXIX, 1–2.

60–32a. "En passant," *Ohio state weekly journal,* July 31, 1860, L, 1.

Letter dated Niagara Falls, July 19. Unsigned: see 60–37.

60–33. "Glimpses of summer travel," Cincinnati *Gazette,* Aug. 1, 1860, LXXI, 1.

Letter dated Montreal, July 25. Signed Chispa. Reprinted Ashtabula *Sentinel,* Aug. 15, 1860, XXIX, 1–2.

60–34. "En passant," *Ohio state journal,* Aug. 4, 1860, XXIV, 1.

Letter dated Quebec, July 26. Unsigned: for attribution see Cincinnati *Gazette,* 60–26 and 60–37.

60–35. "Glimpses of summer travel," Cincinnati *Gazette,* Aug. 6, 1860, LXXI, 1.

Letter dated Portland, July 28. Signed Chispa. Reprinted Ashtabula *Sentinel,* Aug. 15, 1860, XXIX, 1–2.

60–36. "En passant," *Ohio state journal,* Aug. 6, 1860, XXIV, 1.

Letter dated Portland, July 29. Unsigned (but note Ashtabula *Sentinel* reprint): for attribution see Cincinnati *Gazette,* 60–26 and 60–37. Reprinted Ashtabula *Sentinel,* Aug. 15, 1860, XXIX, 1–2, with Chispa signature.

60–37. "En passant," *Ohio state journal,* Aug. 7, 1860, XXIV, 1.

Letter dated Boston, Aug. 1. For attribution see Cincinnati *Gazette,* 60–26. We are indebted to Robert Price for the discovery of this letter. Price has noted that in a letter of Howells to J. M. Comly of Sept. 5, 1869 (MS. at Ohio State Archaeological and Historical Society), Howells mentioned six such newsletters; we had found only five.

60–38. "Glimpses of summer travel," Cincinnati *Gazette,* Aug. 9, 1860, LXXI, 1.

Letter dated Portland, July 30. Signed Chispa. Reprinted Ashtabula *Sentinel,* Aug. 15, 1860, XXIX, 1–2.

60–39. "The pilot's story," *Atlantic,* Sept., 1860, VI, 323–325.

Reprinted Ashtabula *Sentinel,* Aug. 29, 1860, XXIX, 1, with note that Howells derived idea from an 1858 series of letters from Mississippi published in Ashtabula *Sentinel.* Reprinted 73–B.

60–40. "Misanthropy," *Dial,* Sept., 1860, I, 555.

Poem. Signed W. D. H.

60–E. [Poems and notices,] *The poets and poetry of the West,* Sept. 1.

60–41. "The poets and poetry of the West," *Ohio state journal,* Sept. 1, 1860, xxiv, 2.

Unsigned: attribution on basis of identity of writer with writer of 60–22.

60–42. "Some western poets of today, — William Wallace Harney," *Ohio state journal,* Sept. 25, 1860, xxiv, 1.

Unsigned: see 58–14 and 60–41.

60–43. "Some western poets of today, Helen H. Bostwick," *Ohio state journal,* Oct. 1, 1860, xxiv, 2.

First printed 60–E.

60–44. [The moonlight is full of the fragrance,] *Dial,* Nov., 1860, i, 708 [710].

Signed W. D. H. Reprinted *Saturday press,* Nov. 10, 1860, iii, 1, and *Ohio state journal,* Nov. 14, 1860, xxiv, 4.

60–45. "Lamartine and American literature," *Ohio state journal,* Nov. 3, 1860, xxiv, 2.

Mentions Cervantes and Dante. Unsigned: for attribution see 58–14.

60–46. [Clipping from *Ohio state journal* on *Saturday press* closing,] *Saturday press,* Nov. 17, 1860, iii, 1.

Unsigned: attribution on basis of Howells' interest and dual connection. Date of first printing unknown.

1861

61–1. "Literary gossip," *Ohio state journal,* Jan. 18 (p. 2), 28, Feb. 4, 9, 11, 13, 20, 23, 1861, xxiv, p. 1 except as noted.

Unsigned: for attribution see 58–14 and 58–17.

61–2. "The old homestead," *Atlantic,* Feb., 1861, vii, 213.

Reprinted 73–B.

61–3. "Bubbles," *Atlantic,* April, 1861, vii, 415.

Reprinted 73–B.

61–4. "From Ohio (from our own correspondent), Columbus, April 16," New York *World,* April 22, 1861, i, 3.

Ohio's reaction to the war; D. L. Wood; cadet corps. For attribution see 61–6.

61–5. "War movements in Ohio (from our own correspondent), Columbus, May 11," New York *World,* May 15, 1861, i, 6.

John Brown, jr., Donn Piatt; camps Taylor, Jackson, Dennison, and Harrison. Compare 59–27. For attribution see 61–6.

61–6. "From Ohio (from our own correspondent)," New York *World,* May 21, 1861, i, 3.

War matters, "droll events"; quotes sentimental ballad. Attribution made through letter from E. C. Stedman to Howells dated May 20, 1861, in Harvard Library, which states that Howells' newspaper letter "will appear tomorrow" in the New York *World.*

61–7. "From Ohio (from our own correspondent), Columbus, June 5," New York *World,* June 10, 1861, i, 8.

Carrington, Wood; Governor Dennison's war preparations defended. Military situation in Ohio and Washington. For attribution see 61–6.

61–8. "From Ohio (from our own correspondent)," New York *World,* July 17, 1861, ii, 4.

Rebel FFV prisoners from Virginia at Camp Chase; their release. Military activity in Columbus. For attribution see 61–6.

61–9. "A dream," *Knickerbocker,* Aug., 1861, lviii, 146–150.

Probably the story referred to in *Literary friends and acquaintance,* p. 79.

61–A. *Three years in Chili,* edited and rewritten.

1862

62–1. "Letter from Europe — the ocean 'transit'," *Ohio state journal,* Jan. 9, 1862, xxv, 2.

The passage, the English customs office, poetry; one of a promised series. Dateline "At Venice, December, 1861." Unsigned as series: attribution made through subject matter, place of writing, and republication in Howells' father's paper. Reprinted Ashtabula *Sentinel,* Jan. 22, 1862, xxxi, 1.

62–2. "Letter from Europe — three days in England," *Ohio state journal,* Jan. 30, 1862, xxv, 1.

Liverpool and Dickens. Reprinted Ashtabula *Sentinel,* Feb. 5, 1862, xxxi, 1.

62–3. "Letter from Europe, still in London — the Golden Cross — visit to Westminster Abbey — the 'Poets' corner'," *Ohio state journal,* Jan. 31, 1862, xxv, 1.

Dateline, Venice, Dec. 23, 1861. Reprinted Ashtabula *Sentinel,* Feb. 12, 1862, xxxi, 1.

62–4. "Letter from Europe," Ashtabula *Sentinel,* May 14, 1862, xxxi, 1.

"Extracted from a private letter from Venice dated April 13, 1862." Trieste and Venice. See *Life in letters,* i, 47.

62–5. "From Europe," Ashtabula *Sentinel,* July 30, 1862, xxxi, 1.

"Extracted from a letter dated Venice, June 29th, 1862." The Lido and Malamocco. See 62–4.

62–6. "Louis Lebeau's conversion," *Atlantic,* Nov., 1862, x, 534–538.

Reprinted 73–B.

1863

63–1. "A poet," *Commonwealth,* Feb. 14, 1863, i, 1.

First printed 60–24. Reprinted 73–B.

63–2. "Letters from Venice," Boston *Advertiser,* March 27, 1863, ci, 2.

Dateline, Venice, March 2. Domenico Turrazza, the Instituto, Miani discovery, Duc de Levis obituary. Signed W. D. H.

63–3. "The bag of gold," Ashtabula *Sentinel,* April 22, 1863, xxxii, 1.

Short story. Unsigned: attribution on basis of Italian setting and Venetian references.

63–4. "For the Commonwealth, By the sea," *Commonwealth,* May 1, 1863, i, 1.

Dateline, Venice, March 24. Reprinted Boston *Advertiser,* May 6, 1863, ci, 1. Reprinted 73–B.

63–5. "The revival of mosaic painting in Venice," Boston *Advertiser,* May 2, 1863, ci, 2.

Dateline, April 5. Unsigned. Reprinted Ashtabula *Sentinel,* May 13, 1863, xxxii, 1.

63–6. "From Venice to Florence and back again," Boston *Advertiser,* May 25, 1863, ci, 2.

Dateline, May 3. Reprinted Ashtabula *Sentinel,* June 3, 1863, xxxii, 1. One paragraph and phrases reprinted 67–B.

63–7. "Letters from Venice. — iv," Boston *Advertiser,* June 29, 1863, cii, 3.

Dateline, June 4. Reprinted Ashtabula *Sentinel,* July 8, 1863, xxxii, 1. Reprinted 66–A.

63–8. "Letters from Venice," Boston *Advertiser,* July 28, 1863, cii, 2.

Dateline, July 6. Holiday celebration, poem reported, more on Miani. Unsigned.

63–9. "Letters from Venice. — vi," Boston *Advertiser,* Sept. 11, 1863, cii, 2.

Dateline, Aug. 19. An anniversary, an exhibition, Beecher. In part reprinted 66–A.

63–10. "Letters from Venice. — vii," Boston *Advertiser,* Sept. 29, 1863, cii, 2.

Dateline, Sept. 9. Reprinted Ashtabula *Sentinel,* Oct. 13, 1863, xxxii, 1. With revisions reprinted 66–A.

63–11. "For the Commonwealth, The fair prisoner to the swallow, from the Italian of Tommasso Grossi, translated by W. D. Howells," *Commonwealth,* Oct. 9, 1863, ii, 1.

Reprinted 67–7 and 87–C.

63–12. "Letters from Venice. — vɪɪɪ," Boston *Advertiser,* Nov. 21, 1863, cɪɪ, 2.

Dateline, Oct. 24. On painter Coake. In part reprinted 66–A.

63–13. "Letters from Venice. — ɪx," Boston *Advertiser,* Nov. 26, 1863, cɪɪ, 2.

Dateline, Nov. In part reprinted Ashtabula *Sentinel,* Dec. 23, 1863, xxxɪɪ, 7. All reprinted 66–A.

63–14. "Saint Christopher," *Harper's monthly,* Dec., 1863, xxvɪɪɪ, 1–2.

Reprinted 73–B.

63–15. "Letters from Venice. — x," Boston *Advertiser,* Dec. 8, 1863, cɪɪ, 2.

Except paragraph reprinted 66–A.

63–A. [Report,] *Commercial relations of the United States with foreign countries.*

63–B. [Zeni-Foratti pamphlet.]

63–C. [Translation of a guidebook.]

1864

64–1. "Letters from Venice. — xɪ," Boston *Advertiser,* Jan. 18, 1864, cɪɪɪ, 2.

Dateline, Dec. 23, 1863. Reprinted 66–A.

64–2. "For the Commonwealth, Some Italian epigrams, translated by W. D. Howells," *Commonwealth,* Jan. 22, 1864, ɪɪ, 1.

Epigrams by Giuseppe Capparoggo and Clementino Vannetti.

64–3. "Letters from Venice. — xɪɪɪ," Boston *Advertiser,* Feb. 4, 1864, cɪɪɪ, 2.

Reprinted 66–A.

64–4. "Letters from Venice. — xɪɪ," Boston *Advertiser,* Feb. 6, 1864, cɪɪɪ, 2.

Dateline, Jan. 2. Renan's *Life of Jesus* noted. In large part reprinted 66–A.

64–5. "Letters from Venice. — xvɪ," Boston *Advertiser,* Feb. 27, 1864, cɪɪɪ, 2.

With revisions reprinted 66–A.

64–6. "Letters from Venice. — xɪv," Boston *Advertiser,* March 5, 1864, cɪɪɪ, 2.

Dateline, Feb. 6. Reprinted 66–A.

64–7. "Letters from Venice. — xv," Boston *Advertiser,* March 12, 1864, cɪɪɪ, 2.

Dateline, Feb. 12. On singer Frezzolini and painter Miner Kellogg. In part reprinted 66–A.

64–8. "Letters from Venice. — xvɪɪ," Boston *Advertiser,* March 19, 1864, cɪɪɪ, 2.

Except paragraph reprinted 66–A.

64–9. "Letters from Venice. — xvɪɪ [xvɪɪɪ]," Boston *Advertiser,* March 26, 1864, cɪɪɪ, 2.

Dateline, Feb. 26. Reprinted 66–A.

64–10. "For the Commonwealth, A springtime," *Commonwealth,* April 1, 1864, ɪɪ, 1.

Dateline: "Columbus, O., June, 1861." Reprinted 73–B.

64–11. "Letters from Venice. — xɪx," Boston *Advertiser,* April 7, 1864, cɪɪɪ, 2.

Dateline, March 11. Reprinted Ashtabula *Sentinel,* April 27, 1864, xxxɪɪɪ, 2. Reprinted 66–A.

64–12. "Letters from Venice. — xx," Boston *Advertiser,* April 22, 1864, cɪɪɪ, 2.

Dateline, March 25. Reprinted Ashtabula *Sentinel,* May 4, 1864, xxxɪɪɪ, 5. Reprinted 66–A.

64–13. "Letters from Venice. — xxɪ," Boston *Advertiser,* May 7, 1864, cɪɪɪ, 2.

Dateline, April 4. Reprinted Ashtabula *Sentinel,* May 18, 1864, xxxɪɪɪ, 2. Except two paragraphs reprinted 66–A.

64–14. "Letters from Venice. — xxii," Boston *Advertiser*, June 16, 1864, ciii, 2.

Dateline, May 14. Nobles, women, Goethe. Reprinted Ashtabula *Sentinel*, June 29, 1864, xxxiii, 1. In part reprinted 66–A.

64–15. "John Butler Howells," Ashtabula *Sentinel*, June 29, 1864, xxxiii, 1.

Reprinted 73–B.

64–16. "Letters from Venice. — xxiii," Boston *Advertiser*, June 25, 1864, ciii, 2.

Dateline, May 28. Reprinted Ashtabula *Sentinel*, July 6, 1864, xxxiii, 2. In part reprinted 66–A.

64–17. "Letters from Venice.–xxiv," Boston *Advertiser*, July 2, 1864, civ, 2.

Dateline, June 4. Reprinted Ashtabula *Sentinel*, July 13, 1864, xxxiii, 1. Reprinted 66–A.

64–18. "Letters from Venice. — xiv [xxv]," Boston *Advertiser*, July 9, 16, 23, 1864, civ, p. 2.

Dateline, June 11. Reprinted Ashtabula *Sentinel*, July 20, 27, Aug. 3, 1864, xxxiii, p. 1. Reprinted 66–A.

64–19. "Recent Italian comedy," *North American review*, Oct., 1864, xcix, 304–401.

Reviews of *Opere drammatiche* di Paolo Ferrari, *Teatro salto* di Paolo Giacometti, *Le commedie* del Teobaldo Ceceni, *Florilegio drammatico*, F. Dall' Ongaro's *Intorno alla natura e all' ufficio dell' arte drammatica*. Unsigned as all early *North American review* items: attribution through *North American review* index.

64–20. "Venetia," Ashtabula *Sentinel*, Oct. 26, 1864, xxxiii, 5.

Private letter, dated Sept. 22.

64–21. "The two wives," Boston *Advertiser*, Nov. 12, 1864, civ, 2.

Dateline, Venice, Oct. 13. Reprinted 73–B.

64–22. "Rhyme of the New Year," Ashtabula *Sentinel*, Dec. 28, 1864, xxxiii, 1.

Poem.

64–A. The battle in the clouds, song and chorus inscribed to the Army of the Cumberland.

1865

65–1. "The road to Rome and home again," Boston *Advertiser*, March 4, April 13, May 3, 1865, cv, 2, 1, 2.

In part reprinted Ashtabula *Sentinel*, May 3, 17, 1865, xxxiv, p. 1. Reprinted 67–B.

65–2. "Italian brigandage," *North American review*, July, 1865, ci, 162–189.

Reviews of David Hilton's *Brigandage in south Italy;* A. D. di Saint Jorioz's *Il brigantaggio alla frontiera pontificia dal 1860 al 1863;* Marco Monnier's *Notizie storiche documentate sul brigantaggio nelle provincie Napoletane.*

65–3. "Spanish-Italian amity," New York *Times*, Sept. 23, 1865, xv, 4.

Editorial. Unsigned as with all New York *Times* items in 1865: attribution for this and others through *Literary friends and acquaintance*, p. 105: "I wrote editorials on European and literary topics for different papers, but mostly for the *Times...*"

65–4. "Esthetic reporting — the French propagandists," New York *Times*, Sept. 28, 1865, xv, 4.

Dramatic, literary reporting of the guillotining of one Picot in Marseilles. Attribution made by comparison with crime interests in *Nation* articles.

65–5. "Proposed purchase of Venetia," New York *Times*, Sept. 29, 1865, xv, 4.

Sentiment pro and con in Italy.

65–6. "Dante as philosopher, patriot, and poet," *Round table*, Sept. 30, 1865, n. s. no. 4, 51–52.

Review of Vincenzo Botta's *Dante*. Signed W. D. H.; *Life in letters*, i, 98, indicates this as the first article in *Round table*.

65–7. "A day in Pompeii," *Nation*, Oct. 5, 1865, i, 430–432.

Reprinted 67–B.

65–8. "Consolation," *Saturday press,* Oct. 17, 1865, p. 157.

Poem. Signed W. D. H.: attribution made by F. C. Marston, jr., through Lowell's letter to Howells of the same date.

65–9. "The discomforts of New-York and their remedies," New York *Times,* Oct. 18, 1865, xv, 4.

Attribution made through phrase "often noticed by American travellers returning to this country," and treatment of subject matter.

65–10. "A visit to the Cimbri," *Nation,* Oct. 19, 1865, I, 495–497.

Reprinted 67–B.

65–11. "Marriage among the Italian priesthood," New York *Times,* Oct. 19, 1865, xv, 4.

Sentiment and tendency towards it in Italy. Attribution made because of the definitely Howellsian subject and manner.

65–12. "Two men," *Nation,* Oct. 26, 1865, I, 537–538.

Review of Elizabeth Stoddard's novel. Unsigned: attribution made by E. H. O'Neill through *Nation* office.

65–13. "Doses for children," *Round table,* Oct. 28, 1865, n. s. no. 8, 116.

Review of A. J. Davis' *The children's progressive lyceum, a manual.* Signed W. D. H.

65–14. "Our consuls in China and elsewhere," *Nation,* Nov. 2, 1865, I, 551–552.

Chinese incident gives rise to remarks on salary and personnel. Unsigned: attribution made by E. H. O'Neill through *Nation* office.

65–15. "The drama, the new play at Wallack's," *Nation,* Nov. 2, 1865, I, 570–571.

Review of H. T. Craven's *The needful.* Unsigned: attribution made through *Life in letters,* I, 102.

65–16. "Drum taps," *Round table,* Nov. 11, 1865, n. s. no. 10, 147–148.

Review of Walt Whitman's book. Signed W. D. H.

65–17. "Letter from New York. The late George Arnold — Bohemianism — the Saturday Press — the Round Table and the Nation — literary — personal, &c.," Cincinnati *Gazette,* Nov. 20, 1865, LXXVII, 1.

Dateline, New York, Nov. 15. The first letter in a series from Nov. 20, 1865 to Feb. 20, 1866. Signed, "Wondering, therefore, if any old reader of the Gazette remembers me, I am yours, Chispa."

65–18. "Concerning Timothy Titcomb," *Nation,* Nov. 23, 1865, I, 659.

Review of J. G. Holland's *Plain talks on familiar subjects.* Unsigned: attributed through marked copy in *Nation* office.

65–19. "Letter from New York. Art matters — General Grant's reception — the World's Fair at Paris, &c.," Cincinnati *Gazette,* Nov. 25, 1865, LXXVII, 1.

Dateline, New York, Nov. 22. Discusses Quincy Ward as a sculptor. Signed Chispa.

65–20. "Minor topics," *Nation,* Nov. 30, 1865, I, 677.

Concealed weapons. Unsigned as with all items in this department: attribution is made on the basis of *Literary friends and acquaintance,* p. 106: "I amused myself very much with the treatment of social phases and events in a department which grew up under my hand." "Minor topics" runs from Nov. 30, 1865 to April 26, 1866. Further evidence that it is written by Howells is the use of a poem (*Nation,* Dec. 7, 1865, I, 708–709) which appears in the 1873 *Poems.* Upon another occasion the author refers to an article on Pompeii as his own (*Nation,* Jan. 11, 1866, II, 37, referring to Oct. 5, 1865, I, 430–432), which appears later in *Italian journeys.* That up until the very end Howells continued to conduct the department is indicated by his referring upon another occasion back to an earlier "Minor topics" which is indubitably his own (*Nation,* April 26, 1866, II, 517, referring to Dec. 7, 1865, I, 708–709). A possible source of further Howells items in the *Nation* is the Wendell Phillips Garrison diary, which LeRoy Phillips in A *bibliography of the writings of Henry James* (New York, 1930), p. viii–ix, implies covers other authorship than that of James.

65–21. "A pilgrimage to Petrarch's house at Arquà," *Nation,* Nov. 30, 1865, I, 685–688.
Reprinted 67–B.

65–22. "The royal portraits," *Harper's monthly,* Dec., 1865, XXXII, 43.
Reprinted 73–B.

65–23. "Letter from New York. Crime in New York — the Otero murder — the Strong scandal — art matters — city politics," Cincinnati *Gazette,* Dec. 2, 1865, LXXVII, 1.
Dateline, New York, Nov. 29. Signed Chispa.

65–24. "Our mutual friend," *Round table,* Dec. 2, 1865, n. s. no. 13, 200–201.
Review of Dickens' novel. Signed W. D. H.

65–25. "Minor topics," *Nation,* Dec. 7, 1865, I, 708–709.
Thanksgiving; the Otero murder case. "Thanksgiving" is reprinted 73–B.

65–26. "Minor topics," *Nation,* Dec. 14, 1865, I, 740–741.
Benjamin Rhett's opinions on labor contracts; New Jersey Central accident.

65–27. "Letter from New York. The election for mayor — metropolitan accidents — street cars in New York — the Fenians of Seventeenth Street and their troubles — Thanksgiving — Stoddard's 'Melodies and madrigals'," Cincinnati *Gazette,* Dec. 18, 1865, LXXVII, 1.
Dateline, New York, Dec. 13. Signed Chispa. Reprinted Ashtabula *Sentinel,* Dec. 27, 1865, XXXIV, 1.

65–28. "Minor topics," *Nation,* Dec. 21, 1865, I, 772–773.
Christmas and the troubles of the Fenian brotherhood.

65–29. "One branch of native industry that needs protection," *Nation,* Dec. 21, 1865, I, 774–775.
Authors and artists. Unsigned: attribution made by E. H. O'Neill through *Nation* office.

65–30. "Letter from New York. Christmas — a new fashion — the mayoralty again — the collectorship — something about stamps — the Strongs and their divorce," Cincinnati *Gazette,* Dec. 25, 1865, LXXVII, 1.
Dateline, New York, Dec. 20. Signed Chispa. Reprinted Ashtabula *Sentinel,* Jan. 3, 1866, XXXV, 1.

65–31. "Minor topics," *Nation,* Dec. 28, 1865, I, 804–805.
The effect of proximity of subject on literature, as the Civil War; the rascality of F. T. Winkelman.

65–A. [Report,] *Commercial relations of the United States with foreign countries.*

65–B. [Report,] *Commercial relations of the United States with foreign nations.*

1866

66–1. "Ducal Mantua," *North American review,* Jan., 1866, CII, 48–100.
Reprinted 72–B.

66–2. "Letter from New York [with another letter by another correspondent]. New submarine invention — the Broadway underground railroad — reorganization of the Board of Health — a fantastic crime," Cincinnati *Gazette,* Jan. 1, 1866, LXXVII, 1.
Dateline, New York, Dec. 28. Signed Chispa.

66–3. "Minor topics," *Nation,* Jan. 4, 1866, II, 4–5.
New Year's visiting, a murder, and beer-drinking.

66–4. "A little German capital," *Nation,* Jan. 4, 1866, II, 11–13.
Travel sketch. Unsigned: see *Letters of James Russell Lowell* (New York, 1894), I, 355, for attribution.

66–5. "Letter from New York. New Year's calls and callers — the traveler's clubs — literary gossip — po-

Periodical Publications... — 1866, continued

litical gossip — Edwin Booth's appearance," Cincinnati *Gazette*, Jan. 9, 1866, LXXVII, 1.

Dateline, New York, Jan. 5. Booth in *Hamlet*. Signed Chispa.

66–6. "Minor topics," *Nation*, Jan. 11, 1866, II, 37.

Blond hair.

66–7. "Minor topics," *Nation*, Jan. 18, 1866, II, 68–69.

Colds; the Mrs. Lincoln scandal.

66–8. "Literariana — American," *Round table*, Jan. 20, 1866, III, 37.

Review of W. D. O'Connor's *Good gray poet*. Unsigned: attribution through implication that authorship is same as in 65–16.

66–9. "Fast and firm — a romance at Marseilles," Ashtabula *Sentinel*, Jan. 24, 31, 1866, XXXV, p. 1.

Unsigned: attribution on basis of manner and travel itinerary closely following *Italian journeys*.

66–10. "Minor topics," *Nation*, Jan. 25, 1866, II, 100–101.

A boy singer's visit to President Johnson; criticism of things not paid for.

66–11. "Certain things in Naples," *Nation*, Jan. 25, 1866, II, 108–110.

Reprinted 67–B.

66–12. "Letter from New York. Literary gossip — art — Paris exposition — stamps and stamped envelopes," Cincinnati *Gazette*, Jan. 27, 1866, LXXVII, 1.

Dateline, New York, Jan. 24. Signed Chispa. Reprinted Ashtabula *Sentinel*, Feb. 7, 1866, XXXV, 1.

66–13. "Literary criticism," *Round table*, Jan. 27, 1866, III, 49.

Unsigned: attribution on basis of style.

66–14. "Sweet clover," *Harper's monthly*, Feb., 1866, XXXII, 322.

Reprinted 73–B.

66–15. "Minor topics," *Nation*, Feb. 1, 1866, II, 132–133.

American progress and decadence; the bloody shirt is waved at General Delafield.

66–16. "Letter from New York. Sleighing and skating — price of life in New York — literary gossip," Cincinnati *Gazette*, Feb. 3, 1866, LXXVII, 1.

Dateline, New York, Jan. 31. Signed Chispa.

66–17. "Minor topics," *Nation*, Feb. 8, 1866, II, 164–165.

Teachers' employment agencies; a contribution on music.

66–18. "Minor topics," *Nation*, Feb. 15, 1866, II, 196–197.

Newspaper libel and A. T. Stewart; a railroad accident deplored.

66–19. "Men and manners on the way from Ferrara to Genoa," *Nation*, Feb. 15, 1866, II, 205–207.

Reprinted 67–B.

66–20. "Massimo d'Azeglio," *Nation*, Feb. 15, 1866, II, 202–204.

Obituary. Unsigned: attribution made by E. H. O'Neill through *Nation* office.

66–21. "The poetry of love," *Round table*, Feb. 17, 1866, III, 81–82.

Unsigned: attribution on basis of matter and allusions.

66–22. "Letter from New York," Cincinnati *Gazette*, Feb. 20, 1866, LXXVII, 1.

Dateline, New York, Feb. 16. A. T. Stewart's libel suits, health bill, Cole's engraving "Voyage of life," literary gossip. Signed Chispa.

66–23. "Minor topics," *Nation*, Feb. 22, 1866, II, 228–229.

Defense of negro; euphemisms.

66–24. "Minor topics," *Nation*, March 1, 1866, II, 261.

Labor; shaking hands.

66–25. "Minor topics," *Nation*, March 8, 1866, ɪɪ, 292–293.

Imitation of famous men; Proudhon and overstatement; Democrats and Johnson.

66–26. "Minor topics," *Nation*, March 15, 1866, ɪɪ, 325.

Love of human nature for titles.

66–27. "Minor topics," *Nation*, March 22, 1866, ɪɪ, 357.

Lay criticism of painting, an answer to G. H. Hall.

66–28. "Minor topics," *Nation*, March 29, 1866, ɪɪ, 388–389.

Poverty; model tenements.

66–29. "Minor topics," *Nation*, April 5, 1866, ɪɪ, 421.

Dining habits; criminal insanity.

66–30. "A half-hour at Herculaneum," *Nation*, April 5, 1866, ɪɪ, 429–430.

Reprinted 67–B.

66–31. "Minor topics," *Nation*, April 12, 1866, ɪɪ, 453.

Greeley reproved; compounding felonies.

66–32. "Minor topics," *Nation*, April 19, 1866, ɪɪ, 485.

Behavior of ex-soldiers; lurid journalism.

66–33. "Minor topics," *Nation*, April 26, 1866, ɪɪ, 517.

Sentimental justice; drunkenness in Congress.

66–34. "Question of monuments," *Atlantic monthly*, May, 1866, xvɪɪ, 646–649.

Civil War commemoration; comparison of Roman and American civilizations.

66–35. Review of J. J. Piatt's *Poems in sunshine and firelight*. *Atlantic monthly*, May, 1866, xvɪɪ, 653–655.

Unsigned and not indexed: attribution made through Howells' letter to E. C. Stedman, May 27, 1866 (ᴍs. at Columbia University Library).

66–36. "The coming translation of Dante," *Round table*, May 19, 1866, ɪɪɪ, 305–306.

Unsigned: attribution through style, allusions, and Howells' relation with Longfellow.

66–37. Review of Bayard Taylor's *The story of Kennett*. *Atlantic monthly*, June, 1866, xvɪɪ, 775–778.

66–38. "Clement," *Galaxy*, June 1, 1866, ɪ, 210–212.

Reprinted 73–B.

66–A. *Venetian life*, first English edition, June 2.

66–39. Reviews of G. P. Fisher's *Life of Benjamin Silliman; Fifteen days, an extract from Edward Colvil's journal*. *Atlantic monthly*, July, 1866, xvɪɪɪ, 126–128.

66–40. "Capri and Capriotes," *Nation*, July 5, 12, 1866, ɪɪɪ, 14–15, 33–34.

Reprinted 67–B.

66–41. Reviews of *The poems of Thomas Bailey Aldrich*; August Laugel's *The United States during the war*; Goldwin Smith's *The Civil War in America*. *Atlantic monthly*, Aug., 1866, xvɪɪɪ, 250–253.

66–42. "Forlorn," *Nation*, Aug. 16, 1866, ɪɪɪ, 134–135.

Literary friends and acquaintance, p. 85, gives a history of the poem. Reprinted 73–B.

66–B. *Venetian life*, Aug. 24.

66–43. "Roman pearls," *Nation*, Sept. 27, Nov. 29, Dec. 27, 1866, ɪɪɪ, 253–254, 433–435, 523–525.

Reprinted 67–B.

66–44. Reviews of W. J. C. Moens' *English travellers and Italian brigands*; A. O. Abbott's *Prison life in the South*. *Atlantic monthly*, Oct., 1866, xvɪɪɪ, 518–520.

Periodical Publications... — 1866, continued

66–45. "Modern Italian poets," *North American review*, Oct., 1866, CIII, 313–345.

Reviews of Paolo Emiliani-Giudici's *Storia della letteratura italiana;* Cesare Cantù's *Della letteratura italiana;* Giuseppe Arnaud's *I poeti patriottici dell' Italia; I contemporanei italiani;* Marc-Monnier's *L'Italie est-elle la terre des morts?;* F. P. Cobbe's *Italics.* See 67–7. In part reprinted 87–C.

66–46. "Busily engaged, a plot for a farce," Ashtabula *Sentinel,* Oct. 3, 10, 1866, xxxv, p. 1.

Unsigned: attribution on the basis of completely Howellsian manner.

66–47. "Why he married," Ashtabula *Sentinel,* Oct. 31, 1866, xxxv, 1.

Story. Unsigned: attribution on the basis of completely Howellsian manner.

66–48. Reviews of Charles Reade's *Griffith Gaunt, or, Jealousy;* Barry Cornwall's *Charles Lamb, a memoir. Atlantic monthly,* Dec., 1866, XVIII, 767–769, 771–772.

Unsigned and second review un-indexed: attribution made through Howells' letter to J. T. Fields, Oct. 22, 1866 (MS. at Huntington Library).

66–C. [Report,] *Commercial relations of the United States with foreign nations.*

1867

67–A. *Venetian life,* second edition, circa Jan. 1.

67–1. Reviews of J. R. Lowell's *The Biglow papers, second series; Harvard memorials,* ed. T. W. Higginson; Bayard Taylor's *The picture of St. John;* J. H. Ward's *The life and letters of James Gates Percival. Atlantic monthly,* Jan., 1867, XIX, 123–127, 127–128.

67–2. "Forza Maggiore," *Atlantic monthly,* Feb., 1867, XIX, 220–227.

Reprinted 67–B.

67–3. Reviews of Herman Melville's *Battle-pieces and aspects of the war;* H. C. Lea's *Superstition and force. Atlantic monthly,* Feb., 1867, XIX, 252–254.

67–4. "A glimpse of Genoa," *Atlantic monthly,* March, 1867, XIX, 359–363.

Reprinted 67–B.

67–5. Review of W. P. Fetridge's *Harper's hand-book for travellers in Europe and the East, fifth year. Atlantic monthly,* March, 1867, XIX, 380–383.

67–6. Reviews of *The book of the sonnet,* eds., Leigh Hunt and S. A. Lee; I. I. Hayes' *The open polar sea. Atlantic monthly,* April, 1867, XIX, 510–512.

67–7. "Modern Italian poets," *North American review,* April, 1867, CIV, 317–354.

Alessandro Manzoni, Tomasso Grossi, Silvio Pellico, Luigi Carrer, Aleardo Aleardi, Giulio Carcano; reference to books in 66–45 *North American review* review. In large part reprinted 87–C.

67–8. "Henry Wadsworth Longfellow," *North American review,* April, 1867, CIV, 531–540.

Review of the 1866 collected works.

67–9. Reviews of James Parton's *Famous Americans of recent times;* Charles Gayarré's *Philip II. of Spain,* introduction by George Bancroft; C. C. Felton's *Greece, ancient and modern. Atlantic monthly,* May, 1867, XIX, 636–640.

67–10. "Mr. Longfellow's translation of the Divine Comedy," *Nation,* June 20, 1867, IV, 492–494.

Unsigned: attributed through marked copy in *Nation* office; cf. *Life in letters,* I, 117, and 66–36.

67–11. "At Padua," *Atlantic monthly*, July, 1867, xx, 25–32.

Reprinted 67–B.

67–12. Reviews of J. W. De Forrest's [*sic*] *Miss Ravenel's conversion from secession to loyalty;* W. I. Paulding's *The literary life of James K. Paulding*. *Atlantic monthly*, July, 1867, xx, 120–122, 124–125.

67–13. Reviews of A. O. Morse's *A vindication of the claim of Alexander M. W. Ball...to the authorship of the poem "Rock me to sleep, mother;"* Thomas Purnell's *Literature and its professors*. *Atlantic monthly*, Aug., 1867, xx, 252–255.

67–14. "Minor Italian travels," *Atlantic monthly*, Sept., 1867, xx, 337–348.

Reprinted 67–B.

67–15. Reviews of R. W. Emerson's *May-day and other pieces;* Jean Ingelow's *A story of doom, and other poems*. *Atlantic monthly*, Sept., 1867, xx, 376–378, 383–384.

67–16. Review of *The New Life of Dante Alighieri*, trans., C. E. Norton. *Atlantic monthly*, Nov., 1867, xx, 638–639.

Longfellow's translation compared.

67–17. Reviews of *The first canticle of the Divine Comedy of Dante Alighieri*, trans., T. W. Parsons; J. G. Holland's *Kathrina, her life and mine, in a poem*. *Atlantic monthly*, Dec., 1867, xx, 759–761, 762–764.

67–B. Italian journeys, Dec. 8.

1868

68–1. "Mrs. Johnson," *Atlantic monthly*, Jan., 1868, xxi, 97–106.

Reprinted 71–A.

68–2. Reviews of Francesco dall'Ongaro's *Stornelli italiani; Fantasie drammatiche e liriche;* and *Poesie*. *North American review*, Jan., 1868, cvi, 26–42.

In large part reprinted 87–C.

68–3. Reviews of Whitelaw Reid's *Ohio in the war;* F. Hassaurek's *Four years among Spanish Americans*. *Atlantic monthly*, Feb., 1868, xxi, 252–255.

68–4. Review of Mr. and Mrs. Louis Agassiz's *A journey in Brazil*. *Atlantic monthly*, March, 1868, xxi, 383–384.

68–5. Reviews of G. W. Greene's *The life of Nathanael Greene*, vol. i; *Life and letters of Wilder Dwight*. *Atlantic monthly*, April, 1868, xxi, 506–508, 509–510.

68–6. "Letters from eminent persons," *Prang's chromo*, April, 1868, i, 6.

To L. Prang & Co., dated Jan. 1, 1867; congratulates accomplishments and applauds purposes. This letter appeared earlier in newspapers.

68–7. "The next president," *Atlantic monthly*, May, 1868, xxi, 628–632.

Grant and the Republican party.

68–8. Reviews of J. L. Motley's *History of the United Netherlands*, vols. iii, iv; John Ruskin's *Time and tide, by Weare and Tyne, twenty-five letters to a workingman*. *Atlantic monthly*, May, 1868, xxi, 632–638, 639–640.

68–9. Review of H. W. Beecher's *Norwood, or Village life in New England*. *Atlantic monthly*, June, 1868, xxi, 761–764.

68–10. "Tonelli's marriage," *Atlantic monthly*, July, 1868, xxii, 96–110.

Reprinted 81–A.

Periodical Publications . . . — 1868, continued

68–11. Reviews of John Durand's *Italy, Rome, and Naples, from the French of Henri Taine; Autobiography of Benjamin Franklin*, ed., John Bigelow; H. W. Bellows' *The old world in its new face. Atlantic monthly*, July, 1868, xxii, 124–127, 127–128.

68–12. "George William Curtis," *North American review*, July, 1868, cvii, 104–117.

Reviews of *Nile notes of a Howadji; The Howadji in Syria; Lotus-eating, a summer-book; The Potiphar papers; Prue and I;* and *Trumps, a novel.*

68–13. Review of Charles Reade's and Dion Boucicault's *Foul play. Atlantic monthly*, Aug., 1868, xxii, 254–255.

68–14. Reviews of *Life in the Argentine Republic*, from the Spanish of Domingo F. Sarmiento, with a biographical sketch of the author, by Mrs. Mary Mann; George Eliot's *The Spanish gypsy, a poem. Atlantic monthly*, Sept., 1868, xxii, 374–377, 380–384.

68–15. Reviews of D. G. Brinton's *The myths of the new world;* C. G. Leland's *Hans Breitmann's party, with other ballads. Atlantic monthly*, Oct., 1868, xxii, 509–512.

68–16. Reviews of E. E. Hale's *If, yes, and perhaps;* John Bartlett's *Familiar quotations*, fifth edition; A. D. Richardson's *A personal history of Ulysses S. Grant; Modern women and what is said of them*, ed., Mrs. L. G. Calhoun. *Atlantic monthly*, Nov., 1868, xxii, 634–635, 638–640.

68–17. "No love lost, a romance of travel," *Putnam's*, Dec., 1868, n. s. ii, 641–651.

Reprinted 69–A.

1869

69–A. *No love lost, a romance of travel*, by Nov. 12, 1868.

69 – 1. "Gnadenhütten," *Atlantic monthly*, Jan., 1869, xxiii, 95–115.

Reprinted 84–C.

69–2. Reviews of Frances Bunsen's *A memoir of Baron Bunsen;* H. W. Longfellow's *The New England tragedies;* A. E. Dickinson's *What answer?; The civil service*, report of Mr. Jenckes, of Rhode Island. *Atlantic monthly*, Jan., 1869, xxiii, 129–132, 132–136.

69–3. Review of Paolo Fambri's *The free press and duelling in Italy. North American review*, Jan., 1869, cviii, 299–302.

69–4. Reviews of Horace Greeley's *Recollections of a busy life;* J. R. Lowell's *Under the willows and other poems. Atlantic monthly*, Feb., 1869, xxiii, 260–264.

69–5. Reviews of *Historical account of Bouquet's expedition*, ed., Francis Parkman; N. H. Bishop's *The Pampas and Andes. Atlantic monthly*, March, 1869, xxiii, 389–392.

69–6. "Doorstep acquaintance," *Atlantic monthly*, April, 1869, xxiii, 484–493.

Reprinted 71–A.

69–7. Reviews of Raphael Semmes' *Memoirs of service afloat during the War between the States; The letters of Lady Mary Wortley Montagu* and *The letters of Madame Sévigné to her daughter and friends,* ed., Mrs. S. J. Hale; J. L. Motley's *Historic progress and American democracy. Atlantic monthly,* April, 1869, XXIII, 515–520.

69–8. "The new taste in theatricals," *Atlantic monthly,* May, 1869, XXIII, 635–644.
Reprinted 72–E.

69–9. Reviews of W. H. Dixon's *Her majesty's tower;* E. C. Stedman's *The blameless prince and other poems. Atlantic monthly,* May, 1869, XXIII, 645–648.

69–10. Reviews of Berthold Auerbach's *Edelweiss,* trans., Ellen Frothingham; Bayard Taylor's *By-ways of Europe;* Victor Rydberg's *The last Athenian,* trans., Widgery Thomas, Jr.; W. H. Murray's *Adventures in the wilderness. Atlantic monthly,* June, 1869, XXIII, 762–765, 767–768, 770.

69–11. Reviews of L. A. Gobright's *Recollections of men and things at Washington during the third of a century;* E. E. Hale's *The Ingham papers. Atlantic monthly,* July, 1869, XXIV, 125–128.

69–12. "Before the gate," *Atlantic monthly,* Aug., 1869, XXIV, 176.
Reprinted 73–B.

69–13. "Jubilee days," *Atlantic monthly,* Aug., 1869, XXIV, 245–254.
Reprinted 71–A.

69–14. "Recent travels," *Atlantic monthly,* Aug., 1869, XXIV, 254–260.
Reviews of travel books by A. R. Wallace, C. C. Coffin, A. K. McClure, C. L. Brace, R. H. Dana, Jr.

69–15. "The first cricket," *Atlantic monthly,* Sept., 1869, XXIV, 351.
Reprinted 73–B.

69–16. "A poetical lot," *Atlantic monthly,* Sept., 1869, XXIV, 382–388.
Reviews of *Poetry of the Pacific,* ed., Mary Wentworth; Henry Abbey's *Stories in verse;* Nicholas Michell's *Sybil of Cornwall; Colour, or, The island of humanity;* [J. McD. Leavitt's] *The seige of Babylon;* G. H. Calvert's *Ellen, a poem;* George Eliot's *How Lisa loved the king;* C. G. Leland's *Hans Breitmann's ballads.*

69–17. "A pedestrian tour," *Atlantic monthly,* Nov., 1869, XXIV, 591–603.
Reprinted 71–A.

69–18. Reviews of W. E. H. Lecky's *History of European morals, from Augustus to Charlemagne; Col. George Rogers Clark's sketch of his campaign in the Illinois in 1778–9,* ed., Henry Pirtle; T. W. Higginson's *Army life in a black regiment. Atlantic monthly,* Nov., 1869, XXIV, 639–644.

69–B. "Bopeep, a pastoral," *The Atlantic almanac 1870,* by Dec.

69–19. Reviews of Henry James' *The secret of Swedenborg;* W. H. Dixon's *Her majesty's tower,* second series; H. . Scudder's *Stories from my attic;* J. G. Whittier's *Ballads of New England. Atlantic monthly,* Dec., 1869, XXIV, 762–768.
Review of Clements' [sic] *Innocents abroad* reprinted 10–C.

1870

70–1. "By horse-car to Boston," *Atlantic monthly,* Jan., 1870, XXV, 114–122.
With revisions reprinted 71–A.

70–2. Reviews of Francis Parkman's *The discovery of the great West;* T. B. Aldrich's *The story of a bad boy. Atlantic monthly,* Jan., 1870, XXV, 122–125.

70–3. Reviews of W. M. Thackeray's *Miscellanies;* Ikey Solomons, Esq., Jr.'s [Thackeray's] *Catherine, a story;* Alfred Tennyson's *The Holy Grail, and other poems. Atlantic monthly,* Feb., 1870, xxv, 246–248, 249–250.

70–4. "A romance of real life," *Atlantic monthly,* March, 1870, xxv, 305–312.
Reprinted 71–A.

70–5. Reviews of Björnstjerne Björnson's *Arne; The happy boy; The fisher-maiden. Atlantic monthly,* April, 1870, xxv, 504–512.

70–6. Reviews of Bret Harte's *The luck of Roaring Camp;* Leigh Hunt's *A day by the fire. Atlantic monthly,* May, 1870, xxv, 633–635, 639–640.

70–7. Reviews of J. R. Lowell's *Among my books; Goethe's Hermann and Dorothea,* trans., Ellen Frothingham. *Atlantic monthly,* June, 1870, xxv, 757–758, 761–762.

70–8. "A day's pleasure," *Atlantic monthly,* July – Sept., 1870, xxvi.
Reprinted 71–A.

70–9. Reviews of D. G. Rossetti's *Poems; The Bazar book of decorum. Atlantic monthly,* July, 1870, xxvi, 115–118, 122–123.

70–10. Reviews of W. H. Dall's *Alaska and its resources;* S. A. Allibone's *A critical dictionary of English literature,* vol. ii. *Atlantic monthly,* Aug., 1870, xxvi, 245–249, 255–256.

70–11. Reviews of [Mary Allan-Olney's] *The private life of Galileo;* H. C. Andersen's *In Spain and a visit to Portugal* and *O. T., a Danish*

romance. Atlantic monthly, Sept., 1870, xxvi, 375–379, 383–384.

70–12. Reviews of W. M. Baker's *The new Timothy;* W. M. Darlington's *An account of...the life and travels of Colonel James Smith;* Daniel Drake's *Pioneer life in Kentucky. Atlantic monthly,* Oct., 1870, xxvi, 504–509.

70–13. Reviews of H. C. Andersen's *Only a fiddler;* M. Goldschmidt's *The flying mail;* Magdalen Thoreson's *Old Olaf;* Björnstjerne Björnson's *The railroad and the churchyard,* trans., Carl Larsen. *Atlantic monthly,* Nov., 1870, xxvi, 632–634, 637–638.

70–14. "Flitting," *Atlantic monthly,* Dec., 1870, xxvi, 734–739.
Reprinted 71–A.

70–15. Reviews of Edmund De Schweinitz's *The life and times of David Zeisberger;* Ralph Keeler's *Vagabond adventures. Atlantic monthly,* Dec., 1870, xxvi, 755–757, 759–760.

1871

71–A. Suburban sketches, Dec. 19, 1870.

71–1. "A year in a Venetian palace," *Atlantic monthly,* Jan., 1871, xxvii, 1–14.
Reprinted 72–C.

71–2. Reviews of J. G. Whittier's *Miriam and other poems;* H. W. Longfellow's *The poets and poetry of Europe;* Sylvester Judd's *Margaret, a tale of the real and ideal, of blight and bloom. Atlantic monthly,* Jan., 1871, xxvii, 137–138, 142–143, 144.

71–3. "Scene," *Every Saturday,* Jan. 7, 1871, x, 11.
First printed 71–A.

71–4. Reviews of Goethe's *Faust,* trans., Bayard Taylor; G. Z. Gray's *The Children's Crusade;* seven illustrated books. *Atlantic monthly,* Feb., 1871, xxvii, 258–260, 261–262, 269–271.

71–5. "The mulberries," *Atlantic monthly,* March, 1871, xxvii, 377–379.

Reprinted 73–B.

71–6. Reviews of Bret Harte's *Poems;* R. G. White's *Words and their uses, past and present; Frederick S. Cozzens' Works,* 3 vols.; Hippolyte Taine's *Art in the Netherlands,* trans., J. Durand; C. D. Warner's *My summer in a garden. Atlantic monthly,* March, 1871, xxvii, 392–397.

71–7. Review of Francis Parkman's *The conspiracy of Pontiac. Atlantic monthly,* April, 1871, xxvii, 522–523.

71–8. "Some traits of a good, brisk day," *Balloon post,* April 12, 1871, no. 2, 3.

71–9. Reviews of O. W. Holmes' *Mechanism in thought and morals; Regimen sanitatis Salernitanum,* trans., John Ordronaux. *Atlantic monthly,* May, 1871, xxvii, 653–654, 655–656.

71–10. Reviews of J. R. Lowell's *My study windows;* G. W. Greene's *The life of Nathanael Greene,* vol. ii. *Atlantic monthly,* June, 1871, xxvii, 778–780.

71–11. "Their wedding journey," *Atlantic monthly,* July – Dec., 1871, xxviii.

Reprinted 72–A.

71–12. Reviews of *William Winston Seaton, of the "National intelligen-*

cer"; Goethe's *Faust, a tragedy,* trans., Bayard Taylor, part ii; J. A. Garfield's *Oration on the life and character of General George H. Thomas;* W. H. Trescot's *Memorial of the life of J. Johnston Pettigrew, Brig. Gen. of the Confederate States Army* and *In memoriam, General Steven Elliott. Atlantic monthly,* July, 1871, xxviii, 122–126.

71–13. Reviews of *The journal of John Woolman,* introduction, J. G. Whittier; John Burroughs' *Wakerobin;* James McBride's *Pioneer biography;* John Espy's, Samuel Williams' and R. H. Taneyhill's *Miscellanies. Atlantic monthly,* Aug., 1871, xxviii, 251–252, 254, 255–256.

71–14. Reviews of Mrs. H. B. Stowe's *Pink and white tyranny;* H. C. Andersen's *The story of my life;* Charles Reade's *A terrible temptation. Atlantic monthly,* Sept., 1871, xxviii, 377–378, 379–380, 383–384.

71–15. Review of G. W. Greene's *The life of Nathanael Greene,* vol. iii. *Atlantic monthly,* Oct., 1871, xxviii, 510–512.

71–16. Reviews of John Hay's *Castilian days;* T. W. Higginson's *Atlantic essays. Atlantic monthly,* Nov., 1871, xxviii, 636–638, 639–640.

71–17. Review of Joaquin Miller's *Songs of the Sierras. Atlantic monthly,* Dec., 1871, xxviii, 770–772.

1872

72–A. Their wedding journey, Dec. 27, 1871.

72–1. "Some Arcadian shepherds," *Atlantic monthly,* Jan., 1872, xxix, 84–89.

In large part reprinted 87–C.

72–2. Reviews of Alfred Tennyson's *The last tournament;* H. W. Longfellow's *The divine tragedy;* John Forster's *The life of Charles Dickens,* vol. I; Hippolyte Taine's *History of English literature,* trans., H. Van Laun, and *Art in Greece. Atlantic monthly,* Feb., 1872, XXIX, 236–242.

72–3. Reviews of Edward Eggleston's *The Hoosier schoolmaster;* J. W. DeForest's *Kate Beaumont;* Celia Thaxter's *Poems. Atlantic monthly,* March, 1872, XXIX, 364–365, 367.

72–4. Reviews of J. T. Fields' *Yesterdays with authors;* Clarence King's *Mountaineering in the Sierra Nevada;* P. H. Hayne's *Legends and lyrics. Atlantic monthly,* April, 1872, XXIX, 498–499, 500–502.

72–5. "In earliest spring," *Atlantic monthly,* May, 1872, XXIX, 619.
Reprinted 73–B.

72–6. Review of *Passages from the French and Italian notebooks of Nathaniel Hawthorne. Atlantic monthly,* May, 1872, XXIX, 624–626.

72–B. *Italian journeys,* enlarged ed., May 18.

72–C. *Venetian life,* enlarged ed., May 18.

72–7. Review of Bayard Taylor's *The masque of the gods. Atlantic monthly,* June, 1872, XXIX, 750–751, 754–755.
Review of Mark Twain's *Roughing it* reprinted 10–C.

72–8. Reviews of Frédéric Mistral's *Mirèio, a Provençal poem,* trans., H. W. Preston; H. W. Longfellow's *Three books of song. Atlantic monthly,* July, 1872, XXX, 110–113.

72–9. "Politics," *Atlantic monthly,* July, 1872, XXX, 127–128.
Howells for neither Grant nor Greeley.

72–10. "The Florentine satirist, Giusti," *North American review,* July, 1872, CXV, 31–47.
Reprinted 87–C.

72–D. *Jubilee days,* written and ed. with T. B. Aldrich, July 4.

72–11. Reviews of Hippolyte Taine's *Notes on England,* trans., W. F. Rae; C. D. Warner's *Saunterings;* I. S. Turgeneff's *Smoke,* trans., W. F. West. *Atlantic monthly,* Aug., 1872, XXX, 240–243, 243–244.

72–12. Review of W. H. Lamon's *The life of Abraham Lincoln. Atlantic monthly,* Sept., 1872, XXX, 364–369.

72–13. Reviews of [Mrs. P. H. Gibbons'] *"Pennsylvania Dutch" and other essays;* Francis Parkman's *The Oregon trail;* H. R. Casgrain's *Francis Parkman;* Edward Whymper's *Scrambles amongst the Alps. Atlantic monthly,* Oct., 1872, XXX, 488–491, 494–495.

72–14. "Niccolini's anti-papal tragedy," *North American review,* Oct., 1872, CXV, 333–366.
Reprinted 87–C. Howells edited this number of the *North American review* in Henry Adams' absence; see *North American review,* July, 1920, CCXII, 16.

72–15. Review of J. G. Palfrey's *A compendious history of New England* [vol. III]. *Atlantic monthly,* Nov., 1872, XXX, 621–624.

72–16. "Politics," *Atlantic monthly,* Nov., 1872, XXX, 638–640.
Mr. Greeley farceur.

72–17. Reviews of O. W. Holmes' *The poet at the breakfast-table;*

Edward Eggleston's *The end of the world. Atlantic monthly*, Dec., 1872, xxx, 745–747.

72–E. *Suburban sketches*, enlarged ed.

1873

73–1. "A chance acquaintance," *Atlantic monthly*, Jan. – June, 1873, xxxi.

Reprinted 73–A.

73–2. "Among the ruins," *Atlantic monthly*, Jan., 1873, xxxi, 97–101.

Boston fire.

73–3. Reviews of C. K. Tuckerman's *The Greeks of today;* Victor Cherbuliez's *Joseph Noirel's revenge*, trans., W. F. West. *Atlantic monthly*, Jan., 1873, xxxi, 104–106.

73–4. Reviews of John Forster's *The life of Charles Dickens*, vol. ii; I. S. Turgénieff's *Liza*, trans., W. R. S. Ralston; John Fiske's *Myth and mythmakers. Atlantic monthly*, Feb., 1873, xxxi, 237–242.

73–5. Reviews of William Morris' *Love is enough;* Mary C. Ames' *A memorial of Alice and Phoebe Cary. Atlantic monthly*, March, 1873, xxxi, 359–361.

73–6. Review of C. D. Warner's *Backlog studies. Atlantic monthly*, April, 1873, xxxi, 494–496.

73–7. Review of Leigh Hunt's *The wishing-cap papers. Atlantic monthly*, May, 1873, xxxi, 624–625.

73–A. *A chance acquaintance*, May 27.

73–8. Review of J. G. Palfrey's *A compendious history of New England*, vol. iv. *Atlantic monthly*, June, 1873, xxxi, 743–746.

73–9. Reviews of John Morley's *Rousseau;* Celia Thaxter's *Among the Isles of Shoals;* Robert Browning's *Red cotton night-cap country. Atlantic monthly*, July, 1873, xxxii, 104–106, 114–115.

73–10. Reviews of *Scintillations from the prose works of Heinrich Heine*, trans., S. A. Stern; R. M. M. Houghton's *Monographs, personal and social. Atlantic monthly*, Aug., 1873, xxxii, 237–239.

73–11. Reviews of I. S. Turgénieff's *Dimitri Roudine; Old New England traits*, ed., George Lunt; H. W. Preston's *Love in the nineteenth century. Atlantic monthly*, Sept., 1873, xxxii, 369–370, 372–373, 375–376.

73–B. *Poems*, Sept. 30.

73–12. Reviews of W. H. Pater's *Studies in the history of the Renaissance;* W. C. Bryant's *Orations and addresses. Atlantic monthly*, Oct., 1873, xxxii, 496–500.

73–13. Reviews of H. W. Longfellow's *Aftermath;* T. B. Aldrich's *Marjorie Daw and other people. Atlantic monthly*, Nov., 1873, xxxii, 622–626.

73–14. Review of G. H. Boyland's *Six months under the Red Cross. Atlantic monthly*, Dec., 1873, xxxii, 748–750.

1874

74–A. *A chance acquaintance*, illustrated ed., Nov. 17, 1873.

74–1. Reviews of *The poetical works of Edmund Clarence Stedman;* J. B. O'Reilly's *Songs from the southern seas;* Joaquin Miller's *Songs of the sunlands. Atlantic monthly*, Jan., 1874, xxxiii, 103–108.

74–2. Reviews of R. D. Owen's *Threading my way;* C. W. Butterfield's *An historic account of the expedition against Sandusky;* J. L. Pike's *The prostrate state, South Carolina under Negro government; The poems of Charles Fenno Hoffman,* ed., E. F. Hoffman. *Atlantic monthly,* Feb., 1874, xxxiii, 231–235.

74–3. "Ralph   Keeler,"   *Atlantic monthly,* March, 1874, xxxiii, 366–367.
Obituary.

74–4. Reviews of *Cameos, selected from the works of Walter Savage Landor,* ed., E. C. Stedman and T. B. Aldrich; C. P. Cranch's *Satan, a libretto. Atlantic monthly,* March, 1874, xxxiii, 368–371.

74–5. Reviews of Edward Bulwer-Lytton's *The Parisians;* John Forster's *The life of Charles Dickens,* vol. iii. *Atlantic monthly,* May, 1874, xxxiii, 616–617, 621–622.

74–6. "The long days," *Atlantic monthly,* June, 1874, xxxiii, 663.
Reprinted 86–C.

74–7. Reviews of Edward Eggleston's *The circuit rider;* C. D. Warner's *Baddeck and that sort of thing. Atlantic monthly,* June, 1874, xxxiii, 745–747, 748.

74–8. "A foregone conclusion," *Atlantic monthly,* July – Dec., 1874, xxxiv.
Reprinted 75–A.

74–9. "While the oriole sings," *Atlantic monthly,* July, 1874, xxxiv, 83–84.
Reprinted 86–C.

74–10. Reviews of George Eliot's *The legend of Jubal;* Mrs. S. M. B. Piatt's *A voyage to the fortunate isles;* H. R. Hudson's *Poems;* James Parton's *Life of Thomas Jefferson. Atlantic monthly,* July, 1874, xxxiv, 102–106, 110–111.

74–11. Reviews of T. B. Aldrich's *Prudence Palfrey;* J. W. DeForest's *The Wetherel affair;* W. M. Baker's *Moses Evans. Atlantic monthly,* Aug., 1874, xxxiv, 227–230.

74–12. Review of F. H. Underwood's *Lord of himself. Atlantic monthly,* Sept., 1874, xxxiv, 362–363.

74–13. Review of Aubrey De Vere's *Alexander   the   Great.   Atlantic monthly,* Oct., 1874, xxxiv, 492–493.

74–14. "Mr. Parkman's histories," *Atlantic monthly,* Nov., 1874, xxxiv, 602–610.

74–15. Review of H. H. Boyesen's *Gunnar. Atlantic monthly,* Nov., 1874, xxxiv, 624–625.

74–16. Reviews of Bayard Taylor's *The prophet, a tragedy;* H. W. Longfellow's *The hanging of the crane;* Celia Thaxter's *Poems,* new and enlarged edition. *Atlantic monthly,* Dec., 1874, xxxiv, 743–746.

74–17. "Atlantic   dinner,"   Boston *Transcript,* Dec. 17, 1874, xlvii, 1.
Speech (quoted and paraphrased).

1875

75–A. *A foregone conclusion,* Dec. 3, 1874.

75–1. Reviews of O. W. Holmes' *Songs of many seasons;* J. G. Whittier's *Hazel-blossoms. Atlantic monthly,* Jan., 1875, xxxv, 105–107.

75–2. Reviews of Bret Harte's *Echoes of the foot-hills;* J. T. Trowbridge's *The emigrant's story, and other poems;* G. C. Eggleston's *A rebel's recollections. Atlantic monthly*, Feb., 1875, xxxv, 234–238.

75–3. Review of Henry James, Jr.'s *A passionate pilgrim. Atlantic monthly*, April, 1875, xxxv, 490–495.

75–4. "Alfieri," *Atlantic monthly*, May, 1875, xxxv, 533–549.
Reprinted 77–E.

75–5. Review of W. C. Gannett's *Ezra Stiles Gannett, Unitarian minister. Atlantic monthly*, May, 1875, xxxv, 620–621.

75–6. Reviews of C. F. Woolson's *Castle Nowhere, lake-country sketches; Baedeker's handbooks for travelers*, 9 vols. *Atlantic monthly*, June, 1875, xxxv, 736–738.

75–7. "Drama," *Atlantic monthly*, June, 1875, xxxv, 749–751.
Discussion of Mr. Raymond's Colonel Sellers in *The gilded age*. Reprinted 10–C.

75–8. "An obsolete fine gentleman," *Atlantic monthly*, July, 1875, xxxvi, 98–106.
Reprinted 87–C.

75–9. Reviews of E. S. Phelps' *Poetic studies;* G. A. Baker, Jr.'s *Point-lace and diamonds;* G. E. Waring, Jr.'s *Whip and spur. Atlantic monthly*, July, 1875, xxxvi, 108–111.

75–10. Reviews of Alfred Tennyson's *Queen Mary, a drama;* Lucy Larcom's *An idyl of work;* William Morris' *The defence of Guinevere;* J. M. Bugbee's and O. W. Holmes' *Memorial, Bunker Hill;* A. S. Richardson's *The history of our country. Atlantic monthly*, Aug., 1875, xxxvi, 240–245.

75–11. "Private theatricals," *Atlantic monthly*, Nov., 1875 – May, 1876, xxxvi–xxxvii.
Reprinted 21–B.

75–12. Reviews of *Mark Twain's sketches* and A. P. Russell's *Library notes. Atlantic monthly*, Dec., 1875, xxxvi, 749–751, 753–754.
Review of *Mark Twain's sketches* reprinted 10–C.

1876

76–A. "Dorothy Dudley," *Theatrum Majorum, The Cambridge of 1776*, Nov., 1875.

76–1. "Four new books of poetry," *Atlantic monthly*, Jan., 1876, xxxvii, 105–111.
Reviews of R. W. Gilder's *The new day;* G. P. Lathrop's *Rose and roof-tree;* Bayard Taylor's *Home pastorals, ballads and lyrics;* H. W. Longfellow's *The masque of Pandora*.

76–B. *A day's pleasure*, Feb. 18.

76–2. Review of Robert Browning's *The inn album. Atlantic monthly*, March, 1876, xxxvii, 372–374.

76–3. Review of J. R. Lowell's *Among my books, second series. Atlantic monthly*, April, 1876, xxxvii, 493–494.

76–4. Reviews of Mark Twain's *The adventures of Tom Sawyer* and [Wilkie Collins'] *The queen of hearts. Atlantic monthly*, May, 1876, xxxvii, 621–622.
Review of Mark Twain's *The adventures of Tom Sawyer* reprinted 10–C.

76–5. "A Shaker village," *Atlantic monthly*, June, 1876, xxxvii, 699–710.
Reprinted 84–C.

76–6. "A sennight of the centennial," *Atlantic monthly*, July, 1876, xxxviii, 92–107.

76–7. Review of C. D. Warner's *Mummies and Moslems. Atlantic monthly,* July, 1876, xxxviii, 108–112.

76–8. Review of *Men and manners in America one hundred years ago,* ed., H. E. Scudder. *Atlantic monthly,* Aug., 1876, xxxviii, 243.

76–9. "The parlor car, farce," *Atlantic monthly,* Sept., 1876, xxxviii, 290–300.
Reprinted 76–D.

76–C. *Sketch of the life and character of Rutherford B. Hayes,* Sept. 15.

76–D. *The parlor car, farce,* Dec. 4.

1877

77–1. "Some new books of poetry," *Atlantic monthly,* Jan., 1877, xxxix, 87–94.
Reviews of Mrs. S. M. B. Piatt's *That new world;* T. B. Aldrich's *Flower and thorn;* R. K. Weeks' *Twenty poems;* Bayard Taylor's *The echo club; The poetical works of James Russell Lowell.*

77–2. "Out of the question, comedy," *Atlantic monthly,* Feb. – April, 1877, xxxix.
Reprinted 77–A.

77–3. Review of Alfred Tennyson's *Harold, a drama. Atlantic monthly,* Feb., 1877, xxxix, 242–243.

77–4. Reviews of J. R. Lowell's *Three memorial poems; Poems of places,* ed., H. W. Longfellow; *The American architect and building news,* vol. i; *Libraire de l'art, deuxième année. Atlantic monthly,* March, 1877, xxxix, 374–378.

77–A. *Out of the question, a comedy,* April 25.

77–5. Review of Maria W. Chapman's *Harriet Martineau's autobi-* ography. *Atlantic monthly,* May, 1877, xxxix, 624–628.

77–6. Reviews of *Charles Kingsley, his letters and memories of his life;* S. O. Jewett's *Deephaven. Atlantic monthly,* June, 1877, xxxix, 752–753, 759.

77–7. "At the sign of the Savage," *Atlantic monthly,* July, 1877, xl, 36–48.
Reprinted 81–A.

77–8. Reviews of *Afterglow, no name series; L'Art, troisième année;* Albert Racinet's *Le costume historique. Atlantic monthly,* July, 1877, xl, 109–110, 112–113.

77–9. "A counterfeit presentment, comedy," *Atlantic monthly,* Aug. – Oct., 1877, xl.
Reprinted 77–B.

77–10. Reviews of Fieldat's [Eduardo Premio Real] and Aitiaiche's [Annie T. Howells] *Popular sayings from old Iberia;* G. W. Greene's *A short history of Rhode Island. Atlantic monthly,* Sept., 1877, xl, 377–379.

77–11. Review of Francis Parkman's *Count Frontenac and New France under Louis xiv. Atlantic monthly,* Oct., 1877, xl, 496–498.

77–B. *A counterfeit presentment, comedy,* Oct. 5.

77–C. [Essay], *Memoirs of Frederica Sophia Wilhelmina,* Oct. 12.

77–D. [Essay], *Lives of Lord Herbert of Cherbury and Thomas Ellwood,* Oct. 15.

77–12. "Carlo Goldoni," *Atlantic monthly,* Nov., 1877, xl, 601–613.
Reprinted 77–F.

77–13. Review of James Baker's *Turkey. Atlantic monthly,* Nov., 1877, XL, 628–630.

77–E. [Essay], *Life of Vittorio Alfieri,* Nov. 6.

77–F. [Essay], *Memoirs of Carlo Goldoni,* Nov. 13.

77–14. Reviews of Nathaniel Hawthorne's *The scarlet letter,* illustrated ed.; B. P. Avery's *Californian pictures;* C. Vosmaer's *Works of William Unger;* Albert Racinet's *Le costume historique,* vol. III; *L'Art,* vol. II (1877); C. D. Warner's *Being a boy. Atlantic monthly,* Dec., 1877, XL, 753–757, 763–764.

77–15. "The Atlantic dinner, honors to Whittier," Boston *Transcript,* Dec. 18, 1877, L, 1, 3.

Speech, with introductions for others.

77–G. [Essay], *Memoirs of Edward Gibbon, Esq.,* Dec. 20.

1878

78–1. "Edward Gibbon," *Atlantic monthly,* Jan., 1878, XLI, 99–111.

Reprinted 77–G.

78–2. Reviews of James Parton's *Caricature and other comic art;* S. G. W. Benjamin's *Contemporary art in Europe;* [J. E. Millais'] *The Millais gallery;* [Thomas Faed's] *The Faed gallery;* J. G. Whittier's *The river path;* G. C. Eggleston's *The signal boys; The wings of courage,* ed., M. E. Field; Mrs. A. M. Diaz's *The Jimmyjohns;* J. J. Piatt's *Western windows and landmarks, the lost farm;* T. B. Aldrich's *The queen of Sheba. Atlantic monthly,* Jan., 1878, XLI, 135–136, 137, 139–142.

78–3. "A French poet of the old régime," *Atlantic monthly,* March, 1878, XLI, 332–343.

Reprinted 78–A.

78–4. Review of G. E. Waring, Jr.'s *The bride of the Rhine. Atlantic monthly,* April, 1878, XLI, 550–551.

78–5. "Some recent volumes of verse," *Atlantic monthly,* May, 1878, XLI, 629–635.

Reviews of J. T. Trowbridge's *The book of gold;* L. C. Moulton's *Poems;* Mrs. S. M. B. Piatt's *Poems in company with children;* Edgar Fawcett's *Fantasy and passion.*

78–6. Review of *Works of Charles Dickens,* new illustrated library edition. *Atlantic monthly,* May, 1878, XLI, 669.

78–A. [Essay], *Memoirs of Jean François Marmontel,* May 17.

78–7. Review of F. W. Palfrey's *Memoir of William Francis Bartlett. Atlantic monthly,* June, 1878, XLI, 801–802.

78–8. Reviews of Henry James, Jr.'s *French poets and novelists;* H. W. Longfellow's *Keramos and other poems;* William Winter's *Thistledown, a book of lyrics. Atlantic monthly,* July, 1878, XLII, 118–119, 120–122.

78–9. Review of C. D. Warner's *In the wilderness. Atlantic monthly,* Sept., 1878, XLII, 377.

78–10. "The lady of the Aroostook," *Atlantic monthly,* Nov., 1878 – March, 1879, XLII–XLIII.

Reprinted 79–A.

78–11. Reviews of *The family library of British poetry,* eds., J. T. Fields and E. P. Whipple; J. G. Whittier's *The vision of Echard; Letters from*

Periodical Publications... — 1878, continued

Muskoka, by an emigrant lady. *Atlantic monthly,* Dec., 1878, XLII, 775–776, 778.

1879

79–1. Reviews of A. M. Toplady's *Rock of ages;* O. W. Holmes' *The school-boy;* W. C. Bryant's *Thanatopsis; L'Art, quatrième année,* tome III; Albert Racinet's *Le costume historique,* Part 5; H. E. Scudder's *The Bodleys on wheels; Mother Goose's melodies,* illustrations by Alfred Kappes. *Atlantic monthly,* Jan., 1879, XLIII, 119–122, 123–124.

79–A. *The lady of the Aroostook,* Feb. 27.

79–B. [Letters,] *Editorial right,* June.

79–2. "Buying a horse," *Atlantic monthly,* June, 1879, XLIII, 741–750.
Reprinted 81–D.

79–3. Reviews of John Burroughs' *Locusts and wild honey;* J. L. Motley's *The rise of the Dutch republic; Mary Wollstonecraft, Letters to Imlay,* ed., C. K. Paul; L. W. Bacon's *A life worth living, memorials of Emily Bliss Gould. Atlantic monthly,* July, 1879, XLIV, 123–125.

79–4. Reviews of W. H. Bishop's *Detmold, a romance;* Anthony Trollope's *Thackeray;* Alfred Tennyson's *The lover's tale;* Maurice Thompson's *The witchery of archery. Atlantic monthly,* Aug., 1879, XLIV, 264–265, 267–269.

1880

80–1. "The undiscovered country," *Atlantic monthly,* Jan. – July, 1880, XLV–XLVI.
Reprinted 80–A.

80–2. "Holiday books," *Atlantic monthly,* Jan., 1880, XLV, 124–128.
Reviews of F. O. C. Darley's *Compositions in outline from Hawthorne's Scarlet letter;* Charles Yriarte's *Venice;* G. E. Waring, Jr.'s *Tyrol and the skirt of the Alps;* Elaine and Dora Goodale's *In Berkshire with the wild flowers;* H. E. Scudder's *The Bodleys afoot;* J. P. Ballard's *Insect lives.*

80–3. "Dickens's letters," *Atlantic monthly,* Feb., 1880, XLV, 280–282.
Review.

80–4. "James's Hawthorne," *Atlantic monthly,* Feb., 1880, XLV, 282–285.
Review.

80–5. "Literary and philological manuals [in part]," *Atlantic monthly,* March, 1880, XLV, 357–361.
Reviews of *American poems,* [ed., H. E. Scudder]; J. A. Weisse's *Origin, progress, and destiny of the English language and literature;* W. D. Adams' *Dictionary of English literature;* George Crabb's *English synonymes.*

80–6. "Mark Twain's new book," *Atlantic monthly,* May, 1880, XLV, 686–688.
Reprinted 10–C.

80–7. "A new observer," *Atlantic monthly,* June, 1880, XLV, 848–849.
Review of J. B. Harrison's *Dangerous tendencies in American life, and other papers.*

80–7a. "Contributors' club," *Atlantic monthly,* June, 1880, XLV, 859–860.
Recurrent dreams. Unsigned and unindexed: attribution by Mr. A. B. Fox through *Impressions and experiences,* p. 125.

80–8. "The Holmes breakfast, Mr. Howells's response," *Atlantic monthly,* (supplement, 1880), XLV, 6–7 and throughout.

80–A. *The undiscovered country,* June 24.

80–9. "Literature for the schools," *Atlantic monthly,* July, 1880, XLVI, 134–136.
Reviews of *American prose,* [ed., H. E. Scud-

der]; H. C. Lodge's *Ballads and lyrics;* William Swinton's *Masterpieces of English literature.*

80–10. "Goldwin Smith's Cowper," *Atlantic monthly,* Sept., 1880, XLVI, 425–427.

In Morley's "English men of letters series."

80–11. "Mr. Aldrich's fiction," *Atlantic monthly,* Nov., 1880, XLVI, 695–698.

1881

81–1. Review of H. E. Scudder's *Mr. Bodley abroad. Atlantic monthly,* Jan., 1881, XLVII, 126.

81–2. "Henry Wadsworth Longfellow," *Harvard register,* Jan., 1881, III, 1–2.

81–3. "A fearful responsibility," *Scribner's,* June, July, 1881. XXII, 276–293, 390–414.

Reprinted 81–A.

81–A. *A fearful responsibility and other stories,* July 13.

81–4. "Dr. Breen's practice," *Atlantic monthly,* Aug. – Dec., 1881, XLVIII.

Reprinted 81–C.

81–5. Review of Clemens' *The prince and the pauper.* New York *Tribune,* Oct. 25, 1881, p. 6.

Unsigned: attribution through *Life in letters,* I, 303.

81–6. "Garfield," *Atlantic monthly,* Nov., 1881, XLVIII, 707–709.

Obituary.

81–B. "My first friend in Cambridge," *"The city and the sea" with other Cambridge contributions,* Nov. 9.

81–7. "A modern instance," *Century,* Dec., 1881 – Oct., 1882, XXIII–XXIV.

Reprinted 82–B.

81–C. *Dr. Breen's practice, a novel,* Dec. 2.

81–D. *A day's pleasure and other sketches.*

1882

82–1. "Police report," *Atlantic monthly,* Jan., 1882, XLIX, 1–16.

Reprinted 96–E.

82–2. "Note," *Atlantic monthly,* April, 1882, XLIX, 518.

Letter to E. S. Phelps, dated Oct. 28, 1881, explains *Dr. Zay's* independence of *Dr. Breen's practice.*

82–A. "Introduction," *Living truths from the writings of Charles Kingsley,* July 20.

82–3. "Mark Twain," *Century,* Sept., 1882, XXIV, 780–783.

Reprinted 10–C.

82–B. *A modern instance, a novel,* Oct. 7.

82–4. "Henry James, Jr.," *Century,* Nov., 1882, XXV, 25–29.

Biographical, critical.

82–5. "Pordenone," *Harper's monthly,* Nov., 1882, LXV, 829–835.

Reprinted 86–C.

82–6. "Lexington," *Longman's,* Nov., 1882, I, 41–61.

Reprinted 84–C.

82–C. "The sleeping-car, a farce," *Harper's Christmas,* Nov.

82–7. "Literary gossip," *Athenæum,* Nov. 25, 1882, no. 2874, 700.

Letter on Dickens and Thackeray in reference to 82–4. See *Life in letters,* I, 336.

1883

83–1. "A woman's reason," *Century,* Feb. – Oct., 1883, XXV – XXVI.

Reprinted 83–B.

83–A. *The sleeping car, a farce,* March 21.

83–2. "Niagara revisited, twelve years after their wedding journey," *Atlantic monthly,* May, 1883, LI, 598–610.

Reprinted 84–D.

83–3. "The late Horatio S. Noyes," Newton *Journal,* Aug. 18, 1883, p. 2.

Obituary. Unsigned: letter to Mrs. Noyes acknowledges authorship.

83–B. *A woman's reason, a novel,* Sept. 24.

83–4. "Maurice Thompson and his poems," *Independent,* Oct. 4, 1883, XXXV, 1249–1250.

Review of *Songs of fair weather.*

83–5. "The register," *Harper's monthly,* Dec., 1883, LXVIII, 70–86.

Reprinted 84–B.

1884

84–A. *A little girl among the old masters,* Nov. 15, 1883.

84–B. *The register, farce,* March 17.

84–1. "Recent American novels, 'The breadwinners,'" *Century,* May, 1884, XXVIII, 153–154.

A letter signed W: Tyler Dennett, *John Hay* (New York, 1933), p. 115, thinks "most probably" by Howells.

84–C. *Three villages,* May 22.

84–2. "Two notable novels," *Century,* Aug., 1884, XXVIII, 632–634.

Review of E. W. Bellamy's *Miss Ludington's sister.* Review of E. W. Howe's *The story of a country town* reprinted 17–C.

84–3. "The rise of Silas Lapham," *Century,* Nov., 1884 – Aug., 1885, XXIX–XXX.

Reprinted 85–B.

84–4. "The elevator (a farce)," *Harper's monthly,* Dec., 1884, LXX, 111–125.

Reprinted 85–A.

84–D. *Niagara revisited.*

1885

85–1. "'Anachronism,'" *Century,* Jan., 1885, XXIX, 477.

Letter answering charge of "anachronism" in Howells' using "Daisy Millerism" before *Daisy Miller* appeared.

85–A. *The elevator, farce,* Jan. 30.

85–2. "A Florentine mosaic," *Century,* Feb., April, June, 1885, XXIX–XXX.

Reprinted 86–A.

85–3. "Indian summer," *Harper's monthly,* July, 1885 – Feb., 1886, LXXI–LXXII.

Reprinted 86–D.

85–4. "Panforte di Siena," *Century,* Aug., Sept., 1885, XXX, 534–549, 659–673.

Illustrations by Joseph Pennell. Reprinted 86–A.

85–B. *The rise of Silas Lapham,* Aug. 21.

85–5. "'Silas Lapham' and the Jews," *American Hebrew,* Sept. 4, 1885, XXIV, 50–51.

Letter dated Old Orchard, Maine, July 17, 1885, defends passage in Nov. *Century* excised in published work. In part reprinted *New England quarterly,* March, 1943, XVI, 118–122.

85–6. "Tuscan cities," *Century,* Oct., 1885, XXX, 890–910.

Illustrations by Joseph Pennell. Reprinted 86–A.

85–7. "The laureate of death," *Atlantic monthly,* Sept., 1885, LVI, 311–322.

Reprinted 87–C.

85–8. "The garroters (a farce)," *Harper's monthly*, Dec., 1885, LXXII, 146–162.

Reprinted 86–B.

85–C. *Venetian life*, Aldine ed.

1886

86–A. *Tuscan cities*, Oct. 26, 1885.

86–B. *The garroters, farce*, Dec. 18, 1885.

86–1. "Editor's study," *Harper's monthly*, Jan., 1886, LXXII, 321–326.

Scope of department. Reviews of M. N. Murfree's *Prophet of the Great Smoky Mountain* and *Across the chasm;* S. W. Mitchell's *In war time;* Arlo Bates' *A wheel of fire;* G. H. Picard's *A mission flower;* B. C. Greene's *A New England conscience;* Edgar Fawcett's *Social silhouettes.* Literary decentralization; American English. Reviews of illustrated "holliday books," as *Tuscan cities* (Pennell). Unsigned as all "Editor's studies": the authorship is clear in view of portions reprinted in *Criticism and fiction* (see 91–B); it was, of course, quite generally known at the time. In part reprinted 91–B.

86–2. "Christmas every day," *Saint Nicholas*, Jan., 1886, XIII, 163–167.

Reprinted 93–A.

86–C. *Poems*, enlarged ed., by Jan. 30.

86–3. "The minister's charge; or, The apprenticeship of Lemuel Barker," *Century*, Feb. – Dec., 1886, XXXI–XXXIII.

Reprinted 87–A.

86–4. "International copyright," *Century*, Feb., 1886, XXXI, 630.

Letter with forty-four others (Lowell, Twain, Warner, *et al.*).

86–5. "Editor's study," *Harper's monthly*, Feb., 1886, LXXII, 481–487.

Reviews of *Life and correspondence of Louis Agassiz;* M. de Bacourt's *Souvenirs of a diplomate* (with foreign criticism of United States);

William Black's *White heather;* Grant Allen's *Babylon* (American English); [W. H. White's] *Autobiography of Mark Rutherford* and *Mark Rutherford's deliverance.* In part reprinted 91–B.

86–D. *Indian summer*, Feb. 19.

86–6. "Editor's study," *Harper's monthly*, March, 1886, LXXII, 646–650.

Reviews of Holmes' *A mortal antipathy* (lack of sharp criticism of young poet's work); E. C. Stedman's *Poets of America;* W. J. Courthope's *Liberal movement in English literature.* Howells' shift from poetry to novels. Reviews of Edmund Gosse's *From Shakespeare to Pope;* J. C. Ropes' *The first Napoleon.* In part reprinted 91–B.

86–7. "Editor's study," *Harper's monthly*, April, 1886, LXXII, 808–812.

Reviews of John Fiske's *The destiny of man as viewed in the light of his origin* and *The idea of God as affected by modern knowledge.* Christianity and Tolstoï: *Anna Karenine* [sic], *My religion,* and *The confession of an author.* Gogol. Reviews of Henry Hayes' [E. W. Kirk] *Margaret Kent;* A. P. Valdés' *Marta y Maria;* T. W. Higginson's *Larger history of the United States;* Edwin Pears' *Story of the fourth crusade;* J. R. Seeley's *A short history of Napoleon the First;* E. S. Morse's *Japanese homes and their surroundings;* Percival Lowell's *Chösen, the land of the morning calm.* In small part reprinted 91–B.

86–8. "Howells' meeting Miss Murfree," *Literary news*, April, 1886, VII, 122.

Interview excerpt. First printed Chicago *News.*

86–9. "Nassau," "New York letter," *Literary world*, April 17, 1886, XVII, 135.

Interview on America as field for writers. First printed *Mail and express.*

86–E. "Sketch of George Fuller's life," *George Fuller's life and works*, April 19.

86–10. "Editor's study," *Harper's monthly*, May, 1886, LXXII, 972–976.

Reviews of R. L. Stevenson's *The strange case of Dr. Jekyll and Mr. Hyde;* Edward Bellamy's *Miss Ludington's sister;* Balzac's *The*

Periodical Publications... — 1886, continued

Duchesse de Langeais. Tennyson; Max Müller on John Lubbock's "Best hundred books." Reviews of Georges Noufflard's *Berlioz et le mouvement de l'art contemporain;* J. A. Froude's *Oceana.* In part reprinted 91–B.

86–11. "Mr. Howells' work," *Literary news,* May, 1886, VII, 155.

Interview excerpt: he works hard and does his best. First printed Chicago *News.*

86–12. "New York letter," *Literary world,* May 1, 1886, XVII, 152.

Speech at Author's Club reception.

86–13. "Editor's study," *Harper's monthly,* June, 1886, LXXIII, 153–157.

Reviews of *Life and genius of Goethe,* lectures of the Concord School of Philosophy; Samuel Longfellow's *Life of Longfellow;* Longfellow's *Poems on slavery;* M. Ernest Dupuy's *Les grands maîtres de la littérature russe.* In part reprinted 91–B.

86–14. Frederick Wedmore, "To Millicent, from America," *Temple Bar,* June, 1886, LXXVII, 241.

Informal interview on Björnson, Murfree, Hardy, Zola, W. S. Gilbert. Reprinted *Critic,* July 3, 1886, n. s. VI, 10.

86–15. "Editor's study," *Harper's monthly,* July, 1886, LXXIII, 314–319.

Reviews of Sidney Luska's *Mrs. Peixada* (contemporary theater); Edward Harrigan's *Dan's tribulations* and *The leather patch* (compared with Goldoni); Bronson Howard's *One of our girls;* Wolcott Balestier's *A victorious defeat;* H. M. Posnett's *Comparative literature;* T. S. Perry's *English literature in the eighteenth century* and *From Opitz to Lessing.* In small part reprinted 91–B.

86–16. "Editor's study," *Harper's monthly,* Aug., 1886, LXXIII, 475–480.

Literary average perhaps higher than in past. Reviews of A. W. Greely's *Three years of Arctic service;* C. F. Woolson's *East angels;* [E. P. Tenney's] *Constance of Arcadia;* H. H. Boyesen's *Story of Norway;* Josiah Royce's *History of California.* In part reprinted 91–B.

86–17. "Editor's study," *Harper's monthly,* Sept., 1886, LXXIII, 639–643.

Russian fiction. Reviews of Dostoïevsky's *Le crime et le châtiment* and *Les humiliés et*

offensés; Vernon Lee's *Baldwin;* L. L. Hunt's *Memoir of Mrs. Edward Livingston;* Adam Badeau's *Aristocracy of England.* In part reprinted 91–B.

86–18. "Editor's study," *Harper's monthly,* Oct., 1886, LXXIII, 801–805.

Reviews of *Il libro dell' amore,* trans., M. A. Canini; J. L. Gilder's *Representative poems of living poets,* introduction by G. P. Lathrop. Reference to James article (82–4).

86–19. "Editor's study," *Harper's monthly,* Nov., 1886, LXXIII, 961–967.

Reviews of Hardy's *The mayor of Casterbridge;* Juan Valera's *Pepita Ximeniz* and *Doña Luz;* Valdés' *Marta y Maria, Reverita, José,* and Verga's *I Malavoglia;* L. D. Ventura's and S. Shovitch's *Misfits and remnants;* E. J. Reid's *Judge Richard Reid, a biography;* C. M. Clay's *The life of Cassius Marcellus Clay.* In part reprinted 91–B.

86–20. "The mouse-trap, a farce," *Harper's monthly,* Dec., 1886, LXXIV, 64–75.

Reprinted 89-B.

86–21. "Editor's study," *Harper's monthly,* Dec., 1886, LXXIV, 157–162.

Reviews of H. W. S. Cleveland's *Voyage of a merchant navigator* (a democratic type); Edmund Gosse's *Raleigh; Memoirs and letters of Dolly Madison;* [L. L. Hunt's] *Memoir of Mrs. Edward Livingston;* T. S. Perry's *Evolution of the snob; Gateley's* [sic] *World's progress,* with T. S. Perry's "The progress of literature." Subscription books in the United States.

1887

87–A. *The minister's charge, or, The apprenticeship of Lemuel Barker,* Dec. 11, 1886.

87–1. "Editor's study," *Harper's monthly,* Jan., 1887, LXXIV, 321–325.

Holiday literature; Dickens; American type graphic rather than literary; miscellaneous illustrated work. In part reprinted 91–B.

87–2. Harriet Earheart Monroe, "Statesman and novelist, a talk between Senator Ingalls and Mr. Howells," *Lippincott's*, Jan., 1887, XXXIX, 128–132.

Cleveland, Mugwumps; New England group.

87–3. "April hopes," *Harper's monthly*, Feb. – Nov., 1887, LXXIV–LXXV.

Reprinted 88–A.

87–4. "Editor's study," *Harper's monthly*, Feb., 1887, LXXIV, 482–486.

Reviews of C. F. Woolson's *Castle Nowhere* and *Rodman the keeper*; L. C. Wyman's *Poverty grass*; S. O. Jewett's *A white heron and other stories*. The novel and the short story. American short story writers. T. B. Aldrich, W. H. Bishop, R. T. Cooke, C. E. Craddock, Alice Cary, Rebecca H. Davis, J. W. De Forest, Philander Deming, Bret Harte, E. E. Hale, E. H. House, Henry James, S. O. Jewett, Ralph Keeler, G. P. Lathrop, S. W. Mitchell, Mrs. Prescott Spofford, Fitz-James O'Brien, Charles DeKay, E. S. Phelps, F. R. Stockton, J. T. Trowbridge, J. C. Harris, T. N. Page, O. A. Wadsworth, S. B. Wister. Review of Tolstoï's *Deux générations* and *La mort d'Ivan Illitch*. In part reprinted 91–B.

87–5. "Editor's study," *Harper's monthly*, March, 1887, LXXIV, 647–651.

Reviews of volumes of poetry by Margaret Deland, C. P. Cranch, Nora Perry, Celia Thaxter, Mrs. Akers Allen, Rachel Reynear, Arlo Bates, and Tennyson.

87–6. "Editor's study," *Harper's monthly*, April, 1887, LXXIV, 824–829.

Reviews of C. E. Craddock's *In the clouds*; Margaret Holmes' *The chamber over the gate*; *Towards the gulf*; H. W. Preston's *Year in Eden*; [E. P. Tenney's] *Agatha and the shadow*; Charlotte Dunning's *A step aside*; H. C. Bunner's *Midge*; W. H. Bishop's *The Golden justice*; Henry James' *The princess Casamassima*; W. H. Mallock's *The old order changes*. In part reprinted 91–B.

87–7. "Lyof Tolstoï," *Harper's weekly*, April 23, 1887, XXXI, 299–300.

Reprinted 87–B.

87–8. "Editor's study," *Harper's monthly*, May, 1887, LXXIV, 983–987.

Reviews of *Early letters of Thomas Carlyle*, ed., C. E. Norton; Lowell's *Democracy and other addresses*; Brooks Adams' *Emancipation of Massachusetts; Day in Athens with Socrates; Talks with Socrates about life*. Letter from "one of our chief novelists [De Forest]" on Tolstoï's *War and peace*. In small part reprinted 91–B.

87–9. "Year in a log-cabin, a bit of autobiography," *Youth's companion*, May 12, 1887, LX, 213–215.

Reprinted 93–F.

87–10. "Editor's study," *Harper's monthly*, June, 1887, LXXV, 155–158.

With revisions reprinted 91–B.

87–11. "Editor's study," *Harper's monthly*, July, 1887, LXXV, 315–320.

Reviews of Lee Meriwether's *Tramp trip*; Samuel Samuels' *From the forecastle to the cabin*; Tolstoï's *Que faire*; *Memoirs of Charles Reade*; Hardy's *The woodlanders*. Rider Haggard. Edgar Fawcett's quarrel with his critics; play criticism in general. In part reprinted 91–B.

87–B. "Leo Tolstoï," *Sebastopol*, July 2.

87–12. "Mr. Howells on realism, a talk with the novelist. Rider Haggard, a counter current — a Russian Shakespeare," New York *Tribune*, July 10, 1887, p. 12.

Interview mentions Hardy, Tolstoi, Turgenieff, Bjornson, Zola. In part reprinted *Critic*, July 16, 1887, n. s. VIII, 32.

87–13. "Editor's study," *Harper's monthly*, Aug., 1887, LXXV, 476–480.

Economic levels of the American reading public; Tolstoï. Reviews of A. F. Heard's *The Russian church and Russian dissent*; Frank Wilkeson's *Recollections of a Private*; *Correspondence between Goethe and Carlyle*, ed., C. E. Norton.

87–14. "Editor's study," *Harper's monthly*, Sept., 1887, LXXV, 638–642.

Recent southern fiction "narrow"; Henry James, J. W. De Forest, Cable, W. H. Bishop. Reviews of M. E. Wilkins' *A humble romance and other stories*; B. P. Poore's *Reminiscences*; H. B. Stanton's *Random recollections*; *Letters of Horatio Greenough to his brother Henry Greenough*. In part reprinted 91–B.

Periodical Publications... — 1887, continued

87–15. "Editor's study," *Harper's monthly*, Oct., 1887, LXXV, 801–806.

Reviews of Sidney Colvin's *Life of John Keats;* [W. H. White's] *The revolution in Tanner's Lane.* Emerson on the common, familiar, and low; J. W. De Forest's recent letter to the press, and international copyright; naval officer's letter and intelligent reading; M. J. Savage on Christ and Tolstoï. In part reprinted 91–B.

87–C. *Modern Italian poets, essays and versions,* Oct. 1.

87–16. "Editor's study," *Harper's monthly*, Nov., 1887, LXXV, 962–967.

"Autographic criticism." Reviews of J. A. Symonds' *Renaissance in Italy;* M. A. Ward's *Dante, and his life and works;* F. C. Baylor's *Behind the Blue Ridge; Society verse,* ed., Ernest De L. Pierson. In part reprinted 91–B.

87–17. "Clemency for the anarchists, a letter from Mr. W. D. Howells," New York *Tribune*, Nov. 6, 1887, p. 5.

Dated Dansville, New York, Nov. 4. Reprinted 28–A.

87–18. "Five o'clock tea," *Harper's monthly*, Dec., 1887, LXXVI, 86–96.

Reprinted 89–B.

87–19. "Editor's study," *Harper's monthly*, Dec., 1887, LXXVI, 153–155.

Reprinted 91–B.

87–D. *Their wedding journey,* enlarged ed., by Dec. 25.

1888

88–A. *April hopes,* Dec. 10, 1887.

88–B. *Mark Twain's library of humor,* edited, with introduction, Dec. 15, 1887.

88–1. "Editor's study," *Harper's monthly*, Jan., 1888, LXXVI, 316–321.

Reviews of Valdés' *Maximina;* Tolstoï's *The invaders;* E. B. Carpenter's *South county neighbors;* Octave Thanet's *Knitters in the sun.* In small part reprinted 91–B.

88–2. "Anglo-American copyright," *North American review,* Jan., 1888, CXLVI, 78.

Approves R. Pearsall Smith's plan.

88–3. "Execution by electricity," *Harper's weekly,* Jan. 14, 1888, XXXII, 23.

Bitter opposition in letter dated Christmas, 1887.

88–4. "A little Swiss sojourn," *Harper's monthly,* Feb., March, 1888, LXXVI, 452–467, 572–587.

Reprinted 92–F.

88–5. "Editor's study," *Harper's monthly*, Feb., 1888, LXXVI, 476–482.

Reviews of J. E. Cabot's *Memoir of Ralph Waldo Emerson;* Henry James, Sr.'s essay on Emerson in *Literary remains* (relation to Whitman and Tolstoï); Cervantes' *Don Quixote,* trans., John Ormsby; Tappan-Zee edition of Irving; Holmes' *Our hundred days in Europe.* In small part reprinted 91–B.

88–6. "Editor's study," *Harper's monthly*, March, 1888, LXXVI, 640–644.

Reviews of H. C. Lea's *History of the Inquisition of the Middle Ages,* vol. I; Zola's *La terre;* Tolstoï's *La puissance des tenebres;* W. P. Frith's *My autobiography.* August [*sic*] St. Gaudens on art criticism; correction in criticism of Octave Thanet's *Knitters in the sun.*

88–7. "Editor's study," *Harper's monthly*, April, 1888, LXXVI, 801–806.

Reviews of Laurence Gronlund's *Ça ira* and *Co-operative commonwealth;* R. T. Ely's *Land, labor, and taxation;* Adolphus Trollope's *What I remember* (Fanny Wright and New Harmony); Mrs. Trollope's *Domestic manners of the Americans;* J. B. McMaster's *Life of Franklin;* Marion [*sic*] Wilcox's *Gray, an Oldhaven romance;* H. W. Chaplin's *Five hundred dollars;* R. M. Johnston's *Mr. Absalom Billingslea.*

88–8. "Was there nothing to arbitrate?" *Harper's weekly,* April 21, 1888, XXXII, 286.

Blames C. B. & Q. for refusing to arbitrate with Brotherhood of Engineers.

88–9. "Editor's study," *Harper's monthly,* May, 1888, LXXVI, 964–969.

Reviews of H. C. Lea's *History of the Inquisition of the Middle Ages,* vol. II; Perez Galdós' *Leon Roch;* Tolstoï's essay on Napoleon and the Russian campaign, recently translated; poetry of Coates Kinney and Madison Cawein.

88–C. Library of universal adventures by sea and land, edited with T. S. Perry, May 17.

88–10. "Annie Kilburn," *Harper's monthly,* June – Nov., 1888, LXXVII.

Reprinted 89–A.

88–11. "Editor's study," *Harper's monthly,* June, 1888, LXXVII, 151–155.

Review of J. R. Lowell's *Heartsease and rue. Critic* symposium on author's identification with his characters. Reviews of Joseph Kirkland's *Zury;* Mrs. [E. W.] Kirke's [*sic*] *Queen money;* E. W. Bellamy's *Looking backward;* Mr. and Mrs. Joseph Pennell's *Our sentimental journey.* In small part reprinted 91–B.

88–12. "Editor's study," *Harper's monthly,* July, 1888, LXXVII, 314–318.

Death of Matthew Arnold. Review of Theodore Roosevelt's *Gouverneur Morris.* Franklin; Tourguénief; democracy and democratic art.

88–13. "A sea-change, a lyricated farce," *Harper's weekly,* July 14, 1888, XXXII, 505, (supplement) 521–524.

Reprinted 88–E.

88–14. "Editor's study," *Harper's monthly,* Aug., 1888, LXXVII, 476–480.

Review of *Library of American literature,* vols. I–III, eds., E. C. Stedman and E. M. Hutchinson (with particular comment on Roger Williams).

88–D. A sea change, or Love's stowaway, a lyricated farce, Aug. 8.

88–15. "Editor's study," *Harper's monthly,* Sept., 1888, LXXVII, 637–642.

Decline of the influence of Tennyson on American poets. Coates Kinney. Reviews of Madison Cawein's *The triumph of music and other lyrics;* R. B. Wilson's *Life and love;* L. W. Reese's [*A branch of May*]; O. W. Holmes' *Before the curfew and other poems; Poems of Rose Terry Cooke.*

88–16. E. J. C., "Howells at Nahant," Boston *Advertiser,* Sept. 20, 1888, p. 5.

Interview on New York vs. Boston and on British copyrights. In small part reprinted *Critic,* Oct. 6, 1888, n. s. x, 166–167.

88–17. "Editor's study," *Harper's monthly,* Oct., 1888, LXXVII, 799–804.

Henry James' recent short stories. Reviews of T. S. Denison's *The man behind;* S. O. Jewett's *The king of Folly Island;* G. W. Cable's *Bonaventure* and *The Grandissimes;* A. W. Rollins' *Uncle Tom's tenement;* Henry James' *The Reverberator;* A. P. Valdés' *El cuarto poder;* Stepniak's *The Russian peasantry;* George Pellew's *In castle and cabin, or, Talks in Ireland in 1887;* W. E. Curtis' *Capitals of South America.*

88–18. "Editor's study," *Harper's monthly,* Nov., 1888, LXXVII, 962–967.

Further mention of *Il libro dell' amore,* ed., M. A. Canini. Shakespeariana for the Stratford Memorial. Reviews of Mrs. Humphry Ward's *Robert Elsmere;* Margaret Deland's *John Ward, preacher;* C. L. Moore's *Book of day-dreams;* R. H. Lathrop's *Along the shore;* W. E. Henley's *Book of verses.* In small part reprinted 91–B.

88–19. "Mr. Howells and the anarchist meeting," *Harper's weekly,* Nov. 24, 1888, XXXII, 887.

Reprints Boston *Transcript* (?) letter from Howells, dated Nov. 3, declining invitation to speak at anarchist memorial meeting.

88–20. "A likely story, a farce," *Harper's monthly,* Dec., 1888, LXXVIII, 26–38.

Reprinted 89–B.

88–21. "Editor's study," *Harper's monthly,* Dec., 1888, LXXVIII, 158–160.

Soporific Christmas literature. Review of Walter Besant's *Fifty years ago.* Tolstoï, Ruskin, Morris, Hugo, and the healing of the plague bred by luxury and poverty, waste and want. In part reprinted 91–B.

1889

89–A. Annie Kilburn, a novel, Dec. 15, 1888.

89–1. "Editor's study," Harper's monthly, Jan., 1889, LXXVIII, 319–322.

Reviews of F. C. Gooch's Face to face with the Mexicans (introduction of American "civilization" into Mexico); T. A. Janvier's The Mexican guide; Mrs. E. Laszowska-Gerard's The land beyond the forest; Olive Schreiner's The story of an African farm (compared with E. W. Howe's The story of a country town).

89–2. "Editor's study," Harper's monthly, Feb., 1889, LXXVIII, 488–492.

Reviews of Walt Whitman's November boughs; Edmund Gosse's "Has America produced a poet?"; Edward Eggleston's The Graysons; Björnstjerne Björnson's Sigurd Slembe, trans., W. M. Payne; Mark Twain's library of American humor; C. D. Warner's On horseback.

89–3. "Editor's study," Harper's monthly, March, 1889, LXXVIII, 658–663.

Reviews of J. K. Hosmer's Life of young Sir Henry Vane; John Fiske's A critical period in American history; M. D. Conway's Life and papers of Edmund Randolph; James Bryce's The American commonwealth.

89–4. "A hazard of new fortunes," Harper's weekly, March 23 – Nov. 16, 1889, XXXIII.

Reprinted 90–A.

89–5. "Editor's study," Harper's monthly, April, 1889, LXXVIII, 820–825.

Reviews of M. E. and W. A. Brown's Musical instruments and their homes; C. H. Webb's Vagrom verse; Archibald Lampman's Among the millet and other poems; Clinton Scollard's Old and new world lyrics; F. D. Sherman's Madrigals and catches; Old songs, eds., E. A. Abbey and Alfred Parsons; Letters, poems, and selected writings of David Gray, ed., J. N. Larned.

89–B. The mouse trap and other farces, April 17.

89–6. "Editor's study," Harper's monthly, May, 1889, LXXVIII, 982–987.

Scott vs. Flaubert, Tolstoï, and Manzoni. Reviews of George Meredith's Beauchamp's career; Ibsen's Ghosts, The pillars of society, and The enemy of society [sic]; M. N. Murfree's The despot of Broomsedge Cove; Margaret Wood's A village tragedy; Joseph Kirkland's The MacVeys; R. T. Cooke's Steadfast; Elizabeth Stoddard's stories; Edward House's Yone Santo; Henry Harland's (Sidney Luska) A Latin Quarter courtship and Grandison Mather. In part reprinted 91–B.

89–C. The sleeping-car and other farces, May 13.

89–7. "Editor's study," Harper's monthly, June, 1889, LXXIX, 151–154.

Reprinted 91–B.

89–8. "Editor's study," Harper's monthly, July, 1889, LXXIX, 314–319.

Review of Brander Matthews' and A. M. Palmer's articles. Drama in the United States. Reviews of Edward Harrigan's Waddy Googan; Denman Thompson's The old homestead; [Charles Barnard's and Neil Burgess'] The country fair; [F. W. Bacon's] Vim (with Burgess); C. H. Hoyt's A midnight bell, The rag baby, A tin soldier, A hole in the ground, and The brass monkey.

89–9. Walter Brooks, "A talk with Mr. Howells," Author, July 15, 1889, I, 103–105.

Interview. First printed Brooklyn Citizen.

89–10. "Editor's study," Harper's monthly, Aug., 1889, LXXIX, 476–481.

H. H. Boyesen. Reviews of Henry James' A London life; E. W. Emerson's Emerson in Concord; W. M. Salter's Ethical religion; Lee Meriwether's The tramp at home; Helen Campbell's Prisoners of poverty abroad; Carlyle's letters, ed., C. E. Norton.

89–11. "Editor's study," Harper's monthly, Sept., 1889, LXXIX, 639–643.

Reviews of A. R. Aldrich's The rose of flame and other poems of love; Madison Cawein's Accolon of Gaul; William Sharp's Romantic ballads and poems of phantasy; American sonnets, ed., William Sharp; S. W. Mitchell's The cup of youth.

89–12. "Editor's study," *Harper's monthly,* Oct., 1889, LXXIX, 800–805.

Reviews of H. C. Lodge's *George Washington;* John Fiske's *The beginnings of New England;* Theodore Roosevelt's *Winning of the West;* C. O. Ward's *History of the ancient working-people.*

89–D. *Samson, a tragedy in five acts,* translated, Oct. 19.

89–13. "Editor's study," *Harper's monthly,* Nov., 1889, LXXIX, 962–967.
Reprinted 91–B.

89–14. "Editor's study," *Harper's monthly,* Dec., 1889, LXXX, 155–159.
History of Christmas and Thanksgiving: fiction dealing with each. In part reprinted 91–B.

89–15. "The Albany depot, farce," *Harper's weekly,* Dec. 14, 1889, XXXIII, 989, (supplement) 1005–1008.
Reprinted 92–A.

1890

90–A. *A hazard of new fortunes, a novel,* paper, Nov. 27, 1889.

90–1. "Editor's study," *Harper's monthly,* Jan., 1890, LXXX, 318–323.
Reviews of P. G. Hamerton's *French and English;* J. T. Morse's *Life of Franklin; Harper's fifth reader;* illustrated holiday books. Quotes William Morris. In part reprinted 10–C.

90–B. *A hazard of new fortunes, a novel,* 2 vols., Jan. 27.

90–2. "Editor's study," *Harper's monthly,* Feb., 1890, LXXX, 480–485.
Reviews of Boswell's *Life of Johnson,* ed., G. B. Hill; Eilian Hughes' *Some aspects of humanity;* De Maupassant's *The odd number,* trans., Jonathan Sturges; G. P. Lathrop's *Would you kill him?;* C. D. Warner's *A little journey in the world;* R. T. Ely's *Social aspects of Christianity;* D. G. Mitchell's *English lands, letters, and kings.*

90–3. "The shadow of a dream," *Harper's monthly,* March – May, 1890, LXXX.
Reprinted 90–D.

90–4. "Editor's study," *Harper's monthly,* March, 1890, LXXX, 642–647.
Review of E. J. Phelps' "The age of words;" a defense of American authors, literature, and criticism.

90–5. "Editor's study," *Harper's monthly,* April, 1890, LXXX, 804–810.
Reviews of *God in His world;* Tennyson's *Demeter, and other poems;* Browning's *Asolando;* poetry of "Ironquill" [E. F. Ware]; Mrs. J. G. Wilson's *Themes and variations;* L. C. Moulton's *In the garden of dreams;* Walter Learned's *Between whiles;* T. B. Aldrich's *Wyndham Towers.*

90–C. "The prose poem," *Pastels in prose,* April 5.

90–6. "A boy's town," *Harper's young people,* April 8 – Aug. 26, 1890, XI.
Reprinted 90–G.

90–7. "Editor's study," *Harper's monthly,* May, 1890, LXXX, 966–971.
Reviews of Carl Lumholz's *Among cannibals;* Reuben Davis' *Recollections of Mississippi and Mississippians;* Henry Adams' *History of the United States,* vol. I; John Bigelow's *William Cullen Bryant.*

90–D. *The shadow of a dream, a story,* paper, May 31.

90–8. "Editor's study," *Harper's monthly,* June, 1890, LXXXI, 152–157.
Promise of American comedy. Reviews of J. A. Herne's *Drifting apart; Old Jed Prouty;* Bronson Howard's *Shenandoah;* Lloyd's and Rosenfeld's *The senator;* [David Belasco's and H. C. De Mille's] *The charity ball* (compared with Sudermann's *Die Ehre* and [Paolo Giacometti's] *La morte civile*).

90–E. *The shadow of a dream, a story,* cloth, June 7.

90–9. "Editor's study," *Harper's monthly,* July, 1890, LXXXI, 314–318.
Four letters from correspondents; Howells' "flaws of judgements, sins of ignorance, and inaccuracies of expression;" review of Grant Allen's article in *The Speaker.* In small part reprinted 91–B.

90–10. "Editor's study," *Harper's monthly*, Aug., 1890, LXXXI, 476–481.
In part reprinted 91–B.

90–F. "Introduction," *The house by the medlar-tree*, Aug. 13.

90–11. "Editor's study," *Harper's monthly*, Sept., 1890, LXXXI, 638–643.
Reviews of John Hay's *Poems;* Henry James' *The tragic muse;* Baroness Deichmann's [life of Carmen Sylva], trans., Baroness Stachelberg; Shinkichi Shigemi's *A Japanese boy;* Balzac's *Sons of the soil;* Lafcadio Hearn's *Youma;* George Pellew's *Life of John Jay.* In part reprinted 91–B.

90–12. "Editor's study," *Harper's monthly*, Oct., 1890, LXXXI, 800–804.
Reviews of Harold Frederic's *In the valley, Seth's brother's wife,* and *The Lawton girl;* Kipling; Giovanni Verga's *The house by the medlar-tree;* Tolstoï's *The Kreutzer sonata;* W. E. Henley's *Views and reviews;* E. O. White's *Miss Brooks.* In part reprinted 91–B.

90–G. *A boy's town,* Oct. 11.

90–13. "Editor's study," *Harper's monthly*, Nov., 1890, LXXXI, 962–967.
Reviews of Isaac Taylor's *Origin of the Aryans;* J. W. DeForest's article indicating weakness of philological evidence. Science and creeds.

90–14. "Editor's study," *Harper's monthly*, Dec., 1890, LXXXII, 152–156.
Critics, creative authors, the anonymous critic, visiting authors, the last of the romanticists, and the "Editor's study" on perpetual copyright *et al.* in the "Synthetized sympathies of Altruria."

90–H. "W. D. Howells," *The art of authorship*.

1891

91–1. "Editor's study," *Harper's monthly*, Jan., 1891, LXXXII, 316–321.
Reviews of E. B. Custer's *Following the guidon;* Charles King's *Campaigning with Crook.* Military and civic ideals (Ruskin). Reviews of Kipling's *Departmental ditties and other verses; Poems of Emily Dickinson,* ed.,

M. L. Todd (compared with Blake, Emerson, Heine); J. MacN. Whistler's *The gentle art of making enemies.*

91–A. [*Winifred Howells,*] by Feb.

91–2. "What shall it profit," *Harper's monthly*, Feb., 1891, LXXXII, 384.
Reprinted 95–F.

91–3. "Editor's study," *Harper's monthly*, Feb., 1891, LXXXII, 478–483.
Reviews of Nicolay's and Hay's *Abraham Lincoln;* Björnstjerne Björnson's *In God's ways;* De Maupassant's *Notre coeur;* Valdés' *Scum.*

91–4. "Moods," *Harper's monthly*, March, 1891, LXXXII, 608–609.
Six poems. Reprinted 95–F.

91–5. "Editor's study," *Harper's monthly*, March, 1891, LXXXII, 640–644.
Reviews of B. E. Martin's *In the footprints of Charles Lamb; The journal of Sir Walter Scott,* ed., David Douglas; Ward McAllister's *Society as I have found it; The autobiography of Joseph Jefferson;* Lawrence Hutton's *Curiosities of the American stage; A sketch of Chester Harding, artist, drawn by his own hand;* G. W. Smalley's *London letters.*

91–6. "Editor's study," *Harper's monthly*, April, 1891, LXXXII, 802–806.
Reviews of T. S. Perry's *History of Greek literature;* S. O. Jewett's *Strangers and wayfarers; Tales by François Coppée,* ed., Guy de Maupassant; Emilia Pardo Bazán's *Morriña* and *La cuestión palpitante;* Armando Palacio Valdés' *Scum;* Tolstoï's *The fruits of culture.*

91–7. Foster Coates, "The novel of the future," *Author*, April 15, 1891, III, 47–49.
Response to questionnaire. First printed Springfield *Homestead.*

91–8. "Mortality," *Harper's monthly*, May, 1891, LXXXII, 848–849.
Reprinted 95–F.

91–9. "Editor's study," *Harper's monthly*, May, 1891, LXXXII, 964–968.
Reviews of F. D. Sherman's *Lyrics for a lute;* E. M. Thomas' *The inverted torch;* Henry Austin's *Vagabond verses;* J. W. Riley's *Rhymes*

of childhood; Eugene Field's *Little book of western verse;* T. B. Aldrich's *The sister's tragedy and other poems;* Danske Dandridge's *Rose Brake;* William Watson's *Wordsworth's grave and other poems.*

91–B. *Criticism and fiction,* May 9.

91–10. "Editor's study," *Harper's monthly,* June, 1891, LXXXIII, 152–156.

Reviews of *The writings of James Russell Lowell,* vols. VII–X, *Poems; Gentlemen* (compared with Ward McAllister); M. E. Wilkins' *A New England nun and other stories.*

91–11. "An imperative duty," *Harper's monthly,* July – Oct., 1891, LXXXIII.

Reprinted 92–C.

91–12. "Editor's study," *Harper's monthly,* July, 1891, LXXXIII, 314–318.

Reviews of William James' *The principles of psychology;* Mrs. A. M. Richards' *Letter and spirit;* S. W. Mitchell's *A psalm of deaths and other poems;* H. H. Boyesen's *The mammon of unrighteousness.*

91–13. "Editor's study," *Harper's monthly,* Aug., 1891, LXXXIII, 476–479.

Morality in American fiction and on American stage: Thompson, Harrigan, Howard. Reviews of Clyde Fitch's *Beau Brummel;* Arthur Jones' *The middleman* and *Judah;* J. A. Herne's *Margaret Fleming.*

91–14. "Editor's study," *Harper's monthly,* Sept., 1891, LXXXIII, 638–642.

Reviews of Hamlin Garland's *Main-travelled roads;* R. H. Davis' *Gallegher;* J. L. Allen's *Flute and violin;* Rudyard Kipling's *Mine own people,* introduction by Henry James; Thomas Hardy's *A group of noble dames;* Fanny Murfree's *Felicia.* In part reprinted 93–J.

91–15. "Editor's study," *Harper's monthly,* Oct., 1891, LXXXIII, 800–805.

Reviews of Mrs. Oliphant's *The life of Laurence Oliphant;* Mrs. Sutherland Orr's *The life and letters of Robert Browning;* A. M. Bacon's *Japanese girls and women;* E. R. Scidmore's *Jinriksha days;* Elizabeth Bisland's *A flying trip round the world.*

91–16. "The quality of mercy, a story of contemporary American life," New York *Sun,* Oct. 4, 1891 – Jan. 3, 1892.

Reprinted 92–D.

91–C. *Venetian life,* English and American eds., 2 vols., illustrated, Oct. 7.

91–17. "November — impression," *Harper's monthly,* Nov., 1891, LXXXIII, 906.

Reprinted 95–F.

91–18. "Editor's study," *Harper's monthly,* Nov., 1891, LXXXIII, 962–966.

Whitman. Arthur Quiller-Couch in *The Speaker,* Aug. 1, 1891, IV, 143–144, and the national literature of the United States.

91–19. "Editor's study," *Harper's monthly,* Dec., 1891, LXXXIV, 153–156.

Dialogue between Christmas boy and Study in 2091 in the "United sympathies of Altruria" on international copyright.

1892

92–A. *The Albany depot, farce,* first printed issue, Oct., 1891.

92–B. *The Albany depot,* Oct. 10, 1891.

92–C. *An imperative duty, a novel,* Nov. 14, 1891.

92–1. "A letter of introduction, farce," *Harper's monthly,* Jan., 1892, LXXXIV, 243–256.

Reprinted 92–E.

92–2. "Editor's study," *Harper's monthly,* Jan., 1892, LXXXIV, 315–320.

Reviews of O. C. Stevens' *An idyl of the sun;* Meredith Nelson's *Short flights;* W. W. Campbell's *Lake lyrics;* D. J. Snider's *Homer in Chios;* J. P. Irvine's *The green leaf and the gray;* J. W. Riley's *Old-fashioned roses;* Madison Cawein's *Days and dreams;* Gertrude Hall's *Verses; A garden of Hellas,* trans., L. C.

Perry; William Sharp's *Sospiri di Roma;* Maurice Maeterlinck's *The intruder,* trans., Mary Violé; *In middle harbor;* R. W. Gilder's *Two worlds and other poems.*

92–3. Hamlin Garland, "Mr. Howells's plans," Boston *Transcript,* Jan. 1, 1892, p. 6.

Interview on *Cosmopolitan* relation. In part reprinted *Critic,* Jan. 9, 1892, n. s. xvii, 28 (cf. *ibid.,* Jan. 16, 1892, 41).

92–4. "Editor's study," *Harper's monthly,* Feb., 1892, lxxxiv, 478–482.

Reviews of T. A. Janvier's *The uncle of an angel and other stories;* G. A. Hibbard's *Iduna and other stories;* R. T. Cooke's *Huckleberries;* W. M. Griswold's *Descriptive lists of novels.* Letter on T. L. Harris, as described in *The life of Laurence Oliphant.* Review of George Du Maurier's *Peter Ibbetson;* Dante's *Divine comedy,* trans., C. E. Norton.

92–5. Franklin Smith, "An hour with Mr. Howells," *Frank Leslie's,* March 17, 1892, lxxiv, 118–119.

Interview: Boston vs. New York, criticism, college as training for writing, heroines.

92–6. "The world of chance," *Harper's monthly,* March – Nov., 1892, lxxxiv–lxxxv.

Reprinted 93–B.

92–D. *The quality of mercy, a novel,* March 26.

92–7. "Editor's study," *Harper's monthly,* March, 1892, lxxxiv, 640–643.

William Morris. Tribute to G. W. Curtis and C. D. Warner. Reflections on "the cause of common honesty in literature." Last "Editor's study."

92–8. "Evening dress, farce," *Cosmopolitan,* May, 1892, xiii, 116–127.

Reprinted 93–G.

92–9. "Materials of a story," *Harper's monthly,* May, 1892, lxxxiv, 942.

Reprinted 95–F.

92–10. "The Wit supreme, and sovereign Sage," New York *Times,* May 1, 1892.

Four-line poem in Press Club album. Reprinted *Critic,* May 7, 1892, xx, 270.

92–11. T. C. Crawford, "Mr. Howells, his carer [*sic*], his present work, and his literary opinions," New York *Tribune,* June 26, 1892, p. 14.

Interview: reminiscences, literary forms and methods, New York, western writing. In part reprinted *Critic,* July 16, 1892, n. s. xviii, 36–37.

92–E. *A letter of introduction, farce,* July 25.

92–12. "George Pellew," *Cosmopolitan,* Sept., 1892, xiii, 527, 530.

Reprinted 93–E.

92–13. "George William Curtis," *Harper's weekly,* Sept. 10, 1892, xxxvi, 868, 870.

92–F. *A little Swiss sojourn,* Sept. 28.

92–14. "A traveller from Altruria," *Cosmopolitan,* Nov., 1892 – Oct., 1893, xiv–xv.

Reprinted 94–B.

92–15. "Mr. Howells's new novel," *Ladies' home journal,* Nov., 1892, ix, 2.

Note to editor on *The coast of Bohemia.*

92–16. "The coast of Bohemia," *Ladies' home journal,* Dec., 1892 – Oct., 1893, x.

Illustrations by Frank O. Small. Reprinted 93–I.

92–G. "Introductory letter," *Southsea idyls,* after Aug. 11.

1893

93–A. *Christmas every day and other stories told for children,* Dec. 7, 1892.

93–1. "The unexpected guests, farce," *Harper's monthly,* Jan., 1893, LXXXVI, 211–225.

Reprinted 93–C.

93–2. "Mr. Howells on forest preservation," Boston *Transcript,* Jan. 7, 1893, p. 6.

Undated letter to J. B. Harrison: conservation and socialism. In part reprinted *Critic,* Jan. 14, 1893, n. s. XIX, 22.

93 – 3. "Monochromes," *Harper's monthly,* March, 1893, LXXXVI, 547–550.

Nine poems. Reprinted 95–F.

93–B. *The world of chance, a novel,* March 29.

93–4. "The country printer," *Scribner's,* May, 1893, XIII, 539–558.

Illustrations by A. B. Frost. Reprinted 96–E.

93–C. *The unexpected guests, a farce,* May 17.

93–5. "Real conversations. — I, A dialogue between William Dean Howells and Hjalmar Hjorth Boyesen," *McClure's,* June, 1893, I, 3–11.

Biographical, reminiscent. In part reprinted *Bookman* (London), June, 1893, IV, 79–81. Reprinted *Human documents* (S. S. McClure, 1896), p. 140–147.

93–D. "Niagara, first and last," *The Niagara book, a complete souvenir of Niagara Falls,* June 27.

93–E. "Introduction," *The poems of George Pellew,* July 1.

93–6. "Bride roses, scene," *Harper's monthly,* Aug., 1893, LXXXVII, 424–430.

Illustrations by W. H. Hyde. Reprinted 00–B.

93–7. "The man of letters as a man of business," *Scribner's,* Oct., 1893, XIV, 429–445.

Reprinted 02–C.

93–F. *My year in a log cabin,* Oct. 10.

93–G. *Evening dress, farce,* Oct. 25.

93–8. "The cliff-dwellers," *Harper's bazar,* Oct. 28, 1893, XXVI, 883.

Review of H. B. Fuller's novel.

93–H. "Judgment day," *The first book of the Authors Club, Liber scriptorum,* Oct. 31.

93–9. "Letters of an Altrurian traveller," *Cosmopolitan,* Nov., 1893 – Sept., 1894, XVI–XVII.

Illustrations by Otto H. Bacher, Sonntag, jr., and Reginald Coxe. In part reprinted 96–E and 07–B.

93–I. *The coast of Bohemia, a novel,* Nov. 3.

93–10. "Letters of James Russell Lowell," *Harper's weekly,* Nov. 18, 1893, XXXVII, 1102.

Review of the C. E. Norton edition.

93–11. "My literary passions," *Ladies' home journal,* Dec., 1893 – March, 1895, XI–XII.

Reprinted 95–E.

93–J. "Introduction," *Main-travelled roads,* Dec. 4.

93–K. "Folksong, The sea, Through the meadow," *Eight songs,* Dec. 30.

1894

94–1. "The edge of the future," *McClure's,* Jan., 1894, II, 214.

Symposium letter on the coming year.

94–2. "A masterpiece of diplomacy, farce," *Harper's monthly,* Feb., 1894, LXXXVIII, 371–385.

Illustrations by A. E. Sterner. Reprinted 07–G.

94–3. "Are we a plutocracy?" *North American review,* Feb., 1894, CLVIII, 185–196.

Votes, classes, millionaires, corruption, business, politics.

94–4. A. R. Calhoun, "W. Dean Howells talks on literature," Philadelphia *Press*, Feb. 25, 1894, p. 24.

Interview on "sub-cellar fiction."

94–5. Clifton Johnson, "The writer and the rest of the world," *Outlook*, March 31, 1894, xLIX, 580–582.

Interview.

94–6. "Race," *Harper's monthly*, April, 1894, LXXXVIII, 677.

Illustrations by Mildred Howells. Reprinted 95–F.

94–7. Edward Marshall, "A great American writer," Philadelphia *Press*, April 15, 1894, p. 27.

Interview: views on a variety of matters, especially Crane's *Maggie*.

94–8. "My first visit to New England," *Harper's monthly*, May – Aug., 1894, LXXXVIII–LXXXIX.

Reprinted 00–F.

94–A. A likely story, farce, first separate ed., May 28.

94–B. A traveler from Altruria, romance, May 28.

94–C. The mouse trap, farce, first separate ed., June 8.

94–9. Marrion Wilcox, "W. D. Howells's first romance," *Harper's bazar*, June 16, 1894, xxvII, 475.

Review quotes Howells on Jacob Coxey's army.

94–D. Five o'clock tea, farce, first separate ed., June 19.

94–10. "Politics, but a good thing, W. D. Howells's views on the women's movement to aid Dr. Parkhurst," New York *Times*, Oct. 13, 1894, p. 9.

Interview.

94–11. Stephen Crane, "Fears realists must wait, an interesting talk with William Dean Howells," New York *Times*, Oct. 28, 1894, p. 20.

Interview. Reprinted *Americana*, April, 1943, xxxvII, 270–274.

94–12. "A parting and a meeting," *Cosmopolitan*, Dec., 1894 – Feb., 1895, xvIII.

Illustrations by C. Y. Turner. Reprinted 96–C.

94–13. "Stops of various quills," *Harper's monthly*, Dec., 1894, xc, 35–39.

Eleven poems. Reprinted 95–F.

94–E. Tuscan cities, new preface.

1895

95–A. Their wedding journey, illustrated edition, Oct. 26, 1894.

95–B. "Introduction" and "Chapter xvIII," *Recollections of life in Ohio from 1813 to 1840,* Feb. 13.

95–1. Clifton Johnson, "Sense and sentiment," *Outlook*, Feb. 23, 1895, LI, 304–305.

Interview: men and women, love and marriage.

95–2. "Society," *Harper's monthly*, March, 1895, xc, 630.

Two poems. Reprinted 95–F.

95–3. "A circle in the water," *Scribner's*, March, April, 1895, xvII, 293–303, 428–440.

Reprinted 01–B.

95–4. "The play and the problem," *Harper's weekly*, March 30, 1895, xxxIX, 294.

Reviews of Shaw's *Arms and the man;* H. A. Jones' *The case of rebellious Susan* and *The masqueraders;* Oscar Wilde's *An ideal husband.*

95–5. "At the American artists'," *Harper's weekly*, April 6, 1895, xxxIX, 318.

They are becoming more American.

95 – 6. "Degeneration," *Harper's weekly*, April 13, 1895, xxxix, 342.

Review of Max Nordau's book.

95–7. "The Ibsen influence," *Harper's weekly*, April 27, 1895, xxxix, 390.

Review of *The enemy of the people* with Beerbohm Tree.

95–8. "True, I talk of dreams," *Harper's monthly*, May, 1895, xc, 836–845.

Reprinted 96–E.

95–9. "Life and letters," *Harper's weekly*, May 4, 1895, xxxix, 416–417.

The new woman and smoking; review of [M. M. Dowie's] *A girl in the Carpathians*.

95–10. "Life and letters," *Harper's weekly*, May 11, 1895, xxxix, 436.

Joseph Jefferson's speech; art on the stage, in the novel.

95–C. "Introduction," *Master and man*, May 17.

95–11. "Life and letters," *Harper's weekly*, May 18, 1895, xxxix, 460.

Reviews of William Minto's *The literature of the Georgian era;* H. H. Boyesen's *Essays on Scandinavian literature*.

95–12. "Life and letters," *Harper's weekly*, May 25, 1895, xxxix, 485.

Reviews of Paul Bourget's *Outre-mer;* Isabel Hapgood's *Russian rambles;* Henry Norman's *Peoples and politics of the Far East*.

95–13. "Tribulations of a cheerful giver," *Century*, June, July, 1895, L, 181–185, 417–421.

Reprinted 96–E.

95–14. "First impressions of literary New York," *Harper's monthly*, June, 1895, xci, 62–74.

Reprinted 00–F.

95–15. "Life and letters," *Harper's weekly*, June 1, 1895, xxxix, 508.

Reviews of H. B. Fuller's *With the procession;* E. W. Townsend's Chimmie Fadden stories; H. W. Nevison's [sic] *Slum stories;*

Zangwill's *The children of the ghetto;* Conrad's *Almayer's folly;* C. E. Craddock's *Phantoms of the foot-bridge*.

95–16. "Life and letters," *Harper's weekly*, June 8, 1895, xxxix, 532–533.

Bad spelling vs. dialect; Crane's *Maggie*.

95–17. "Life and letters," *Harper's weekly*, June 15, 1895, xxxix, 556–557.

Review of *Memoirs of Barras*, ed., George Duruy.

95–18. "Life and letters," *Harper's weekly*, June 22, 1895, xxxix, 580–581.

Dialect in English and continental literature.

95–19. "Life and letters," *Harper's weekly*, June 29, 1895, xxxix, 604.

On symposium "Should husbands kill adulterers?"

95–20. "Life and letters," *Harper's weekly*, July 6, 1895, xxxix, 628.

Reprinted 02–C.

95–21. "Life and letters," *Harper's weekly*, July 13, 1895, xxxix, 653.

Reprinted 02–C.

95–22. "Life and letters," *Harper's weekly*, July 20, 1895, xxxix, 677.

Reviews of José Echegaray's *Mariana;* C. B. Luffman's *A vagabond in Spain;* on Cuba.

95–23. "Life and letters," *Harper's weekly*, July 27, 1895, xxxix, 701.

Reviews of Henry James' *Terminations;* George Moore's *Celibates* and *Esther Waters*.

95–24. "Roundabout to Boston," *Harper's monthly*, Aug., 1895, xci, 427–438.

Reprinted 00–F.

95–25. "Life and letters," *Harper's weekly*, Aug. 3, 1895, xxxix, 725–726.

Reviews of Brander Matthews' *His father's son* (serialization in *Harper's weekly*); H. R. Marshall's *Aesthetic principles*.

Periodical Publications... — 1895, continued

95–26. "Life and letters," *Harper's weekly*, Aug. 10, 1895, xxxix, 748–749.

On women cycling.

95–27. "Life and letters," *Harper's weekly*, Aug. 17, 1895, xxxix, 772–773.

On summer hotels and marital separation.

95–D. [*Don't wake the children, song,*] Aug. 19.

95–28. "Life and letters," *Harper's weekly*, Aug. 24, 1895, xxxix, 796.

On summer hotels.

95–29. "Life and letters," *Harper's weekly*, Aug. 31, 1895, xxxix, 820.

Review of J. T. Codman's *Brook Farm.*

95–30. "Pebbles," *Harper's monthly*, Sept., 1895, xci, 517–520.

Seven poems. Reprinted 95–E.

95–31. "An editor's relations with young authors," *Youth's companion*, Sept. 5, 1895, lxviii, 418–419.

With a little reminiscence.

95–32. "Life and letters," *Harper's weekly*, Sept. 7, 1895, xxxix, 844.

City children vacationing in country; socializing process in United States; parks.

95–33. "Life and letters," *Harper's weekly*, Sept. 14, 1895, xxxix, 868–869.

Review of John Corbin's *The Elizabethan Hamlet.*

95–34. "Life and letters," *Harper's weekly*, Sept. 21, 1895, xxxix, 892.

The comic and the cruel: *Hamlet.*

95–35. "Life and letters," *Harper's weekly*, Sept. 28, 1895, xxxix, 916–917.

Reprinted 96–E.

95–36. "The day of their wedding," *Harper's bazar*, Oct. 5 – Nov. 16, 1895, xxviii.

Illustrations by T. de Thulstrup. Reprinted 96–B.

95–37. "Life and letters," *Harper's weekly*, Oct. 5, 1895, xxxix, 941.

Reprinted 96–E.

95–38. "Life and letters," *Harper's weekly*, Oct. 12, 1895, xxxix, 965.

Review of H. M. Alden's *A study of death.*

95–39. "Life and letters," *Harper's weekly*, Oct. 19, 1895, xxxix, 988–989.

Reprinted 96–E.

95–E. *My literary passions*, Oct. 19.

95–F. *Stops of various quills*, Oct. 25.

95–40. "Life and letters," *Harper's weekly*, Oct. 26, 1895, xxxix, 1012–1013.

Reviews of Brander Matthews' *His father's son;* Anthony Hope's *A change of air;* R. S. Hitchins' *An imaginative man;* Tighe Hopkins' *Lady Bonnie's experiment;* Stephen Crane's *Red badge of courage;* M. C. Graham's *Stories of the foothills;* E. W. Thompson's *Old man Savarin;* Frank Stockton's *Adventures of Captain Horn;* Maarten Maartens' *My lady nobody;* Henryk Sienkiewicz's *Children of the soil.*

95–41. "Equality as the basis of good society," *Century*, Nov., 1895, li, 63–67.

Social inequality.

95–42. "Literary Boston thirty years ago," *Harper's monthly*, Nov., 1895, xci, 865–879.

Reprinted 00–F.

95–42a. "A great novel," *Harper's bazar*, Nov. 2, 1895, xxviii, 886.

Review of Galdós' *Doña Perfecta.* Reprinted 96–A.

95–43. "Life and letters," *Harper's weekly*, Nov. 2, 1895, xxxix, 1037.

Spelling, usage, diction in England and America.

95–44. "Life and letters," *Harper's weekly*, Nov. 9, 1895, xxxix, 1060.

Jefferson in *The cricket on the hearth;* Francis Wilson in *The chieftain;* John Drew and Maude Adams.

95–45. "Life and letters," *Harper's weekly*, Nov. 16, 1895, xxxix, 1084–1085.

Recent political plays.

95–46. "Life and letters," *Harper's weekly*, Nov. 23, 1895, xxxix, 1109.

American-European marriage.

95–47. "Life and letters," *Harper's weekly*, Nov. 30, 1895, xxxix, 1133.

Reviews of Alice Brown's *Meadow-grass;* S. O. Jewett's *The life of Nancy;* K. D. Wiggins' *The village watch-tower;* Gertrude Smith's *The rousing of Mrs. Potter;* Julian Ralph's *People we pass;* John Fox, Jr.'s *A Cumberland vendetta;* F. H. Smith's *A vagabond gentleman;* Owen Wister's *Red men and white.*

95–48. "The nature of liberty," *Forum*, Dec., 1895, xx, 401–409.

Economic liberty.

95–49. "A previous engagement, comedy," *Harper's monthly*, Dec., 1895, xcii, 29–44.

Reprinted 97–B.

95–50. "Life and letters," *Harper's weekly*, Dec. 7, 1895, xxxix, 1156.

Review of Thomas Hardy's *Jude the obscure.*

95–51. "Life and letters," *Harper's weekly*, Dec. 14, 1895, xxxix, 1177, 1180.

Dialogue with the Christmas muse.

95–52. "Life and letters," *Harper's weekly*, Dec. 21, 1895, xxxix, 1212–1213.

Possibility of teaching authorship.

95–53. "Life and letters," *Harper's weekly*, Dec. 28, 1895, xxxix, 1236–1237.

The present theatre; reviews of Clemens' *Pudd'nhead Wilson; His Excellency;* Clyde Fitch's *Runaway colt; Don Quixote* with Henry Irving; Conan Doyle's *Story of Waterloo;* Mrs. [P. R.] Craigie's *Journeys end in lovers' meeting;* Lorimer Stoddard's *Napoleon;* Dostoyevsky's *Rodion the student.*

1896

96–A. "Introduction," *Doña Perfecta*, Nov. 8, 1895.

96–1. "Life and letters," *Harper's weekly*, Jan. 4, 1896, xl, 6–7.

Venezuela boundary dispute; patriotism.

96–2. "Life and letters," *Harper's weekly*, Jan. 11, 1896, xl, 30–31.

Review of Pinero's *The notorious Mrs. Ebbsmith.*

96–3. "Life and letters," *Harper's weekly*, Jan. 18, 1896, xl, 54.

Marriage of "economical disparates."

96–4. "Hjalmar Hjorth Boyesen," *Harper's bazar*, Jan. 25, 1896, xxix, 70–71.

Obituary with reminiscence and criticism.

96–5. "Life and letters," *Harper's weekly*, Jan. 25, 1896, xl, 79.

Alfred Austin; the year in poetry; reviews of Stephen Crane's *The black riders;* George Horton's *In unknown seas;* C. P. Stetson's *In this our world.*

96–6. "Life and letters," *Harper's weekly*, Feb. 1, 1896, xl, 102–103.

Public spitting and women's hats in theaters.

96–7. "Life and letters," *Harper's weekly*, Feb. 8, 1896, xl, 126.

Reviews of Fyles' *The governor of Kentucky;* H. A. Jones' *Michael and his lost angel;* Pinero's *Benefit of the doubt.*

96–B. *The day of their wedding, a novel*, Feb. 14.

96–8. "Life and letters," *Harper's weekly*, Feb. 15, 1896, xl, 150.

Society of Colonial Dames and American titles.

96–9. "Life and letters," *Harper's weekly*, Feb. 22, 1896, xl, 175.

High price of theater seats.

96–10. "Life and letters," *Harper's weekly*, Feb. 29, 1896, XL, 199.

A public theater, but with censorship.

96–11. "Life and letters," *Harper's weekly*, March 7, 1896, XL, 223.

Reviews of Hamlin Garland's *Rose of Dutcher's Coolly;* M. H. Foote's *The cup of trembling;* W. S. Rossiter's *An accidental romance;* Kenneth Graham's *The golden age;* Gertrude Smith's *The Arabella and Araminta studies;* J. K. Bangs' *A houseboat on the Styx;* W. D. McCracken's *Little idyls of the big world.*

96–12. "Life and letters," *Harper's weekly*, March 14, 1896, XL, 246.

Fiction standards higher than play standards; need for government-subsidized theater.

96–13. "Life and letters," *Harper's weekly*, March 21, 1896, XL, 270.

Reprinted 02–C.

96–14. "Life and letters," *Harper's weekly*, March 28, 1896, XL, 294.

Reviews of Brander Matthews' *An introduction to the study of American literature;* A. H. Smyth's *Bayard Taylor.*

96–15. "Who are our brethren?" *Century*, April, 1896, LI, 932–936.

Liberty, equality, fraternity.

96–16. "Life and letters," *Harper's weekly*, April 4, 1896, XL, 318–319.

The Juliet of Mrs. Marlowe-Taber; the Pamela (Goldoni) of Signora Duse.

96–C. *A parting and a meeting, story*, April 7.

96–17. "Life and letters," *Harper's weekly*, April 11, 1896, XL, 342.

Reviews of Violet Hunt's *A hard woman;* W. P. Ridge's *A clever wife;* Holger Drachmann's *Paul and Virginia of a northern zone;* Rebecca H. Davis' *Dr. Warrick's daughters.*

96–18. "Life and letters," *Harper's weekly*, April 18, 1896, XL, 390.

American artists and National Academy exhibits.

96–19. "Life and letters," *Harper's weekly*, April 25, 1896, XL, 415.

Reprinted 02–C.

96–20. "Life and letters," *Harper's weekly*, May 2, 1896, XL, 438.

Matthew Arnold and Thomas Hughes; Augustus Hoppin.

96–21. "Life and letters," *Harper's weekly*, May 9, 1896, XL, 462.

Reprinted 02–C.

96–22. "Life and letters," *Harper's weekly*, May 16, 1896, XL, 486.

Tipping.

96–23. "Life and letters," *Harper's weekly*, May 23, 1896, XL, 510.

Review of J. T. Morse's *Life and letters of Oliver Wendell Holmes.*

96–24. "Life and letters," *Harper's weekly*, May 30, 1896, XL, 535–536.

Reprinted 10–D.

96–D. "An appreciation," *Maggie, a child of the streets*, June.

96–25. "Life and letters," *Harper's weekly*, June 6, 1896, XL, 558.

The "summer girl" — a pretty barbarian.

96–26. "Life and letters," *Harper's weekly*, June 13, 1896, XL, 582.

Czar's coronation; democracy and autocracy.

96–27. "Life and letters," *Harper's weekly*, June 20, 1896, XL, 606.

On the home; "home science" in schools and special instruction in civility.

96–28. "Life and letters," *Harper's weekly*, June 27, 1896, XL, 630.

Review of P. L. Dunbar's *Majors and minors.*

96–29. "An open-eyed conspiracy, an idyl of Saratoga," *Century*, July – Oct., 1896, LII.

Illustrations by Irving R. Wiles. Reprinted 97–D.

96–30. Marrion Wilcox, "Works of William Dean Howells," *Harper's weekly*, July 4, 1896, XL, 655–656.

Quotes directly and indirectly on change in social direction.

96–31. "The landlord at Lion's Head," *Harper's weekly,* July 4 – Dec. 5, 1896, XL.
Illustrations by W. T. Smedley. Reprinted 97–C.

96–32. "Life and letters," *Harper's weekly,* July 11, 1896, XL, 678.
Reprinted 02–C.

96–33. "Life and letters," *Harper's weekly,* July 25, 1896, XL, 724, 726.
New York City in summer.

96–34. "New York low life in fiction," New York *World,* July 26, 1896, II, 18.
Reviews of Abraham Cahan's *Yekl;* Stephen Crane's *Maggie.*

96–35. "The white Mr. Longfellow," *Harper's monthly,* Aug., 1896, XCIII, 327–343.
Reprinted 00–F.

96–36. "Life and letters," *Harper's weekly,* Aug. 8, 1896, XL, 774.
Reprinted 02–C.

96–37. "Life and letters," *Harper's weekly,* Aug. 22, 1896, XL, 822.
Landscape from Long Island to New Hampshire.

96–38. "Life and letters," *Harper's weekly,* Sept. 5, 1896, XL, 870.
Reprinted 02–C.

96–39. "Life and letters," *Harper's weekly,* Sept. 12, 1896, XL, 894.
Reprinted 02–C.

96–E. Impressions and experiences, Sept. 25.

96–40. "Men and letters, on coming back," *Atlantic monthly,* Oct., 1896, LXXVIII, 562–565.
On returning to *Atlantic monthly* columns.

96–41. "Life and letters," *Harper's weekly,* Oct. 3, 1896, XL, 966.
Reprinted 02–C.

96–42. "Life and letters," *Harper's weekly,* Oct. 10, 1896, XL, 997–998.
Reviews of Edward Harrigan's *Marty Malone;* Bret Harte's *Sue.*

96–43. "W. D. Howells — reviews James Whitcomb Riley's new book, A child world," *Daily tatler,* Nov. 7, 1896, I, 5–7.

96–44. "Life and letters," *Harper's weekly,* Nov. 7, 1896, XL, 1094.
George Du Maurier.

96–45. "Life and letters," *Harper's weekly,* Nov. 28, 1896, XL, 1171.
Reprinted 02–C.

96–46. "Oliver Wendell Holmes," *Harper's monthly,* Dec., 1896, XCIV, 120–134.
Reprinted 00–F.

96–F. "Introduction," *Lyrics of lowly life,* Dec. 2.

96–47. "Life and letters," *Harper's weekly,* Dec. 19, 1896, XL, 1243.
Dialogue with the Christmas muse: the state of the world.

1897

97–A. "George du Maurier," *English society,* Dec. 17, 1896.

97–1. "Indian giver, comedy," *Harper's monthly,* Jan., 1897, XCIV, 235–252.
Illustrations by W. T. Smedley. Reprinted 00–D.

97–2. "Life and letters," *Harper's weekly,* Jan. 23, 1897, XLI, 83.
Reprinted 02–C.

97–B. A previous engagement, comedy, Jan. 29.

97–3. "Life and letters," *Harper's weekly,* Jan. 30, 1897, XLI, 107–108.
Reviews of William Gillette's *Secret service;* Pinero's *The hobby horse.*

97–4. "Life and letters," *Harper's weekly*, Feb. 13, 1897, XLI, 155.

Clemens, especially *Tom Sawyer, Huckleberry Finn,* and *Connecticut Yankee.*

97–5. "The laureate of the larger England," *McClure's*, March, 1897, VIII, 453–455.

Review of Rudyard Kipling's *The seven seas.*

97–6. "The story of a play," *Scribner's*, March – Aug., 1897, XXI–XXII.
Reprinted 98–A.

97–7. "Life and letters," *Harper's weekly*, March 13, 1897, XLI, 270.

Review of *Works of Lord Byron,* vol. I, *Letters, 1804–13,* ed., W. E. Henley.

97–8. "Life and letters," *Harper's weekly*, March 20, 1897, XLI, 291.

Mrs. Maddern Fiske in Lorimer Stoddard's dramatization of Hardy's *Tess of the D'Urbervilles.*

97–9. "My favorite novelist and his best book," *Munsey's*, April, 1897, XVII, 18–25.

In *My literary passions* vein; especially Tolstoy.

97–10. [Testimonial letter to R. H. Stoddard,] *Critic*, April 3, 1897, XXX, 231.

97–11. "Life and letters," *Harper's weekly*, April 3, 1897, XLI, 338–339.
Reprinted 02–C.

97–C. *The landlord at Lion's Head, a novel*, April 9.

97–12. "Life and letters," *Harper's weekly*, May 29, 1897, XLI, 538.

Review of F. R. Stockton's *A story teller's pack.*

97–13. "Life and letters," *Harper's weekly*, June 12, 1897, XLI, 590–591.
Stroll about New York City.

97–14. "The rambler," *Bookbuyer*, July, 1897, XIV, 558–559.

Quotes series of brief opinions of Howells of his own works. Reprinted as "Mr. Howells his own critic," *Literary news,* Oct., 1897, XVIII, 313.

97–15. "The modern American mood," *Harper's monthly*, July, 1897, XCV, 199–204.

Buoyant but not uncritical survey of the United States' past and its future possibilities.

97–16. "Life and letters," *Harper's weekly*, July 17, 1897, XLI, 706.
Reprinted 02–C.

97–17. "Life and letters," *Harper's weekly*, July 24, 1897, XLI, 730.

Review of George Du Maurier's *The Martian.*

97–D. *An open-eyed conspiracy, an idyl of Saratoga,* Sept. 3.

97–18. "A pair of patient lovers," *Harper's monthly*, Nov., 1897, XCV, 832–851.
Reprinted 01–B.

97–19. "Mr. Howells's trip abroad, he gives some of his impressions in an entertaining chat," New York *Tribune,* Nov. 10, 1897, p. 6.

Interview: travel itinerary, new novel. In part reprinted (with abstract from "a Paris paper" interview on American literary scene) *Critic,* Nov. 13, 1897, n. s. XXVIII, 290.

97–20. "Life and letters," *Harper's weekly*, Nov. 13, 1897, XLI, 1134.
Reprinted 02–C.

97–21. "Life and letters," *Harper's weekly*, Nov. 20, 1897, XLI, 1147.
Reprinted 02–C.

97–22. "Life and letters," *Harper's weekly*, Dec. 4, 1897, XLI, 1194.

Review of William Gillette's *Secret service* (Paris performance).

97–E. *Stories of Ohio,* Dec. 15, 1897.

97–23. "Life and letters," *Harper's weekly*, Dec. 25, 1897, XLI, 1297–1298.

Dialogue with the Christmas muse; illustrations by Mildred Howells.

97–F. "Lyof Tolstoy," *A library of the world's best literature*, vol. 27, Feb. 17, 1898.

1898

98–1. "Notes," *Literary digest*, Jan. 29, 1898, XVI, 133.

Seven lines defending Alfred Austin's appointment as poet laureate. First printed?

98–1a. G. [W. J. Ghent?], "Mr. Howells' socialism," *American Fabian*, Feb., 1898, IV, 1–2.

Interview.

98–2. "Life and letters," *Harper's weekly*, Feb. 19, 1898, XLII, 174.

Review of E. C. Stedman's *Poems now first collected*; his position and career.

98–3. "Life and letters," *Harper's weekly*, Feb. 26, 1898, XLII, 202.

Theater trust and the trust principle.

98–4. Theodore Dreiser, "How he climbed fame's ladder, William Dean Howells tells the story of his long struggle for success, and his ultimate triumph," *Success*, April, 1898, p. 5–6.

Interview. With revisions reprinted 01–A.

98–4a. "W. D. Howells at home," *Current literature*, May, 1898, XXIII, 402–403.

Interview. Howells' habits of writing; current American authors. First printed in New York *Times*.

98–5. "American letter, Puritanism in fiction," *Literature*, May 14, 1898, n. s. II, 563–564.

Reprinted 02–C.

98–6. "Pictures for Don Quixote," *Century*, June, 1898, LVI, 177–185.

On Vierge's illustrations; review of A. F. Jaccaci's *On the trail of Don Quixote*.

98–7. "American letter, American literary centres," *Literature*, June 4, 18, 1898, II, 649–651, 704–706.

Reprinted 02–C.

98–8. "Mr. Howells on Mr. Bellamy," *Critic*, June 11, 1898, n. s. XXIX, 391.

Address, June 7, at Social Reform Club, partially reported.

98–A. *The story of a play, a novel*, June 15.

98–9. "Ragged lady," *Harper's bazar*, July 2 – Nov. 5, 1898, XXXI.

Reprinted 99–A.

98–10. "American letter, Chicago in fiction," *Literature*, July 2, 1898, II, 758–759.

Herrick, Fuller, Ade.

98–11. "American letter, the politics of American authors," *Literature*, July 16, 1898, III, 41–42.

Reprinted 02–C.

98–12. "American letter, from New York into New England," *Literature*, July 30, 1898, III, 87–90.

Reprinted 02–C.

98–13. "Edward Bellamy," *Atlantic monthly*, Aug., 1898, LXXXII, 253–256.

Reprinted 98–B.

98–14. "Life and letters, our Spanish prisoners at Portsmouth," *Harper's weekly*, Aug. 20, 1898, XLII, 826–827.

Reprinted 02–C.

98–15. "American letter, the southern states in recent American literature," *Literature*, Sept. 10, 17, 24, 1898, III, 231–232, 257–258, 280–281.

Cable, Harris, Murfree, Page, Allen, Cawein, Lanier.

98–16. "In honor of Tolstoy," *Critic*, Oct., 1898, n. s. XXX, 288.

Letter dated "York Harbor, Maine, August 21, 1898," written for Tolstoy celebration of Sept. 8. Also printed in part, *Bookman*, Oct., 1898, VIII, 107.

98–B. "Edward Bellamy," *The blind-man's world and other stories,* Oct. 5.

98–17. "American letter, the nature of American literary criticism," *Literature,* Oct. 22, Nov. 5, 1898, III, 378–379, 424–425.

98–18. "American letter, American civic life," *Literature,* Nov. 19, 1898, III, 474–475.

Review of J. J. Chapman's *Causes and consequences.*

98–19. "Confessions of a summer colonist," *Atlantic monthly,* Dec., 1898, LXXXII, 742–750.

Reprinted 02–C.

98–20. "The smoking car, a farce," *Frank Leslie's,* Dec., 1898, XLVII, 183–199.

Illustrations by Charles Grunwald. Reprinted 00–E.

98–21. "The abandoned watermelon patch," *Youth's companion,* Dec. 1, 1898, LXXII, 602–603.

Reprinted 02–B.

98–22. "American letter, a human document," *Literature,* Dec. 3, 1898, III, 528–529.

Review of W. A. Wyckoff's *The workers, the East* and *The workers, the West.*

98–23. "American letter, some recent novels," *Literature,* Dec. 17, 1898, III, 577–579.

Reviews of Frank Norris' *Moran of the Lady Letty;* Will Payne's *The money captain;* J. W. De Forest's *A lover's revolt.*

98–24. "American letter, some books of short stories," *Literature,* Dec. 31, 1898, III, 628–629.

Reviews of David Gray's *Gallops;* Lilian Bell's *The instinct of step-fatherhood;* Gertrude Hall's *The hundred, and other stories;* M. E. Wilkins' *The people of our neighborhood;* Abraham Cahan's *The imported bridegroom, and other stories;* Morgan Robertson's *Spun-yarn.*

1899

99–1. "Their silver wedding journey," *Harper's monthly,* Jan. – Dec., 1899, XCVIII–C.

Reprinted 99–C.

99–2. "Destiny of the letter R in America," *Literature,* Jan. 17, 1899, n. s. I, 25–26.

An amusing and accurate paper on the pronunciation of R throughout the United States.

99–3. "American prose," *Literature,* Jan. 27, 1899, n. s. I, 49–50.

Review of *American prose,* ed., G. R. Carpenter.

99–4. "Garland's Grant," *Literature,* Feb. 3, 1899, n. s. I, 73–74.

Review of *Ulysses S. Grant, his life and character.*

99–5. "Rosenfeld's Songs from the ghetto," *Literature,* Feb. 10, 1899, n. s. I, 97–98.

Review of Morris Rosenfeld's book.

99–A. Ragged lady, a novel, Feb. 16.

99–6. "Mr. Remington's wild men," *Literature,* Feb. 17, 1899, n. s. I, 121–122.

Review of Frederic Remington's *Sundown Leflare.*

99–7. "Suggestions of a patriotic play," *Literature,* Feb. 24, 1899, n. s. I, 145–146.

Anglo-American relations; patriotism; review of [Clyde Fitch's?] play on Nathan Hale.

99–8. "American literature in exile," *Literature,* March 3, 1899, n. s. I, 169–170.

Reprinted 02–C.

99–9. "Problems of existence in fiction," *Literature,* March 10, 1899, n. s. I, 193–194.

In answer to charge that the American novel never handles important problems firmly, Howells cites Fuller, Payne, Herrick, Crane, Frederic, Wilkins, Cable, and James.

99–10. "The passing of a poet," *Literature*, March 17, 1899, n. s. I, 217–219.

Obituary of Archibald Lampman.

99–11. "A case in point," *Literature*, March 24, 1899, n. s. I, 241–242.

Review of Frank Norris' *McTeague.*

99–12. "A new kind of play," *Literature*, March 31, 1899, n. s. I, 265–266.

Review of J. A. Herne's *Rev. Griffith Davenport.*

99–13. Ellen Burns Sherman, "To the use of edifying," *Critic*, April, 1899, n. s. XXXI, 319–320.

Report of speech at Social Reform Club.

99–14. "Concerning a counsel of imperfection," *Literature*, April 7, 1899, n. s. I, 289–290.

Advises writing for both an English and American audience — the international note and realism.

99–15. "A subscription theatre," *Literature*, April 14, 1899, n. s. I, 313–314.

Favors a popular theater — preferably state — for social criticism; remarks on Ibsen, Hauptmann, Sudermann, Shaw.

99–16. "The Canadian habitant in recent fiction," *Literature*, April 21, 1899, n. s. I, 337–338.

Review of French-Canadian literature.

99–17. "An opportunity for American fiction," *Literature*, April 28, May 5, 1899, n. s. I, 361–362, 385–386.

Review of Thorstein Veblen's *Theory of a* [*sic*] *leisure class.*

99–18. "The new poetry," *North American review*, May, 1899, CLXVIII, 581–592.

Kipling, William Watson, F. B. Money-Coutts, E. H. Coleridge, Stephen Phillips, John Davidson; Cawein, Mrs. C. P. Stetson, Garland, Dunbar. English and American imperialism.

99–19. "A charming Spanish novel," *Literature*, May 12, 1899, n. s. I, 409–410.

Review of A. P. Valdés' *La alegría del Capitán Ribot.*

99–20. "Arms and the men," *Literature*, May 19, 1899, n. s. I, 433–434.

War literature in periodicals.

99–21. "The new sort of stories," *Literature*, May 26, 1899, n. s. I, 457–458.

Essay on faked news stories, arising from J. L. Williams' *The stolen story and other newspaper stories.*

99–21a. "Poetry, war, and Mr. Howells," *Literary digest*, May 27, 1899, XVIII, 607–608.

Interview. The decline in poetry; war and literature with reference to Kipling. First printed New York *Sun.*

99–22. "Vengeance of the female," *Literature*, June 2, 1899, n. s. I, 481–482.

Review of Marrion Wilcox's book.

99–23. "Old Cambridge," *Literature*, June 9, 1899, n. s. I, 505–506.

Review of T. W. Higginson's *Old Cambridge:* Lowell, Longfellow, Holmes.

99–24. "A second apparition of 'Ghosts,'" *Literature*, June 16, 1899, n. s. I, 529–530.

Review of Ibsen's play.

99–25. "A new poet out of the West," *Literature*, June 23, 1899, n. s. I, 553–554.

Review of Edwin Markham's *The man with the hoe and other poems.*

99–26. "Are the Americans Bible readers?" *Literature*, June 30, 1899, n. s. I, 585–586.

Riches vs. the kingdom of heaven.

99–27. "A question of propriety," *Literature*, July 7, 1899, n. s. I, 609.

Defence of Ibsen's *Ghosts* on all grounds.

99–28. "Some suggestions from Mr. McCarthy," *Literature*, July 14, 21, 1899, n. s. II, 9, 33.

Review of Justin McCarthy's *Reminiscences;* comment on the New York *Tribune, Atlantic monthly, Nation, North American review;* literary circles.

99–29. "The latest avatar of American girlhood," *Literature*, July 28, 1899, n. s. II, 57–58.

Review of C. D. Warner's *That fortune*, with remarks on *Daisy Miller.*

99–30. "Breakfast is my best meal," *Frank Leslie's*, Aug., 1899, XLVIII, 388–391.

Illustrations by Charles Grunwald. Reprinted 16–C.

99–31. "Literary outlawry," *Literature*, Aug. 4, 1899, n. s. II, 81–82.

On Hay-Austin correspondence in matter of international copyright.

99–32. "Aesthetic New York fifty years ago," *Literature*, Aug. 11, 1899, n. s. II, 105–106.

Reprinted 02–C.

99–33. "The psychology of plagiarism," *Literature*, Aug. 18, 1899, n. s. II, 129–130.

Reprinted 02–C.

99–34. "Southwest and Northwest in recent verse, first paper," *Literature*, Aug. 25, 1899, n. s. II, 153–154.

Review, especially of Madison Cawein's *Myth and romance.*

99–35. "The Southwest and Northwest in recent poetry, second paper," *Literature*, Sept. 1, 1899, n. s. II, 177–178.

Review, especially of Hamlin Garland's *The trail of the goldseekers.*

99–36. "Letters of Ralph Waldo Emerson to a friend," *Literature*, Sept. 8, 1899, n. s. II, 201–202.

Review of the book, ed., C. E. Norton.

99–37. "Nothing to wear, and other poems," *Literature*, Sept. 15, 1899, n. s. II, 225–226.

Review of W. A. Butler's book.

99–38. "An obsolescent American type," *Literature*, Sept. 22, 1899, n. s. II, 249.

Review of George Ade's *Doc' Horne.*

99–39. "Portsmouth town," *Literature*, Sept. 29, 1899, n. s. II, 273–274.

Review of James De Normandie's [*et al.*] *Portsmouth book.*

99–40. "Our real grievance with England," *Literature*, Oct. 6, 1899, n. s. II, 297.

On William Archer's article, "America of today."

99–41. "Staccato notes of a vanished summer," *Literature*, Oct. 13 – Nov. 10, 1899, n. s. II.

In part reprinted 02–C.

99–B. The coast of Bohemia, biographical ed., Nov. 2.

99–42. "A pocketful of money," *Youth's companion*, Nov. 16, 23, 1899, LXXIII, 602–603, 617–618.

Reprinted 02–B.

99–43. "Room forty-five, (a farce)," *Frank Leslie's*, Dec., 1899, XLIX, 132–148.

Illustrations by F. W. Read. Reprinted 00–C.

99–44. "The magic of a voice," *Lippincott's*, Dec., 1899, LXIV, 901–928.

Reprinted 01–B.

99–C. Their silver wedding journey, Dec. 8.

1900

00–1. "Mr. Stockton and all his works," *Bookbuyer*, Feb., 1900, XX, 19–21.

Review of the Shenandoah edition.

00–2. Theodore Dreiser, "The real Howells," *Ainslee's*, March, 1900, V, 137–142.

Interview. Reprinted *Americana*, April, 1943, XXXVII, 274–282.

00–3. "The pursuit of the piano," *Harper's monthly*, April, 1900, c, 725–746.

Illustrations by Lucius Hitchcock. Reprinted 01–B.

00–3a. "Personals," *Literary digest*, April 7, 1900, xx, 438.

Seven-line letter, undated, to the Anti-Death Penalty League of Massachusetts. First printed?

00–4. "Mr. Charles W. Chesnutt's stories," *Atlantic monthly*, May, 1900, LXXXV, 699–701.

00–5. "Father and mother, a mystery," *Harper's monthly*, May, 1900, c, 869–874.

Reprinted 09–A.

00–6. "Heroines of nineteenth-century fiction," *Harper's bazar*, May 5, 1900 – Jan., 1902, xxxiii–xxxvi.

Reprinted 01–C.

00–7. "The hairbreadth escape of Jim Leonard," *Youth's companion*, May 10, 1900, LXXIV, 237–238.

Reprinted 02–B.

00–A. "Success and unsuccess," "The mulberries in Pay's garden," *The Hesperian tree*, May 17.

00–B. Bride roses, a scene, May 21.

00–C. Room forty-five, a farce, May 21.

00–7a. "A novelist on art," *Literary digest*, June 2, 1900, xx, 662–663.

Speech on art before the National Sculpture Society. First printed New York *Post*, May 16.

00–8. "A difficult case," *Atlantic monthly*, July, Aug., 1900, LXXXVI, 24–36, 205–217.

Reprinted 01–B.

00–D. An Indian giver, a comedy, Aug. 15.

00–E. The smoking car, a farce, Aug. 15.

00–9. "A personal retrospect of James Russell Lowell," *Scribner's*, Sept., 1900, xxviii, 363–378.

Reprinted 00–F.

00–10. "Some literary memories of Cambridge," *Harper's monthly*, Nov., 1900, ci, 823–839.

Reprinted 00–F.

00–11. "Mark Twain," New York *Times*, Nov. 17, 1900, p. 789.

Introduction of Clemens' Nov. 10 "Lotos Club speech."

00–F. Literary friends and acquaintance, a personal retrospect of American authorship, Nov. 17.

00–12. "Editor's easy chair," *Harper's monthly*, Dec., 1900, cii, 153–158.

Unsigned as with all items in this department until Sept., 1915; but the authorship was an open secret. Reprinted 10–D.

00–13. "The new historical romances," *North American review*, Dec., 1900, CLXXI, 935–948.

De Forest, Bellamy, and many others.

00–14. "The surprise party to Mark Twain," *Harper's weekly*, Dec. 15, 1900, XLIV, 1205.

Howells' "Lotos Club speech" with Clemens' comments.

00–15. W. S. Walsh, "William Dean Howells believes in the future," New York *Herald*, Dec. 30, 1900, v, 13.

Interview. Ranking of contemporary authors: among Americans James "most consummate artist," Twain "greater perhaps than Cervantes."

1901

01–1. "Editor's easy chair," *Harper's monthly*, Jan., 1901, cii, 316–320.

Manners; review of Henry James' *The soft side;* obituary of C. D. Warner.

01–2. "A hundred years of American verse," *North American review,* Jan., 1901, CLXXII, 148–160.

Review of *An American anthology, 1787–1899,* ed., E. C. Stedman.

01–3. "At third hand, a psychological inquiry," *Century,* Feb., 1901, LXI, 496–506.

Reprinted 03–B.

01–4. "Editor's easy chair," *Harper's monthly,* Feb., 1901, CII, 478–482.

Review of Lord Rosebery's *Napoleon, the last phase;* Anglophobia; review of Mrs. Humphry Ward's *Eleanor.*

01–5. "Mark Twain, an inquiry," *North American review,* Feb., 1901, CLXXII, 306–321.

Reprinted 10–C.

01–5a. "Is New York 'a city without a face'?" New York *Herald,* Feb. 3, 1901, v, 6.

A statement, in reply to E. H. Crosby, on literature in New York.

01–5b. "New York the loneliest city in the world...a symposium," New York *Herald,* Feb. 10, 1901, v, 1.

A city of coteries and cliques: slight autobiographical references.

01–6. "Editor's easy chair," *Harper's monthly,* March, 1901, CII, 640–643.

Reprinted 02–C.

01–7. "The recent dramatic season," *North American review,* March, 1901, CLXXII, 468–480.

Reviews of Pinero's *The gay Lord Quex;* Herne's *Sag Harbor;* Augustus Thomas' *Arizona;* Clyde Fitch's *The climbers;* Robert Grant's *Unleavened bread;* Robert Marshall's *A royal family;* H. A. Jones' *Mrs. Dane's defence;* [R. C. Critchett's] *Lady Huntworth's experiment.*

01–8. "Editor's easy chair," *Harper's monthly,* April, 1901, CII, 802–806.

Popular and trashy books; review of José Rizal's *An eagle flight;* anti-imperialism.

01–9. "Professor Barrett Wendell's notions of American literature," *North American review,* April, 1901, CLXXII, 623–640.

Review of *A literary history of America.*

01–A. "How William Dean Howells worked to secure a foothold," *How they succeeded,* April 25.

01–10. "Editor's easy chair," *Harper's monthly,* May, 1901, CII, 966–970.

Review of N. S. Shaler's *The individual, a study of life and death;* war, wealth, lynching.

01–11. "The new poetic drama," *North American review,* May, 1901, CLXXII, 794–800.

Superiority of Stephen Phillips to Rostand.

01–12. "Young contributors and editors," *Youth's companion,* May 9, 23, 1901, LXXV, 245, 267–268.

Reminiscence.

01–B. A *pair of patient lovers,* May 23.

01–13. "Editor's easy chair," *Harper's monthly,* June, 1901, CIII, 146–151.

Reprinted 02–C.

01–14. "An earlier American," *North American review,* June, 1901, CLXXII, 934–944.

Review of W. J. Stillman's *The autobiography of a journalist.* The end of an epoch in American life; the Philippines.

01–15. "Editor's easy chair," *Harper's monthly,* July, 1901, CIII, 311–314.

Senator Depew on classes.

01–16. "A possible difference in English and American fiction," *North American review,* July, 1901, CLXXIII, 134–144.

Mrs. Humphry Ward's *Eleanor* is really American.

01–17. "John Fiske," *Harper's weekly,* July 20, 1901, XLV, 732.

Obituary.

01–18. "Editor's easy chair," *Harper's monthly,* Aug., 1901, CIII, 490–495.

The hall of fame – old America and the "dying republic."

01–19. "An exemplary citizen," *North American review,* Aug., 1901, CLXXIII, 280–288.

Reviews of B. T. Washington's *Up from slavery;* F. M. Holland's *Frederick Douglass;* C. W. Chesnutt's *Frederick Douglass.*

01–20. "Editor's easy chair," *Harper's monthly,* Sept., 1901, CIII, 655–659.

Libraries and readers.

01–21. "Some anomalies of the short story," *North American review,* Sept., 1901, CLXXIII, 422–432.

Reprinted 02–C.

01–22. "Editor's easy chair," *Harper's monthly,* Oct., 1901, CIII, 822–827.

Reviews of Edith Wyatt's *Every one his own way;* Edith Wharton's *Crucial instances;* Henry B. Fuller's *The last refuge;* Frank Norris' *The octopus;* A. S. Pier's *The sentimentalists;* Kenneth Brown's and H. B. Booth's [Boone's] *Eastover Courthouse;* Will Harben's *Westerfelt;* Vaughan Kester's *The manager of the B. and A.*

01–23. "An Italian view of humor," *North American review,* Oct., Nov., 1901, CLXXIII, 567–576, 709–720.

Review of Paolo Bellezza's *Humour;* Mark Twain and others. In part reprinted 10–C.

01–C. Heroines of fiction, two volumes, Oct. 26.

01–24. "Editor's easy chair," *Harper's monthly,* Nov., 1901, CIII, 1004–1008.

Women, education, and Stanley Hall.

01–D. Italian journeys, revised and illustrated ed., Nov. 12.

01–E. Italian journeys, illustrated English ed., Nov.

01–25. "Editor's easy chair," *Harper's monthly,* Dec., 1901, CIV, 162–166.

Reprinted 02–C.

01–26. "A psychological counter-current in recent fiction," *North American review,* Dec., 1901, CLXXIII, 872–888.

Realism in the tide of romantic "historical" novels: Gilbert Parker, Henry Van Dyke, W. A. White, Maxim Gorky, S. W. Mitchell, Onoto Watana [*sic*], C. W. Chesnutt, Bertha von Süttner, Basil King.

01–F. Florence in art and literature, ed. with Russell Sturgis, Dec. 13.

1902

02–1. "How to win success in literature," *Booklover's,* Jan., Feb., 1902, II, 570.

Thirty lines of platitude; probably reprinted.

02–2. "Editor's easy chair," *Harper's monthly,* Jan., 1902, CIV, 334–338.

State of the nation, especially the presidency.

02–3. "Some new volumes of verse," *North American review,* Jan., 1902, CLXXIV, 136–144.

Review of *A history of American verse,* J. C. Onderdonk; Edwin Markham, Thomas Hardy, Madison Cawein, Gelett Burgess, Oliver Herford.

02–3a. "Does entertaining entertain?" *Harper's weekly,* Jan. 11, 1902, XLVI, 37.

Difficulties of cabinet members' entertaining on eight thousand a year. Unsigned: see 02–4 and note the expression "higher journalism."

02–4. "The militant muse," *Harper's weekly,* Jan. 18, 1902, XLVI, 69.

Anti-imperialism and Kipling's "The islanders."

Unsigned as all *Harper's weekly* 1902 and 1903 items except 02–27, 47, 51, 52, and 03–22, 26, 27, 28, 43, 51. On nearly all the numbers of *Harper's weekly* for this period (and on all those from which items are attributed except 02–45a, 03–12, and 03–12a) Howells' name appears on the cover as a contributor. However, in only three cases is there external proof of authorship: 02–9 (see *Life in letters,* II, 153); 03–17 (the article is promised in an earlier number); and the "Diversions of the

Periodical Publications... – 1902, continued
higher journalist" articles, 03–26 to 03–53 *passim* (the first three are signed, the rest are anonymous).

A folder in the Howells collection at Harvard (which was brought to our attention by Mr. R. H. Ballinger) contains sheets from *Harper's weekly* for this period. These appear to have been collected by Howells, perhaps as material for a projected book. Since whole leaves are filed without marking, ascription still cannot be made with absolute certainty, but the case for the inclusion of this body of material is strengthened. The file contains articles signed by Howells or ascribable from external evidence, but it does not contain *all* the articles of this sequence so signed or ascribed. We thus feel justified both in regarding the material in the folder as Howells' and in listing articles not in the folder. The following articles of the sequence are those found on the sheets in the folder: 95–5; 02–29, 36a, 40, 41, 42 (two sheets: p. 1547–1550), 45a, 53; 03–4, 4a, 5, 7, 8, 9, 11, 12, 12a, 17, 18, 21, 22, 23, 25, 26, 27, 28, 30, 32, 33, 35, 37; 04–3, 5, 10.

Although this scarcity of external proof and the fact that none of the unsigned articles is reprinted in a Howells book may cause some scepticism about the authorship, examination of the articles here attributed will remove all doubts, for with the possible exception of three (02–36a, 03–4a, 13–12a) found in the folder, they are thoroughly Howellsian in manner and attitude. (In regard to their anti-imperialism, see W. M. Gibson, "Mark Twain and William Dean Howells, anti-imperialists.") The material in question has been thoroughly read and discussed by the collaborators in this bibliography and in cases of slightest doubt has indeed been so summarily rejected that it is certain that many articles in this series by Howells remain unidentified here.

In suggesting two additions (02–3a, 5a) to our original list, Mr. A. B. Fox has remarked: "Every Howells contribution seems to have occupied the last position on page 5 in the magazine, and all the articles in this position which I have examined point to Howells."

02–5. "Editor's easy chair," *Harper's monthly,* Feb., 1902, CIV, 500–504.
The rich; review of H. E. Scudder's *James Russell Lowell.*

02–5a. "The limitations of irony," *Harper's weekly,* Feb. 1, 1902, XLVI, 133.
Examples in 02–3a and in a comment on the Boer War replied to by Labouchere in *Truth* (London).

02–6. "The turning of the dove," *Harper's weekly,* Feb. 8, 1902, XLVI, 165.
On Philippine matter.

02–7. "His apparition," *Harper's monthly,* March, 1902, CIV, 621–648.
Reprinted 03–B.

02–8. "Editor's easy chair," *Harper's monthly,* March, 1902, CIV, 670–674.
Review of T. R. Lounsbury's *Shakespeare as a literary artist.*

02–9. "The worst of being poor," *Harper's weekly,* March 1, 1902, XLVI, 261.
Fear of want.

02–10. "The premature preference of the Rev. Dr. Bagnell," *Harper's weekly,* March 8, 1902, XLVI, 293.
Bagnell wants an empire under Roosevelt.

02–11. "A fatal ignorance of liberty," *Harper's weekly,* March 15, 1902, XLVI, 325.
Anti-imperialism; civil liberty.

02–12. "The grand old name of gentleman," *Harper's weekly,* March 29, 1902, XLVI, 389.

02–13. "Editor's easy chair," *Harper's monthly,* April, 1902, CIV, 833–837.
Review of G. R. Carpenter's *Longfellow;* deaths of Clarence King and H. E. Scudder.

02–14. "The disadvantages of heroism," *Harper's weekly,* April 12, 1902, XLVI, 457.
Rapidly declining fame of Dewey and others.

02–A. *The Kentons, a novel,* April 18.

02–15. "The new phase of the labor problem," *Harper's weekly,* April 26, 1902, XLVI, 521.
Hartford election.

02–16. "Editor's easy chair," *Harper's monthly,* May, 1902, CIV, 995–999.

Review of Baldassare Castiglione's *The courtier.*

02–17. "Race-patriotism," *Harper's weekly,* May 10, 1902, XLVI, 585.

Wants world union and no Anglo-Saxon empire.

02–18. "Some considerations for monarchical countries," *Harper's weekly,* May 17, 1902, XLVI, 617.

The Dutch queen; Howells' typical, mild, political Anglophobia.

02–19. "An anxious inquiry," *Harper's weekly,* May 24, 1902, XLVI, 651.

On honor vs. honour.

02–20. "Editor's easy chair," *Harper's monthly,* June, 1902, CV, 146–151.

Reprinted 02–C.

02–21. "Philippine casuistry," *Harper's weekly,* June 7, 1902, XLVI, 715.

02–22. "A suggestion from the Boer War," *Harper's weekly,* June 14, 1902, XLVI, 747.

02–23. "Ping-pong and popular fiction," *Harper's weekly,* June 21, 1902, XLVI, 779.

02–24. "Without our special wonder," *Harper's weekly,* June 28, 1902, XLVI, 811.

General matters of the day; Philippines and Negroes.

02–25. "Editor's easy chair," *Harper's monthly,* July, 1902, CV, 308–312.

Literary revivals. Dickens.

02–26. "Superfluous partings," *Harper's weekly,* July 5, 1902, XLVI, 864.

Public good-byes.

02–27. "The Fourth-of-July boy," *Harper's weekly,* July 5, 1902, XLVI, 867–870.

Reprinted 02–B.

02–28. "The turning of the tide," *Harper's weekly,* July 12, 1902, XLVI, 907.

Approves of N. S. Shaler's Phi Beta Kappa poem.

02–29. "Some modest misgivings," *Harper's weekly,* July 19, 1902, XLVI, 946.

God as an avenger; anti-imperialism.

02–30. "Anticipative history," *Harper's weekly,* July 26, 1902, XLVI, 986.

Postponed coronation; a peer's daughter's report printed too early.

02–31. "Editor's easy chair," *Harper's monthly,* Aug., 1902, CV, 479–483.

Samuel Richardson.

02–32. "A little mistake," *Harper's weekly,* Aug. 2, 1902, XLVI, 1029.

On Garland's supposed condemning of Longfellow, with "later" retraction.

02–33. "Puritanic influences on American literature," *Harper's weekly,* Aug. 16, 1902, XLVI, 1110.

02–34. "Editor's easy chair," *Harper's monthly,* Sept., 1902, CV, 640–645.

Neglect of poetry.

02–35. "Will the novel disappear?" *North American review,* Sept., 1902, CLXXV, 291–294.

A symposium with Allen, Garland, Mabie, Bangs.

02–36. "Reminiscences of Bret Harte, fac-simile of letter from William Dean Howells," *Overland monthly,* Sept., 1902, XL, 226–227.

To Wallace Irwin, editor, dated June 2, 1902: Harte had literary finish.

02–36a. "An imperial opportunity," *Harper's weekly,* Sept. 6, 1902, XLVI, 1236–1237.

The Kaiser's proposed international congress on earthquakes.

02–B. The flight of Pony Baker, a boy's town story, Sept. 26.

02–37. "Editor's easy chair," *Harper's monthly,* Oct., 1902, cv, 802–805.
Copyright and American fiction.

02–38. "Evidences of civilization," *Harper's weekly,* Oct. 4, 1902, xlvi, 1405–1406.

02–39. "The literary outlook," *Harper's weekly,* Oct. 4, 1902, xlvi, 1407.
Henry James and N. S. Shaler.

02–40. "Woman's limitations in burlesque," *Harper's weekly,* Oct. 11, 1902, xlvi, 1465.

02–C. Literature and life, studies, Oct. 14.

02–41. "The appeal to women," *Harper's weekly,* Oct. 18, 1902, xlvi, 1506–1507.
The revolt of domestic servants.

02–42. "Can a crime be expiated?" *Harper's weekly,* Oct. 25, 1902, xlvi, 1547.
Prison matters; review of R. W. Kauffman's *The things that are Caesar's.*

02–43. "Editor's easy chair," *Harper's monthly,* Nov., 1902, cv, 963–967.
Review of Leslie Stephen's *George Eliot;* W. C. Brownell.

02–44. "What should girls read?" *Harper's bazar,* Nov., 1902, xxxvi, 956–960.
Howells at his most liberal on sex.

02–45. "Émile Zola," *North American review,* Nov., 1902, clxxv, 587–596.
Discussion of naturalism. Reprinted 24–A.

02–45a. "A new touch," *Harper's weekly,* Nov. 15, 1902, xlvi, 1696.
Review of R. R. Gilson's *In the morning glow.*

02–46. "The threatening aspect of the servant problem," *Harper's weekly,* Nov. 22, 1902, xlvi, 1754.
Cf. 02–41.

02–47. "City and country in the fall," *Harper's weekly,* Nov. 29, 1902, xlvi, 1792.
Reprinted 16–C.

02–48. "The mother," *Harper's monthly,* Dec., 1902, cvi, 21–26.
Reprinted 09–A.

02–49. "Editor's easy chair," *Harper's monthly,* Dec., 1902, cvi, 163–167.
Fairs in America.

02–50. "Frank Norris," *North American review,* Dec., 1902, clxxv, 769–778.

02–51. "The Christmas spirit," *Harper's weekly,* Dec. 6, 1902, xlvi, 1822–1824.
Ironic poem on the condition of the world.

02–52. "A double-barrelled sonnet to Mark Twain," *Harper's weekly,* Dec. 13, 1902, xlvi, 1943.
Read at the sixty-seventh birthday.

02–53. "The vulgarity of wealth," *Harper's weekly,* Dec. 27, 1902, xlvi, 2021–2022.
Opinions of Marie Corelli; compare Clemens'.

1903

03–A. "Success — a parable," "Hot," "Awaiting his exequatur," *The Hesperian tree,* Dec. 10, 1902.

03–1. "Editor's easy chair," *Harper's monthly,* Jan., 1903, cvi, 324–328.
A woman's club (the Muses) discussing modern literature; review of Mrs. Katherine Hooker's *Wayfarers of Italy;* Norris, Howells, Wilkins. In part reprinted 10–D.

03–2. "Mr. Henry James's later work," *North American review,* Jan., 1903, clxxvi, 125–137.
In part conversation on James presenting pro's and con's; reviews especially of *Wings of the dove, Awkward age,* and *Sacred fount.*

03–3. "Good resolutions," *Harper's weekly,* Jan. 3, 1903, xlvii, 20.
At the new year.

03–4. "The latest royal scandal," *Harper's weekly,* Jan. 10, 1903, xlvii, 61.
Crown Princess of Saxony's adultery.

03–4a. "The passing of the beard," *Harper's weekly,* Jan. 17, 1903, xlvii, 102.

03–5. "To the Jews a stumbling-block and to the Greeks foolishness," *Harper's weekly,* Jan. 31, 1903, xlvii, 189.
Wealth.

03–6. "Editor's easy chair," *Harper's monthly,* Feb., 1903, cvi, 486–490.
Reprinted 10–D.

03–7. "The unreality of reality," *Harper's weekly,* Feb. 7, 1903, xlvii, 229.
Property.

03–8. "The law and the penalty," *Harper's weekly,* Feb. 14, 1903, xlvii, 269.
Review of Benjamin Howard's *Prisoners of Russia.*

03–9. "The making over of a minx," *Harper's weekly,* Feb. 21, 1903, xlvii, 307–308.
Review of Mrs. Humphry Ward's *Lady Rose's daughter* (in serialization).

03–10. "Editor's easy chair," *Harper's monthly,* March, 1903, cvi, 649–653.
Country origins extolled.

03–11. "A personal question," *Harper's weekly,* March 7, 1903, xlvii, 388–389.
Roosevelt and the size of families.

03–12. "The spread of the hook-bug," *Harper's weekly,* March 14, 1903, xlvii, 429.
Review of Harvey Sutherland's *Book of bugs.*

03–12a. "The last work of Frank Norris," *Harper's weekly,* March 14, 1903, xlvii, 433.
Review of *The pit.*

03–13. "Tainted money," *Harper's weekly,* March 21, 1903, xlvii, 468.
Endowments; Lowell.

03–14. "Though one rose from the dead," *Harper's monthly,* April, 1903, cvi, 724–738.
Reprinted 03–B.

03–15. "Editor's easy chair," *Harper's monthly,* April, 1903, cvi, 810–815.
Reprinted 10–D.

03–16. "Letters home," *Metropolitan,* April – Sept., 1903, xviii.
Illustrations by William Glackens. Reprinted 03–C.

03–17. "The literary outlook and in-look," *Harper's weekly,* April 11, 1903, xlvii, 607–608.

03–18. "Entertaining on thirty-five hundred a year," *Harper's weekly,* April 25, 1903, xlvii, 691.

03–19. "Editor's easy chair," *Harper's monthly,* May, 1903, cvi, 972–976.
Philanthropy; author-publisher relationship. Reviews of Boileau's *Les héros de roman,* ed., T. F. Crane; T. R. Lounsbury's *Shakespeare and Voltaire;* G. S. Lee's *The lost art of reading.*

03–20. "Certain of the Chicago school of fiction," *North American review,* May, 1903, clxxvi, 734–746.
Edith Wyatt, George Ade, F. P. Dunne; reference to H. B. Fuller, Will Payne, Robert Herrick, Brand Whitlock, Frank Norris.

03–21. "A triad of admirable books," *Harper's weekly,* May 2, 1903, xlvii, 732–733.
Reviews of G. S. Wasson's *Captain Simeon's store;* G. L. Collins' *Putnam Place;* J. D. Barry's *A daughter of Thespis.*

Periodical Publications... — 1903, continued

03–22. "Impressions of Emerson," *Harper's weekly,* May 16, 1903, XLVII, 784.

03–B. *Questionable shapes,* May 19.

03–23. "An embarrassing situation," *Harper's weekly,* May 30, 1903, XLVII, 916.

Deals leniently with divorce and has sidelight on socialism.

03–24. "Editor's easy chair," *Harper's monthly,* June, 1903, CVII, 146–150.

Immortality, with mention of John Bigelow's "On the mystery of sleep"; review of Helen Keller's *The story of my life.*

03–25. "Public billing and cooing," *Harper's weekly,* June 6, 1903, XLVII, 956.

Suggests — "pure socialism" — bowers for park-lovers.

03–26. "Diversions of the higher journalist, a change in the insular attitude," *Harper's weekly,* June 13, 1903, XLVII, 997.

H. G. Wells' and Auberon Herbert's criticism of Americans.

03–27. "Diversions of the higher journalist, world-power weather," *Harper's weekly,* June 20, 1903, XLVII, 1055.

03–28. "Diversions of the higher journalist, a grain of wheat in the heap of chaff," *Harper's weekly,* June 27, 1903, XLVII, 1093.

The glamorous South in American literature; H. B. Boone's and Kenneth Brown's *The Redfields succession* an exception.

03–29. "Editor's easy chair," *Harper's monthly,* July, 1903, CVII, 308–312.

Symposium on reliving life; review of *Letters and memorials of Jane Welsh Carlyle,* introduction, James Crichton-Browne (with mention of J. A. Froude).

03–30. "Diversions of the higher journalist, the apotheosis of M. Rostand," *Harper's weekly,* July 4, 1903, XLVII, 1112.

Higher journalist and shade of Émile Zola discuss Rostand's getting into the French Academy.

03–31. "Diversions of the higher journalist, two contrasting and fascinating books," *Harper's weekly,* July 11, 1903, XLVII, 1148.

Reviews of Carl Snyder's *New conceptions in science* and Howard Pyle's *Rejected of men.*

03–32. "Diversions of the higher journalist, litera scripta manet," *Harper's weekly,* July 18, 1903, XLVII, 1184.

On letters of Margaret Fuller and John Ruskin; the open letter of J. A. Froude about the Carlyles.

03–33. "Diversions of the higher journalist, a scientific city," *Harper's weekly,* July 25, 1903, XLVII, 1220.

A South Carolina utopia.

03–34. "Editor's easy chair," *Harper's monthly,* Aug., 1903, CVII, 480–483.

C. G. Leland's translations of Heine.

03–35. "Diversions of the higher journalist, decay of American manners," *Harper's weekly,* Aug. 1, 1903, XLVII, 1256.

"Shirtsleeves," paradoxes in American life.

03–36. "Editor's easy chair," *Harper's monthly,* Sept., 1903, CVII, 641–645.

Reprinted 10–D.

03–37. "Diversions of the higher journalist, reversible proverbs," *Harper's weekly,* Sept. 12, 1903, XLVII, 1472.

"New teeth for old saws."

03–C. *Letters home,* Sept. 18.

03–38. "Diversions of the higher journalist, wanted, a name," *Harper's weekly,* Sept. 19, 1903, XLVII, 1508.

Place names in the United States; apartment names.

03–39. "Editor's easy chair," *Harper's monthly,* Oct., 1903, cvii, 802–806.

Review of Carl Snyder's *New conceptions in science.* In part reprinted 10–D.

03–40. "Diversions of the higher journalist, a new evil," *Harper's weekly,* Oct. 3, 1903, xlvii, 1580.

Puffs of popular books.

03–41. "Diversions of the higher journalist, the age of a book," *Harper's weekly,* Oct. 17, 1903, xlvii, 1660.

Review of George Horton's *In Argolis.*

03–42. "Diversions of the higher journalist, an eye for an eye," *Harper's weekly,* Oct. 24, 1903, xlvii, 1696.

The Van Wormer boy's murder of an uncle and electrocution.

03–43. "An immortal of Boston," *Harper's weekly,* Oct. 31, 1903, xlvii, 1737.

Samuel Gridley Howe in Maude Howe's and F. H. Hall's *Laura Bridgman, Dr. Howe's famous pupil and what he taught her.*

03–44. "Editor's easy chair," *Harper's monthly,* Nov., 1903, cvii, 964–968.

Reading of poetry: a symposium discussed.

03–45. "Diversions of the higher journalist, the thing which hath been," *Harper's weekly,* Nov. 14, 1903, xlvii, 1816.

Review of T. A. Janvier's *The Dutch founding of New York.*

03–46. "Diversions of the higher journalist, the American field for English fiction," *Harper's weekly,* Nov. 28, 1903, xlvii, 1896.

Review of E. F. Benson's *The relentless city;* American novelists should return to their native fields.

03–46a. "Reading for a grandfather," *Harper's bazar,* Dec., 1903, xxxvii, 1153–1157.

03–47. "Sorrow, my sorrow," *Harper's monthly,* Dec., 1903, cviii, 147.

Poem.

03–48. "Editor's easy chair," *Harper's monthly,* Dec., 1903, cviii, 153–159.

Review of C. W. Stoddard's *Exits and entrances.* Bret Harte in Cambridge. Reprinted with revisions 11–F.

03–49. "The personality of Hawthorne," *North American review,* Dec., 1903, clxxvii, 872–882.

Review of Julian Hawthorne's *Hawthorne and his circle.*

03–50. "Diversions of the higher journalist, the livable sort of city," *Harper's weekly,* Dec. 5, 1903, xlvii, 1936.

"The Tarsus of New England."

03–51. "Christmas," *Harper's weekly,* Dec. 12, 1903, xlvii, 18 (Christmas number).

Sonnet.

03–52. "Diversions of the higher journalist, the superstition of the society page," *Harper's weekly,* Dec. 19, 1903, xlvii, 2056.

Review of J. L. Ford's *The brazen calf.*

03–53. "Diversions of the higher journalist, the serial story and its shrinkage," *Harper's weekly,* Dec. 26, 1903, xlvii, 2090.

Defends serialization of novels.

1904

04–1. "Editor's easy chair," *Harper's monthly,* Jan., 1904, cviii, 317–320.

Reprinted 10–D.

04–2. "The son of Royal Langbrith," *North American review,* Jan. – Aug., 1904, clxxviii–clxxix.

Reprinted 04–B.

04–3. "A painful subject," *Harper's weekly,* Jan. 9, 1904, XLVIII, 48.

H. G. Wells on author-publisher relation leads Howells to believe that time is ripe for author's union if not for publisher's syndicate.

04–4. "Some new American plays," *Harper's weekly,* Jan. 16, 1904, XLVIII, 88, 90.

Reviews of Clyde Fitch's *Her own way* and *Glad of it;* George Ade's *The county chairman;* Augustus Thomas' *The other girl.*

04–5. "Some new English plays," *Harper's weekly,* Jan. 23, 1904, XLVIII, 124, 126.

Reviews of Barrie's *The admirable Crichton;* H. A. Jones' *Whitewashing Julia;* Zangwill's *Merely Mary Ann;* Shaw's *Candida.*

04–6. "Privileges of the theatre," *Harper's weekly,* Jan. 30, 1904, XLVIII, 160, 162.

Review of Brander Matthews' *The development of the drama.*

04–7. "Editor's easy chair," *Harper's monthly,* Feb., 1904, CVIII, 478–482.

Reviews of R. H. Stoddard's *Recollections, personal and literary;* J. T. Trowbridge's *Story of my own life.*

04–8. A. Schade Van Westrum, "Mr. Howells on love and literature," *Lamp,* Feb., 1904, XXVIII, 26–31.

Interview.

04–9. "State manslaughter," *Harper's weekly,* Feb. 6, 1904, XLVIII, 196, 198.

Capital punishment.

04–10. "Spoiling the rod and sparing the child," *Harper's weekly,* Feb. 13, 1904, XLVIII, 232.

On member of Society of Medical Jurisprudence who recommends whipping children for criminal acts.

04–11. "What shall we do with our sympathies?" *Harper's weekly,* Feb. 27, 1904, XLVIII, 321.

Russo-Japanese war: the soldiers on both sides have no more real interest in the outcome than we have.

04–12. "Editor's easy chair," *Harper's monthly,* March, 1904, CVIII, 640–644.

Review of A. R. Wallace's *Man's place in the universe.*

04–13. "Editor's easy chair," *Harper's monthly,* April, 1904, CVIII, 802–806.

Review of Luigi Cornaro's *The temperate life.*

04–14. "Experience," *Harper's monthly,* May, 1904, CVIII, 929.

Poem.

04–15. "Editor's easy chair," *Harper's monthly,* May, 1904, CVIII, 964–968.

Reprinted 10–D.

04–A. "Meetings with Clarence King," *Clarence King memoirs,* May 9.

04–16. "Editor's easy chair," *Harper's monthly,* June, 1904, CIX, 147–151.

Reviews of G. B. McClellan's *The oligarchy of Venice;* James Howell's *Survey of the Signorie of Venice.*

04–17. "Editor's easy chair," *Harper's monthly,* July, 1904, CIX, 309–312.

Morals and manners in travel.

04–18. "Editor's easy chair," *Harper's monthly,* Aug., 1904, CIX, 480–483.

Education.

04–19. "Editor's easy chair," *Harper's monthly,* Sept., 1904, CIX, 642–645.

Reviews of Philip Burne-Jones' *Democracy and dollars;* G. O. Trevelyan's *History of the American Revolution;* A. R. Colquhoun's *Greater America.*

04–20. "Editor's easy chair," *Harper's monthly,* Oct., 1904, CIX, 803–806.

Reprinted 10–D.

04–B. *The son of Royal Langbrith, a novel,* Oct. 6.

04–21. "In Folkestone out of season," *Harper's monthly,* Nov., 1904, CIX, 821–830.
Reprinted 06–F.

04–22. "Editor's easy chair," *Harper's monthly,* Nov., 1904, CIX, 965–969.
Reprinted 10–D.

04–23. "London films," *Harper's monthly,* Dec., 1904, CX, 67–78.
Reprinted 06–A.

04–24. "Editor's easy chair," *Harper's monthly,* Dec., 1904, CX, 159–161.
Charity; copyright laws.

04–25. "English feeling toward Americans," *North American review,* Dec., 1904, CLXXIX, 815–823.
Reprinted 06–A.

04–26. "A seasonable moral," *Harper's weekly,* Dec. 10, 1904, XLVIII, 42 (Christmas number).
Poem on giving.

1905

05–1. "Editha," *Harper's monthly,* Jan., 1905, CX, 214–224.
Reprinted 07–D.

05–2. "Editor's easy chair," *Harper's monthly,* Jan., 1905, CX, 317–320.
On symposium on thinking-process.

05–3. "Editor's easy chair," *Harper's monthly,* Feb., 1905, CX, 479–483.
On symposium on marriage.

05–4. "In the season, London films. – Part II," *Harper's monthly,* March, 1905, CX, 559–569.
Reprinted 06–A.

05–5. "Editor's easy chair," *Harper's monthly,* March, 1905, CX, 641–645.
Variety in life; the pioneer age.

05–6. "The landing of a pilgrim," *Harper's monthly,* April, 1905, CX, 707–718.
Reprinted 06–F.

05–7. "Editor's easy chair," *Harper's monthly,* April, 1905, CX, 803–806.
Review of Louis Dyer's *Machiavelli and the modern state;* extended remarks on religion and society.

05–8. "Editor's easy chair," *Harper's monthly,* May, 1905, CX, 965–968.
Reprinted 10–D.

05–9. "In summer, London films. – Part III," *Harper's monthly,* June, 1905, CXI, 104–116.
With changed order reprinted 06–A.

05–10. "Editor's easy chair," *Harper's monthly,* June, 1905, CXI, 147–150.
Age and usefulness; William Osler.

05–A. Miss Bellard's inspiration, June 8.

05–11. "A day at Henley," *Harper's weekly,* June 10, 1905, XLIX, 826–828, 843.
Reprinted 06–A.

05–12. "American origins, London films. – Part IV," *Harper's monthly,* July, 1905, CXI, 185–197.
Reprinted 06–A.

05–13. "Editor's easy chair," *Harper's monthly,* July, 1905, CXI, 309–312.
Reprinted 10–D.

05–14. "American origins, London films. – Part V," *Harper's monthly,* Aug., 1905, CXI, 368–380.
With slight changes reprinted 06–A.

05–15. "Editor's easy chair," *Harper's monthly,* Aug., 1905, CXI, 471–473.
Reprinted 10–D.

05–16. "The peacemakers at Portsmouth," *Harper's weekly,* Aug. 26, 1905, XLIX, 1225, 1244.

05–17. "Twenty-four hours at Exeter," *Harper's monthly,* Sept., 1905, CXI, 497–506.
Reprinted 06–F.

06–12. "Editor's easy chair," *Harper's monthly,* June, 1906, cxiii, 148–151..
State of literature.

06–13. "An English country town and country house," *Harper's monthly,* July, 1906, cxiii, 165–175.
Reprinted 06–F.

06–14. "Editor's easy chair," *Harper's monthly,* July, 1906, cxiii, 310–313.
Reprinted 10–D.

06–15. "Henrik Ibsen," *North American review,* July, 1906, clxxxiii, 1–14.

06–16. "The eidolons of Brooks Alford," *Harper's monthly,* Aug., 1906, cxiii, 387–397.
Reprinted 07–D.

06–17. "Editor's easy chair," *Harper's monthly,* Aug., 1906, cxiii, 473–475.
Reprinted 10–D.

06–D. "Introduction," *Different girls,* Aug. 17.

06–E. "Introduction," *Quaint courtships,* Aug. 17.

06–18. "Kentish neighborhoods, including Canterbury," *Harper's monthly,* Sept., 1906, cxiii, 550–563.
Reprinted 06–F.

06–19. "Editor's easy chair," *Harper's monthly,* Sept., 1906, cxiii, 634–637.
Spelling reform.

06–20. Review of R. H. Hutton's *Brief literary criticism. North American review,* Sept. 7, 1906, clxxxiii, 404–406.

06–21. "Editor's easy chair," *Harper's monthly,* Oct., 1906, cxiii, 795–798.
Review of Aeschylus' *Agamemnon* (Harvard performance).

06–22. "Our daily speech," *Harper's bazar,* Oct., 1906, xl, 930–934.
American women lectured.

06–23. "Oxford," *North American review,* Oct. 5, 1906, clxxxiii, 620–638.
Reprinted 06–F.

06–24. Review of H. G. Wells' *Kipps. North American review,* Oct. 19, 1906, clxxxiii, 795–798.

06–F. Certain delightful English towns with glimpses of the pleasant country between, Oct. 26.

06–25. "By way of Southampton to London," *Harper's monthly,* Nov., 1906, cxiii, 892–903.
Reprinted 06–F.

06–26. "Editor's easy chair," *Harper's monthly,* Nov., 1906, cxiii, 957–960.
Noise.

06–27. "The season's plays, three differently interesting plays," *Harper's weekly,* Nov. 24, 1906, l, 1682–1683.
Reviews of Pinero's *His house in order;* H. A. Jones' *The hypocrites;* [Jacob Gordin's] *The Kreutzer sonata* [trans., Langdon Mitchell].

06–28. "After the wedding," *Harper's monthly,* Dec., 1906, cxiv, 64–69.
Reprinted 09–A.

06–29. "Editor's easy chair," *Harper's monthly,* Dec., 1906, cxiv, 155–158.
The Greek and American minds.

06–G. "Introduction" and "The amigo," *The heart of childhood,* Dec. 1.

06–30. "A sleep and a forgetting," *Harper's weekly,* Dec. 15, 1906 – Jan. 5, 1907, l–li.
Reprinted 07–D.

06–31. "The fiction of John Oliver Hobbes," *North American review,* Dec. 21, 1906, clxxxiii, 1251–1261.
Mrs. P. R. Craigie.

1907

07–1. "Editor's easy chair," *Harper's monthly,* Jan., 1907, cxiv, 317–320.

Canada and Ottawa.

07–2. "An autobiographical view of the 'Weekly,'" *Harper's weekly,* Jan. 5, 1907, li, 19–20.

07–3. "Address of William Dean Howells," *Cambridge Historical Society Publications,* Feb., 1907, ii, 60–72.

On Longfellow. Reprinted (or first printed) 07–6.

07–4. "Editor's easy chair," *Harper's monthly,* Feb., 1907, cxiv, 479–482.

Review of Paul Birukoff's *Leo Tolstoy, his life and works;* Stendhal, Whitman.

07–A. "Introduction," *Southern lights and shadows,* Feb. 28.

07–5. "Editor's easy chair," *Harper's monthly,* March, 1907, cxiv, 641–644.

Reprinted 10–D.

07–6. "The art of Longfellow," *North American review,* March 1, 1907, clxxxiv, 472–485.

First printed (or reprinted) 07–3.

07–7. "Editor's easy chair," *Harper's monthly,* April, 1907, cxiv, 803–806.

Review of Mrs. F. H. Hall's *Social usages at Washington.*

07–8. "The editor's diary, Saturday, March 30, 'The turn of the balance,'" *North American review,* April 5, 1907, clxxxiv, 781–783.

Review of Brand Whitlock's novel. Unsigned: attribution through letter to Whitlock dated March 17, 1907, in Rutgers University Library.

07–B. *Through the eye of the needle, a romance with an introduction,* April 18.

07–9. "Her opinion of his story," *Harper's bazar,* May, 1907, xli, 429–437.

Drama. Reprinted 07–G.

07–10. "Editor's easy chair," *Harper's monthly,* May, 1907, cxiv, 965–968.

Reprinted 10–D.

07–11. "A great New York journalist," *North American review,* May 3, 1907, clxxxv, 44–53.

Review of *Life and letters of Edwin Lawrence Godkin,* ed., Rollo Ogden.

07–12. "A day at Doncaster and an hour out of Durham," *Harper's monthly,* June, 1907, cxv, 58–66.

Reprinted 09–B.

07–13. "Editor's easy chair," *Harper's monthly,* June, 1907, cxv, 147–150.

Survival of poetry.

07–C. "Introduction," *Shapes that haunt the dusk,* June 14.

07–14. "The fiction of Leonard Merrick," *North American review,* June 21, 1907, clxxxv, 378–386.

07–15. "A good natured correction by Mr. Howells," New York *Sun,* June 26, 1907, p. 6.

Letter dated June 23 denies he wants Hughes to succeed Roosevelt as president.

07–16. "Editor's easy chair," *Harper's monthly,* July, 1907, cxv, 309–312.

Reprinted 10–D.

07–17. "A memory that worked overtime," *Harper's monthly,* Aug., 1907, cxv, 415–418.

Reprinted 07–D.

07–18. "Editor's easy chair," *Harper's monthly,* Aug., 1907, cxv, 481–483.

Happiness and psychology.

07–19. "Editor's easy chair," *Harper's monthly,* Sept., 1907, cxv, 641–644.

Human conscience.

07–20. "Editor's easy chair," *Harper's monthly,* Oct., 1907, cxv, 803–806.
Meeting an ocean-liner.

07–21. "On reading the plays of Mr. Henry Arthur Jones," *North American review,* Oct., 1907, clxxxvi, 205–212.

07–D. Between the dark and the daylight, romances, Oct. 24.

07–22. "Recollections of an Atlantic editorship," *Atlantic monthly,* Nov., 1907, c, 594–606.

07–23. "Editor's easy chair," *Harper's monthly,* Nov., 1907, cxv, 965–968.
Internationalism; Japan.

07–E. Venetian life, enlarged and illustrated ed., Nov. 1.

07–24. "Editor's easy chair," *Harper's monthly,* Dec., 1907, cxvi, 148–151.
Reprinted 10–D.

07–25. "The whole family, a novel in twelve parts, chapter one — The father," *Harper's bazar,* Dec., 1907, xli, 1161–1170.
Reprinted 08–C.

07–26. "Talking of presentiments," *Harper's monthly,* Dec., 1907, cxvi, 76–81.
Reprinted 16–C.

07–27. "For Professor Norton's eightieth birthday," *Harvard graduates magazine,* Dec., 1907, xvi, 225–226.
Letter to W. R. Thayer, dated Oct. 29, 1907. In part reprinted *Letters of Charles Eliot Norton* (Boston, 1913), ii, 388–389.

07–28. "The face at the window," *Harper's weekly,* Dec. 14, 1907, li, 1825.
Reprinted 16–C.

07–F. Life at high tide, edited with H. M. Alden, Dec. 24.

07–G. Minor dramas, 2 vols., English ed.

07–H. The mulberries in Pay's garden.

1908

08–1. "Editor's easy chair," *Harper's monthly,* Jan., 1908, cxvi, 309–312.
Reprinted 10–D.

08–2. "The poetry of Mr. Madison Cawein," *North American review,* Jan., 1908, clxxxvii, 124–131.
Review of *The poems of Madison Cawein.* In part reprinted 11–H.

08–3. "Nine days' wonder in York," *Harper's monthly,* Feb., 1908, cxvi, 349–361.
Reprinted 09–B.

08–4. "Editor's easy chair," *Harper's monthly,* Feb., 1908, cxvi, 471–474.
Reprinted 10–D.

08–5. "Editor's easy chair," *Harper's monthly,* March, 1908, cxvi, 633–636.
Horticulture.

08–6. [Roman holidays and others,] New York *Sun,* March 8 – Oct. 18, 1908.
Reprinted 08–D.

08–A. Fennel and rue, a novel, March 13.

08–7. "Editor's easy chair," *Harper's monthly,* April, 1908, cxvi, 795–798.
Great Lakes trip.

08–8. "Editor's easy chair," *Harper's monthly,* May, 1908, cxvi, 957–960.
Review of W. A. Jenner's *The publisher against the people;* copyright.

08–9. W. de Wagstaff ("Pendennis"), "The personality of Mr. Howells, a study at close range," *Book news monthly,* June, 1908, xxvi, 739–741.
Interview.

Periodical Publications... — 1908, continued

08–10. "Editor's easy chair," *Harper's monthly*, June, 1908, CXVII, 147–150.
Lock-outs and unemployment.

08–11. "The justice of a friend," *North American review*, June, 1908, CLXXXVII, 880–885.
Review of G. O. Trevelyan's *The American Revolution*, vol. III.

08–12. "Editor's easy chair," *Harper's monthly*, July, 1908, CXVII, 309–312.
Reprinted 10–D.

08–13. "William Dean Howells a literary optimist," New York *Times*, July 26, 1908, v, 5.
Interview: current literary errors and virtues; glimpses of Maine life.

08–14. "Editor's easy chair," *Harper's monthly*, Aug., 1908, CXVII, 473–475.
Theater audiences.

08–15. "Some unpalatable suggestions," *North American review*, Aug., 1908, CLXXXVIII, 254–261.
Criminals, jails, and the state.

08–16. "The mother of the American Athens," *Harper's monthly*, Sept., 1908, CXVII, 514–525.
Reprinted 09–B.

08–17. "Editor's easy chair," *Harper's monthly*, Sept., 1908, CXVII, 632–636.
George Harvey on journalism.

08–18. "Editor's easy chair," *Harper's monthly*, Oct., 1908, CXVII, 795–798.
English-American backgrounds in fiction.

08–B. Christmas every day, a story told a child, illustrated ed., Oct. 15.

08–C. "The father," *The whole family, a novel by twelve authors,* Oct. 15.

08–D. Roman holidays and others, Oct. 22.

08–19. "Editor's easy chair," *Harper's monthly*, Nov., 1908, CXVII, 957–960.
The election and democracy.

08–20. "Editor's easy chair," *Harper's monthly*, Dec., 1908, CXVIII, 155–158.
Reprinted 10–D.

08–21. "Lyof N. Tolstoy," *North American review*, Dec., 1908, CLXXXVIII, 842–859.

08–22. "Saved, an emotional drama," *Harper's weekly*, Dec. 26, 1908, LII, 22–24.

1909

09–1. "Editor's easy chair," *Harper's monthly*, Jan., 1909, CXVIII, 317–320.
Reprinted 10–D.

09–2. "Edgar Allan Poe," *Harper's weekly*, Jan. 16, 1909, LIII, 12–13.
Personal reactions: thinks four good poems, but modern magazines would reject stories.

09–3. "Editor's easy chair," *Harper's monthly*, Feb., 1909, CXVIII, 479–482.
Reprinted 10–D.

09–4. "Editor's easy chair," *Harper's monthly*, March, 1909, CXVIII, 641–644.
Reprinted 10–D.

09–5. "Editor's easy chair," *Harper's monthly*, April, 1909, CXVIII, 803–806.
Reprinted 10–D.

09–6. "In the house of mourning," *Harper's bazar*, April, 1909, XLIII, 360–363.
Reprinted 10–A.

09–7. "Our Italian assimilators," *Harper's weekly*, April 10, 1909, LIII, 28.
Paper read at New York Society for Italian Immigrants.

09–8. "Three English capitals of industry," *Harper's monthly*, May, 1909, CXVIII, 891–902.
Reprinted 09–B.

09–9. "Editor's easy chair," *Harper's monthly*, May, 1909, cxviii, 965–968.
Woman's rights, reform, and revolution.

09–10. V. W. Brooks, "Mr. Howells at work at seventy-two," *World's work*, May, 1909, xviii, 11547–11549.
Interview. Reprinted *Americana*, April, 1943, xxxvii, 282–287.

09–A. *The mother and the father, dramatic passages*, May 20.

09–11. "Editor's easy chair," *Harper's monthly*, June, 1909, cxix, 147–150.
Reprinted 10–D.

09–12. "The novels of Robert Herrick," *North American review*, June, 1909, clxxxix, 812–820.

09–13. "Two little English episodes," *Harper's monthly*, July, 1909, cxix, 241–244.
Reprinted 09–B.

09–14. "Editor's easy chair," *Harper's monthly*, July, 1909, cxix, 309–312.
Music with meals; ships.

09–15. "The fiction of Eden Philpotts," *North American review*, July, 1909, cxc, 15–22.

09–16. "Editor's easy chair," *Harper's monthly*, Aug., 1909, cxix, 473–475.
Women in politics; the presidency.

09–17. "Editor's easy chair," *Harper's monthly*, Sept., 1909, cxix, 633–636.
Reprinted 10–D.

09–18. "Editor's easy chair," *Harper's monthly*, Oct., 1909, cxix, 795–798.
Review of F. B. Sanborn's *Recollections of seventy years.*

09–B. *Seven English cities*, Oct. 22.

09–19. "A true hero, melodrama," *Harper's monthly*, Nov., 1909, cxix, 866–875.
Illustrations by Lucius W. Hitchcock.

09–20. "Editor's easy chair," *Harper's monthly*, Nov., 1909, cxix, 957–960.
Collective effort in society.

09–21. "The mother-bird," *Harper's monthly*, Dec., 1909, cxx, 126–128.
Reprinted 16–C.

09–22. "Editor's easy chair," *Harper's monthly*, Dec., 1909, cxx, 149–151.
George Meredith, *et al.*

1910

10–1. "The night before Christmas, a morality," *Harper's monthly*, Jan., 1910, cxx, 207–216.
Reprinted 16–C.

10–2. "Editor's easy chair," *Harper's monthly*, Jan., 1910, cxx, 309–312.
Reprinted 10–D.

10–3. "Mr. Pett Ridge's clever books," *North American review*, Jan., 1910, cxci, 64–74.

10–4. "Editor's easy chair," *Harper's monthly*, Feb., 1910, cxx, 471–474.
Reprinted 10–D.

10–5. "Professor Cross's life of Sterne," *North American review*, Feb., 1910, cxci, 273–276.
Review of W. L. Cross' *Life and times of Laurence Sterne.*

10–A. "A counsel of consolation," *In after days, thoughts on the future life*, Feb. 11.

10–6. "Editor's easy chair," *Harper's monthly*, March, 1910, cxx, 633–636.
Reprinted 10–D.

10–7. "The turning point of my life," *Harper's bazar*, March, 1910, xliv, 165–166.
Fresh reminiscence of his life in 1864.

10–8. "Mr. Harben's Georgia fiction," *North American review*, March, 1910, cxci, 356–363.

Periodical Publications... – 1910, continued

10–9. "Editor's easy chair," *Harper's monthly*, April, 1910, cxx, 795–798.
Callers; review of C. H. Towne's "Manhattan."

10–10. "Editor's easy chair," *Harper's monthly*, May, 1910, cxx, 957–960.
Reprinted 10–D.

10–11. "Some new volumes of verse," *North American review*, May, 1910, cxci, 652–658.
Reviews of Thomas Hardy's *Time's laughing-stocks and other verses;* C. Y. Rice's *Many Gods* and *Nirvana days;* Richard Le Gallienne's *New poems.*

10–B. "Introduction," *Mark Twain's speeches*, May 24.

10–12. "Editor's easy chair," *Harper's monthly*, June, 1910, cxxi, 149–152.
Reprinted 16–C.

10–13. "Opening address of the President, William Dean Howells,"

American Academy proceedings, June 10, 1910, i, 5–8.
Purpose of the academy; address given in Washington, Dec. 14, 1909.

10–14. "My memories of Mark Twain," *Harper's monthly*, July – Sept., 1910, cxxi.
Reprinted 10–C.

10–15. "Editor's easy chair," *Harper's monthly*, July, 1910, cxxi, 309–312.
Chit-chat in the park.

10–16. "A political novelist and more," *North American review*, July, 1910, cxcii, 93–100.
Brand Whitlock.

10–17. "Editor's easy chair," *Harper's monthly*, Aug., 1910, cxxi, 473–475.
Review of George Schock's *Hearts contending.*

10–18. "Editor's easy chair," *Harper's monthly*, Sept., 1910, cxxi, 633–636.
Love and marriage.

10–C. *My Mark Twain, reminiscences and criticisms*, Sept. 10.

10–19. "Parting friends, tragedy," *Harper's monthly*, Oct., 1910, cxxi, 670–677.
Reprinted 11–A.

10–20. "Editor's easy chair," *Harper's monthly*, Oct., 1910, cxxi, 795–798.
Woman's suffrage.

10–D. *Imaginary interviews*, Oct. 15.

10–21. "Editor's easy chair," *Harper's monthly*, Nov., 1910, cxxi, 957–960.
Roosevelt and hunting.

10–22. "The impossible, a mystery play," *Harper's monthly*, Dec., 1910, cxxii, 116–125.

10–23. "Editor's easy chair," *Harper's monthly*, Dec., 1910, cxxii, 149–151.
Sailing for Venice; autobiographical.

1911

11–1. "Editor's easy chair," *Harper's monthly*, Jan., 1911, cxxii, 309–312.
Review of Henry Fielding's *Voyage to Lisbon;* sea-travel.

11–2. "John Brown after fifty years," *North American review*, Jan., 1911, cxciii, 26–34.
Review of O. G. Villard's *John Brown, 1800–1859;* capitalism compared to slavery.

11–3. "Editor's easy chair," *Harper's monthly*, Feb., 1911, cxxii, 471–474.
Review of Laura Stedman's and G. M. Gould's *Life of Stedman;* mention of Melville and Henry Harland.

11–4. "Editor's easy chair," *Harper's monthly*, March, 1911, cxxii, 633–636.
Arnold Bennett praised.

11–5. "Self-sacrifice, a farce tragedy," *Harper's monthly*, April, 1911, cxxii, 748–757.
Reprinted 16–C.

11–6. "Editor's easy chair," *Harper's monthly,* April, 1911, CXXII, 795–798.

An American advertising man's autobiography (unnamed); autobiography discussed.

11–7. "Editor's easy chair," *Harper's monthly,* May, 1911, CXXII, 957–960.

Criticism (Howells, Brownell, Matthews, Phelps); proposal of belles-lettres commission to eliminate bad books by trial.

11–8. "Editor's easy chair," *Harper's monthly,* June, 1911, CXXIII, 148–151.

Review of Marguerite Audoux's *Marie-Claire,* preface by Arnold Bennett.

11–9. "Some last drops in Tunbridge Wells," *North American review,* June, 1911, CXCIII, 879–892.

11–A. Parting friends, a farce, June 17.

11–10. "Editor's easy chair," *Harper's monthly,* July, 1911, CXXIII, 310–313.

Review of Holman Day's *The skipper and the skipped;* American humor.

11–B. "Bibliographical," *My literary passions* [and] *Criticism and fiction,* Library ed., July 26.

11–C. "Bibliographical," *The landlord at Lion's Head, a novel,* Library ed., July 26.

11–D. "Bibliographical," *Literature and life, studies,* Library ed., July 26.

11–E. "Bibliographical," *London films and certain delightful English towns,* Library ed., July 26.

11–F. "Bibliographical," *Literary friends and acquaintance* [and *My Mark Twain*], Library ed., July 26.

11–G. "Bibliographical," *A hazard of new fortunes,* Library ed., July 26.

11–11. "Editor's easy chair," *Harper's monthly,* Aug., 1911, CXXIII, 473–475.

On peace.

11–12. "The human interest of Buxton," *North American review,* Aug., 1911, CXCIV, 227–238.

Also printed *Cornhill magazine,* Aug., 1911, n. s. XXXI, 203–214.

11–13. "The daughter of the storage," *Harper's monthly,* Sept., 1911, CXXIII, 572–583.

Reprinted 16–C.

11–14. "Editor's easy chair," *Harper's monthly,* Sept., 1911, CXXIII, 634–637.

Review of Havelock Ellis' "Love and the woman's movement;" romantic love.

11–H. "The poetry of Madison Cawein," *Poems,* Sept. 14.

11–15. "Editor's easy chair," *Harper's monthly,* Oct., 1911, CXXIII, 796–799.

On firearms ownership law.

11–16. "The city of the royal pavilion," *North American review,* Oct., 1911, CXCIV, 602–611.

Brighton.

11–I. "Introduction," *Tom Brown's school-days,* Oct. 16.

11–17. "Editor's easy chair," *Harper's monthly,* Nov., 1911, CXXIII, 958–961.

Spanish literature; penal employment.

11–18. "In memory of Mark Twain," *American Academy Proceedings,* Nov. 1, 1911, I, 5–6 and *passim.*

Reprinted 22–A.

11–19. "A Bermudan sojourn," *Harper's monthly,* Dec., 1911, CXXIV, 16–27.

Travel sketch.

11–20. "Editor's easy chair," *Harper's monthly,* Dec., 1911, CXXIV, 148–151.

Review of R. M. Johnson's *The Corsican* (Napoleon).

11–21. "The waters of Blackpool," *North American review,* Dec., 1911, CXCIV, 872–881.

11–J. [Prefaces for incomplete Library edition.]

1912

12–1. "Editor's easy chair," *Harper's monthly*, Jan., 1912, cxxiv, 309–312.
Tolstoy, non-resistance, and war; unmartial heroism.

12–2. "Experiences of a true Baconian in Shakespeare's town," *North American review*, Jan., 1912, cxcv, 120–127.

12–3. "Editor's easy chair," *Harper's monthly*, Feb., 1912, cxxiv, 471–474.
Woman's suffrage.

12–A. [Letter,] *The house of Harper*, Feb. 17.

12–4. Henry Rood, "W. D. Howells, at 75, talks of old literary New York," New York *Times*, Feb. 25, 1912, v, 4.
Interview: richly reminiscent.

12–5. "W. D. Howell's [*sic*] birthday, author makes it the occasion of a letter to city school children," New York *Times*, Feb. 28, 1912, p. 6.
Letter, dated Feb. 23, warns against false patriotism.

12–6. "Editor's easy chair," *Harper's monthly*, March, 1912, cxxiv, 634–637.
Rankling criticism; regionalism in literature.

12–7. "Mr. Howells beaming on seventy-fifth birthday," New York *Sun*, March 3, 1912, p. 10.
Interview: chit-chat.

12–8. "A tribute to William Dean Howells," *Harper's weekly*, March 9, 1912, lvi, 27–34.
Speech on March 2. Reprinted *North American review*, April, 1912, cxcv, 550–558.

12–9. "Editor's easy chair," *Harper's monthly*, April, 1912, cxxiv, 796–799.
Review of Eliot Norton's *Lincoln, a lover of mankind;* revenge codes and lynching.

12–10. "The austere attraction of Burgos," *Harper's monthly*, May, 1912, cxxiv, 813–827.
Reprinted 13–B.

12–11. "Editor's easy chair," *Harper's monthly*, May, 1912, cxxv, 958–961.
Review of A. M. Simons' *Social forces in American history;* capitalism and imperialism.

12–12. "A pair of pageants," *North American review*, May, 1912, cxcv, 607–617.
Chester and Stroud.

12–13. "Editor's easy chair," *Harper's monthly*, June, 1912, cxxv, 148–151.
Reviews of Arnold Bennett's *Hilda Lessways;* H. O. Taylor's *The mediaeval mind;* J. H. Harper's *The house of Harper;* Walt Mason's *Prose poems* and *Business prose poems.*

12–14. "The coming," *Bookman*, July, 1912, xxxv, 510–514.
First printed 60–6.

12–15. "The variety of Valladolid," *Harper's monthly*, July, 1912, cxxv, 165–178.
Reprinted 13–B.

12–16. "Editor's easy chair," *Harper's monthly*, July, 1912, cxxv, 310–313.
State of poetry.

12–17. "Recent Russian fiction, a conversation," *North American review*, July, 1912, cxcvi, 85–103.
By Howells and T. S. Perry. Artsibashef, Gogol, Kuprin.

12–18. "A night and a day in Toledo," *Harper's monthly*, Aug., 1912, cxxv, 429–442.
Reprinted 13–B.

12–19. "Editor's easy chair," *Harper's monthly*, Aug., 1912, cxxv, 473–475.
Spanish hotel chit-chat.

12–20. "Editor's easy chair," *Harper's monthly*, Sept., 1912, cxxv, 634–637.
Morals, art, and education in the cinema.

12–B. "One of the public to the author," *The Henry James year book*, Sept. 27.

12–21. "Editor's easy chair," *Harper's monthly*, Oct., 1912, cxxv, 796–799.
Summer hotel reflections; motoring.

12–22. "Mr. Garland's books," *North American review*, Oct., 1912, cxcvi, 523–528.

12–C. [Introduction,] *Artemus Ward's best stories*, Oct. 5.

12–23. "Editor's easy chair," *Harper's monthly*, Nov., 1912, cxxv, 958–961.
Spiritualism.

12–24. "Phases of Madrid," *North American review*, Nov., 1912, cxcvi, 608–634.
Reprinted 13–B.

12–25. "Cordova and the way there," *Harper's monthly*, Dec., 1912, cxxvi, 112–125.
Reprinted 13–B.

12–26. "Editor's easy chair," *Harper's monthly*, Dec., 1912, cxxvi, 149–151.
The 1912 campaign.

12–27. "The fulfilment of the pact," *Harper's weekly*, Dec. 14, 1912, lvi, 9–10. Illustrations by Harvey Emrich.

1913

13–1. "Editor's easy chair," *Harper's monthly*, Jan., 1913, cxxvi, 310–312.
Mark Twain, with reference to Paine's biography.

13–2. "Editor's easy chair," *Harper's monthly*, Feb., 1913, cxxvi, 472–475.
American and European travel; capital punishment.

13–A. *New Leaf Mills, a chronicle*, Feb. 21.

13–3. "First days in Seville," *Harper's monthly*, March, 1913, cxxvi, 568–581.
Reprinted 13–B.

13–4. "Editor's easy chair," *Harper's monthly*, March, 1913, cxxvi, 634–637.
Effects of too much fiction; love in fiction.

13–5. "Editor's easy chair," *Harper's monthly*, April, 1913, cxxvi, 796–799.
Reviews of Arnold Bennett's [*Your United States*]; Mrs. Trollope's [*Domestic manners of the Americans*]; François Jean Chastellux's *Travels in North-America;* Dickens' *American notes.*

13–6. "To and in Granada," *North American review*, April, 1913, cxcvii, 501–521.
Reprinted 13–B.

13–7. "Editor's easy chair," *Harper's monthly*, May, 1913, cxxvi, 958–961.
Reviews of Barrie's *The twelve pound look;* Shaw's *Fanny's first play;* Charles Kline's *Maggie Pepper;* George Cohan's *Broadway Jones;* [Edward Locke's] *The case of Becky; Years of discretion;* [E. A. Bennett's and Edward Knoblauch's] *Milestones;* [L. N. Parker's] *Disraeli* (Arliss).

13–8. "Some Sevillan incidents," *Harper's monthly*, June, 1913, cxxvii, 71–86.
Reprinted 13–B.

13–9. "Editor's easy chair," *Harper's monthly*, June, 1913, cxxvii, 148–151.
Suffrage apropos English riots.

13–10. "Editor's easy chair," *Harper's monthly*, July, 1913, cxxvii, 310–313.
Tipping.

13–11. "The critical bookstore," *Harper's monthly*, Aug., 1913, cxxvii, 431–442.
Reprinted 16–C.

13–12. "Editor's easy chair," *Harper's monthly*, Aug., 1913, cxxvii, 473–475.
Poll on ten most useful Americans commented on.

13–13. "Editor's easy chair," *Harper's monthly*, Sept., 1913, cxxvii, 634–637.
Insects.

13–14. "Editor's easy chair," *Harper's monthly*, Oct., 1913, cxxvii, 796–799.
Newspaper murders, Tolstoy, old age.

13–B. *Familiar Spanish travels*, Oct. 18.

13–C. "Introduction," *Gulliver's travels*, Oct. 18.

13–15. "On a bright winter day," *Harper's monthly*, Nov., 1913, cxxvii, 835.
Poem.

13–16. "Editor's easy chair," *Harper's monthly*, Nov., 1913, cxxvii, 958–961.
Jane Austen; visit to Winchester.

13–17. "A high-minded public man," *North American review*, Nov., 1913, cxcviii, 657–663.
Review of Horace White's *The life of Lyman Trumbull*.

13–18. "Editor's easy chair," *Harper's monthly*, Dec., 1913, cxxviii, 149–151.
Review of E. W. Maunder's *Are the planets inhabited?*

13–19. "Charles Eliot Norton, a reminiscence," *North American review*, Dec., 1913, cxcviii, 836–848.
Review of *Letters of Charles Eliot Norton*, eds., Sara Norton and M. A. de Wolfe [sic] Howe.

1914

14–1. "Editor's easy chair," *Harper's monthly*, Jan., 1914, cxxviii, 310–313.
Reviews of Basil King's *The war home*; Mrs. Humphry Ward's *The Coryston family*.

14–2. "Editor's easy chair," *Harper's monthly*, Feb., 1914, cxxviii, 472–475.
Reviews of Mrs. Ethel B. Alec-Tweedie's [*America as I saw it*]; F. A. Kemble's [*Journal*].

14–3. "Editor's easy chair," *Harper's monthly*, March, 1914, cxxviii, 634–637.
Reviews of H. C. Chatfield-Taylor's *Life of Goldoni*; [G. M. Cohan's and E. D. Biggers'] *Seven keys to Baldpate; A clever woman*; [Shaw's] *Androcles and the lion*.

14–4. "Editor's easy chair," *Harper's monthly*, April, 1914, cxxviii, 796–799.
Sailing for Europe; London.

14–5. "Editor's easy chair," *Harper's monthly*, May, 1914, cxxviii, 958–961.
Review of C. E. Shorter's *George Borrow and his circle*.

14–A. *The seen and unseen at Stratford-on-Avon, a fantasy*, May 11.

14–6. "Editor's easy chair," *Harper's monthly*, June, 1914, cxxix, 148–151.
Charities.

14–7. "Editor's easy chair," *Harper's monthly*, July, 1914, cxxix, 310–313.
Reviews of Brand Whitlock's *Forty years of it*; M. T. Higginson's *Memoir of Thomas Wentworth Higginson*.

14–8. "Editor's easy chair," *Harper's monthly*, Aug., 1914, cxxix, 473–475.
Summer talk; child labor.

14–9. "Letter from W. D. Howells," *American Academy Proceedings*, Aug. 1, 1914, ii, 6.
Dated Nov. 11, 1913.

14–10. "In an old-time state capital," *Harper's monthly*, Sept. – Nov., 1914, cxxix.
With changes reprinted 16–F.

14–11. "Editor's easy chair," *Harper's monthly,* Sept., 1914, cxxix, 634–637.
Barataria, a penal utopia; review of Arturo Giovanitti's *Arrows in the gale.*

14–12. "Editor's easy chair," *Harper's monthly,* Oct., 1914, cxxix, 796–799.
The middleman.

14–13. "The archangelic censorship," *North American review,* Oct., 1914, cc, 559–565.

14–14. "Editor's easy chair," *Harper's monthly,* Nov., 1914, cxxix, 958–961.
World unification to prevent war.

14–15. Joyce Kilmer, "War stops literature, says William Dean Howells," New York *Times,* Nov. 29, 1914, v, 8.
Interview. Reprinted *Literature in the making* (New York, 1917), p. 3–15.

14–16. "Editor's easy chair," *Harper's monthly,* Dec., 1914, cxxx, 149–151.
Christmas, 1913, on Beacon Hill; the war.

14–17. "A number of interesting novels," *North American review,* Dec., 1914, cc, 908–922.
Archibald Marshall, Kathleen Norris, Robert Herrick, Arnold Bennett, Basil King, W. N. Harben. Paragraph reprinted 17–A.

1915

15–1. "Editor's easy chair," *Harper's monthly,* Jan., 1915, cxxx, 309–312.
Chit-chat on New Year's; religion.

15–2. "Part of which I was," *North American review,* Jan., 1915, cci, 135–141.
Centennial celebration of *North American review.*

15–3. "Editor's easy chair," *Harper's monthly,* Feb., 1915, cxxx, 472–475.
Reviews of Henry Holt's *On the cosmic relations;* George Harris' *A century's change in religion.*

15–4. "Editor's easy chair," *Harper's monthly,* March, 1915, cxxx, 634–637.
Capital punishment.

15–5. "The plays of Eugene Brieux," *North American review,* March, 1915, cci, 402–411.

15–6. "Editor's easy chair," *Harper's monthly,* April, 1915, cxxx, 796–799.
Reviews of Edward Garnett's "Some remarks on English and American fiction;" Booth Tarkington's *The turmoil;* Ernest Poole's *The harbor.*

15–7. "Editor's easy chair," *Harper's monthly,* May, 1915, cxxx, 958–961.
Jews in literature: Zangwill, Cahan, Glass, Hurst; reviews of J. L. Ford's *The great mirage;* Booth Tarkington's *The turmoil.*

15–8. "Why?" *North American review,* May, 1915, cci, 676–682.
Favors allies.

15–9. "Editor's easy chair," *Harper's monthly,* June, 1915, cxxxi, 148–151.
Berea College; Wilson on society.

15–10. "The return to favor," *Harper's monthly,* July, 1915, cxxxi, 278–280.
Reprinted 16–C.

15–11. "Editor's easy chair," *Harper's monthly,* July, 1915, cxxxi, 310–313.
Review of Samuel Johnson's *Rasselas.*

15–12. "Editor's easy chair," *Harper's monthly,* Aug., 1915, cxxxi, 473–476.
Review of Gaillard Hunt's *Life in America one hundred years ago;* and the present.

15–13. "Somebody's mother," *Harper's monthly,* Sept., 1915, cxxxi, 523–526.
Reprinted 16–C.

15–14. "Editor's easy chair," *Harper's monthly,* Sept., 1915, cxxxi, 634–637.
Reviews of Amy Lowell's *Sword blades and poppy seeds;* E. L. Masters' *Spoon River anthology;* Robert Frost's *North of Boston* and *A boy's will;* Dana Burnet's *[Poems]*; Conrad Aiken's *Earth triumphant;* James Oppenheim's *Songs for the new age;* Vachel Lindsay's *Adventures while preaching the gospel of beauty.* Mention of A. H. Branch, A. D. Ficke, E. A. Robinson, J. G. Fletcher, Brian Hooker.

15–15. "Address of W. D. Howells," *American Academy Proceedings,* Sept. 1, 1915, ɪɪ, 7.

Given Nov. 19, 1914.

15–16. "In Charleston," *Harper's monthly,* Oct., 1915, cxxxɪ, 747–757.

Travel sketch.

15–17. "Editor's easy chair," *Harper's monthly,* Oct., 1915, cxxxɪ, 796–799.

Reprinted 16–C.

15–18. "An experience," *Harper's monthly,* Nov., 1915, cxxxɪ, 940–942.

Reprinted 16–C.

15–19. "Editor's easy chair," *Harper's monthly,* Nov., 1915, cxxxɪ, 957–960.

Blasco Ibañez.

15–20. "Editor's easy chair," *Harper's monthly,* Dec., 1915, cxxxɪɪ, 149–151.

Christmas stories.

15–21. "Bars Ford party from war zone, answers to invitations," New York *Times,* Dec. 2, 1915, p. 2.

Undated letter (or telegram) declines peace ship invitation.

15–A. [Letter,] *Sixty American opinions on the war.*

1916

16–1. "Editor's easy chair," *Harper's monthly,* Jan., 1916, cxxxɪɪ, 310–313.

Review of W. R. Thayer's *Life of John Hay.*

16–A. "The little children," *The book of the homeless,* Jan. 25.

16–2. "Editor's easy chair," *Harper's monthly,* Feb., 1916, cxxxɪɪ, 473–476.

Reprinted 16–C.

16–3. "The boarders," *Harper's monthly,* March, 1916, cxxxɪɪ, 540–543.

Reprinted 16–C.

16–4. "Editor's easy chair," *Harper's monthly,* March, 1916, cxxxɪɪ, 634–637.

Reviews of Shaw's *Major Barbara;* [H. A. Vachell's] *The Quinneys;* [H. Brighouse's] *Hobson's choice;* [G. U. Hobart's and Edna Ferber's] *Our Mrs. McChesney;* [R. C. Megrue's and Montague Glass'] *Abe and Mawruss;* G. M. Cohan's *Hit-the-trail Holliday;* [Thomas Taylor's] *Our American cousin;* [William Gillette's] *Secret service.*

16–5. "Leatherwood god," *Century,* April – Nov., 1916, xcɪ–xcɪɪɪ.

Reprinted 16–E.

16–6. "Editor's easy chair," *Harper's monthly,* April, 1916, cxxxɪɪ, 796–799.

Poets' incomes.

16–B. "Preface," *They of the high trails,* April 20.

16–C. The daughter of the storage and other things in prose and verse, April 27.

16–7. "Around the council table, another correction," *Authors League of America Bulletin,* May, 1916, ɪv, 11.

Howells authorizes indirect quotation on relation of Harper's and "Authors' Union."

16–8. "Editor's easy chair," *Harper's monthly,* May, 1916, cxxxɪɪ, 958–961.

Censorship; review of Alfred [Albert] Mordell's *Dante and other waning classics;* social Christianity.

16–9. "The Irish executions," New York *Post,* May 8, 1916, p. 8.

Letter, dated New York, May 6, condemns British tactics. Reprinted *Nation,* May 18, 1916, cɪɪ, 541. Reprinted 28–A.

16–10. "Editor's easy chair," *Harper's monthly,* June, 1916, cxxxɪɪɪ, 146–149.

Brander Matthews, ed., series of books on drama; the cinema.

16–11. "Editor's easy chair," *Harper's monthly,* July, 1916, cxxxɪɪɪ, 306–309.

New York in summer and winter; a Florida air-service.

16–12. "The pearl," *Harper's monthly,* Aug., 1916, cxxxiii, 409–413.

Autobiographical story.

16–13. "Editor's easy chair," *Harper's monthly,* Aug., 1916, cxxxiii, 456–459.

Reviews of Rupert Brooke's *Letters from America;* C. W. Jansen's *The stranger in America; Charles Francis Adams, 1835–1915, an autobiography;* Harriet Martineau's [*Society in America*]; J. J. Jusserand's *With Americans of past and present days.*

16–14. "Editor's easy chair," *Harper's monthly,* Sept., 1916, cxxxiii, 626–629.

Reviews of J. L. Williams' *Remating time;* Edwin Lefevre's *Wall Street stories;* Hamlin Garland's *They of the high trails.*

16–D. Buying a horse, first separate ed., Sept. 21.

16–15. "The rotational tenants, a Hallowe'en mystery," *Harper's monthly,* Oct., 1916, cxxxiii, 770–777.

16–16. "Editor's easy chair," *Harper's monthly,* Oct., 1916, cxxxiii, 786–789.

Suffrage and the election.

16–17. "Letter from Mr. Howells in acceptance of the medal," *American Academy Proceedings,* Nov., 1916, ii, 53.

Undated; the medal was given Nov. 19, 1915.

16–18. "Editor's easy chair," *Harper's monthly,* Nov., 1916, cxxxiii, 938–941.

Democracy, monarchy, international government, and war.

16–19. "The passengers of a retarded submersible," *North American review,* Nov., 1916, cciv, 741–742.

Poem.

16–E. The leatherwood god, Nov. 2.

16–F. Years of my youth, first issue, Nov. 7.

16–20. "Editor's easy chair," *Harper's monthly,* Dec., 1916, cxxxiv, 138–141.

Automobiling.

16–21. "A conjecture of intensive fiction," *North American review,* Dec., 1916, cciv, 864–880.

16–G. [Letter,] *Tributes to Canada,* Dec. 9.

16–H. The country printer, an essay, first separate ed.

1917

17–1. "Editor's easy chair," *Harper's monthly,* Jan., 1917, cxxxiv, 289–293.

More automobiling and state-owned inns.

17–2. "Editor's easy chair," *Harper's monthly,* Feb., 1917, cxxxiv, 442–445.

American humor; Twain, T. C. Haliburton, Lowell, F. P. Dunne, Ade.

17–3. "Editor's easy chair," *Harper's monthly,* March, 1917, cxxxiv, 594–597.

Language; words and usage.

17–A. [Paragraph,] *The books of Kathleen Norris,* prior to April.

17–4. "A confession of St. Augustine," *Harper's monthly,* April, May, 1917, cxxxiv, 680–688, 877–885.

Travel essay.

17–5. "Editor's easy chair," *Harper's monthly,* April, 1917, cxxxiv, 746–749.

Magazine of contemporary verse.

17–6. "Editor's easy chair," *Harper's monthly,* May, 1917, cxxxiv, 899–902.

Doctors.

17–B. "Introduction," *The second odd number,* May 5.

17–7. "Editor's easy chair," *Harper's monthly,* June, 1917, cxxxv, 138–141.

Harper anniversary; relationship with publishing firm and review of history of *Harper's monthly.*

17–8. "Editor's easy chair," *Harper's monthly,* July, 1917, cxxxv, 291–293.

J. J. Piatt.

17–9. "A tale untold," *Atlantic monthly,* Aug., 1917, cxx, 236–242.

17–10. "Editor's easy chair," *Harper's monthly,* Aug., 1917, cxxxv, 434–437.

Reviews of William McFee's *Casuals of the sea;* Paul Kester's *His own country.*

17–11. "An appreciation," New York *Times,* Aug. 26, 1917, vii, 309, 315.

Review of Hamlin Garland's *Son of the middle border.*

17–12. "Editor's easy chair," *Harper's monthly,* Sept., 1917, cxxxv, 578–582.

The war.

17–C. "Letter" and "An appreciation," *The story of a country town,* Sept. 25.

17–13. "Editor's easy chair," *Harper's monthly,* Oct., 1917, cxxxv, 730–734.

Autobiographical sketch.

17–14. "An appreciation," New York *Times,* Oct. 21, 1917, iv, 405, 415.

Review of Brander Matthews' *These many years.*

17–15. "Editor's easy chair," *Harper's monthly,* Nov., 1917, cxxxv, 882–885.

Review of Oliver Lodge's *Raymond Lodge;* immortality. In part reprinted 20–B.

17–D. Years of my youth, illustrated ed., Nov. 5.

17–16. "Editor's easy chair," *Harper's monthly,* Dec., 1917, cxxxvi, 146–149.

Review of W. S. Braithwaite's *The poetic year for 1916, a critical anthology;* memories of C. W. Stoddard.

17–E. [Letter,] *The Harper centennial,* December.

17–17. "War as seen by famous authors," New York *Times,* Dec. 2, 1917, ii, 8.

Quotes Howells: "May the war for liberty win equality and fraternity, too." Reprinted?

1918

18–A. [Letter,] *Defenders of democracy,* late in 1917.

18–1. "Editor's easy chair," *Harper's monthly,* Jan., 1918, cxxxvi, 299–301.

Christmas and change.

18–2. "Editor's easy chair," *Harper's monthly,* Feb., 1918, cxxxvi, 450–453.

Women and work.

18–3. "Editor's easy chair," *Harper's monthly,* March, 1918, cxxxvi, 602–605.

Reviews of *Mark Twain's letters,* ed., A. B. Paine; *Letters of John Holmes.*

18–4. "Editor's easy chair," *Harper's monthly,* April, 1918, cxxxvi, 754–757.

Comment on the year 1917: "a mad world."

18–B. "Introduction," *Pride and prejudice,* April 4.

18–5. "Howells sticks to buying, tells Liberty Loan boosters he is too old for press agent job," New York *Times,* April 19, 1918, p. 11.

Parts of two (?) undated letters.

18–6. "Editor's easy chair," *Harper's monthly,* May, 1918, cxxxvi, 906–909.

The board of health and socialism.

18–7. "Editor's easy chair," *Harper's monthly*, June, 1918, cxxxvii, 138–141.
Review of H. L. Wilson's *Ruggles of Red Gap*, with digressions on war and democracy.

18–8. "Editor's easy chair," *Harper's monthly*, July, 1918, cxxxvii, 290–293.
Review of Sidney Colvin's *John Keats*, second ed., enlarged.

18–9. "Editor's easy chair," *Harper's monthly*, Aug., 1918, cxxxvii, 444–446.
War. In part reprinted 19-C.

18–10. "Editor's easy chair," *Harper's monthly*, Sept., 1918, cxxxvii, 589–592.
Altruria footnote on war and conscription.

18–11. "Editor's easy chair," *Harper's monthly*, Oct., 1918, cxxxvii, 734–736.
The country trolley.

18–12. "Overland to Venice," *Harper's monthly*, Nov., 1918, cxxxvii, 837–845.
Autobiographical sketch.

18–13. "Editor's easy chair," *Harper's monthly*, Nov., 1918, cxxxvii, 878–880.
Current evidences of socialism.

18–14. "Editor's easy chair," *Harper's monthly*, Dec., 1918, cxxxviii, 134–136.
Review of G. R. B. Charnwood's *Abraham Lincoln*.

18–C. "Introduction," *Daisy Miller* [and] *An international episode*.

1919

19–1. "Editor's easy chair," *Harper's monthly*, Jan., 1919, cxxxviii, 278–280.
Reviews of H. L. Wilson's *Somewhere in Red Gap*; W. A. White's *Martial adventures*

of *Henry and me*; Homer Croy's *Boone stop*; Katherine Mayo's *The standard bearers*.

19–A. "Introduction," *The shadow of the cathedral*, Jan. 14.

19–2. "Savannah twice visited," *Harper's monthly*, Feb., 1919, cxxxviii, 310–332.
Travel essay.

19–3. "Editor's easy chair," *Harper's monthly*, Feb., 1919, cxxxviii, 422–424.
Reviews of Henry Adams' *The education of Henry Adams*; F. H. Hall's *Memories grave and gay*; W. H. Hudson's *Far away and long ago*.

19–4. "Editor's easy chair," *Harper's monthly*, March, 1919, cxxxviii, 566–568.
Vacationing spots.

19–5. "An old Venetian friend," *Harper's monthly*, April, 1919, cxxxviii, 634–640.
Autobiographical sketch.

19–6. "Editor's easy chair," *Harper's monthly*, April, 1919, cxxxviii, 714–716.
Post-war jobs, war literature, prohibition.

19–7. "A young Venetian friend," *Harper's monthly*, May, 1919, cxxxviii, 827–833.
Autobiographical sketch.

19–8. "Editor's easy chair," *Harper's monthly*, May, 1919, cxxxviii, 854–856.
Review of E. W. Emerson's *The early years of the Saturday Club, 1855–1870*.

19–9. "Editor's easy chair," *Harper's monthly*, June, 1919, cxxxix, 133–136.
Domestic employment.

19–10. "Editor's easy chair," *Harper's monthly*, July, 1919, cxxxix, 286–288.
Hotel service; American versus European plan.

19–11. "Editor's easy chair," *Harper's monthly*, Aug., 1919, cxxxix, 445–448.

Immortality. In part reprinted *19–C.*

19–B. "Introduction," *The actor-manager*, Aug. 4.

19–C. "The incredible cruelty of the Teutons," *The World War*, Aug. 18.

19–12. "Editor's easy chair," *Harper's monthly*, Sept., 1919, cxxxix, 605–608.

Review of Rudolph Schevill's *Cervantes.*

19–13. "Editor's easy chair," *Harper's monthly*, Oct., 1919, cxxxix, 765–768.

The cinema and contemporary civilization.

19–14. "Editor's easy chair," *Harper's monthly*, Nov., 1919, cxxxix, 925–928.

A course in short story writing offered to Howells.

19–15. "Eight years and after," *Harper's monthly*, Dec., 1919, cxl, 21–28.
Reprinted *21–A.*

19–16. "Editor's easy chair," *Harper's monthly*, Dec., 1919, cxl, 133–136.

Henry M. Alden obituary.

20–1. "Editor's easy chair," *Harper's monthly*, Jan., 1920, cxl, 278–280.

Post-Civil War period compared with present.

20–A. Hither and thither in Germany, Jan. 16.

20–2. "A memory of San Remo," *Harper's monthly*, Feb., 1920, cxl, 321–327.

Travel sketch.

20–3. "Editor's easy chair," *Harper's monthly*, Feb., 1920, cxl, 422–424.

San Remo sketch.

20–4. "Editor's easy chair," *Harper's monthly*, March, 1920, cxl, 566–568.

Reviews of Robert Grant's *The law and the family;* Brooks Adams' *Emancipation of Massachusetts.*

20–B. Immortality and Sir Oliver Lodge, March 1.

20–5. "Editor's easy chair," *Harper's monthly*, April, 1920, cxl, 710–712.

Post-war conditions observed by Martians.

20–C. "A reminiscent introduction," *The great modern American stories,* July 13.

20–D. The vacation of the Kelwyns, an idyl of the middle eighteen-seventies, Sept. 25.

SELECTED CRITICAL WRITINGS

The bibliography of critical writings is a selection from about eight hundred items which the editors have listed during their course of investigation. The choice of the comparatively few resultant items has necessarily been arbitrary. An attempt has been made to follow as consistently as possible three criteria, intrinsic importance, the authority of the writers, and representativeness, but few articles satisfy all three of these criteria, or even the first two.

A certain number of biographical and reminiscent sketches have been included. Work in progress that is known and that promises importance is also listed. Histories of American literature and of its special phases — such as those by Blankenship, Boynton, Brooks, Calverton, Hartwick, Hicks, Lewisohn, Michaud, Mott, Parrington, Pattee, Quinn, Bernard Smith, Taylor, and Van Doren — have not been entered.

When known, both magazine and book publication of articles have been given, since in many cases one or the other may not be immediately available. An attempt has been made to locate certain reprinted items in their first printing, but it has not always proved successful. Authors under *American Academy, Book news monthly*, Boston *Transcript, Harper's weekly*, and the New York *Sun* have not been separately listed.

ADAMS, BROOKS. "The undiscovered country," *International review*, Aug., 1880, IX, 149–154.

Review.

[ADAMS, HENRY.] Review of *Their wedding journey, North American review*, April, 1872, CXIV, 444–445.

ALDEN, H. M. "Editor's study," *Harper's monthly*, May, 1917, CXXXIV, 903–904.

At his eightieth birthday.

— "William Dean Howells," *Bookman*, July, 1919, XLIX, 549–554.

Critical and biographical generalizations.

[ALDRICH, T. B.] "Mr. Howells's new book," *Atlantic monthly*, Sept., 1881, XLVIII, 402–405.

Review of *A fearful responsibility*.

AMERICAN ACADEMY OF ARTS AND LETTERS. "Public meeting held at the Stuart Gallery, New York Public Library, New York, March 1st, 1921, in memory of William D. Howells," *American Academy Proceedings*, July 1, 1921, II, 1–21.

Tributes by W. M. Sloane, Juan Riano, A. M. Huntington, Rolandi Ricci, Giovanni Verga, Ciro Trabalza, R. U. Johnson, H. C. de Wiart, Brand Whitlock, Stephen Leacock, J. J. Jusserand, Rudyard Kipling, John Burroughs, Robert Grant, Augustus Thomas, J. L. Williams, Brander Matthews, and Henry Van Dyke. Reprinted *Public meeting...in honor of William Dean Howells* (New York, 1922).

ANONYMOUS. "American literature in England," *Blackwood's magazine*, Jan., 1883, CXXXIII, 136–161.

Reprinted *Studies in literature*, ed., T. M. Coan (New York, 1883), p. 1–66. Review of Edinburgh edition, with emphasis on *The lady of the Aroostook* and *A modern instance*.

— "Novel-writing as a science," *Catholic world*, Nov., 1885, XLII, 274–280.

Review of *The rise of Silas Lapham*.

— "Mr. Howells's 'Americanisms'," *Critic*, Sept. 27, 1894, n. s. XXII, 193.

First printed Springfield *Republican*.

— "Mr. Howells's views," *Critic*, Jan. 2, 1897, n. s. XXVII, 5.

Review of *Impressions and opinions* [sic].

— "Howells' *A hazard of new fortunes*," *Explicator*, Nov., 1942, I, 14.

— "The earlier and later work of Mr. Howells," *Lippincott's*, Dec., 1882, XXX, 604–608.

Review of *A modern instance*.

— "Mr. Howells," *Literary digest*, May 29, 1920, LXV, 34–35.

Abstracts of tributes.

— "William Dean Howells, printer, journalist, poet, novelist," *Literary digest*, June 12, 1920, LXV, 53, 54, 57.

Abstracts of biographical accounts.

Selected Critical Writings, continued
ANONYMOUS, *continued*

— "Mr. Howells in England," *Literary digest,* June 19, 1920, LXV, 37.
Abstracts of English tributes.

— "Mr. Howells's latest novel," *Nation,* June 5, 1890, L, 454–455.
Review of *A hazard of new fortunes.*

— "Howells at home," New York *Tribune,* Jan. 25, 1880, p. 3.
Descriptive. First printed Boston *Herald.*

— Review of *Poems of two friends,* *Saturday press,* Jan. 28, 1860, III, 1.

— "Scott's latest critics," *Saturday review,* May 4, 1889, LXVII, 521–522.

— "William Dean Howells," *Saturday review of literature,* March 13, 1937, XV, 8.
Assays reputation.

ARCHER, WILLIAM. "The novelist as critic," *Illustrated London news,* Aug. 8, 1891, XCIX, 175.

ARMS, GEORGE. "Further inquiry into Howells's socialism," *Science and society,* Spring, 1939, III, 245–248.

— "The social criticism of William Dean Howells." Unpublished dissertation (New York University, 1939).

— "The literary background of Howells's social criticism," *American literature,* Nov., 1942, XIV, 260–276.

— and W. M. GIBSON. "'Silas Lapham,' 'Daisy Miller,' and the Jews," *New England quarterly,* March, 1943, XVI, 118–122.

— "Five interviews with William Dean Howells," *Americana,* April, 1943, XXXVII, 257–295.

ARMS, GEORGE. "A novel and two letters," *Journal of the Rutgers University Library,* Dec., 1944, VIII, 9–13.

— "Howells's unpublished prefaces," *New England quarterly,* Dec., 1944, XVII, 580–591.

— "Ever devotedly yours, the Whitlock-Howells correspondence," *Journal of the Rutgers University Library,* Dec., 1946, X, 1–19.

ARVIN, NEWTON. "The usableness of Howells," *New republic,* June 30, 1937, XCI, 227–228.
Re-establishes significance in American letters.

ATHERTON, GERTRUDE. "Why is American literature bourgeois?" *North American review,* May, 1904, CLXXVIII, 771–781.
Notable early opposition to Howells' genteelness.

— "Gertrude Atherton assails 'the powers,'" New York *Times,* Dec. 29, 1907, V, 2.
Reprinted *Current literature,* Feb., 1908, XLIV, 158–160. Continues her attack in interview.

BADGER, G. H. "Howells as an interpreter of American life," *International review,* May – June, 1883, XIV, 380–386.
Attacks purported misrepresentation.

BALLINGER, R. H. "A calendar and a study of the William Dean Howells collection." (Harvard University dissertation in progress.)

BANGS, J. K. "The rise of Hop o' My Thumb," *New waggings of old tales* (Boston, 1888), p. 18–46.
Parody.

— Review of *The story of a play,* *Harper's monthly,* Aug. [?], 1898, XCVII, supplement, 1.

— "The overcoat, being the contribution of Mr. Bedford Parke," *The dreamers, a club* (New York, 1900), p. 59–79.

Parody of farces.

BASS, A. L. "The social consciousness of William Dean Howells," *New republic,* April 13, 1921, XXVI, 192–194.

Ability to keep social consciousness in artistic perspective.

BEACH, J. W. Review of Cooke's *Howells, Journal of English and Germanic philology,* July, 1923, XXII, 451–454.

— "An American master," *Yale review,* Jan., 1926, n. s. xv, 399–401.

Reviews of Firkins' *Howells* and Phelps' *Howells, James, Bryant.*

BELCHER, H. G. "William Dean Howells, magazine writer." Unpublished dissertation (University of Michigan, 1942).

— "Howells's opinions on the religious conflicts of his age as exhibited in magazine articles," *American literature,* Nov., 1943, xv, 262–278.

BISHOP, W. H. "Mr. Howells in Beacon street, Boston," *Critic,* Nov. 27, 1886, n. s. VI, 259–261.

Reprinted in *Authors at home,* eds., L. and J. B. Gilder (New York [c. 1888]), p. 193–210.

BLACK, ALEXANDER. "The king in white," *American husbands* (Indianapolis, 1925), p. 173–182.

Reminiscent.

[BLANC, M. T.] "William D. Howells," *Les nouveaux romanciers Americains* par "Th. Bentzon" (Paris, 1885), p. 7–70.

On *The undiscovered country, A modern instance, The lady of the Aroostook, et al.*

BLODGETT, HAROLD. "A note on *Mark Twain's library of American humor,*" *American literature,* March, 1938, x, 78–80.

Howells' part in the book.

BOLTON, S. K. "William Dean Howells," *Famous American authors* (New York [c. 1887]), p. 258–285.

Biographical.

BOOK NEWS MONTHLY, June, 1908, XXVI.

A "Howells number" with articles by H. M. Alden, H. W. Mabie, P. Maxwell, and W. de Wagstaff.

BOSTON *Transcript,* "William Dean Howells at 75, tributes from eminent Americans to our foremost man of letters," Feb. 24, 1912, III, 2.

Contributions by W. S. Braithwaite, J. D. Long, M. E. W. Freeman (reprinted *Literary digest,* q.v.), H. M. Alden, F. E. Coates (poem), G. W. Cable, Henry Van Dyke, R. U. Johnson, Robert Herrick ("A warm champion of the truth"), G. E. Woodberry, Alice Brown, Bliss Perry, J. B. Esenwein, W. E. B. DuBois ("As a friend of the colored man").

BOYD, ERNEST. "Readers and writers," *Independent,* Jan. 3, 1925, CXIV, 20.

Review of Firkins' *Howells.*

BOYESEN, H. H. "Mr. Howells and his work," *Cosmopolitan,* Feb., 1892, XII, 502–503.

Emphasizes broadening sympathies.

— "Mr. Howells at close range," *Ladies' home journal,* Nov., 1893, x, 7–8.

Biographical.

BOYNTON, P. H. "William Dean Howells," *Literary review* (New York *post*), April 23, 1921, I, 22.

Attacks Garland's standard of praise.

— "William Dean Howells," *New republic,* Jan. 31, 1923, XXXIII, 256–257.

Review of Cooke's *Howells.*

[BROWNELL, W. C.] "The novels of Mr. Howells," *Nation,* July 15, 1880, XXXI, 49–51.

Review of *The undiscovered country.*

play," *Literary digest,* June 19, 1920, LXV, 56–58.

First printed in New York *World.* Assistance for *A Hazard of new fortunes,* with seven letters.

EDWARDS, HERBERT. "Howells and the controversy over realism in American fiction," *American literature,* Nov., 1931, III, 237–248.

His eventual triumph through Norris' success.

EKSTROM, W. F. "The social philosophies of William Morris and W. D. Howells." (University of Illinois dissertation in progress.)

ERSKINE, JOHN. "William Dean Howells," *Bookman,* June, 1920, LI, 385–389.

Manifold nature of his accomplishments.

FAWCETT, WALDON. "Mr. Howells and his brother," *Critic,* Nov., 1899, XXXV, 1026–1028.

FERGUSON, J. D. "New letter of Paul Hamilton Hayne," *American literature,* Jan., 1934, V, 368–370.

To Howells, dated May 21, 1873.

FIRKINS, O. W. *William Dean Howells, a study* (Cambridge, 1924).

— "Last of the mountaineers," *Saturday review of literature,* March 16, 1929, V, 774–775.

Review of *Life in letters.* Reprinted *Selected essays* (Minneapolis [1933]), p. 94–108.

Fox, A. B. "The progress of thought in William Dean Howells." (New York University dissertation in progress.)

FRÉCHETTE, A. H. "William Dean Howells," *Canadian bookman,* July, 1920, II, 9–12.

Reminiscence by Howells' sister.

FREEMAN, M. W. "A woman's tribute to Mr. Howells," *Literary digest,*

March 9, 1912, XLIV, 485.

First printed Boston *transcript,* Feb. 24, 1912, III, 2.

FRENCH, J. C. Review of Firkins' *Howells, Modern language notes,* June, 1925, XL, 375–377.

GARLAND, HAMLIN. "Mr. Howells's latest novels," *New England magazine,* May, 1890, n. s. II, 243–250.

Howells' growth.

— "Sanity in fiction," *North American review,* March, 1903, CLXXVI, 336–348.

Defense of Howells' methods.

— "William Dean Howells, master craftsman," *Art world,* March, 1917, I, 411–412.

Celebrates birthday.

— "Meetings with Howells," *Bookman,* March, 1917, XLV, 1–7.

With changes reprinted in *A son of the middle border* (New York, 1917), p. 383–390.

— "A great American," *Literary review* (New York *post*), March 5, 1921, I, 1–2.

See P. H. Boynton for reply.

— "Roadside meetings of a literary nomad. II, William Dean Howells and other memories of Boston," *Bookman,* Nov., 1929, LXX, 246–250.

Reprinted *Roadside meetings* (New York, 1930), p. 55–65.

— "Howells," *American writers on American literature,* ed. John Macy (New York, 1931), p. 285–297.

GETTMAN, R. A. "Turgenev in England and America," *University of Illinois studies in language and literature,* 1941, XXVII, 51–63.

Howells' relationship.

GETZELS, J. W. "William Dean Howells and socialism," *Science and society,* Summer, 1938, II, 376–386.

164

The New York Public Library

Selected Critical Writings, continued

GIBSON, W. M. "Mark Twain and William Dean Howells, anti-imperialists." Unpublished dissertation (University of Chicago, 1940).

— "Materials and form in Howells's first novels," *American literature,* May, 1947, xix, 158–166.

— "Mark Twain and Howells, anti-imperialists," *New England quarterly,* Dec., 1947, xx, 435–470.

— *See also* ARMS, GEORGE.

GILMAN, LAWRENCE. "Dean of American letters," New York *Times,* May 16, 1920, v, 254–255.
Sketch.

GOSSE, E. W. "To W. D. Howells," *From Shakespeare to Pope* (New York, 1885), p. iii.
Dedicatory poem. Reprinted *Critic,* Sept. 19, 1885, n. s. iv, 139.

— "The passing of William Dean Howells," *Living age,* July 10, 1920, cccvi, 98–100.

— "The world of books, W. D. Howells," *Sunday Times* (London), March 8, 1925, p. 8.
Reprinted *Silhouettes* (New York [1925]), p. 191–199.

GRATTAN, C. H. "Howells, ten years after," *American mercury,* May, 1930, xx, 42–50.
Howells superficial and genteel.

HACKETT, FRANCIS. "William Dean Howells," *New republic,* April 21, 1917, x, supplement, 3–5.
Review of Harvey's *Howells.* Reprinted *Horizons, a book of criticism* (New York, 1918), p. 21–30.

HARPER'S WEEKLY. "A tribute to William Dean Howells, souvenir of a dinner given to the eminent author in celebration of his seventy-fifth birthday," March 9, 1912, lvi, 27–34.
Speeches by George Harvey, Taft, Howells, James Barnes (verses), Winston Churchill, H. W. Mabie, W. A. White, Basil King. Letters by Arnold Bennett, T. W. Dunton, Arthur Pinero, Thomas Hardy, J. M. Barrie, A. T. Richie, H. G. Wells, Israel Zangwill, Anthony Hope, W. J. Locke, Andrew Lang, Lord Curzon of Kedleston, Mrs. Humphry Ward, L. M. Sill (verses), Henry Van Dyke, G. W. Cable, John Burroughs, S. W. Mitchell, H. H. Furness. See also Henry James and F. B. Sanborn.

HARVEY, ALEXANDER. *William Dean Howells, a study of the achievement of a literary artist* (New York, 1917).

HAZARD, LUCY L. "Howells a hundred years later," *Mills quarterly,* Feb., 1938, xx, 167–172.

HEARN, LAFCADIO. *Essays on American literature,* eds., Albert Mordell and Sanki Ichikawa (Tokyo, 1929), p. 189–193, 238–244, 248–250.
First printed New Orleans *Times-Democrat,* June 6, 1886, April 12, 1887, May 29, 1887.

HELLMAN, G. S. "The reminiscences of Mr. Howells," *Bookman,* March, 1901, xiii, 67–71.
Review of *Literary friends and acquaintance.*

HERFORD, OLIVER. "Celebrities I have not met," *American magazine,* March, 1913, lxxv, 95.
Satiric poem and drawing.

HERRICK, ROBERT. "Mr. Firkins on Howells," *New republic,* March 4, 1925, xlii, 47–48.
Review.

HIGGINSON, T. W. "Howells," *Literary world,* Aug. 2, 1879, x, 249–250.
Reprinted *Short studies of American authors* (Boston [1879]), p. 32–39.

[—] "Howells's Modern Italian poets," *Nation,* Jan. 5, 1888, xlvi, 18–19.
Review.

[—] "Howells's 'Undiscovered country,'" *Scribner's*, Sept., 1880, xx, 793–795.
Review.

HOMBERGER, HEINRICH. "William Dean Howells," *Deutsche Rundschau*, June, 1877, xi, 510–513.
The first (*A foregone conclusion*) of several reviews.

[JAMES, HENRY.] Review of *Italian journeys*, *North American review*, Jan., 1868, cvi, 336–339.

— "Howells' Poems," *Independent*, Jan. 8, 1874, xxvi, 9.
Review.

[—] Review of *A foregone conclusion*, *North American review*, Jan., 1875, cxx, 207–214.

[—] "Howells's *Foregone conclusion*," *Nation*, Jan. 7, 1875, xx, 12–13.
Review.

— "William Dean Howells," *Harper's weekly*, June 19, 1886, xxx, 394–395.

— "American letter," *Literature*, July 9, 1898, iii, 18.
Review of *The story of a play*.

— "A letter to Mr. Howells," *North American review*, April, 1912, cxcv, 558–562.
Indebtedness of James to Howells.

JONES, H. M. "A study of Howells," *Freeman*, April 25, 1923, vii, 163.
Review of Cooke's *Howells*.

JOSEPHSON, MATTHEW. "Those who stayed," *Portrait of the artist as American* (New York [1930]), p. 161–166.
Relation with James.

KAZIN, ALFRED. "Howells, a late portrait," *Antioch review*, Summer, 1941, i, 216–233.
Reprinted in *On native ground* (New York [1942]), p. 3–50, *passim*.

KELLEY, C. P. "The early development of Henry James," *University of Illinois studies in language and literature*, 1930, xv, 73–80.

KILMER, JOYCE. "Shakespeare and Bacon," New York *Times*, May 10, 1914, vii, 225.
Review of *The seen and unseen at Stratford-on-Avon*.

KIRK, RUDOLF AND CLARA. "'Poems of two friends,'" *Journal of the Rutgers University Library*, June, 1941, iv, 33–44.

— "American writers series" volume in preparation.

[KIRK, S.] "America, Altruria, and The coast of Bohemia," *Atlantic monthly*, Nov., 1894, lxxiv, 701–704.
Review of *A traveler from Altruria* and *The coast of Bohemia*.

KÖNIGSBERGER, SUZANNE. *Die Romantechnik von William Dean Howells* (Düsseldorf, 1933).

LANG, ANDREW. "At the sign of the ship," *Longman's*, April, 1892, xix, 682–684.
Reprinted *Critic*, April 16, 1892, xx, 233. On Howells' leaving the "Editor's study," with humorous poem.

— "The new fiction," *Illustrated London news*, Aug. 3, 1895, cvii, 141.

LESSING, O. E. "William Dean Howells," *Das literarische Echo*, Nov. 1, 1912, xv, 155–161.
Reprinted *Brücken über den Atlantik* (Berlin, 1927), p. 139–149.

LEWIS, SINCLAIR. "The American fear of literature," in E. A. Karlfeldt, *Why Sinclair Lewis got the Nobel prize* (New York [1931]), p. 20–22.
The Howells influence, an address delivered Dec. 12, 1930.

[LOWELL, J. R.] Review of *Poems by [sic] two friends, Atlantic monthly,* April, 1860, v, 510–511.

[—] Review of *Venetian life, North American review,* Oct., 1866, CIII, 610–613.

Reprinted J. R. Lowell's *The function of the poet,* ed., Albert Mordell (Boston, 1920), p. 146–152. G. W. Cooke, A *bibliography of James Russell Lowell* (Boston, 1906), p. 27, ascribes to Lowell; the *North American review* index ascribes to C. E. Norton.

[—] Review of *Suburban sketches, North American review,* Jan., 1871, CXII, 236–237.

MABIE, H. W. "A typical novel," *Andover review,* Nov., 1885, IV, 417–429.
Review of *The rise of Silas Lapham.*

— "William Dean Howells," *Outlook,* Dec., 1915, CXI, 786–787.
Reprinted *American Academy Proceedings,* Nov., 1916, II, 51–52.

McCABE, L. R. "Literary and social recollections of William Dean Howells," *Lippincott's,* Oct., 1887, XL, 547–552.

— "One never can tell," *Outlook,* May 14, 1898, LIX, 131–132.
On *Poems of two friends.*

MACY, JOHN. "Howells," *The spirit of American literature* (Garden City, 1913), p. 278–295.

MALONE, CLIFTON. "The critical opinions of William Dean Howells." (University of Oklahoma dissertation in progress.)

MARSTON, F. C., JR. "The early life of William Dean Howells, a chronicle, 1837–1871." Dissertation, to be published in 1947 (Brown University, 1944).

— "An early Howells letter," *American literature,* May, 1946, XVIII, 163–165.
A letter to his brother from Cincinnati, dated April 10, 1857.

MARTIN, E. S. "Twenty-five years after," *Bookbuyer,* Dec., 1899, XIX, 378–381.
Review of *Their silver wedding journey.*

— "W. D. Howells," *Harper's monthly,* July, 1920, CXLI, 265–266.

MATHER, F. J., JR. Review of *The Kentons, Forum,* Oct., 1902, XXXIV, 221–223.

MATTHEWS, BRANDER. "Bret Harte and Mr. Howells as dramatists," *Library table,* Sept. 13, 1877, III, 174–175.
Reprinted *American theatre as seen by its critics, 1752–1934,* eds., M. J. Moses and J. M. Brown (New York [1934]), p. 147–148.

— "Mr. Howells as a critic," *Forum,* Jan., 1902, XXXII, 629–638.

— "American character in American fiction," *Munsey's,* Aug., 1913, XLIX, 794–797.
Review of *New Leaf Mills.*

MATTHIESSEN, F. O. "A monument to Howells," *New republic,* April 24, 1929, LVIII, 284–285.
Review of *Life in letters.*

MEDRANO, H. J. "William Dean Howells," *Cuba contemporánea,* July, 1920, XXIII, 252–256.

MENCKEN, H. L. "The Dean," *Prejudices, first series* (New York, 1919), p. 52–58.
Menckenesque attack.

— *American language, fourth edition* (New York, 1938), p. 168 n.
Contemporaries on Howells' English.

MILLER, C. T. "Howells' theory of the novel." Unpublished dissertation (University of Chicago, 1947).

MORBY, E. S. "William Dean Howells and Spain," *Hispanic review,* July, 1946, XIV, 187–212.

MORDELL, ALBERT. "William Dean Howells and the classics," *Stratford monthly,* Sept., 1924, n. s. II, 199–205.
Comments on "Editor's easy chair."

MUIRHEAD, J. F. "W. D. Howells, the American Trollope," *Landmark,* Dec., 1920 – Jan., 1921, II–III, 53–56, 812–816.
Reprinted *Living age,* Jan. 29, 1921, CCCVIII, 304–309.

MUNFORD, H. M. "The genesis and development of Howells' basic ideas to 1891." (Harvard University dissertation in progress.)

NEVINS, ALLAN. "Howells an exponent of Americanism, our greatest novelist of manners merits a wider appreciation as a social historian," New York *Post,* Dec. 26, 1922, p. 6.
Review of Cooke's *Howells.*

NEW YORK *Sun.* "His friends greet William Dean Howells at eighty," Feb. 25, 1917, V, 10.
Comment by M. B. Mullett, Booth Tarkington, D. Z. Doty, Hamlin Garland; reminiscence by C. H. Towne and T. S. Perry.

[NORTON, C. E.] Review of Venetian life, *Nation,* Sept. 6, 1866, III, 189.
Unsigned; attributed through marked copy in *Nation* office. See also under Lowell.

ORCUTT, W. D. "Italian dividends," *Celebrities off parade* (Chicago, 1935), p. 121–128.
Reminiscent.

ORR, A. [MRS. SUTHERLAND]. "International novelists and Mr. Howells," *Contemporary review,* May, 1880, XXXVII, 741–765.
Reprinted *Living age,* June 5, 1880, CXLV, 599–615.

PECK, H. T. "Mr. Howells as a poet," *Bookman,* Feb., 1896, II, 525–527.
Review of *Stops of various quills.*

— "Living critics, XII — William Dean Howells," *Bookman,* Feb., 1897, IV, 529–541.
Analysis of his faults.

PENNELL, JOSEPH. "Adventures of an illustrator, with Howells in Italy," *Century,* May, 1922, CIV, 135–141.
More on Pennell than on Howells.

[PERRY, T. S.] "William Dean Howells," *Century,* March, 1882, XXIII, 680–685.
More biographical than critical.

PHELPS, W. L. "William Dean Howells," *Essays on modern novelists* (New York, 1910), p. 56–81.

— "Howells," *Howells, James, Bryant, and other essays* (New York, 1924), p. 156–180.
In large part first printed as "An appreciation," *North American review,* July, 1920, CCXII, 17–20; and as "William Dean Howells as a novelist," *Yale review,* Oct., 1920, n. s. X, 99–109.

POWYS, LLEWELYN. "The style of Howells," *Nation,* June 17, 1925, CXX, 694.
Review of Firkins' *Howells.*

PRITCHARD, J. P. "William Dean Howells," *Return to the fountains* (Durham, 1942), p. 135–147.
Relation of Horace and Aristotle.

QUILLER-COUCH, A. T. "A literary causerie," *Speaker,* Aug. 1, 1891, IV, 143–144.
Review of *Criticism and fiction.*

QUINN, A. H. "The thirst for salvation," *Dial,* Dec. 14, 1916, LXI, 534–535.
Review of *The leatherwood god.*

— "The art of William Dean Howells," *Century,* Sept., 1920, C, 675–681.

REED, H. B. "The critical theory and practice of William Dean Howells." (University of Southern California dissertation in progress.)

RICHARDSON, L. N. "Men of letters and the Hayes administration," *New England quarterly*, March, 1942, xv, 117–127.

ROBERTSON, J. M. "Mr. Howells' novels," *Westminster review*, Oct., 1884, n. s. cxxxII, 347–375.

Reprinted *Essays toward a critical method* (London, 1889), p. 149–199.

— "Mr. Howells' recent novels (1890)," *Criticisms* (London, 1902), I, 111–121.

Notes improvement with social themes.

ROOD, HENRY. "William Dean Howells, some notes of a literary acquaintance," *Ladies' home journal*, Sept., 1920, xxxvII, 42, 154, 157.

Biographical.

SANBORN, F. B. "A letter to the chairman," *North American review*, April, 1912, cxcv, 562–566.

Reminiscent letter at birthday.

[SCUDDER, H. E.] "A modern instance," *Atlantic monthly*, Nov., 1882, L, 709–713.

Review.

[—] "The East and West in recent fiction," *Atlantic monthly*, Nov., 1883, LII, 704–705.

Review of *A woman's reason*.

[—] Review of *The rise of Silas Lapham*, *Atlantic monthly*, Oct., 1885, LVI, 554–556.

[—] "James, Crawford, and Howells," *Atlantic monthly*, June, 1886, LVII, 855–857.

Review of *Indian summer*.

[—] "New York in recent fiction," *Atlantic monthly*, April, 1890, LXV, 563–567.

Review of *A hazard of new fortunes*.

[—] "Mr. Howells' literary creed," *Atlantic monthly*, Oct., 1891, LXVIII, 566–569.

Review of *Criticism and fiction*.

[—] Review of *The quality of mercy*, *Atlantic monthly*, May, 1892, LXIX, 702–704.

[—] "Mr. Howells under tutors and governors," *Atlantic monthly*, Nov., 1895, LXXVI, 701–703.

Review of *My literary passions*.

SHAW, G. B. "Told you so," *Saturday review*, Dec. 7, 1895, LXXX, 761–762.

Review of *The garroters*. Reprinted *Dramatic opinions and essays* (New York, 1906), I, 265–266.

SINCLAIR, R. B. "William Dean Howells as a literary critic." (University of North Carolina dissertation in progress.)

— "Howells in the Ohio valley," *Saturday review of literature*, Jan. 6, 1945, xxxvIII, 22–23.

SMITH, BERNARD. "Howells, the genteel radical," *Saturday review of literature*, Aug. 11, 1934, XI, 41–42.

SNELL, GEORGE. "Howells' grasshopper," *College English*, May, 1946, VII, 444–452.

Howells historically rather than critically important. Reprinted *The Shapers of American fiction, 1798–1947* (New York, 1947).

STANTON, ELIZABETH B. "William Dean Howells, a study of his literary theories and practices during his *Atlantic monthly* years." Unpublished dissertation (Ohio State University, 1943).

STARKE, A. H. "William Dean Howells and Sidney Lanier," *American literature*, March, 1931, III, 79–82.

STILES, MARION L. "Travel in the life and writings of William Dean Howells." Unpublished dissertation (University of Texas, 1946).

STODDARD, R. H., ed., "W. D. Howells," *Poets' homes* (Boston [1877]), p. 119–138.
Reminiscent and biographical.

TARKINGTON, BOOTH. "Mr. Howells," *Harper's monthly*, Aug., 1920, CXLI, 346–350.
Grants Howells' influence on him. Reprinted with revisions and additions as "Introduction," *The rise of Silas Lapham* (Centenary ed.; Boston, 1937), p. v–xv, and *ibid.*, (Riverside literature series; Boston [c. 1937]), p. xiii–xxi.

TAYLOR, W. F. "On the origin of Howells' interest in economic reform," *American literature*, March, 1930, II, 1–14.

— "William Dean Howells and the economic novel," *American literature*, May, 1932, IV, 103–113.

— "William Dean Howells, artist and American," *Sewanee review*, July – Sept., 1938, XLVI, 288–303.

— "William Dean Howells," *The economic novel in America* (Chapel Hill, 1942), p. 214–281.

THOMAS, B. P. "A unique biography of Lincoln," *Bulletin of the Abraham Lincoln Association*, June, 1934, no. 35, 3–8.
Sources and corrections made by Lincoln in the Howells campaign biography.

THOMAS, E. M. "Mr. Howells's way of saying things," *Putnam's*, July, 1908, IV, 443–447.

THOMPSON, MAURICE. "The analysts analyzed," *Critic*, July 10, 1886, n. s. VI, 19–22.
Report of Indianapolis address.

— "Mr. Maurice Thompson on Mr. Howells," *Literary world*, Sept. 3, 1887, XVIII, 281–282.
Opposes him on Tolstoy.

— "Studies of prominent novelists. No. 3. — William Dean Howells," *Book news*, Nov., 1887, VI, 93–94.

TICKNOR, CAROLINE. "William Dean Howells," *Glimpses of authors* (Boston, 1922), p. 169–178.
Reminiscent.

TOWNE, C. H. "The kindly Howells," *Touchstone*, July, 1920, VII, 280–282.
Reminiscent.

TRENT, W. P. "Mr. Howells and romanticism," *The authority of criticism and other essays* (New York, 1899), p. 259–267.

UNDERWOOD, J. C. "William Dean Howells and Altruria," *Literature and insurgency* (New York, 1914), p. 87–129.
Condemns his social outlook and his pessimism.

VAN DOREN, CARL. "Howells his own censor," *Literary review* (New York post), Oct. 23, 1920, I, 3.
Review of *The vacation of the Kelwyns*. Cf. *Nation*, Nov. 3, 1920, CXI, 510–511.

— "Novel killed with kindness," *Literary review* (New York post), Sept. 10, 1921, II, 3.
Review of *Mrs. Farrell*.

— "Howells, May, 1920, eulogium," *The roving critic* (New York, 1923), p. 69–80.

VAN DYKE, HENRY. *See* AMERICAN ACADEMY.
Reprinted *Campfires and guideposts* (New York, 1921), p. 310–319.

VAN WESTRUM, A. S. "Mr. Howells and American aristocracies," *Bookman*, March, 1907, xxv, 67–73.

— "Altruria once more," *Bookman*, June, 1907, xxv, 434–435.
Review of *Through the eye of the needle*.

WAGENKNECHT, EDWARD. "Of Henry James and Howells, 1925," *Virginia quarterly review*, Oct., 1925, I, 453–460.
Review of Firkins' *Howells*.

[WARNER, C. D.] "Editor's study," *Harper's monthly*, April, 1892, LXXXIV, 802–803.
Response to Howells in the "Editor's study."

[—] "Editor's study," *Harper's monthly*, July, 1892, LXXXV, 316–317.
Review of *The quality of mercy*.

[—] "Editor's study," *Harper's monthly*, Sept., 1894, LXXXIX, 801–802.
Review of "Literary friends and acquaintance" serialization.

[WHITELOCK, W. W.] "The otherwise men," *The literary guillotine* (New York, 1903), p. 238–262.

WHITING, L. "W. D. Howells at home," *Author*, Sept. 15, 1891, III, 130–131.
Biographical.

WILCOX, MARRION. "W. D. Howells's first romance," *Harper's bazar*, June 16, 1894, xxvII, 475.
Review of *A traveler from Altruria*.

— "Works of William Dean Howells," *Harper's weekly*, July 4, 1896, XL, 655–656.
Howells' socialist tendency.

WILSON, C. D., and D. B. FITZGERALD. "A day in Howells's 'Boy's town,'" *New England magazine*, May, 1907, xxxVI, 289–297.

WINTER, WILLIAM. "Vagrant comrades," *Old friends* (New York, 1909), p. 89–92.

WISTER, OWEN. "William Dean Howells," *Atlantic monthly*, Dec., 1937, CLX, 704–713.
Reminiscent.

[WOODBERRY, G. E.] "Howells's Modern Italian poets," *Atlantic monthly*, Jan., 1888, LXI, 130–133.
Review.

WOODRESS, J. L., JR. "The Italian phase of William Dean Howells." (Duke University dissertation in progress.)

WRIGHT, CONRAD. "The sources of Mr. Howells's socialism," *Science and society*, Fall, 1938, II, 514–517.

WYATT, EDITH. "A national contribution," *North American review*, Sept., 1912, CXCVI, 339–352.
Reprinted *Great companions* (New York, 1917), p. 113–142.

ZIMMERN, H[ELEN]. "W. D. Howells," *Revue internationale*, April 25, 1884, II, 353–363.
Chronological survey of works.

NAME INDEX, INCLUDING ILLUSTRATORS

Note: The full order of reference under each name is first, to the "Annual register," and second, to the "Collations of works and partial works." Page references in the original work appear immediately after each item of the second category. Thus "Arnaud, Giuseppe, 66–45, 87–C, 98–9" refers, first, to article 66–45 in the "Annual register," and second, to the book 87–C (PAGES 98–9 in *Modern Italian poets*, NOT article 98–9) in the "Collations." "Abbey, E. A., 89–5" refers only to an article in the "Annual register." "Angelo, Michael, 86–A, 75" refers only to a page in a book (*Tuscan cities*, p. 75).

This index excludes reference to "Selected critical writings." Descriptive phrases have frequently been added for persons who are not authors of books (e.g., actor) or who have not been dealt with by Howells (e.g., attributor). See also the "Preface" for general remarks on this index.

Belasco, David, 90–8.
Bell, Lilian, 98–24.
Bellamy, E. W., 84–2, 86–10, 88–11, 98–8, 98–13, 00–13, 94–B, 312, 98–B, v–xiii, 10–C, 43.
Bellezza, Paolo, 01–23.
Bellows, H. W., 68–11.
Benjamin, S. G. W., 78–2.
Bennett, Arnold, 11–4, 11–8, 12–13, 13–5, 14–17.
Bennett, E. A., 13–7.
Benson, E. F., 03–46, 10–D, 128.
Berchet, Giovanni, 87–C, 188–95.
Berlioz, L. H., 86–10.
Besant, Walter, 88–21.
Bigelow, John, 68–11, 90–7, 03–24.
Biggers, E. D., 14–3.
Birukoff, Paul, 07–4.
Bishop, N. H., 69–5.
Bishop, W. H., 79–4, 87–4, 87–6, 87–14.
Bisland, Elizabeth, 91–15.
Björnson, Björnstjerne, 70–5, 70–13, 86–14, 87–12, 89–2, 91–3, 95–E, 225–7, 232, 00–F, 208.
Black, N. I. [illustrator], 13–B.
Black, William, 86–5, 01–C, II, 213–24.
Blackmore, R. D., 01–C, II, 211–12.
Blackstone, William, 95–E, 125.
Blake, William, 91–1.
Blasco Ibañez, Vicente, 15–19, 19–A, v–xiv.
Blodgett, Harold [attributor], 88–B.
Boccaccio, Giovanni, 67–B, 83, 86–A, 44, 10–D, 13–14.
Boileau, Nicholas, 03–19.
Bone, J. H. A., 60–E, 589.
Boone, H. B., 01–22, 03–28.
Booth, Edwin [actor], 66–5, 00–F, 107.
Booth, F. [music], 76–E.
Borrow, George, 14–5.
Bostwick, H. L., 60–43, 60–E, 550.
Boswell, James, 90–2.
Botta, Vincenzo, 65–6.
Boucicault, Dion, 68–13.
Bouquet, Henry, 69–5.
Bourget, Paul, 95–12.
Bowers, C. W. [music], 95–D.
Bowles, Samuel, 00–F, 113.
Boyd, Henry, 87–C, 114–15.
Boyesen, H. H., 74–15, 86–16, 89–10, 91–13, 93–5 [dialogue], 95–11, 96–4, 00–F, 256–65.
Boyland, G. H., 73–14.
Brace, C. L., 69–14, 10–C, 31.
Braithwaite, W. S. B., 17–16.
Branch, A. H., 15–14.
Brever, T. A. [illustrator], 06–A.
Bridgman, Laura, 03–43.
Brieux, Eugène, 15–5.
Brighouse, H., 16–4.
Brinton, D. G., 68–15.
Brontë, Charlotte, 95–E, 35, 01–C, I, 221–9, II, 1–2.

Brontë, Emily, 01–C, I, 229–39, II, 1–2.
Brooke, Rupert, 16–13.
Brooks, Noah, 10–C, 36.
Brooks, V. W. [interviewer], 09–10.
Brooks, Walter [interviewer], 89–9.
Broughton, C. [illustrator], 00–F.
Brown, Alice, 95–47.
Brown, C. B., 01–C, I, 110, 111–12.
Brown, John, 60–7, 11–2, 60–B, 316, 00–F, 59–60, 16–F, 187–8.
Brown, John, Jr. [war], 61–5.
Brown, Kenneth, 01–22, 03–28.
Brown, M. E., 89–5.
Browne, C. F., 00–F, 127–8, 12–C, vii–xvi, 16–F, 213–14.
Brownell, W. C., 02–43, 11–7.
Browning, Robert, 73–9, 76–2, 90–5, 91–15, 95–E, 156, 189, 235–6, 10–C, 16.
Bryant, W. C., 59–18, 73–12, 79–1, 90–7.
Bryce, James, 89–3.
Bugbee, J. M., 75–10.
Bulwer-Lytton, Edward, 74–5, 95–E, 8, 161, 01–C, I, 117–24, II, 8, 16–F, 132.
Bunner, H. C., 87–6.
Bunsen, Baron, 69–2.
Bunsen, Frances, 69–2.
Burgess, Gelett, 02–3.
Burgess, Neil, 89–8.
Burke, Edmund, 91–B, 6–8.
Burne-Jones, Philip, 04–19.
Burnet, Dana, 15–14.
Burney, Francis, 01–C, I, 13–23.
Burns, Robert, 95–E, 6, 16–F, 29, 30.
Burroughs, John, 71–13, 79–3.
Butler, W. A., 99–37.
Butterfield, C. W., 74–2.
Byron, G. G., 59–13b, 97–7, 66–B, 7, 67–B, 16–17, 87–C, 66, 95–E, 6, 60, 66, 16–F, 30, 89.
C-----, E. J. [interviewer], 88–16.
Cable, G. W., 87–14, 88–17, 98–15, 99–9, 01–C, II, 235–44, 10–C, 53, 22–A, 68.
Cabot, J. E., 88–5.
Cady, E. H. [attributor], 53–1, 54–8, 57–10.
Cahan, Abraham, 96–34, 98–24, 15–7.
Calhoun, A. R. [interviewer], 94–4.
Calhoun, Mrs. L. G., 68–16.
Calvert, G. H., 69–16.
Campanella, 94–B, 289, 312.
Campbell, Helen, 89–10.
Campbell, W. W., 92–2.
Canini, M. A., 86–18, 88–18.
Cannon, J. G., 22–A, 44–5.
Cantù, Cesare, 66–45.
Capparoggo, Giuseppe, 64–2.
Carcano, Giulio, 67–7, 87–C, 360–2.
Carleton, Clifford [illustrator], 95–A.
Carlyle, Jane Welsh, 03–29, 03–32.
Carlyle, Thomas, 87–8, 87–13, 89–10, 03–32, 91–B, 102–4, 01–C, I, 162, II, 136.
Carpenter, E. B., 88–1.

Carpenter, G. R., 99–3, 02–13.
Carrer, Luigi, 67–7, 87–C, 184–8.
Carrington [war], 61–7.
Cary, Alice and Phoebe, 73–5, 87–4.
Cary, W. M. [illustrator], 97–E.
Casgrain, H. R., 72–13.
Castaigne, A. [illustrator], 08–D.
Castiglione, Baldassare, 02–16.
Cawein, Madison, 88–9, 88–15, 89–11, 92–2, 98–15, 99–18, 99–34, 02–3, 08–2, 11–H, xiii–xix.
Ceconi, Teobaldo, 64–19.
Cervantes Saavedra, Miguel de, 54–7 [allusion], 57–2 [allusion], 60–45 [allusion], 88–5, 95–53, 98–6, 00–15, 19–12, 91–B, 67–8, 95–E, 10, 19–20, 23, 25, 28, 31, 43, 68, 77, 108, 141, 96–E, 9, 30–31, 16–F, 20, 27, 47, 84, 23–A.
Chaplin, H. W., 88–7.
Chapman, J. J., 98–18.
Chapman, Marie W., 77–5.
Charnwood, G. R. B., 18–14.
Chase, S. P. [politics], 58–4, 16–F, 153–6.
Chastellux, F. J., 13–5.
Chatfield-Taylor, H. C., 14–3.
Chaucer, Geoffrey, 95–E, 108–11, 113.
Cherbuliez, Victor, 73–3.
Chesnutt, C. W., 00–4, 01–19, 01–26.
Child, F. J., 00–F, 252–6, 10–C, 46–7.
Choate, J. H., 22–A, 1–7.
Christy, H. C. [illustrator], 01–C, 10–D.
Clark, Champ, 22–A, 55–6.
Clark, G. R., 69–18.
Clay, C. M., 86–19.
Clemens, Olivia L., 10–C, 10–13.
Clemens, S. L., 66–19, 72–7, 75–7, 75–12, 76–4, 81–5, 86–4 [allusion], 89–2, 95–53, 97–4, 00–11, 00–14, 01–23, 02–52, 05–27, 11–18, 13–1, 17–2, 18–3, 88–B, 02–C, 9, 14, 10–B, vii–viii, 10–C, 22–A.
Cleveland, Grover [politics], 87–2.
Cleveland, H. W. S., 86–21.
Coake [artist], 63–12.
Coates, Foster [interviewer], 91–7.
Cobbe, F. P., 66–45.
Codman, J. T., 95–29.
Coffin, C. C., 69–14.
Coggeshall, W. T. [allusion], 58–14.
Cohan, G. M., 13–7, 14–3, 16–4.
Cole, 66–22.
Coleridge, E. H., 99–18.
Collins, G. L., 03–21.
Collins, Wilkie, 76–4.
Colquhoun, A. R., 04–19.
Colvil, Edward, 66–39.
Colvin, Sidney, 87–15, 18–8.
Comly, J. M., 58–17, 60–37 [allusions], 16–F, 228–9.
Conacher, J. [illustrator], 02–C.
Conde, 95–E, 141.
Conrad, Joseph, 95–15.

Conway, M. D., 57–2, 60–11 [attribution], 89–3, 06–2, 00–F, 99, 101, 10–D, 159, 16–F, 176–7.
Cooke, H. D., 16–F, 145–6.
Cooke, J. E. [allusion], 58–2.
Cooke, R. T., 87–4, 88–15, 89–6, 92–4.
Cooper, J. F., 59–13d, 01–C, I, 111, 115, 10–D, 85–6.
Coppée, François, 91–6.
Corbin, Mrs. C. F., 80–2.
Corbin, John, 95–33.
Corelli, Marie, 02–53.
Cornaro, Luigi, 04–13.
Cornwall, Barry, 66–48.
Corry [politics], 57–2, 16–F, 137–8.
Courthope, W. J., 86–6.
Cowper, William, 80–10, 95–E, 6, 16–F, 30.
Cox, G. C. [illustrator], 11–G.
Coxe, Reginald [illustrator], 93–9.
Coxey, Jacob [politics], 94–9.
Cozzens, F. S., 71–6.
Crabbe, George, 80–5, 10–D, 240–43.
Craddock, C. E., see M. N. Murfree.
Craig, Frank [illustrator], 09–B.
Craigie, Mrs. P. R., 95–53, 06–31.
Cranch, C. P., 74–4, 87–5, 00–F, 285–6.
Crane, Stephen, 94–7, 94–11 [interviewer], 95–16, 95–40, 96–5, 96–34, 99–9, 96–D, v–vii.
Crane, T. F., 03–19.
Craven, H. T., 65–15.
Crawford, T. C. [interviewer], 92–11.
Creevey, Caroline A., 02–C, 89, 91–4.
Crescimbeni, G. M., 87–C, 11–15.
Crichton-Browne, James, 03–29.
Critchett, R. C., 01–7.
Crook, George, 91–1.
Cross, W. L., 10–5.
Croy, Homer, 19–1.
Curtis, G. W., 68–12, 92–7, 92–13, 00–F, 108–11, 95–E, 145–6, 149, 10–D, 1, 128–35.
Curtis, W. E., 88–17.
Custer, E. B., 91–1.
Dall, W. H., 70–10.
Dall' Ongaro, Francesco, 64–19, 68–2, 67–B, 265, 87–C, 300–22.
Dana, R. H., Jr., 69–14, 00–F, 273–5.
Dandolo, Emilio, 87–C, 312–13.
Dandridge, Danske, 91–9.
Dante Alighieri, 60–45, 65–6, 66–36, 67–10, 67–16, 67–17, 72–2, 87–16, 92–4, 16–8, 67–B, 194–5, 86–A, 31, 35–40, 129, 131, 139, 160, 177, 231, 95–E, 160, 200–01, 204.
Darley, F. O. C., 80–2.
Darlington, W. M., 70–12.
Darwin, C. R., 80–2, 10–C, 51.
D'Aste, Ippolito, 89–D.
Daudet, Alphonse, 91–B, 135, 95–E, 247.
Davidson, John, 99–18.
Davis, A. J., 65–13.
Davis, R. H., 91–14.

Jacobson, W. L. [illustrator], 01–C.
James, Henry, 69–19, 88–5, 00–F, 266–9.
James, Henry, Jr., 65–20 [allusion], 75–3, 78–8, 80–4, 82–4, 85–1 [allusion], 86–18, 87–4, 87–6, 87–14, 88–17, 89–10, 90–11, 91–14, 95–23, 99–9, 99–29, 00–15, 01–1, 02–39, 03–2, 91–B, 118–20, 95–E, 224, 01–C, II, 28, 140, 164–76, 12–B, 12–13, 18–C, i–ix.
James, William, 91–12.
Jansen, C. W., 16–13.
Janvier, T. A., 89–1, 92–4, 03–45.
Jay, John, 90–11.
Jefferson, Joseph, 91–5, 95–10, 95–44.
Jefferson, Thomas, 74–10.
Jenckes, T. A., 69–2.
Jenner, W. A., 08–8.
Jewett, S. O., 77–6, 87–4, 88–17, 91–6, 95–47, 02–C, 236, 238.
Johnson, Andrew [politics], 66–10, 66–25.
Johnson, Clifton, 94–5, 95–1 [interviewer], 17–D [illustrator].
Johnson, Merle [attributor], 72–A, 82–B, 85–B, 86–D, 90–G.
Johnson, Samuel, 90–2, 15–11.
Johnston, R. M., 88–7, 11–20.
Jones, H. A., 91–13, 95–4, 96–7, 01–7, 04–5, 06–27, 07–21.
Jones, T. D., 16–F, 216–18.
Jorioz, A. B. di Saint, 65–2.
Judd, Sylvester, 71–2.
Jusserand, J. J., 16–13.
Kappes, Alfred [illustrator], 79–1.
Kauffman, R. W., 02–42.
Keats, John, 87–15, 67–B, 167–8, 87–C, 97, 01–C, II, 9, 10–D, 220.
Keeler, Ralph, 70–15, 74–3, 87–4, 00–F, 275–9, 10–C, 6–7.
Keller, A. I. [illustrator], 97–E, 99–A, 01–C.
Keller, Helen, 03–24.
Keller, M. [music], 64–A.
Kellogg, Miner [artist], 64–7.
Kemble, F. A., 14–2.
Kester, Paul, 17–10.
Kester, Vaughan, 01–22.
Kidder, D. P., 58–18.
Kilmer, Joyce [interviewer], 14–15.
King, Basil, 01–26, 14–1, 14–17.
King, Charles, 91–1.
King, Clarence, 72–4, 02–13, 04–A, 133–56.
Kingsley, Charles, 77–6, 82–A, 3–4, 95–E, 218, 01–C, I, 220, II, 2–13, 16–F, 179.
Kinney, Coates, 88–9, 88–15.
Kipling, Rudyard, 90–12, 91–1, 91–14, 97–5, 99–18, 99–21a, 02–4.
Kirk, E. W., 86–7, 88–11.
Kirkland, Joseph, 88–11, 89–6.
Kjerolf, Halfdan [music], 60–1.
Klapper, Max F. [illustrator], 97–E.
Kline, Charles, 13–7.
Klippert [politics], 58–2.
Knoblauch, Edward, 13–7.

Knowles, Sheridan, 16–F, 36.
Kossuth, Louis, 16–F, 66–8.
Kotzebue, August von, 16–F, 36.
Kuprin, 12–17.
Labouchere, 02–5a.
Lamartine, A. M. L. de, 60–45, 16–F, 27.
Lamb, Charles, 66–48, 91–5, 95–F, 120.
Lamon, W. H., 72–12.
Lampman, Archibald, 89–5, 99–10.
Landor, W. S., 74–4.
Lanier, Sidney, 98–15.
Larcom, Lucy, 75–10, 00–F, 122–4.
Larned, J. N., 89–5.
Larsen, Carl, 70–13.
Lasells, Richard, 86–A, 211–12, 228.
Laszowska-Gerard, Mrs. E., 89–1.
Lathrop, G. P., 76–1, 86–18, 87–4, 90–2, 10–C, 50.
Lathrop, R. H., 88–18.
Laugel, Auguste, 66–41.
Laurence, Samuel [illustrator], 11–B.
Laurik, J. N., 06–9.
Lea, H. C., 67–3, 88–6, 88–9.
Learned, Walter, 90–5.
Leavitt, J. McD., 69–16.
Lecky, W. E. H., 69–18.
Lee, G. S., 03–19.
Lee, S. A., 67–6.
Lee, Vernon, 86–17, 87–C, 23–4.
Lefevre, Edwin, 16–14.
Le Gallienne, Richard, 10–11.
Leland, C. G., 68–15, 69–16, 03–34.
Leopardi, Giacomo, 87–C, 244–74.
Lincoln, Abraham, 72–12, 91–3, 12–9, 18–14, 60–C, 60–D, 00–F, 82, 16–F, 156, 193–4, 202–4, 226.
Lincoln, Mrs. Abraham, 66–7.
Lindsay, Vachel, 15–14.
Linton, W. J., 79–B.
Livingston, Mrs. Edward, 86–17, 86–21.
Lloyd, H. D., 10–D, 64.
Lloyd and Rosenfeld, 90–8.
Locke, Edward, 13–7.
Lodge, H. C., 80–9, 89–12.
Lodge, Oliver, 17–15, 20–B.
Lodge, Raymond, 17–15.
Longfellow, H. W., 59–18a, 66–36, 67–8, 67–10, 67–16, 69–2, 71–2, 72–2, 72–8, 73–13, 74–16, 76–1, 77–4, 78–8, 81–2, 86–13, 99–23, 02–13, 02–32, 07–3, 67–B, 213, 87–C, 24, 94–B, 208, 95–E, 38, 106, 147, 155, 00–F, 10, 14–18, 178–211, 10–C, 46, 59–63, 10–D, 307, 16–F, 53, 179.
Longfellow, Samuel, 86–13.
Lounsbury, T. R., 02–8, 03–19, 16–F, 112.
Lowell, Amy, 15–14.
Lowell, J. R., 65–8 [attributor], 66–4 [attributor], 67–1, 69–4, 70–7, 71–10, 76–3, 77–1, 77–4, 86–4, 87–8, 88–11, 91–10, 93–10, 99–23, 02–5, 03–13, 17–2, 95–E, 57, 107, 108, 172, 179, 239, 00–F, 10, 22–9, 35–40, 88–90,

Smith, Gerrit [politics], 59–34.
Smith, Gertrude, 95–47, 96–11.
Smith, Goldwin, 66–41, 80–10.
Smith, James, 70–12.
Smith, R. Pearsall, 88–2.
Smyth, A. H., 96–14.
Snider, D. J., 92–2.
Snyder, Carl, 03–31, 03–39.
Socrates, 87–8.
Solomons, Ikey, Esq., Jr. [pseud.], see Thackeray, W. M.
Sonntag, Jr. [illustrator], 93–9.
Spenser, Edmund, 10–D, 219.
Spofford, Mrs. Harriet Prescott, 87–4, 00–F, 125–6.
Stachelberg, Baroness, 90–11.
Stanton, H. B., 87–14.
Stedman, E. C., 61–6, 66–35 [attributions], 69–9, 74–1, 74–4, 86–6, 88–14, 98–12, 01–2, 11–3, 95–E, 239, 00–F, 83–6.
Stedman, Laura, 11–3.
Steele, Richard, 95–E, 132.
Stendhal, 07–4.
Stepniak, 88–17.
Stern, S. A., 73–10.
Sterne, Laurence, 10–5, 95–E, 172.
Sterner, A. E. [illustrator], 94–2, 97–B, 01–C, 02–C, 09–B.
Stetson, C. P., 96–5, 99–18.
Stevens, O. C., 92–2.
Stevens, W. D. [illustrator], 07–D.
Stevenson, R. L., 86–10, 01–C, II, 211.
Stewart, A. T. [politics], 66–18, 66–22.
Stewart, G. A., 60–E, 612.
Stillman, W. J., 01–14.
Stockton, F. R., 87–4, 95–40, 97–12, 00–1.
Stoddard, C. W., 03–48, 17–16, 92–G, v–vi.
Stoddard, Elizabeth, 65–12, 89–6.
Stoddard, Lorimer, 95–53, 97–8.
Stoddard, R. H., 65–27, 97–10, 04–7, 95–E, 239, 00–F, 86–8.
Stowe, Mrs. H. B., 71–14, 95–E, 63–4, 00–F, 11, 118, 138–40, 10–C, 36.
Strong [scandal], 65–23, 65–30.
Sturges, Jonathan, 90–2.
Sudermann, Hermann, 90–8, 99–15.
Sutherland, Harvey, 03–12.
Süttner, Bertha von, 01–26.
Swayne, Noah L. [politics], 16–F, 171–2.
Swedenborg, Emanuel, 69–19, 95–E, 4, 235, 16–F, 58, 20–B.
Swift, Jonathan, 95–E, 132, 13–C, xv–xvi, 16–F, 20, 27.
Swinton, William, 80–9.
Sylva, Carmen, 90–11.
Symonds, J. A., 87–16, 91–B, 1–2.
Taine, Hippolyte, 68–11, 71–6, 72–2, 72–11.
Taneyhill, R. H., 71–13.
Tarkington, Booth, 15–6, 15–7.
Tasso, Torquato, 95–E, 216–17.
Tautphoeus, Baroness, 01–C, II, 138–51.

Taylor, Bayard, 66–37, 67–1, 69–10, 71–4, 71–12, 72–7, 74–16, 76–1, 77–1, 96–14, 00–F, 3–10.
Taylor, H. O., 12–13.
Taylor, Isaac, 90–13.
Taylor, Thomas, 16–4.
Tenney, E. P., 86–16, 87–6.
Tennyson, Alfred, 59–24, 70–3, 72–2, 75–10, 77–3, 79–4, 86–10, 87–5, 88–15, 90–5, 95–E, 93, 149, 153, 155, 157, 159, 162–3, 177, 189, 192, 16–F, 99, 132, 163.
Thackeray, W. M., 59–13b, 59–20a, 70–3, 79–4, 82–7, 95–E, 30, 129–38, 218, 01–C, I, 190–220, II, 110, 10–D, 29, 16–F, 132, 164–5.
Thanet, Octave [pseud.], 88–1, 88–6.
Thaxter, Celia, 72–3, 73–9, 74–16, 87–5, 00–F, 124.
Thayer, W. R., 07–27, 16–1.
Thomas, Augustus, 01–7, 04–4.
Thomas, E. M., 91–9.
Thomas, G. H., 71–12.
Thomas, Widgery, Jr., 69–10.
Thompson, Denman, 89–8, 91–13.
Thompson, E. W., 95–40.
Thompson, Maurice, 79–4, 83–4.
Thomson, James, 95–E, 5, 47, 55–6.
Thoreau, Henry David, 00–F, 11, 57–60.
Thoreson, Magdalen, 70–13.
Thulstrup, T. de [illustrator], 95–36, 96–B, 02–C.
Tobin, G. T. [illustrator], 01–C.
Tocqueville, Alexis de, 86–A, 154.
Todd, M. L., 91–1.
Tolstoy, Lyof, 86–7, 87–4, 87–7, 87–8, 87–11, 87–12, 87–13, 87–15, 88–1, 88–5, 88–6, 88–9, 88–21, 89–6, 90–12, 91–6, 97–9, 98–16, 07–4, 08–21, 12–1, 13–14, 87–B, 5–12, 91–B, 142–3, 94–B, 106, 95–C, v–xv, 95–E, 250–54, 256–8, 97–F, 14985–94, 02–C, 3, 10–C, 16, 10–D, 10–11.
Toplady, A. M., 79–1.
Torelli, Giuseppe, 87–C, 15–22.
Towne, C. H., 10–9.
Townsend, E. W., 95–15.
Tree, Beerbohm [actor], 95–7.
Trescot, W. H., 71–12.
Trevelyan, G. O., 04–19, 08–11.
Trollope, Adolphus, 88–7.
Trollope, Anthony, 79–4, 66–B, 215–16, 91–B, 75–6, 95–E, 218–47, 01–C, I, 220, II, 94–137, 10–D, 28.
Trollope, Mrs. Frances, 88–7, 13–5.
Trowbridge, J. T., 75–2, 78–5, 87–4, 04–7, 00–F, 122–3.
Trumbull, Lyman, 13–17.
Tuckerman, C. K., 73–3.
Turgenev, I. S., 72–11, 73–4, 73–11, 87–12, 88–12, 95–E, 229–32, 249.
Turner, C. Y. [illustrator], 94–12, 96–C.
Turner, Ross [illustrator], 91–C.

A NOTE BY THE COMPILERS, 1971

We are pleased that Arno Press and The New York Public Library have reprinted *A Bibliography of William Dean Howells* from the original edition published by The New York Public Library in 1948. At first we had planned to add a list of errors and omissions, but we soon found that such a list—of new items especially—would become much longer than we anticipated. For example we could now list British editions that were unavailable to us under war-time conditions. But once started on this road, we ought certainly to present all collations by signatures and include the dozens of impressions and editions that we and Jacob Blanck and the editors of *A Selected Edition of W. D. Howells* have turned up and are still turning up as a result of the great advances made by bibliographers and editors in the past twenty years.

A Selected Edition of W. D. Howells began to appear in 1968 under the imprint of Indiana University Press. When completed, it will end with a new bibliography that will be as definitive as the research of the textual editors, the contributing editors, and other Howells scholars can make it. But that new work may be ten years in coming. In the meanwhile we believe that the original bibliography is still a useful, mostly reliable guide, particularly when it is supplemented by the following works:·

Jacob Blanck, comp. *Bibliography of American Literature*, IV, 384–448. New Haven: Yale University Press, 1963. As Mr. Blanck generously notes in his acknowledgments, we made available to him our post-1948 discoveries. He in turn will aid the Indiana edition bibliographers with what he finds after 1963.

James Woodress and Stanley P. Anderson. "A Bibliography of Writings about William Dean Howells," American Literary Realism, II (1969), [ii] + [1]–139. This is an annotated list of writing *about* Howells but the section "Bibliographical Items" notices articles that make specific corrections and additions to our 1948 bibliography, while other sections occasionally cite new editions or previously unpublished material by Howells. The critical pieces are presented in two groups: 1860–1919 and 1920–1969.

John K. Reeves, comp. "The Literary Manuscripts of W. D. Howells,

A Descriptive Finding List," *Bulletin of The New York Public Library*, LXII (June-July 1958), 267–278, 350–363, and "The Literary Manuscripts of W. D. Howells, A Supplement to the Descriptive Finding List," *Bulletin of The New York Public Library*, LXV (Sept. 1961), 465–476, have been indispensable to the editors of *A Selected Edition.*

A Selected Edition of W. D. Howells. Bloomington: Indiana University Press, 1968–   Under the successive general editorships of Edwin H. Cady, Ronald Gottesman, and Don L. Cook, with David J. Nordloh the present textual editor, five volumes have now appeared, two more will appear in 1970, and a total of approximately 40 are planned. The textual apparatus of each volume provides full bibliographical information for each title. This edition is supported by Indiana University, and by the Center for Editions of American Authors, Modern Language Association of America, under grants from the National Endowment for the Humanities.

The new edition, with its tracing of Howells's revisions and its study of his relation to publishers, reviewers, and the public, may well make a marked change in our current understanding of Howells's art and personality. Also, the editors of the five volume *Correspondence* in *A Selected Edition* are finding new unsigned periodical pieces from the late 1850's and early 1860's. Clara and Rudolf Kirk have described the guide-book to Venice that Howells translated (see entry 63-C) of which the Houghton Library obtained a copy in 1956 from Miss Mildred Howells; and Edwin Cady has found other pieces we knew existed but had not seen. Jacob Blanck's listing of books and pamphlets includes leaflets on saving American forests and on vivisection, as well as every sort of use of Howells's reviews. And our own thick file of new items includes material so diverse as a strong pro-Filipino statement in the New York Evening *Post,* of 17 October 1899, and a translation of the play *Evening Dress* into German for local reading and production in Milwaukee, authorized and published in 1893.

We take this occasion to thank again people who helped us earlier (pp. 9–10). We thank others who in the intervening years have made contributions as yet unrecorded. We repeat our plea for corrections and additions.

W. M. G., *New York University*
G. A., *University of New Mexico*